SPRINGBOARD
TO WORSHIP

SPRINGBOARD
TO WORSHIP

Ideas and Resources for Sundays & Festivals
A companion to ASB Years 1 & 2

Susan Sayers

Dedication
I would like to dedicate this book to all those
whose lives and ideas have inspired it and
contributed to it, and particularly to John, Eleanor
and Rachel, whose love and encouragement helped
me to write it.

Acknowledgement
The 15 year old playwright whose script appears
on page 36 is Paul Fuggle of Hawkwell, Essex. I
am grateful to him for having allowed me to use
his work in this book.

First published 1989 in Great Britain by
KEVIN MAYHEW LTD.
Rattlesden
Bury St Edmunds, Suffolk IP30 0SZ

ISBN 0 86209 103 9

Cover design by Rob Williams
Drawings for 'Church Decoration' by Mary McCullough;
   drawings for 'Children's Teaching' by Arthur Baker
Typesetting by Typestylers, Ipswich, Suffolk
Music origination by Words & Music, Southend-on-Sea, Essex
Printed in Great Britain by J.B. Offset, (Marks Tey) Ltd.,
   Marks Tey, Essex

FOREWORD

Susan Sayers has produced a most valuable resource for all those who have any responsibility for the planning and conduct of eucharistic worship. She has taken the ASB calendar and assembled additional material to go with the day's prayers. Worship is becoming richer, and more inclusive of the many talents in the congregation — drama, music, poetry, testimony, dance, to name just some. They need informing and blending together around the Sunday's theme. Susan Sayers has gathered together excellent material and her work is full of imaginative ideas. Those who use it will find a mine of good things.

† *Derek Bradwell*
  21 April 1989

Contents

How to use this book

This book is intended as a resource for a parish and the individuals and groups within it. It focuses attention on the theme of each Sunday and the main festivals based on the Alternative Service Book, and covering the two-year cycle of readings. The ASB has provided us with a rich and broad selection of Bible readings which are a valuable resource in themselves; this book aims to help 'unpack' some of that treasure in ways which can nurture a living, growing church.

It is hoped that this resource book will help to encourage the family of Christ to share in the preparation and celebration of worship, even the very young, so that our Christian response is enriched and deepened.

Many of the ideas would be equally useful in parishes where the Book of Common Prayer is preferred. The emphasis throughout is on thoughtful expression of God's Word, based on prayerful and thorough preparation.

TODAY'S THEME

A short paragraph on the theme of the day's readings is provided. This may be added to a weekly handout. It may also be useful for advance planning.

INTERCESSIONS

No mass-produced form for the Intercessions will be right for an individual parish with its own particular needs and forms of expression.

At the same time, those preparing to lead the congregation in prayer need guidelines to help them. Also, if the Intercessions reflect the needs highlighted by the day's readings, the prayer time is likely to be particularly worthwhile.

Accordingly, a response is suggested which picks up the theme of the day. I have also suggested prayer concerns which would be filled out and adapted by those involved in this ministry.

PARISH MUSIC

For each Sunday I have suggested a list of hymns which are appropriate for the ASB themes, based on the Bible readings, which I hope will be a useful timesaver. The lists are far from exhaustive, of course, but the need for such a shortlist has often been expressed.

Sometimes instrumental music can be an alternative to singing a hymn, or an aid to prayer before the service, between the readings or during communion. This may be an opportunity for a group of musicians in the parish to contribute to the worship; alternatively taped music can be used. So there are suggested pieces of music for each Sunday, chosen to reflect the atmosphere of the week's theme. They are mostly well-known pieces which should be widely available. I stress that they are only suggestions to get you started. Once you have prepared the readings other ideas may well spring to mind.

Some parishes are delighted to have the opportunity to sing an anthem from time to time, so suitable music is suggested to fit in with the theme.

CHURCH DECORATION

The church building speaks. Our historical churches are visited and admired by many, and it is important that visitors see evidence of the living church of today as well as the beauty of the building. During services, the mind and heart can be steered quietly towards the message of the day by means of a particular flower arrangement, exhibition of pictures, display or banner.

I have included a suggested flower arrangement for each Sunday (apart from Advent and Lent) along with the outline of what the arrangement aims to express. In this way I hope there is help for the beginner, and freedom for the more experienced to develop the theme in whatever way he or she is inspired.

Apart from flower arrangements, there are many other suggestions for decoration. It might be useful to have a co-ordinator, whose ministry it is to collect necessary items and arrange for different groups or individuals to prepare the display for a particular week. Although clear instructions for each type of decoration are given in the book, they can of course be changed and adapted as required.

NOTES ON THE READINGS AND QUESTIONS FOR DISCUSSION

The worshipping community will be richer for shared preparation of God's Word, ready for the Sunday celebration. The notes on the readings in this book are intended to start discussion, suggest links with the them, and stimulate thought. They may also be helpful for personal preparation of the readings.

The discussion questions may sometimes lead on to further Bible study and research, or suggestions for the future direction of activities in the parish.

Groups are best kept fairly small and varied.

To avoid cliques and to spread gifts and talents, it may be wise to shuffle members round regularly.

Begin with silence, to concentrate attention and focus on Christ, who is present at each group. After some prayer, read the following Sunday's readings aloud. Finish with silence and praise, and avoid running over time.

IDEAS FOR ADULTS

Many of the Old Testament and Gospel readings can be brought to life, if movingly presented through drama, mime or dance. Within every parish the gifts are many and varied, and can be used in worship, once people realise the possibilities.

Those involved will need to study the reading prayerfully before discussing how best to present it. The freshness of original ideas thrown up in the course of such preparation may be most effective, but to start you off, I have given detailed notes for a dramatised rendering of some passages, and choreographed some dances in detail. Once you start, I am convinced that much unknown talent will come to light and you will be amazed by what your parish can do.

None of the dances requires great technical excellence. Anyone capable of learning a country dance will find the steps within their scope. The aim is not to achieve a breathtaking performance, but to help the congregation to grasp a particular truth or spiritual quality — similar, in a way, to the Mediaeval mystery plays.

Sometimes a passage lends itself so readily to dramatisation that I have left the details up to the drama group. If you need help for these occasions, here are a few suggestions to start you off:

— have a narrator to read, and simply mime what he says. Anyone not involved in the action at any one time freezes in his last position, like 'statues';

— give individuals their words to say. During the narration the characters act their parts and speak their own words;

— have one or two instruments (guitar and flute, for instance, or organ) to play quietly as a background to the reading, giving extra time between sentences for mimed action;

— use a few materials as props and costumes. They need not be elaborate, just enough to aid imagination;

— use live or taped music and depict not only the actions, through mime, but also the atmosphere and feelings, through dance. Keep it natural and simple, but controlled;

— invite a local dance or drama company to prepare a presentation for a festival which could be presented during the service.

CHILDREN'S TEACHING

The children's work in this book links closely with the week's theme and readings, so the family of Christ will be sharing the Word and learning together. If teachers are preparing the readings for themselves the children will benefit from their insights. The teaching is aimed at four to nine year olds, but can be adapted to suit the age and needs of each group. The children may produce a display or model as part of their study. It is important, not just for them, but for the whole congregation, that the work is seen and shared. Often the directness of children's work can trigger new understanding among adults. The provision of a fully developed teaching scheme with 'off the peg' materials is beyond the scope of this book. The aim is to provide ideas, suggestions and practical hints to help you create your own 'bespoke tailoring' scheme which will exactly fit your parish.

It may be a good idea to make a resources 'bank' as you work through the two-year course, which you can build on next time round. You can duplicate and copy from the pictures; supplementary material is available in the Palm Tree Instant Art series.

EACH WEEK IS SET OUT LIKE THIS

Today's theme
Parish music
Church decoration

Then follows the ministry of the word for each year, set out like this:

Notes on the readings — **Year 1**
Questions for discussion
Ideas for adults
Children's teaching
Intercessions (for both **Years 1 and 2**)
Notes on the readings — **Year 2**
Questions for discussion
Ideas for adults
Children's teaching

Abbreviations used in referring to sources for songs and hymns:

MWTP — Many Ways To Praise
ONA — Hymns Old & New (Anglican)
SONL — Songs of New Life

BEFORE CHRISTMAS

9th Sunday before Christmas

TODAY'S THEME

... is that God created our universe and everything in it, including us. He gives us both physical and spiritual life and sustains his creation with his constant love. As Lord of life he is worthy of all the praise, honour and worship that we can offer.

PARISH MUSIC

Hymns
All the nations of the earth
He's got the whole world in his hand
I danced in the morning
Jesus is Lord! Creation's voice
Light's abode, celestial Salem
Morning has broken
New every morning is the love
Teach me my God and King
The spacious firmament on high
This world you have made

Recorded music
Creation (Haydn): the first section
Morning has broken (Cat Stevens)

For choirs
Above him stood the seraphim (Dering):
  SS
Holy, holy, holy (Palestrina): SATB

CHURCH DECORATION

Use bright and varied colours in flower arrangements, and include wheat and dried grasses, fruits and seed pods to reflect the theme of God's glory, and the wonder of the world he has made.

NOTES ON THE READINGS Year 1

Genesis 1:1-3, 24-31a
Our world did not arrive by accident. The order which characterises the whole universe is not the result of a number of random coincidences and chance developments. The world has occurred because God wanted it to. This divine, creative life-force planned and willed it all to happen. The beautiful poem of creation in Genesis is written to express this fundamental truth, rather than formulate an exact scientific account of events. The finer details of order and method are far less important than the humbling realisation that some great and powerful being instigated all that we know and a good deal that we don't know. Lovingly it was brought into existence because God knew it was a good idea. He chose to create a you and a me. The world he has made is intrinsically good and fully in accordance with God's will.

Colossians 1:15-20
Paul is claiming for Jesus of Nazareth a far higher and greater identity than that of a good man, fine moral leader or outstanding prophet. To claim that he is actually the image of the unseen God is outrageous and challenging. Sometimes it seems easier to believe in God as a vast and cosmic power, the great Spirit of the Universe, the force of Love and source of Life, separate from the man of Galilee, healing, teaching and dying on a Roman gallows.

As soon as we recognise Jesus as being one with the all-powerful creative God — God with a human face — we are bound to listen intently to Jesus' teachings, follow him doggedly, talk to him and introduce him to our friends. If we are at all interested in our individual and collective purpose, we shall find answers to our questions in the reconciling life and death of Jesus, the Christ.

John 1:1-14
Those who spent a lot of time with Jesus could see the divine glory in the grace and truth of this remarkable person. Jesus, the Word of God, is expressing God's character in his behaviour in Palestine just as he had expressed it at the very beginning of creation. Jesus is amazing proof that God loves us enough to get personally involved with us, without waiting for us to become worthy of such attention. Because of this there is always hope in every situation, which we can claim as soon as we claim Jesus Christ as Lord of our lives.

QUESTIONS FOR DISCUSSION

1. 'Word' has many different meanings and connotations. It can be an expression, a command, a promise, an identification, a direct means of communication. How do each of these relate to John's title for Jesus the Word of God?
2. Why do you think science is often talked of as being in opposition to religion? Is this really the case? In what way are they reconciled?

IDEAS FOR ADULTS

The reading from Colossians is most effective if read chorally. Have a group of six people, divided by voice in Light, Medium and Dark. Arrange them like this:

Medium and	Christ is the image of the
Dark	unseen God *(slowly)*
All	and the first-born of all creation,
Dark	for in him were created all things in heaven and earth; *(getting softer)*
Light	everything visible *(pause)* and everything invisible,
1 Medium	Thrones,
1 Light	Dominations *(loud)*
1 Dark	Sovereignties,
Medium	Powers, *(pause)*
All	all things were created through him and for him.
Light	Before anything was created,
Light and Medium	he existed, *(getting louder)*
All	and he holds all things in unity.
Dark	Now the Church is his body,
Medium	he is its head. *(pause)*
1 Light	As he is the Beginning, *(very loud)*
Light	he was first to be born from the dead,
Medium	so that he should be first in every way; *(loud)*
All	because God wanted all perfection to be found in him *(slowly)*
Light	and all things to be reconciled
Light and Medium	through him and for him
Dark	everything in heaven *(louder)*
Medium	and everything on earth,
All	when he made peace by his death on the cross. *(slowly, quieter)*

CHILDREN'S TEACHING

Read the children the story of creation, either from the Bible, or from a Bible story book such as *God Makes the World* (Palm Tree Press). In prayer together thank God for the wonderful world he has made for us. Then give out lumps of modelling clay and make some models of some of God's plants and creatures. Arrange everything on a large tray which has been covered with green and blue paper to represent the land and sea. Write a title for the display: GOD MADE THE WORLD, and bring it into the church for everyone to see. Try singing: *Fishes of the ocean* (Many Ways to Praise, 34); *Push little seed* (Many Ways to Praise, 6), *Who put the colours in the rainbow?* (Hymns Old and New, 584).

INTERCESSIONS **Years 1 and 2**
Some ideas for prayer

Knowing that when we pray in faith
our loving Father will hear us,
let us pray together
for the church, and for the world he has made.

Bless the work of all who spread
the wonderful news of your love.
May all who profess to be Christians
shine with your light so that others are drawn
to know your glory and experience the joy of
   your peace.
Pause
Lord our maker: **hear our prayer**

Sustain and protect Elizabeth our Queen
and guide all world leaders, advisers and
   politicians
to act with wisdom and integrity.
Pause
Lord our maker: **hear our prayer**

Father, we commend to your loving keeping
all who have died, especially . . .
that they may live for ever
in the glorious peace
and joy of your heaven.
Pause
Lord our maker: **hear our prayer**

We offer you thanks and praise
for the rich and beautiful world
you have provided for us,
and for the many blessings in our lives,
and for the gift of life itself.
Pause
Lord our maker: **hear our prayer**

Merciful Father,
accept these prayers
for the sake of your Son,
our Saviour Jesus Christ, Amen.

NOTES ON THE READINGS **Year 2**

Genesis 2:4b-9, 15-end
This is the older of the two creation stories in Genesis, usually known as the J tradition because it refers to God as Jahweh, or Jehovah. In it we see man and woman working in partnership with God in the very rich and beautiful world he has made. There is a sense of comfortable companionship between these created beings and the Lord who has made them. Under God's authority they are able to enjoy the freedom of the garden, including the tree of life itself. It is only the usurping of God's authority — the challenging of his basic principles of good and evil — that is forbidden, for that is bound to fracture the fine tuning of God's world, disrupt the mutual trust he has created and damage the natural harmony that comes from living life in fellowship with him.

Revelation 4
On earth we are surrounded by the evidence of God's glory, mastery, imagination, humour and order. Just as a close study of an artist's exhibition enables us to grasp something of the way he thinks and feels, so a walk through life provides us with plenty of glimpses into the nature of our creator.

In this vision John the Divine sees God's glory in a rare and startling directness. Obviously the sight is impossible to describe in earthly terms, but John expresses it in terms of purest light, brilliant as jewels, bright with a surrounding rainbow, charged with power like a thunder storm. We are given a wonderful sense of the creative force from which we and all things in heaven and earth spring; God is at the very centre of our universe and his majesty and power are truly awesome. He is no man-sized god, but the infinitely gracious Lord, worthy of all praise and honour.

John 3:1-8
We are spiritual, as well as physical beings, created not just for seventy-odd years in this world but also for eternity. Often people become aware of their spiritual selves by virtue of neglect. There is a gnawing restlessness which refuses to be satisfied by the acquisition of material goods, busy lives or even close relationships, and never finds rest until it encounters the peace of God.

In his conversation with Nicodemus, Jesus explains that spiritual awakening as being born all over again. If we try to grasp spiritual truths entirely in physical terms then it will all seem, as it did to Nicodemus, very puzzling and incredible. But when we remember that God is Spirit, greater than time and space, infinitely present and personally involved with our lives, which he designed and is nurturing at this very moment, then we realise that to live completely the physical is inadequate; like trying to explore Africa by sitting in an armchair with an atlas.

QUESTIONS FOR DISCUSSION

1. What sort of qualities and characteristics of God are suggested by the world he has made? Look at all aspects of his universe, from the galactic to the microscopic. It might be helpful for group leaders to bring pictures of different scenery and wildlife, and a few objects such as feathers, shells, minerals or leaves, just to start the imaginations going.
2. Is there a danger that in making our worship informal and 'friendly' we may lose the sense of God's great glory being reverenced, honoured and adored? How can we make sure that our worship expresses awe and wonder?

IDEAS FOR ADULTS

Display a selection of pictures showing the wonder and variety of God's universe. Use magazines, holiday view postcards, birthday cards and calendars. Entitle the display:
'The earth belongs to the Lord, and all that it contains: the whole earth, and all who live in it.' Psalm 24:1

CHILDREN'S TEACHING

On tables around the edge of the room put a varied collection of things created by God, together with hands-on activities. Let the children spend some time exploring these.

Display suggestions:

Assorted rocks and pebbles: How many colours can you see?
Sea shells: Put a shell to your ear. What can you hear?
Autumn leaves: Find which trees these came from, with a chart.
A globe: Can you find Britain? The Pacific Ocean? Australia?
Feathers: Look for the hooks on the end of the feathers with a magnifying glass.
Animal pictures or models: Which box does each animal belong to? (With boxes labelled "Meat eaters", "Grass eaters")
Prism or cut glass beads: Can you make rainbows?
Containers of sand, dried peas, bird seed, sheep's wool: Feel the different textures.

Magnets and a box of things to test for magnetism: What will the magnet attract?

When everyone has sampled everything, gather in a circle to talk about the amazing world God has made for us to live in and look after. How can we look after it well? Thank God together for all he has made, and help the children write down their thanks to God for the things they find most amazing, beautiful, powerful or clever. Cut round the decorated prayers, stick double-sided sticky tape on the back and bring them into church to add to the adults' Creation display. Try singing: *If I were an astronaut*, or, *There's a seed* (MWTP); or *If I were a Butterfly* (ONA).

enthusiast. Miniature gardens in bowls could also be borrowed for today.

8th Sunday before Christmas

TODAY'S THEME

... is the destructive nature of sin, which separates us from God through our disobedience to his will. It was God's love for us that prompted him to give his only Son so that we could be bought back, or redeemed, from the sentence of death and given the chance of new life in Christ.

PARISH MUSIC

Hymns
All my hope on God is founded
A safe stronghold our God is still
Dear Lord and Father of mankind
Guide me, O thou great Redeemer
If we only seek peace
It is a thing most wonderful
Praise to the holiest in the height

Recorded music
Suite in A minor for flute and strings (Telemann)

For choirs
Jesus Christ the Apple Tree (Anthony Piccolo): SS
Day by day (Martin How): 3 part

CHURCH DECORATION

Use a selection of miniature potted trees if possible, such as orange and lemon (citris mitis), bay, Indian tree of happiness or even a bonsai collection if the parish boasts a bonsai

NOTES ON THE READING **Year 1**

Genesis 4:1-10
In this story we watch the resentment of Cain fester into hatred and then murder, as sin takes control of his life. From the beginning he was grudging. Abel had offered the best of his flock to God, while Cain offered only some of his produce from the soil. Typical of humankind, Cain found it bitter to delight in his brother's joy and success, and instead he allowed his resentment to feed a self-pitying grouse at the unfairness of life.

As soon as we allow sin to master us even in the smallest area of our lives, we increase our vulnerability and polish the slide for a rapid descent into evil. None of us is immune from the risk. None can assume it only happens to all the rest. Murder takes many forms, and though we may not commit it directly, God will expect us to accept responsibility for our fellow humans. If someone dies as a result of our self-indulgence or refusal to share the world's resources, or lack of interest in providing a fresh water supply for all earth's inhabitants, then we cannot try to excuse ourselves from being partly to blame.

I John 3:9-18
In fact, if we do remain blind to the needs of our brothers and sisters, John says we are

proving that we do not really love God, however much we claim to love him. True love is bound to show itself in the way we spend our time, talents and money, and in the way we behave, whether anyone we want to impress is watching us or not.

It would be so depressing to feel we had to struggle ineptly along the right path, knowing our habits and weaknesses and certain of failure. Fortunately, we don't have to. God promises to live within us to work for good in our lives — and we couldn't get more constant and individual help than that!

Such help and encouragement is vital. Not only do we need constant protection against temptation; we are also likely to be disliked, hated or even attacked, as Abel was, once people begin to see our lives starting to shine with the light of Christian love. Bright shining can make us feel bad about our own darkness.

Mark 7:14-23
That bad feeling inside comes out as spiteful words, unkind behaviour or malicious scheming. It is our heart that needs to be right with God, and no amount of ritual, no number of correctly followed rules, can take the place of a genuine sorrow at sin committed and a longing to love and serve God better.

The trouble is, we like making rules because then we can follow them and feel smugly that we have completed our duty. But God's values reach deep into the intentions behind our actions, the hidden resentments and secret refusals to forgive. We may fool other Christians with our empty observance of religious customs, but we do not fool God.

He is longing to save each separate person in our world from the terrible destructiveness of sin. His willingness to die for us proves the extent of his longing and his love.

QUESTIONS FOR DISCUSSION

1. What practical steps can we take to prevent sin taking control in our lives? What is the most important thing to do when we do sin?
2. What kind of love is John talking about when he says it is clearly shown in Christ giving his life for us?

IDEAS FOR ADULTS

The reading from Genesis is effective if mimed as it is read. Begin with Cain and Abel walking up to the altar from the back of the church. Cain carries a bunch of wheat, and Abel a toy lamb or a rolled sheepskin rug. God, represented by the minister, accepts Abel's generous gift warmly. When Cain grudgingly hands over his small bunch of wheat God takes it, looks from it to Cain with sorrow, and gives it back.

Cain turns round to face the congregation, his face sullen and resentful. God puts his arm round him as he explains why Cain is feeling angry and depressed, and warns him of the danger of allowing sin to take over. Cain shrugs him off roughly and goes across to his brother indicating that they could go out for the day. He appears friendly, and Abel smiles and agrees.

They walk across the front of the congregation a few steps and then comes the murder. This needs to be acted with two or three strong and clear moves — rather like you would see in dance — with Cain's hatred obvious. Cain runs from the body of his brother towards the back of the church, and God walks over to Abel's body, touches it gently, and calls to Cain from there. At the end the actors freeze in position until after 'Thanks be to God'. Then Abel gets up and walks down to the back with God.

CHILDREN'S TEACHING

Remind the children of the beautiful world God has made and then talk with them about the way we all sometimes spoil it. Have ready a display of pictures to help the thinking. Cut some from newspapers, or use these drawings:

Tell the children the story of how Cain started off being mean and ungrateful to God, became jealous of his brother, began to hate his brother and eventually killed him. Slide a stone down a tilted tray to show how easy it is to slide down once you've got started. Perhaps they have tried stopping halfway down a slide — it takes a lot of strength.

What can we do to stop ourselves slipping down into sin? Show them a large rolled strip of paper and ask one child to hold an end while another child unrolls it. The others read out what it says:

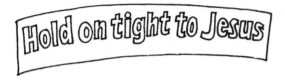

We can talk to Jesus about our bad habits and ask him to help us change them.

We can call to him for strength when we feel tempted to be greedy, unkind or bad-tempered.

We can try to form new habits, such as being helpful, friendly or generous.

Pray together, thanking God for his gifts to us through the last week, asking his forgiveness for times we have spoilt his world, and offering him the coming week for God to use us to spread his love around.

Colour in the letters on the strip of paper and display it in church. Try singing:
Love is something if you give it away
When I needed a neighbour (ONA, 576)
Never let Jesus into your heart unless ...
   (MWTP, 104)

INTERCESSIONS **Years 1 and 2**
Some ideas for prayer

In the Spirit of Jesus Christ, who can save us
   from sin,
let us pray to our heavenly Father
for the Church and for the world.

We pray for all who witness to the truth
of saving love,
especially those whose Christian witness
brings danger, hardship or ridicule.
Pause
Father of Love: **we believe and trust in you**

We pray for our Queen and all who hold
positions of authority in our world;
that they may be led to right and just decisions
in keeping with your will.
Pause
Father of Love: **we believe and trust in you**

We pray for the members of our families,
for all those who are precious to us
and those we find difficult to get on with;
strengthen our love for one another
and give us the grace
to forgive wholeheartedly.
Pause
Father of Love: **we believe and trust in you**

We pray for the vulnerable and the frightened,
for those tormented by guilt and those who
   despair;
give them the comfort of knowing you are with
   them
and draw them to the light of your forgiveness.
Pause
Father of Love: **we believe and trust in you**

We pray for those who have died
and for those who mourn;
grant them peace in your presence for ever.
Pause
Father of Love: **we believe and trust in you**

Thank you, Father, for supplying us always
with the strength we need to do your will,
and for the joy of working with you.
Merciful Father,
accept these prayers
for the sake of your Son
our Saviour Jesus Christ, Amen.

NOTES ON THE READINGS **Year 2**

Genesis 3:1-15
See how subtle the stages of temptation can be. First the seeds of doubt are sown which cast a slur on God's motives in making his rules. Is it really for our own good that we are not to eat of the fruit or indulge ourselves in any activity we please? Or is it perhaps God's way of keeping us in our place and preventing us from becoming like gods ourselves? At once the ambition to be totally powerful takes root, and we look for ways to justify what we have already decided to do. It may look from the outside as if we are doing something for a good reason, but God is never fooled.

The result of Adam and Eve's disobedience is to drive home to them just how naked and vulnerable they are compared with the great power of their creator. That is why they suddenly become frightened of God and hide from him.

Romans 7:7-13
Sin is always deceitful, often using what is intrinsically good to twist our priorities, misguide and coax us into behaving in ways which are contrary to God's law of Love. Paul found that even the Law itself had been used

to tempt him into sin, by spelling out possible evil he hadn't thought about before. Similarly, news reports condemning certain actions may have the effect of starting a rash of such incidences. The point is that while neither the Law nor the news reports are wrong, sin is devastatingly cunning, and we need to be constantly on our guard to avoid being tricked into it.

John 3:13-21
If evil is so cleverly woven into the fabric of our existence, what chance can we possibly have of living good lives? Surely our weakness condemns us before we've even got started. Fortunately, evil is not the strongest force in the universe. God, the supreme Being, is utterly good and loving. Loving enough to risk rejection by creating us with free will to choose right or wrong. Loving enough to confine himself as man in order to save us from the mess of sin we get ourselves into.

For in Christ we are not left to struggle ineptly on our own. Believing in him is a strong, unbreakable life-line that holds us firmly through temptation and rescues us whenever we feel ourselves slipping and falling. The choice between using that life-line and foundering in sin is left to us.

QUESTIONS FOR DISCUSSION

1. Apply the stages of temptation, guilt and blame which are described in the Genesis reading to contemporary sins, such as drug taking, fiddling expenses, adultery, malicious gossip and critical attitudes.
2. After reading John 3:13-21, how would you answer someone who felt that the wrong they had done had put them out of reach of forgiveness from anyone, let alone God. Other useful references: Luke 15:11-24, Luke 23:39-43, Romans 8:1-39).

IDEAS FOR ADULTS

The reading from Genesis is very effective if acted out in the style of the early Mystery Plays. Have God dressed in white, Adam and Eve in brief, simple tunics, and the serpent in leotard and tights of one colour.

Begin with a recording of bird song to create the atmosphere of the lovely garden, which mankind's sin has spoilt. Adam and Eve run up together from the back, looking furtively behind them every so often. At the front they stand pressed against a pew or lectern, as if concealing themselves. (Use a sheet of cardboard to make the sound of distant thunder to suggest inevitable threat.)

God walks slowly up the centre aisle as the narrator starts to read. God's 'Where are you?' is repeated as he nears the front. God stops before he gets really close to Adam, so that they have to call to each other. When God asks why he knows he is naked, Adam and Eve look at each other in silent panic, for they have been found out. They hold hands and agree not to answer.

When God opens the way for Adam to own up, he and Eve release hands and Adam moves slightly away from Eve, so as to disassociate himself from blame. The woman covers her face with her hands. At this point the serpent is seen crawling between Adam and Eve and God. When God asks the woman: 'What is this you have done?' she sees the chance of blaming something else and comes forward pointing accusingly at the serpent as she speaks.

As God addresses the serpent, who writhes in resentment and frustration, Adam and Eve listen in fear, clinging to each other. The thunder crashes as God retraces his steps to the back and Adam and Eve move, weakened and frightened by the silent garden, in another direction. The serpent slinks off a different way.

CHILDREN'S TEACHING

Talk together about how difficult it is to be good. Even quite young children will have discovered the tiresome truth that Paul also found: the things we don't intend to do, we end up doing; and some of the good things we mean to do, don't get done! Such a discussion does not damage a child's self image; rather, it helps him see that doing wrong sometimes is part of being human, and the important thing is to say sorry and put things right quickly.

Now tell them a story of Adam and Eve being disobedient. This is a sin they will readily understand; they may also pick up the way Adam blames Eve and she blames the serpent. They had chosen not to do what God wanted, and that spoilt things. Help them see how we, too, are always free to choose whether to be loving or unloving. Who can help us make the right decision? Jesus can. Why? Show them a picture of Jesus healing, then teaching, so they can see that, though a man like Adam, Jesus was God's Son, and always, without fail, chose to be loving.

Even when people were horrid and cruel to him he went on loving. (Show them a crucifix.) Even when they killed him, he loved and forgave. So if we trust him as our most special friend, he will help us to grow more and more loving.

Using two spent matches and a wire bag-fastener, the children can make a small cross to carry about in a pocket, to remind them to ask Jesus to help when they are tempted to be unkind, mean or selfish.

CHURCH DECORATION

Make one of the flower arrangements an expression of the way God honoured Abraham's act of faith. For *Year I*, lay down a thick plastic sheet with sand and rocks on it. Pile the sand round the vase so it is hidden. Use yellow and white flowers and dried seed heads in the arrangement.

For *Year 2*, lay down driftwood or dead branches to be firewood. Place the vase in the centre and lay a length of coiled rope on the wood. Use reds, oranges, yellows and whites to create an impression of fire.

7th Sunday before Christmas

TODAY'S THEME

. . . is that real faith is bound to be revealed in action. Abraham was prepared to trust God absolutely, even when he could not understand what he was being asked to do, and God honoured such faith. It is no good talking about having faith in God if we are not prepared to translate it into loving action and obedience to his will.

PARISH MUSIC

Hymns
My faith it is an oaken staff
Great is thy faithfulness
The God of Abraham praise
O Jesus I have promised
Lord of my life
I give my hands to do your work

Recorded music
Symphony No. 28 (Mozart): Andante

For choirs
I will lift up mine eyes (Colin Mawby): U
O love of whom is truth and light
(Johann Scheffler) SATB

NOTES ON THE READINGS **Year 1**

Genesis 12:1-9

Abram's obedience is so simply told that it sounds quite easy. In fact, it must have been a great upheaval and a move which was no doubt ridiculed as senseless by many. Why did he want to uproot everything and wander off, leaving all his security behind, for goodness' sake?

Obviously Abram was not like a reed in the wind, easily persuaded by anybody. So he must have recognised that this calling, though unusual and unexpected, was nonetheless full of authority. He sensed the greatness of God, and bowed before it, committing his future security and welfare to God's protection.

If we say that we acknowledge God's greatness, then we must show it to be true in the way we willingly submit to changes, new directions, dangerous or unpleasant undertakings, without grumbling about what we have had to give up.

Whenever we are called forward we shall have to leave something behind. But God will be going with us, so we shall end up not poorer, but richer.

Romans 4:13-end

Abraham is a shining example of faith, since he

believed God's promise in spite of all its seeming impossibility. The practical details were left trustingly in God's capable hands because Abraham had no doubt about either God's power or his unswerving loyalty. It was this great faith which saved, or justified him, as it is our faith which speaks for us.

We may have to begin by wanting to believe, and asking for faith. We may be helped to it by being encouraged to step out, without support being visible, like a beginner on to an ice rink. Gradually we will be encouraged to take greater 'risks' trusting in God, instead of trusting in the more obvious support of our own strength, energy, intelligence or influence. That is not easy, especially if we prize our independence and resourcefulness. But it is essential if we are to learn to trust God. The fruit of that love will be increased love for one another.

John 8:51-end
Sadly, some of those claiming most vehemently to trust God were unable to recognise him when he stood among them in the person of Jesus. Consequently their reaction to hints of his divinity ('before Abraham was born, I am') is such violent anger at his 'blasphemy' that they pick up stones to throw at him.

How was it possible for such a terrible misunderstanding to occur among those who studied God's law? Is it possible that we may act with similar blindness to Christ's presence in the world? For answer we are referred by Jesus back to Abraham once more. He, says Jesus, was overjoyed to see the Christ — God incarnate. His faith allowed him to 'see'. Where we rely only on proved, rational, visible evidence, we are effectively shutting out whole landscapes of insight which we might call Wisdom, or spiritual perception. This is the only way we can hope to stay in touch with God's truth, and it comes through living in his company.

QUESTIONS FOR DISCUSSION

1. Why did Jesus' expression, 'I am', have such a powerful effect on his listeners? (You may like to refer to Exodus 3:13-15 to help you.)
2. Do you think that suffering, insecurity and hardship in our lives can sometimes be spiritually advantageous to us? Could that change our attitude to any present difficulties?

IDEAS FOR ADULTS

On a display board, create this visual meditation on what real faith involves. Use a selection of pictures showing empty or deserted landscapes, candles or lanterns burning in darkness, and flowering and fruiting trees. (Sources: calendars, postcards, greetings cards, advertisements, holiday brochures, magazines and gardening catalogues.)

Write out appropriate quotations on pieces of white card. Here are some suggestions:

'Faith is the root of works. A root that produces nothing is dead.'   (Thomas Wilson)
'As the flower is before the fruit, so is faith before good works.'   (Richard Whately)
'Trouble is only opportunity in work clothes.'   (Anon)
'Going to church doesn't make you a Christian any more than going to a garage makes you an automobile.'   (Billy Sunday)
'Faith opens the door to understanding, unbelief closes it.'   (St. Augustine of Hippo)
'To have found God is not an end in itself but a beginning.'   (Franz Rosenzweig)
'The beginning of anxiety is the end of faith, and the beginning of true faith is the end of anxiety.'   (George Mueller)
Arrange all the material on a contrasting background, and give it a title:
'*O come, all ye faithful!*'

CHILDREN'S TEACHING

First show the children a world map. Establish one or two countries they know of and then point out Haran and the route to Canaan. Also show pictures of the landscape there (the local library should have some books with photographs of the Bible lands). It is important that the children realise these places really exist!

Now tell the children about a man who lived there, called Abraham. Read them just the first paragraph of the Genesis reading. Talk together about how it feels to be starting out somewhere new for the first time, such as a new school, a new class or moving house. Abraham, too, may well have been a bit scared. He may not have particularly wanted to go. But he trusted God and obeyed him. God promised that he would be with Abraham and he kept his word.

Using an old baking tray, sand and stones, make a model of Abraham setting off for the promised land. Abraham and his family are made of pipecleaners and pieces of material, and sheep and goats are made from black and white pipe-cleaners. Write a title for the model:

ABRAHAM TRUSTED GOD

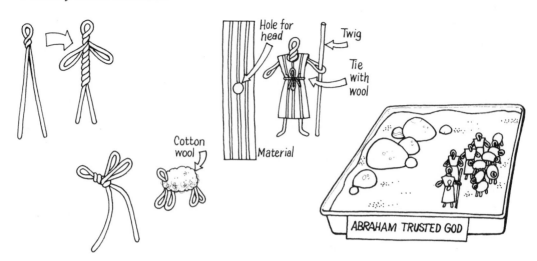

Try singing: *Forward in faith* (MWTP, 54)
I watch the sunrise (Alleluya! 15)

INTERCESSIONS **Years 1 and 2**
Some ideas for prayer

My brothers and sisters in Christ,
bound together in love and faith let us pray for
    the Church
and for the world.

O Lord our God, we trust in your promise to
    hear us
when we pray in faith.

Strengthen us in the certain knowledge of your
    constant presence,
so that we witness to your love by the way
we speak and act each day.
Pause
Merciful Father: **hear us as we pray**

Teach us and guide us to use the resources of
    the world
wisely and unselfishly, sharing its riches
and respecting its beauty.
Pause
Merciful Father: **hear us as we pray**

Alert us to the needs of those around us
and increase our friendliness and understanding
in all our relationships.
Pause
Merciful Father: **hear us as we pray**

Bring your health and wholeness
to those in physical pain
and mental anguish,
and give your inner peace
to those overwhelmed with worries.
Pause
Merciful Father: **hear us as we pray**

Into your hands, Father we commend

those who have died,
for we know that in your care
they are safe.
Pause
Merciful Father: **hear us as we pray**

And now we want to thank you
for your constant love and kindness,
support and protection.
Pause
Merciful Father:
accept these prayers
for the sake of your Son,
our Saviour Jesus Christ, Amen.

NOTES ON THE READINGS **Year 2**

Genesis 22:1-18
It must have seemed utterly incomprehensible
to Abraham that God should ask him to sacrifice
the very son through whom the promise of a
chosen nation was to be fulfilled. If Isaac were
killed, how could God's word possibly come
true?

Perhaps Abraham was on the edge of trusting
more in the means of achieving results than in
the source of the power. Such a drastic threat
to the 'means' threw Abraham's faith squarely
on to the author of the promise. Since he was
prepared to sacrifice even his beloved son,
Abraham proved that even his most cherished
hopes were second to his desire to serve God
faithfully.

It was not any blood-sacrifice that God
required. He needed Abraham to sacrifice 'faith-
in-other-things', however closely those things
may be tied up with his will. And it is all too
easy to start trusting in the means instead of the
source.

If anything seems to be steering our attention

away from God, we may find we are asked to abandon it, even though it is intrinsically good. Perhaps, once we have refocused our priorities, it will be given back abundantly; but by that time we will have sacrificed our faith in it, so our trust in God will have grown.

James 2:14-24 (25,26)

James' sardonic humour drives the point home: faith without action is ridiculously ineffective. Our faith is dead and barren if we think our Christian duty is done by praying for the needs of the world on Sunday and sympathising from a safe distance.

God's idea of faith is rather different. He expects us to take an active part in helping those in need and changing what is wrong in society. A truly Christian community can never be apathetic or complacent. Christians should be positively involved in the community, not instead of church going, but as the natural result of worshipping the God of Love.

Luke 20:9-17

Perhaps the key to this parable is the motive behind the killing of the heir to the vineyard. The tenants figure that if he is out of the way they will be able to own the vineyard themselves. Get rid of your faith in God and you can live as selfishly as you like.

There is another point, too. The people listening are horrified at what Jesus says the owner will do. For some the abuse of the prophets and the rejection of Christ is not deliberate evil but the result of an appalling blindness — a total inability to recognise Christ in everyday situations. We sometimes talk about the 'eye' of faith; that gift of discerning God in daily life is available for the asking, and we need to cultivate it so as to avoid the risk of persecuting and rejecting the very God we claim to worship.

QUESTIONS FOR DISCUSSION

1. What circumstances or events in your life have helped to increase your faith? Are they linked with times when you recognise your human limits and weakness? Trace the way God has used events in your life to draw you towards him.
2. Is the faith of this parish resulting in a more caring community, not just among the congregation but among all who live in the area? If you are doubtful, pray together that God will show you how he needs you to witness to his love. Ideas growing out of such prayer should be very seriously considered.

IDEAS FOR ADULTS

There may be a religious resource centre in your area from which you can borrow a set of 'creation' slides showing the whole range and development of life on earth. Otherwise, collect a set of slides showing the beauty of creation, such as sunsets, trees and animals, the sea and rivers, and people. It does not matter if they don't link precisely with the order of creation — they are there to help awaken people's wonder.

An organist may be able to play sustained chords which complement the reading and slides. Alternatively, try using the slow movement of one of Mahler's symphonies in the background.

The reading from Genesis can be dramatised very effectively. The narrator reads the story while others act it out, speaking their own words.

CHILDREN'S TEACHING

First show some pictures of people in different uniforms (nurses, soldiers, brownies, astronauts, etc.) and ask the children what each person is.

Have the labels ready and stick them on to the pictures as each is named. Talk about what we know about each one because of the uniform worn. (We know, for instance, that the nurse probably works in a hospital, takes temperatures, gives out medicine and changes bandages etc.)

Then show an ordinary group of people. They are Christians (put on label) but their uniform is not their clothes — it is the way they behave. We can't see their faith, but we can see the effect of their faith, in their behaviour.

Discuss with the children what marks a person as being a Christian who has faith in God. (They worship God, pray, behave lovingly, forgive quickly, are happy even when they don't get everything their own way, they are helpful and kind etc.)

Point out that often we don't behave like this, and then we are letting God down, just as a nurse would let the hospital and the patients down if she didn't give out the right medicines. If we say we believe in God then we must show our faith in the way we act.

Now read them the first paragraph of the reading from James 2, first dressing one child up in rags with a begging bowl, so that you call across to this child, 'Good luck to you,' etc. at the appropriate time. Afterwards collect ideas for how a person with real faith in God would help, and act this out.

Organise an event during the week in which

they can all help someone in a practical way.

Suggestions:

★ clearing leaves from paths of elderly people
★ a sponsored silence in aid of a charity
★ a visit to an old people's home to sing to the residents and chat to them

Try singing: *Wanted — Good Hands* (MWTP, 50), *Forward in Faith* (MWTP, 54).

6th Sunday before Christmas

TODAY'S THEME

... is that God promises to save his people, and he can be trusted to keep his word. Moses had faith in God's promise to set his people free from slavery. Our faith in Jesus can set us free from the binding chains of sin. He will lead us and protect us from evil.

PARISH MUSIC

Hymns
Father, hear the prayer we offer
Guide me O thou great Redeemer
Lord Jesus Christ
Moses, I know you're the man
O happy band of pilgrims
The Spirit lives to set us free
Walk with me, O my Lord

Recorded music
The Planets Suite (Holst): Neptune

For choirs
God be in my head (Martin How): U
A prayer of St. Richard of Chichester
(L. J. White): U with descant

CHURCH DECORATION

Make one of the flower arrangements a foliage arrangement instead, using different types of evergreen. Traditionally, evergreen is a symbol of God's unchanging faithfulness, and today is a lovely opportunity to use this symbol. It is surprising to find how colourful and varied an arrangement like this can be, ranging from the dark, shiny green of laurel, right through to the feathery yellow of the golden cedars.

NOTES ON THE READINGS **Year 1**

Exodus 3:7-15
The voice of God sounds full of confident enthusiasm for this escape plan. Having seen the problem and chosen the right time and the right leader, it is as if he can't wait to get started! In contrast, Moses is thoroughly dubious and sceptical. He feels utterly inadequate and unsuitable for the job, and is pretty sure the children of Israel won't accept him anyway.

Well, if he were working in his own strength he would indeed be inadequate and unsuitable — anyone would be. But God has called him, and whenever God asks us to do something, he always provides the strength, gifts and skills necessary.

In Moses' case, the first thing necessary is reassurance. God provides this by identifying himself as the God of Abraham, Isaac and Jacob; this reminds both Moses and the Israelites that God has shown himself to be faithful through many generations, and his promises can be trusted now as then.

Hebrews 3:1-6
Through his faith and obedience Moses is a valuable and respected servant in the 'household' of God. All that he worked for and looked forward to was fulfilled in the coming of Christ, who is not another servant but the Son and heir. As Christians, then, we follow not only the guidelines of the Law but also the living pathway — Jesus himself.

John 6:25-35
In this teaching, following the feeding of the 5,000 Jesus shows how he is indeed the promised Saviour, who provides our sustenance for eternal, spiritual life, just as bread provides us with temporary, physical sustenance. It may seem amazing to us that the people had just been fed miraculously, and many had been healed of diseases, yet they still clamoured for a sign.

Two very human characteristics are in evidence here. One is our desire for the spectacular. Amazing though the multiplying of bread and fishes was, it was not a grand conjuring trick prefaced with a roll of drums. Just Jesus quietly breaking the food up and the people finding they are getting enough to satisfy their hunger. The other is the way we are apt to idolise our heroes and heroines instead of following the direction of their eyes towards God. Moses had constantly reminded the people that it was God who had looked after them so well and here Jesus has to remind them again. But their great regard for one of God's servants is proving an obstacle in their acceptance of the very Saviour Moses foresaw. God often shows himself in ways we are not expecting. It is important that we recognise his presence.

QUESTIONS FOR DISCUSSION

1. Look through Exodus and find some examples of times when God proved himself

faithful to his word: 'But I will be with you'. You may like to share times in your own 'journey' when God has been with you in difficult situations.

2. Jesus said that to do the work of God means to believe in him whom he has sent. Why does he call faith 'work'? (Think of Abraham and Moses. Also such people as Bonhoeffer, Mother Teresa, Martin Luther King.)

IDEAS FOR ADULTS

Coventry cathedral has a series of stone slabs engraved with different words of Jesus. As visitors walk round, these provide profound truths to challenge and inspire. Stone slabs are hardly every parish church's dream, but the idea of an appropriate text being displayed is a very valuable one. Rather than writing the words on a large sheet of paper, try cutting out separate letters from black paper and fixing them to the wall. The words, from today's gospel, are:

CHILDREN'S TEACHING

Talk with the children about what they have eaten for breakfast. Then say something like: 'Well, you won't be needing any more food today, then, will you.' Pretend to be surprised that they are expecting to have more food later on. Why? Because they will get hungry again.

Now show the children a picture of Jesus feeding the 5,000 with bread and fish. Everyone had enough to eat at the time. But would they get hungry again? Yes; one loaf will not keep us alive for ever. Jesus told the people that he was like a loaf of bread — not to keep our bodies alive but to feed the spirit part of us which can

live for ever. If we have Jesus living in us we shall never be spiritually hungry again; he will keep us full of love, peace and joy.

Whenever we eat bread we can remember that we need Jesus, our bread of life as well. Help the children make this bread basket to use at home, and pop a roll into each to eat with their lunch.

INTERCESSIONS

As children and heirs through adoption, let us confide in our heavenly Father who knows us so well.

Father, into your enlightenment and perception we bring all whose faith is limited by fear or prejudice; all whose living faith has been replaced by the empty shell of habit.
Pause
Lord, we believe: **please help our faith to grow**

Father, into the depths of your wisdom and understanding we bring those with responsibilities, and all who have difficult decisions to make; (especially ....) all in charge of hospitals, schools,

factories and all community services.
Pause
Lord, we believe: **please help our faith to grow**

Father, into your tireless faithfulness we bring
the members of our families; any who
rely on us for help, support or guidance;
any whom we are being asked to serve
or introduce to your saving love.
Pause
Lord, we believe: **please help our faith to grow**

Father, into the gentleness of your healing love
we bring all who are in pain;
all those recovering from surgery;
those involved in crippling accidents
or suffering from wasting diseases.
Pause
Lord, we believe: **please help our faith to grow**

Father, into your lasting peace
we bring all those who have died,
especially ...
Pause
Lord, we believe: **please help our faith to grow**

Father, your character is always
full of mercy and faithfulness;
accept these prayers
for the sake of your Son,
our Saviour Jesus Christ, Amen.

NOTES ON THE READINGS **Year 2**

Exodus 6:2-8
From Abraham, starting out in faith, the
promise of God pulses through the generations
and the significant events in this emerging
nation. The covenant between God and his
people is a solemn pledge, and God's faithfulness
has proved constantly trustworthy. Now Moses,
too, is given assurance of God's love and concern
for his people and the promise of escape from
slavery.

God did not just set the creation events in
motion and then drift off, leaving us to get on
with it; he is, and always has been, bound to his
creation in love, like a parent to a child. The
anguish of the starving and oppressed reaches
his ears and evokes deep compassion just as
much in our generation as in the time of Moses.
His power is sufficient for us, now, as it proved
to be for the children of Israel then.

Hebrews 11:17-31
Some of the Jewish Christians for whom this
letter was written no doubt missed the clearly
defined rules of the Law. The Christian way of

love for God and one another, based on life in
Christ, means that the right way forward cannot
be precisely planned in advance. Rather, we
have to learn the water's lesson of flowing —
being willing to go along with God's will,
however odd, difficult or impossible it may
seem.

The writer gives a glowing list of examples of
people who have been prepared to step out in
faith like this, trusting and obeying God, even
in the most dark and dangerous times. In every
case their faith was honoured.

Mark 13:5-13
So, too, will God honour our faith when we
witness, by word and behaviour, to the Good
News of Christ's saving love. We are never
promised a bed of roses, immunity from conflict
and danger, or a charmed life. The tragedies and
world disasters will not suddenly vanish either.
But because we are fixed firmly on the eternal
rock of Christ, we need no longer be panic-
stricken and despairing when they occur.
Rather, God will use us in the mess of hatred,
oppression and deceit, his Spirit speaking
eloquently through our voices.

Nor does this only happen in the more
dramatic arenas of war and persecution. We may
be the only Christian available to witness to a
member of the family, a friend going through
a bad patch, a child at our school, a patient at
our hospital or a colleague at the office.

QUESTIONS FOR DISCUSSION

1. What examples of Christian witness have you
   seen in the news recently? In what ways has
   God been able to use tragedies such as
   earthquakes, fires and famine so as to bring
   some lasting good out of the evil?
2. How does faith grow? Base discussion on
   your own experience and on the life of Moses.

IDEAS FOR ADULTS

Cut out nine footprints from thin card to be
'steps in faith'. Write one word on each, taken
from Psalm 77:13:

WHO IS SO GREAT A GOD AS OUR GOD?

Tape the footprints down in walking and
reading order at the entrance to the church
where people will see them as they come in.

CHILDREN'S TEACHING

Remind the children about Abraham, who was
called by God to leave his home city and travel

to the Promised Land. Explain how, many generations later, the people of Israel settled in Egypt during a long drought; how the Egyptians later began using them as slaves and treating them badly.

(This should be very brief, but it is important for the children to begin to see the 'shape' of God's plan for salvation, rather than a number of unconnected events.)

Show the children a picture of Moses as a baby, hidden in his basket. This was to be the person God had chosen to lead his people to freedom. When he grew up God told him that he had heard his people's groaning and crying, and was going to help them and set them free. (With older children read the Exodus passage here.) Moses trusted God, and God kept his promise.

'Food in the Desert' (Palm Tree Press) emphasises the growth of faith through the hardships in the wilderness. Read this to the children, showing them all the pictures, to give them an idea of how God can be trusted, and how he kept his promise to Moses and his people.

Have ready the separate letters of GOD CAN BE TRUSTED on sheets of thin card, and a length of string. Give the letters out for the children to decorate and cut out, punch two holes in the top of each letter, and string them up in the right order so that the unjumbled message appears. If possible, let the children bring this into church and hang it up between two chairs, so that everyone can see.

Try singing:
Put your hand in the hand
Moses I know you're the man (ONA, 327)
Think big (ONA, 524).

5th Sunday before Christmas

TODAY'S THEME

... is the faithful remnant of God's people, through whom the Good News of God's power and willingness to save is spread to all nations. At every stage of the journey there is bound to be conflict between good and evil, and many will try to lead others astray. But we are to be prepared for this, so that, watchful and alert, we may remain faithful to our calling as followers of Christ.

PARISH MUSIC

Hymns
And now, O Father, mindful of the love
Be thou my guardian and my guide
Dear Lord and Father of mankind
Father, you are living in us now
I cannot tell why he
Let there be peace on earth
Oh when the saints go marching in
Take me, Lord, use my life

Recorded music
Symphony No. 6 (Beethoven): The end of the storm and thanksgiving after it

For choirs
My eyes for beauty pine (Herbert Howells): U opt. SATB
Thou shalt shew me the path of life (Timothy Day)

CHURCH DECORATION

The theme of a faithful remnant will be reflected in a line arrangement, where the eye is led straight up and down a central line of flowers. This is also a practical arrangement for this time of year as fewer blooms are needed. Choose flowers with tall stems, keeping the first one full length and cutting the others progressively shorter. Fill in around the flowers with foliage to give the effect of branching off from the main direction, so that the colour of the blooms looks like a steady, definite path through the distractions. Chrysanthemums would work well, as would Rayonante or Iris.

NOTES ON THE READINGS **Year 1**

I Kings 19:9-18
Elijah is dejected and fearful, doubting his vocation and threatened by his enemies.

Following his superb witness to God in the astonishing and victorious challenge to the worshippers of Baal, Elisha seems to be experiencing the 'sagging' that sometimes comes after much energy and concentration have been used. Satan is ready to use such times of exhaustion to undermine our faith and cause us to collapse in a soggy mass of self-pity, doubt or self-indulgence.

But how tenderly God ministers to his loyal servant, Elijah! Expressing himself as a quiet stillness, he shows Elijah that whatever turmoil and aggression he may be living through, there is a fundamental core of peace which is unshakeable, since it is God himself. Having reassured him, God gives Elijah practical work to do, companionship (in the form of Elisha), and the knowledge that he is supported by a remnant of 7,000 people who have remained faithful to God. Confidence restored, Elijah is empowered to resume God's work.

Romans 11:13-24

It must have been painful to Paul that so many of his own race failed to accept Jesus Christ as the promised Messiah. He reminds the Christians in Rome of the great debt they owe to the Jewish people, through whom Jesus became incarnate. Typical of the way God brings resurrection out of evil, the rejection of Christ by his own people has opened up the way for non-Jews to be reconciled to God through Christ.

But this should never lead us to dismiss God's chosen race. Eventually, not only the faithful remnant but the whole people will be reunited to the 'root', and we can only wonder at what will happen then, when God's great, good plan is fully realised. For the moment, our task is to make sure that we remain faithful, so that we do not risk separation from the true 'olive' — a chosen people, rooted in God.

Matthew 24:37-44

Jesus' teaching about the second coming gives us ample warning, if we will listen. The trouble is, we are always inclined to think that disasters are things that will happen to other people and not to us. There is, too, the temptation to presume rather heavily on God's mercy, forgetting that he is also a God of justice, and our side of the covenant is very important. We tend to tell ourselves that there will be plenty of opportunity to prepare ourselves for death and the second coming of Christ later on — when the children are off our hands, for instance, or once the decorating is finished, or when the ironing is out of the way.

Jesus tells his disciples quite clearly that we will not know when the Son of Man comes until it is too late to start preparing. There is only one time when we can prepare to make sure we are counted among his faithful when he comes: that time is now.

QUESTIONS FOR DISCUSSION

1. Why did God speak to Elijah in the 'still small voice' rather than the strong wind, earthquake or fire? What insight does this story give us of God's character and his relationship with his loved ones?
2. If you knew definitely that the second coming (or your own death) would take place tomorrow, how would your attitudes, behaviour and relationships change? Would you see things differently? We need to live each day like this.

IDEAS FOR ADULTS

The teaching of the reading from 1 Kings 19 can be movingly expressed in dance. This may take place immediately after the reading or just before the sermon.

You will need a group of seven dancers; one represents Elijah, the others represent the powerful elemental forces and God's reassurance. Elijah wears some kind of cloak and the other dancers leotards and tights of any colour. For 'music', you will need a drum, a tambourine, a thunder sheet (large piece of thick card), and xylophone or glockenspiel.

MUSIC and MOVEMENT

Slow drum beat

Elijah walks slowly up the centre, head down, stopping from time to time to look behind him as if scared of being followed.

Drum joined by tambourine

As he reaches the performance area he sits down, holding his head with one hand.

Xylophone/Glockenspiel plays quiet, wandering notes

When music starts Elijah looks up. As if moving to command he gets slowly up and walks across to a more central point, and stands there, waiting.

Thunder sheet, drum and tambourine create sounds of violent wind and storm

Elijah is buffeted and tries to protect himself. The six dancers come racing and twirling up the centre as storm begins, leaping, twisting, always moving. They surround Elijah but take no notice of him, just whirl on and off to one side.

Slow menacing thunder sheet

The dancers enter like this:

moving as if in slow motion. They reach the centre.

Thunder comes in increasing 'waves' of sound, with 3 'peaks'

At each sound peak the two sides overlap their outstretched arms and then recede; each time the movement is slightly bigger.

Thunder continues, 5 drum beats, the last very loud and joined by tambourine

At the drum beats, the dancers' lines split apart in a violent sudden movement, all arms fling up and then down to the floor as dancers kneel, scattered; Elijah staggers back a few steps before gingerly edging forward again.

Tambourine rustles, other shakers join in, gradually accelerating

The dancers move with sharp, jabbing and twisting movements to represent fire. Fingers are extended, and they form small groups, break and re-form, twisting round each other. Gradually the movements become bigger and the dancers spread out, working their way towards the back exit. Elijah watches them, shielding himself whenever they dance near him. When they have gone he slowly scans the sky.

Xylophone plays quietly and slowly. Tambourine, quietly shaken, joins in.

Elijah listens intently, very deliberately kneels down and extends arms down and forward with palms up. Elijah stands up confidently and walks back down the centre to finish.

CHILDREN'S TEACHING

Have ready three parcels, wrapped up in Christmas paper. They should all be the same size and shape — ask a shoe shop to let you have some shoe boxes. Inside one box place a lot of wadding, tissue or scrunched-up newspaper, in another place a tiny jewellery box containing something precious, such as a gold ring, or a diamond. In the third, place a pair of shoes.

Talk with the children about preparing our parcels for Christmas, and the fun of surprises. It is exciting to see a parcel with our name on it and not know what is inside. Often it turns out to be different from what we expect. Now show them the three parcels. Do they think that because they look the same they will have the same things inside? Ask one child to undo the first parcel. At the shoe box stage, guess the contents. When they see all the paper they will still expect something to be tucked inside. It's a surprise to find nothing there. Ask another child to open the second parcel. At the shoe box stage this time some may still expect shoes. Others will expect nothing. This time the contents are much more precious than we expected. A third child opens the last parcel. Stop again at the shoe box stage. Very few will now expect shoes, so it comes as a surprise to find what would normally be expected in a shoe box.

God is full of surprises, too. Sometimes, sadly, we may expect to find him in the lives of people who claim to follow him, but their behaviour shows that he isn't there. (Perhaps others may not find him in OUR behaviour, sometimes.) At other times he surprises us by blessing us richly when we are not expecting it. (On a bad day, when everyone seems cross with you, your pet gives you a special welcome, perhaps.)

We need to keep looking out for God, not just tucking him away into Sunday mornings. Otherwise, when he comes again we won't be ready for him. Read the last paragraph of today's Gospel and pray together that God will help us all stay faithful in our lives.

Help the children make these traffic lights to remind them.

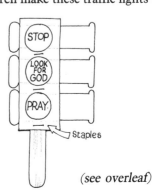

(see overleaf)

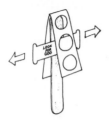

Try singing: *In joy sing of his love* (MWTP, 64),
Love One Another (MWTP, 52).

INTERCESSIONS **Years 1 and 2**
Some ideas for prayer

Companions in Christ
knowing the loyalty and faithfulness
of our Father in Heaven, let us pray to him
for the Church and for our world.

Keep all Christians firm and steadfast
in their faith,
with lives that witness clearly
to the power of your love.
Pause
Hear us, Father: **we come to do your will**

Guide our leaders,
and all those in influential positions,
to uphold and promote Christian values.
Pause
Hear us, Father: **we come to do your will**

Be present in our homes
and our relationships,
and increase our commitment
to reconciliation, encouragement
and understanding of one another.
Pause
Hear us, Father: **we come to do your will**

Give reassurance and peace
to all who are anxious,
depressed or confused;
and make us aware of the needs of others.
Pause
Hear us, Father: **we come to do your will**

Into your safe keeping
we commend all those who have died....
for with you there is eternal life,
peace and joy.
Pause
Hear us, Father: **we come to do your will**

We thank you for all the many blessings
we receive each day,
and in silence we pour out
our individual reasons for gratitude.
Pause

Hear us, Father: **we come to do your will**

Creator God, Lord of our life,
**accept these prayers
for the sake of your Son,
our Saviour Jesus Christ, Amen.**

NOTES ON THE READINGS **Year 2**

Isaiah 10:20-23
Throughout the Old Testament we see God's
people in their swings from fervour to
backsliding, such a familiar pattern of human
behaviour. We are so easily distracted from the
route we have promised to follow, and so ready
to put our trust in anything which is immediate
and obviously powerful.

The prophet sees that eventually, on the day
of the Lord, believers will trust unswervingly
in the one true God. Since he is a God of piercing
purity, righteousness and justice, his coming in
glory is bound to bring a dramatic annihilation
of all that is evil, corrupt or in any way contrary
to his will and character. If we are to look with
eagerness for his coming, then, we need to make
sure that we are reconciled to God whenever we
sin, so that we remain faithful to all the goodness
and love he embodies.

Romans 9:19-28
Not that God is ever destructive. On the
contrary he shows infinite mercy and patience
with those who stubbornly renounce and
disobey him, holding back his judgement to
allow everyone the chance of turning back to
him of their own accord. We are included in this
great harvest, called personally to be sons and
daughters of our heavenly Father, who knows
what will make us eternally happy and at peace,
and longs for us to allow him access, so that he
can make such lasting happiness and peace a
reality.

Many of us prefer being potters to pots, and
will never relax in the hands of our potter long
enough for him to form us as he wants to. If only
we could grasp that he only plans to make us
more fully and joyfully ourselves, perhaps we
would not spend so much energy resisting the
call to be committed and faithful followers of
Christ.

Mark 13:14-23

As nearly 2,000 years have gone past since Jesus was born, it is sometimes tempting to assume that the end of the world is unlikely to happen for thousands of years, and we can dismiss the teaching of Christ about it as an understandable misunderstanding, quite in keeping with the restrictions of being fully human as well as divine. Do we really believe it will happen at all, or is death our individual experience of the coming of Christ in glory?

Surely we ignore the warnings to be alert and watchful at our peril. It is already a lot nearer than in Jesus' time, and we would be fools to reject the possibility of it happening in our own lifetime. No doubt Mary was taken by surprise to find that the Messiah promised for generations was actually going to be born in less than a year. It was important that she kept herself ready so that when the time was right she was both available and receptive. We too need to keep ourselves prepared, with our minds and hearts open and receptive.

QUESTIONS FOR DISCUSSION

1. What does it involve in our lives for us to 'lean upon the Lord'. Are there any areas in which we tend to lean on other supports instead?
2. Jesus warns us that those wishing to lead us astray will use remarkably clever and subtle methods. What can we do to make sure we are not misled? You may like to refer to Matthew 7:15-20.

IDEAS FOR ADULTS

This dance expresses the emergence of a small loyal remnant from the crowd. From the back of the church a crowd of dancers begin moving to the Taizé chant:

'The Lord is my light, my light and salvation
In him I trust, in him I trust.'

The movement is as follows:

The Lord is my light
3 steps forward, slowly raising arms up and forward, palms up, hands straight.
my light and salvation
kneel on one knee, lower arms slowly, but keep stretched forward with palms up. Heads are lowered as well.
In him I trust
Kneel on both knees, slowly bending head forward to touch floor, sitting on heels. On 'trust', raise body to upright, still kneeling and sitting back on heels.
in him I trust

Stand and turn round in circle on the spot, all turning clockwise.

In an unhurried and reverent way repeat these movements right up to the altar. But at each sequence one or two dancers leave the group, stand watching them a moment and then run or saunter to the back of the church again. By the time the group reaches the altar there should be only a small remnant left. For this last time the dancers repeat the first actions but remain on one knee and slowly raise heads and arms during the second half of the chant.

CHILDREN'S TEACHING

Bring in a box of pencils or crayons, most of which are blunt or broken. (In my experience such collections are easy to find!) Ask two or three children to pick out of the box the pencils and crayons which are sharp and unbroken. Out of all that box only a very few were still in a good state. Explain today's readings by referring to the pencils. In a way we are like the pencils, except that we are able to go and get ourselves sharpened and cleaned up when we need to. (Saying sorry to God when we have been selfish or unkind, and making an effort to put things right again.) We can also choose not to bother. But we never know when God is wanting to use us, and if we have let ourselves get into a bad state, he won't be able to use us very easily. It's not enough to be a pencil — we need to be SHARPENED pencils.

On a chart or blackboard write down some ways we can make sure we are keeping ourselves ready. Here are some suggestions, but the children will have ideas as well:

Talking to Jesus and listening to him
Reading the Bible and learning from it
Putting things right quickly when we do wrong
Forgiving people when they hurt us or spoil our toys

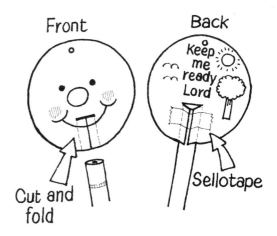

Give the children a new pencil each and help them make this pencil-end for it.

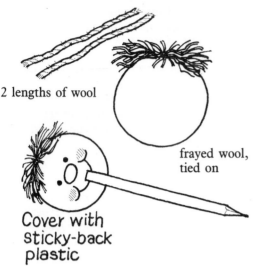

2 lengths of wool

frayed wool, tied on

Cover with sticky-back plastic

While they work, pass round some pencil sharpeners and let each child sharpen one of the blunt pencils. Try singing:
Give me joy in my heart
Shout aloud for Jesus (MWTP, 58)
The builders (MWTP, 30)

ADVENT

1st Sunday in Advent

TODAY'S THEME

... is the urgency and necessity for preparing ourselves right away so that we shall be ready and receptive when Christ comes again in glory at the end of time. The great hope of Israel has already been fulfilled in the first coming of Jesus, born as a baby. We look back to that with wonder. The enormous love it shows, highlights the supreme goodness and compassion of the God whose second coming we await.

PARISH MUSIC

Hymns
Hark! a herald voice is calling
How lovely on the mountains (Our God reigns)
I am the light
Lo, he comes with clouds descending
Mine eyes have seen the glory
Oh Lord, all the world belongs to you
Open your ears, O Christian people
Soldiers of Christ arise
Stand up, stand up for Jesus
Wake, O wake! with tidings thrilling
Wake up, O people, the Lord is very near

Recorded music
Requiem (The end of the Lloyd Webber):
   with the boy's voice sustained

For choirs
I look from afar (Anthony Piccolo)
When the Son of Man (M. Locke):
   SSAATB verse for B

CHURCH DECORATION

Traditionally there are no flower arrangements during Advent. This makes it a good time to have a good clean out and tidy up. Look at any areas of the church which could be used more effectively; any corners where there is unnecessary junk. Could the library/book shelf be made more attractive and more efficient? Is the children's area working well or could it do with a face lift? We now have four weeks to reshape and reorganise, clean and beautify, both in our lives and our building. A work 'party' lightens the load for everyone, and makes it all more fun. Begin with prayer, have some Christian music on tape to listen to while you work and finish with thanksgiving and light refreshments.

NOTES ON THE READINGS **Year 1**

Isaiah 52:7-10
Prophecies often refer to both an immediate and a wider, more far-reaching event at the same time. It is rather like looking at a landscape, where you can focus on the nearest hill or whole mountains on the horizon, but the landscape contains both.

Here the message of hope to the exiled Israelites concerns both the return to their ruined city of Jerusalem, and also the world-wide fulfilment of God's salvation at the end of time. For us, living in the last age (that is, since the life of Jesus Christ) the hope is just as comforting and thrilling. Good ultimately triumphs over evil; the coming of God's kingdom, for which we pray so often, is already in the process of becoming a reality. No one is excluded from the precious gift of God's saving and liberating love.

1 Thessalonians 5:1-11
The early Christians clearly expected the Day of the Lord to take place within a very short time

— they thought in terms of months rather than centuries. Dates and times had therefore become too important an issue, causing unnecessary anxiety. Paul puts things back in perspective by reminding the Thessalonians of the only definite fact: the Day will come as a surprise, not when we are expecting it.

This means, of course, that we cannot live recklessly until the last minute and then build our lives on Christ in a few scrambled seconds. Rather, we have to live now in the light of that Day. As our companionship with Christ gradually floods us with serenity, joy and selfless love, our lives will witness to the reality of salvation. Others will be drawn to reconciliation with their creator, so that for them, too, the Day of the Lord becomes a Day of hope and accomplishment, rather than judgement and terror.

Luke 21:25-33
Many of us do not like to think too much about the second coming of Christ, displaying all the power and glory of God. Even a casual study of our universe hints at such colossal size, force and energy that to think of its final moments, accompanied by the sight of its maker, is utterly terrifying.

Jesus prophesies that it will indeed be a time of appalling terror for the human race, with the physical order chaotic and the whole universe affected. Yet, amazingly, we are encouraged to stand upright and hold our heads high when all this takes place. It is not to be a time of fear but of great excitement and joyful anticipation, for it heralds the fulfilment of all the good that has been planned and cultivated throughout the whole history of the universe. All things are about to come to a glorious completion, where the will of a supreme and loving God is carried out in its entirety, and humankind can join with

its creator in an eternal harmony. Whether we experience this from a standpoint of life or death will not matter. The event is of such cataclysmic magnitude that even the barrier of death will be brushed aside. We can all look forward to it with the thrill of hope, knowing that nothing at all can separate us from the love of God, and that love is eternal.

QUESTIONS FOR DISCUSSION

1. What evidence is there in the church and in the world that the Kingdom of God is already being established? How can we, individually and collectively, encourage the establishment of God's Kingdom?
2. Using atlases and reference books, refresh your awareness of the size and power of the universe. Compare this with Christ's coming at Bethlehem. What can we learn about the character of God?

IDEAS FOR ADULTS

The reading from Isaiah can be effectively dramatised, using a group of readers and also involving the whole congregation. Have the reading duplicated and underline the words to be read by everyone. The group of readers (light, medium and dark voices) stand centrally. Two recorders begin by playing the melody below:

Light How lovely on the mountains are the feet of the herald who comes to proclaim prosperity
Medium and bring good news, the news of deliverance, calling to Zion,
Everyone 'Your God is king.'
Dark Hark, your watchmen raise their voices

Dark and Medium	and shout together in triumph;
Dark	for with their own eyes they shall see the Lord returning in pity to Zion.
Everyone	Break forth together in shouts of triumph, you ruins of Jerusalem;
Light	for the Lord has taken pity on his people and has ransomed Jerusalem.
Medium	The Lord has bared his holy arm in the sight of all nations,
Everyone	and the whole world from end to end shall see the deliverance of our God.

During the last two lines the recorders play again. Their melody continues after the words have finished.

CHILDREN'S TEACHING

Bring in an alarm clock with a really loud ring or buzz. First talk to the children about how lovely it is when you're all warm and asleep in bed in the morning and then suddenly: BRRRRRRR! shatters your peace. Talk about how alarm clocks jerk you awake so you can get ready and not miss the day's activities. Advent (which means 'coming') is like an alarm clock, nudging us to get ready for Christ's coming. Tell them that as well as coming as a baby at Christmas time, 1,990 years ago, Jesus will come again one day with glory and power. We don't know when it will be, so we must be ready for him.

Now read the first paragraph of today's Gospel. You may feel the Good News translation is better suited to children's understanding — it is worth reading a few different versions to choose one most suitable for your particular group.

How can we get ready for Jesus?

Have written on a chart or blackboard:

1. Find out more about him — reading and praying.
2. Try to live the Jesus way — being loving and kind.

If you do not have a church library for children this is a good time to start one. Give each child a card to record which book is read, and ask them to read four Bible story books during Advent. (Families may like to read them together.) On the back of each card print this prayer which the children can decorate. Encourage them to say their prayer each day through Advent.

Try singing:
  You can't stop rain from falling down (ONA, 594)
  When the Lord returns (MWTP, 73)

INTERCESSIONS **Years 1 and 2**

My brothers and sisters in Christ,
as we watch together for his coming
let us pray together for the church
and for the world.

Lord, strengthen and guide your church
in its mission to the world;
that sinners may be alerted
to repentance
and many may be brought to the joy
of living in your love.
Pause
Lord, come to us: **live in us now**

Lord, we pray for the whole
created world and its peoples;
that no evil may thwart your will,
but that rather your kingdom
may be established and your will done.
Pause
Lord, come to us: **live in us now**

Lord, bless this parish
and all who serve our community;
that we may strive each day
to align our lives with the life
of Christ who saves us from sin.
Pause
Lord, come to us: **live in us now**

Lord, we pray for all who suffer —
mentally, physically and spiritually;
for those who see no further than
immediate, material comforts,

and do not realise their spiritual poverty.
Pause
Lord, come to us: **live in us now**

We commend to your love
all who have completed their life on earth,
that they may rest in your peace
and share your risen life.
Pause
Lord, come to us: **live in us now**

Thank you, Lord, for the richness
of your companionship;
for the joy and peace
your constant presence gives.
Pause
Lord, come to us: **live in us now**

Father, we trust in your mercy;
**accept these prayers
for the sake of your Son,
our Saviour Jesus Christ, Amen.**

NOTES ON THE READINGS Year 2

Isaiah 51:4-11
The prophet's vision of the homecoming of
God's people amid great rejoicing and relief, is
no narrow, nationalistic pipe-dream. Certainly
it includes the return of an exiled people to their
ruined city of Jerusalem, but it is much more
than this. Remarkably, it encompasses the idea
of the whole world, with all nations, every coast
and island, every part of God's creation, being
gathered to take part in the greatest homecoming
of all. In the fullness of time God will act with
infinite power and glory so that his will is fully
accomplished.

Running through the prophecy are the words
of encouragement and tremendous hope: though
the final times will be marked by devastating
suffering and terror, God's deliverance lasts for
ever and will not be affected by anything — even
death. No-one seeking to live according to God's
law of love need have anything to fear.

Romans 13:8-end
Paul explains how all the commandments are
different, detailed ways of living the law of love.
If we love someone, that will rule out any
thought or action that would hurt them, so the
entire law can be summed up in the command
to love God and our neighbour. The very fact
that it is a command, rather than a suggestion,
points us towards the kind of loving that is
required. It is not something we can choose to

do if we feel like it, or reserve for use with
attractive neighbours only. God's law of love
involves the will as well as the emotions, and
often begins in earnest only at the point where
liking stops!

Since we have no idea when Christ's second
coming will take place, we need to submit our
lives to God's law of love straight away. Advent
is a good time to do a spiritual stock check and
undertake some reordering of our time,
ambitions and priorities.

Matthew 25:31-end
Having seen the behaviour of Jesus in the
Gospels, we are directed to think of God in terms
of deep, caring and healing love, infinite
compassion and understanding, mercy and
patience. All this is wonderfully true. But we
have to be sure that in concentrating on God's
compassion and mercy we do not neglect other
qualities, also shown to us in Jesus, such as his
zeal for truth, purity and goodness. His
committed obedience to God's will and his
dislike of hypocrisy. We need to trust God to
forgive us but without presuming on his mercy,
for he is utterly good and will never put up with
evil, excusing it as an indulgent parent may spoil
a child.

For God never pretends we have not sinned;
he sees sin for what it is, coaxes us to repentance
and then generously forgives. So when he comes
in glory there is no way that anything evil or
hypocritically smug will survive — the very fact
that God is totally good is bound to result in the
death of evil ultimately. One way or another it
will be wiped out, and obviously it is better for
that to happen through repentance and
forgiveness now rather than inevitable
judgement later.

QUESTIONS FOR DISCUSSION

1. Read through the ten commandments
   together to see how each is a practical
   application of caring love. Why are we
   advised to 'put on Christ' in order to live
   according to this law?
2. Is it possible to uphold what is right without
   condemning what is evil? Can we really live
   God's way without getting involved in
   alleviating the suffering in this world?

IDEAS FOR ADULTS

To aid a better understanding of the Isaiah
reading, use a group of speakers instead of one
reader.

A mixed group of 10-12 people sit, kneel and stand in small groups, wearing blankets or cloths wrapped round them as cloaks. A group of two men and one woman stand together near the altar, wearing either albs or cassocks, and one man stands, leaning on a stick, wrapped in a cloak or blanket, at the side; perhaps near a lectern.

The reading is divided into four main sections. In the first three of these the words are read by the group of two men and one woman, speaking together, and addressing the mixed crowd. They react to the words, showing concentration, wonder, fear etc.

The fourth section (starting: 'Awake, awake . . .') is said by the larger, mixed crowd, preferably learnt by heart. So far the prophet has stood on his own, observing and listening. Now he proclaims the last part of the fourth section (beginning: 'So the Lord's people . . .') and the crowd gets up excitedly, full of relief and joy. As he finishes the passage, the crowd moves with an air of festival up to the altar, where they kneel in worship for a time before dispersing.

CHILDREN'S TEACHING

Tell the children that Advent means 'coming', and remind them that in these weeks before Christmas we are getting ourselves ready for the coming of Jesus, not just as a baby at Christmas time but also the time when he will come again in great glory. We know this will happen because Jesus told us about it, but we don't know when, so we need to be prepared all the time.

With the aid of pictures and/or items of uniform, talk about people who always have to keep themselves ready because they don't know when their help will be needed — such as firemen, police, emergency staff at a hospital, lifeboatmen etc. How do they make sure they are ready?
— by practising rescues
— by keeping themselves fit
— by keeping their equipment well-oiled and repaired

Now read today's Gospel, asking the children to listen out for ways we can get ourselves ready for Jesus' coming. Have the different examples ('When I was hungry, you gave me food' etc) already written out on pieces of card, so that when they are mentioned after the reading you can display them.

Produce an empty carton and place all the cards inside, explaining that all these things are part of LOVING. (Write this in large letters on the carton.) Have some other pieces of card available and help the children write and decorate other practical ways of showing a caring love to others, such as offering to help Mum and Dad, sharing toys with others, being friendly to a child at school who is often lonely, or being pleased at someone else's success.

Carry the carton up to the altar at the offertory, and let the children process to the altar and put their card into the box. If there is time, these could be read out for the congregation to hear. They are offered along with the collection. Try singing:
Love is something if you give it away
When the Lord returns (MWTP, 73)

2nd Sunday in Advent

TODAY'S THEME

. . . is the way God has gradually revealed himself to us through his Word in the Bible. The Old Testament is an unfolding of God's will in creating and leading his people into the way of truth and love. Jesus Christ, in the New Testament, is the fulfilment of all the hopes and prophecies, for in him God lives among his people in person.

PARISH MUSIC
Hymns
A man there lived in Galilee
Come, thou long expected Jesus
Firmly I believe and truly
God's Spirit is in my heart
Hail to the Lord's anointed
Hark, the glad sound!
Hills of the north rejoice
How great is our God
I love to hear the story
Let all mortal flesh keep silence
The Son of God proclaim
Who is this man?

Recorded music
Godspell (Stephen Schwartz)

For choirs
Audivi, Media Nocte (Thomas Tallis):
    SATB
Come, Thou long expected Jesus (Henry
    G. Ley): SATB

NOTES ON THE READINGS **Year 1**

Isaiah 55:1-11
In this prophecy we can see how God calls to us in our need, our thirst, our hunger. He is able to satisfy in a lasting and complete way, and his offer is freely available, so no-one is barred from applying. Neither will stocks run out; surely too good a bargain to miss. Yet often we ignore God's offer, and rush off to sample all kinds of inferior products which promise distraction, admiration or instant success, only to be let down and find that deep down we are still thirsty, restless, and unfulfilled.

When we do respond to his call, we shall find peace activating a desire to align our wills and desires increasingly to God's will. This in turn sets in motion the spreading of God's Good News to the jaded, anxious world. For this has been God's will from the start — that through the binding relationship of God with his people all nations will eventually be drawn to know him and experience his love, peace and joy.

2 Timothy 3:14-4:5
Timothy is what we might call a 'cradle Christian'. Whereas the older generation had made their commitment to Christ as adults, he has been brought up in the Christian faith from childhood. If he can remain true to his early teaching, and use it as a pool of wisdom for the challenges of his missionary work, he will be richly prepared for effective witness in his ministry.

It is important the teaching programmes in our parishes and homes keep pace with the children's development, exploring and explaining the Good News in ways appropriate to their age and understanding. Often the rejection of the Church by teenagers and young adults is actually a very valid rejection of the simplistic and childish image of God they are still being given. We have only to think of the varied and often unsavoury crowds who gathered around Jesus to see that his message is drastically distorted if squashed into a narrow mould of the 'meek, mild and thoroughly nice' variety.

Like Timothy, those who have been reared in the church should have a wonderfully rich knowledge to draw on which can guide and help many in their spiritual journey.

John 5:36b-end
Can it really be that a thorough, detailed knowledge of the scriptures could still leave us spiritually blind? Surely the more knowledgeable we are about our Bible, the better Christians we must be.

Here Jesus explains the dreadful irony that it is indeed possible to scrutinise the scriptures for what we want to find, rather than what God wants to show us. And if this happens we shall fail to recognise the voice of Jesus, either through our Bible reading or in our lives and relationships, just as the scribes and pharisees failed to recognise in this preacher and healer from Nazareth the Messiah described and foretold by Moses and the prophets.

How, then, can we make sure that we do not fall into the same trap? Fortunately it has nothing to do with our I.Q., our status or our qualifications; all that is needed is to want to know and love God more. Everything else will be taken care of by God himself, who leads us by the best route for each one of us to a deeper understanding of his will, his personality and his plans for the world.

QUESTIONS FOR DISCUSSION

1. Referring to a variety of incidents reported recently in the media, see if you can find evidence of God working through his people to touch the world with healing and reconciliation. Are there also cases where opportunities have been squandered or gone unnoticed?
2. Is the practical teaching of the faith in your area working effectively? If not, are there any ways in which the parish could witness to its faith in the living Christ? This may not mean having yet more meetings! It may well involve more prayerful planning in what is already going on.

IDEAS FOR ADULTS

This short drama, intended for performance within today's service, was written by a 15 year old boy, following a discussion about the importance of being ready and receptive if we are to recognise Christ. Involve a group of young people and adults to perform it, possibly straight after the Gospel. Perhaps it will inspire some of the young people in your parish to have a go at expressing the teaching of the readings dramatically. Their directness, humour and honesty can be extremely valuable in alerting the congregation to Christ's teaching.

Characters

Mum, Dad, Andy, Sarah, Scott, Jesus, Voice

(Scott enters from left. Mum enters from left, rushes across stage to grab coat from opposite side.)

Mum Come on, Andy! How long are you going to be?

Andy Won't be a tick. I'm just changing my clothes.

Mum *(Aside)* Third time in one day. The amount of washing I have to do for this family. *(Fed-up sigh.)*

Scott Mum! Why do we have Christmas?

Mum Not now, Scott. Can't you see I'm busy. I've got to get the turkey before the shops shut, and Andy's got to get his Christmas presents. *(Aside)* Where is that boy? *(Aloud)* Come on, Andy! Hurry up!

Andy Alright, alright. I'm coming.

Mum David! I'll take the Volvo and leave you the Mini, alright?

Dad Yes. *(From off-stage.)*

Scott Andy! Why do we have Christmas?

Andy Bye, Scott.

Mum Come on!

(Exit Mum and Andy. Enter Dad, from right.)

Scott Dad! Why do we have...?

Dad Hang on, I've just got to sort out what drink we need to buy.

(Exit Dad, left. Enter Sarah, left.)

Scott Sarah, why do we have Christmas?

Sarah I don't know. I suppose it's just a tradition.

Scott Tradition?

Sarah Yes, you know, tradition, ritual... (pause) like washing.

Scott Oh.

Sarah Hang about. I do remember something about God's Son, Jesus, being born ages ago in Bethlehem.

Scott Where's that?

Sarah Abroad, I think.

Scott Why bother about that now?

Sarah Well, let's see. I think it mentions it somewhere in one of those reference books.

(Gets Bible off shelf. Blows dust off and flicks through, Reads.)

Yes.

Scott Well, why did Jesus come here?

Sarah It says he came to save us, because he loves us.

Scott Why? How?

Sarah Well, we all do things that are wrong, like being selfish, or lying, or hitting your brother. *(Hits Scott playfully.)*

Scott Get off!

Sarah Well, Jesus died, on a cross...

Scott What? When he was a baby?

Sarah No, later on. Anyway, he died, so as to take away our sins.

Scott Sins?

Sarah Yes, sins are all those things we do that are wrong.

Scott Oh. Can Jesus forgive us, then?

Sarah Looks like it. It says here...'God loved the world so much that he gave his only Son, so that everyone who believes in him may not die but have eternal life.'

Scott *(Excited)* Can I tell him I believe in him and I'm sorry about all the things I've done wrong?

Sarah Yes, if you want...I think I will, too. *(Bow their heads, pray silently.)*

Scott I feel different...happy!

Sarah So do I.

(Knocking at door.)

Scott and Sarah We'll go, Dad.

(Enter Jesus, carrying bright light.)

Scott and Sarah *(Run to his arms)* Jesus!

(Jesus knocks again. Enter Dad)

Dad I thought those kids were going.

(Enter Mum and Andy.)

Mum Hello, darling. Scott! Sarah! I've got something for you. *(No answer.)* Scott! Sarah! *(Still no answer.)* Where are they, David? And who is it knocking at the door?

Dad I don't know. I can't see anyone there. Just light — brilliant light! *(He staggers back shielding his eyes as the room is brightly lit. Mum also shields her eyes. They freeze like this as a voice reads Luke 12:35-40.)*

Voice 'Be ready for whatever comes, dressed for action and with your lamps lit, like servants who are waiting for their master to come back from a wedding feast. When he comes and knocks, they will open the door for him at once.'

(Pause.)

'And you can be sure that if the owner of a house knew the time when the thief would come, he would not let the thief break into his house. And you, too, must be ready, because the Son of Man will come at an hour when you are not expecting him.'

(Lights down.)

CHILDREN'S TEACHING

Set up a treasure hunt with clues which direct
the children from one place to another, like this:

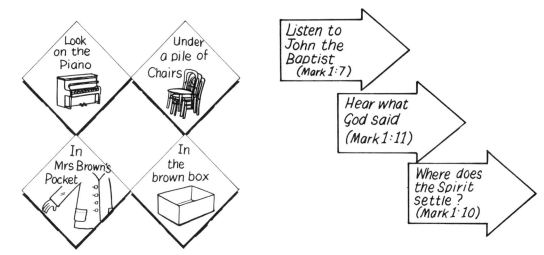

The 'treasure' is a torch or bicycle lamp. Switch
it on and talk with the children about how useful
it is in helping us find our way in the dark,
without tripping over things or causing
accidents.

Now show them several different Bibles,
explaining that in the Bible there are lots of clues
to direct us to find the light of the world —
Jesus. Give out these clues to different children
and help them find the places which lead us to
Jesus. You could have these already written up
on a sheet of paper, each text covered with a
question mark until the child finds the reference
in the Bible.

Tell the children that there are lots of other
clues every day which can lead us to Jesus, such
as the beautiful and amazing things in nature,
kind or unselfish behaviour; Bible stories and
stories of the saints, help given when we need
it, songs and poems etc.

Give the children this duplicated paper with
a picture of Jesus in the centre which they can
colour in. Then each day of the week they fill
in one circle either with words or a drawing,
with something that has directed them to think
of Jesus and know him better. Ask them to bring
these back next week.

INTERCESSIONS **Years 1 and 2**
Some ideas for prayer

As children of our caring, heavenly Father,
let us pray trustfully, now.

Father, inspire all Christians
throughout the world
to follow Christ simply and wholeheartedly,
so their lives witness to the beauty
and peace of his kingdom.
Pause
Father of love: **remake our lives**

May your will be accomplished
through all world leaders, governments
and their advisers;
that they may be enabled
to lead their people wisely and fairly,
with understanding and sensitivity.
Pause
Father of love: **remake our lives**

Father, we bring before you
our own families and loved ones,
especially any from whom we are separated;
that we may learn to see Christ in each face,
and serve him in caring for one another.
Pause
Father of love: **remake our lives**

We pray for all who feel spiritually lost;
for those who feel trapped by emotional,
financial or political circumstances;
that in Christ they may find peace, freedom and
    vitality.
Pause
Father of love: **remake our lives**

Welcome into your kingdom, Father,
all who have died in faith,
and give them the joy
of eternal life with you.
Pause
Father of love: **remake our lives**

With deepest thankfulness
for all that makes our lives
so richly blest,
we give you lasting praise.

Accept these prayers
for the sake of your Son,
our Saviour Jesus Christ, Amen.

NOTES ON THE READINGS **Year 2**

Isaiah 64:1-7
There are times when all of us, faced with
blatant injustice or flagrant disregard for God's
law of love, feel the surge of frustrated zeal for
things to be put right once and for all, with
God's power so dramatically obvious that the
enemies of good will finally be knocked into
sensing their need for repentence. James and
John felt it˗too, when the Samaritan village
wouldn't receive their master, and they were all
ready to call down righteous fire from heaven
to consume the whole lot of them, there and
then.

But Jesus' reaction is to rebuke James and
John, and set off to find another village. And
the prophet in this reading also works through
the understandable desire for immediate
judgement. He recognises that those who trust
God see him acting dramatically in their lives
all the time; that it is our own individual lack
of response to God that cuts us off from him,
blows us like dead leaves further and further
away from his presence; that if we have turned
our faces resolutely away from God we shall not
be able to escape the insidious distortion of our
lives by slavery to the ugly master of sin.

The last line of the reading shows the prophet
turning to God with all the trust of a young
child: in spite of all our doubts and violent
feelings, in spite of all our sin and weakness, we
can turn to God as to a loving parent who knows
and understands us.

Romans 15:4-13
The scriptures can direct us to a better grasp of
this relationship, if we go to them with an open,
receptive mind. Through them we will hear
God, speaking through psalms and prophecies
and through the history of the people of Israel.
We will see God acting in the person of Jesus
in many varied encounters with all kinds of
people and problems. All of which will fill us
with a hope which the world finds strange since
it is independent of comfort and luck. And if
such hope makes people envious, that may be
their first step to acquiring it for themselves.

Luke 4:14-21
Jesus is, at this point, popular with everyone and
beginning to be famous. He chooses to travel
back to his home town and announces that the
words of Isaiah are being fulfilled right in front
of them. Constantly throughout his ministry
Jesus directed the people to see his works and
teaching as the fulfilment of scripture, and never
as isolated or rootless acts of spectacle. Those
who were receptive could begin to grasp the
startling truth that the promised Messiah was
among them, even if he was different from what
they had expected. Never was anyone whipped
up by emotional pressure to accept this. Instead

they were always given clear evidence that complied with God's revelation through scripture, so they could come to believe in him, just as we can, by reading the scriptures and assessing Jesus' 'good fruit'. Anyone merely out to see a miracle show was and is likely to be disappointed.

QUESTIONS FOR DISCUSSION

1. Share with the group one or two passages from scripture which have given you particular encouragement and hope, and why you found them so helpful.
2. Find the passage in Isaiah 61 which Jesus read from in the synagogue at Nazareth. Can you think of events in his ministry which showed that in him the text was being fulfilled?

IDEAS FOR ADULTS

For the reading of today's gospel have a narrator who begins the reading. At 'So he came to Nazareth . . .' have the priest or deacon walking up the centre of the church to the front. One of the servers hands him a scroll which he takes and opens. Then he reads the Isaiah passage from the scroll. Having read it, he mimes Jesus' actions as the narrator continues. Have a pause after 'all eyes in the synagogue were fixed on him'. Jesus' words are spoken by the priest or deacon, after which he holds up the scroll and the narrator holds up his book and both say: 'This is the word of the Lord.'

CHILDREN'S TEACHING

So as to get across the idea of fulfilled prophecy, make a 'scroll' by rolling a sheet of paper stuck on to sticks at either end, with a ribbon or tape on it for fastening. If possible, copy a little Hebrew writing on to it, as well as the prophecy included in today's gospel, (Isaiah 61:1-2a).

Show it to the children, ask them to guess what it is, and explain how, many years before Jesus was born, some people (prophets) were used by God to be messengers. Through them, God told his people that one day he would send someone very important who would save them and show them the right way to live. What they said was written down on scrolls like this one.

Ask one of the older children to read the first part of today's gospel, up to the point when Jesus is handed the scroll. Let one of the younger children hand the reader the home-made scroll. The passage from Isaiah 61:1-2a is read from it. The teacher now tells the last part of the gospel, with the children acting it out.

Recap with them about the kind of things the

promised Saviour would do, matching them up bit by bit with what they know of Jesus. Have lots of pictures, Bible story books, and an illustrated Bible available to refer to. The children will be able to see that the prophecy really was coming true in Jesus.

Help the children make their own scrolls, with the prophecy stuck on. Garden canes, cut to size, make inexpensive sticks, and the paper is best attached with strong glue. Try singing: *All of the people* (MWTP, 39).

3rd Sunday in Advent

TODAY'S THEME

. . . is the Way being prepared for the coming of the Lord. John the Baptist was the promised forerunner to Christ, and his teaching inspired many to turn back to God's ways, making them receptive when Jesus began his ministry. We, too, need to renounce sin and prepare for the time when Christ will come again in glory.

PARISH MUSIC
Hymns
Comfort, comfort my people
Fill thou my life, O Lord my God
God is working his purpose out
Hark! a herald voice is calling
Just as I am without one plea
Lo he comes with clouds descending
Make me a channel of your peace
O Jesus I have promised
On Jordan's bank the Baptist's cry

O thou who camest from above
Rejoice in the Lord always
Spirit of the living God
The advent of our King
The Lord will come and not be slow
The race that long in darkness pined
Thou didst leave thy throne
Thy Kingdom come, O God
We pray thee, heavenly Father

Recorded music
Messiah (Handel)
Godspell (Stephen Schwartz): Prepare ye

For choirs
Be peace on earth (William Crotch, arr.
  Ley): 2-part.
Dearest Lord Jesu (J. S. Bach): SATB

NOTES ON THE READINGS **Year 1**

Isaiah 40:1-11
Although the terrain is far from promising, and
much has to be done before the highway can be
constructed, the overriding message here is of
great joy. The people are given comfort and
consolation. This is because turning towards
God and away from sin has put them in a right
relationship with their creator, and all the hard
work will now be positive: they will be working
with God instead of against him.

We have only to look at the way people throw
themselves into the preparations for a street
party, carnival or Christmas decorating to see
how eagerly we work for something special and
exciting. This is the spirit in which we are urged
to prepare ourselves for the Lord. Having faced
up to sinfulness, having apologised to God for
it and resolved to make amends, we can enjoy
the hard work; enjoy getting our hands dirty by
physical involvement in his service, and be
happy that we are tired at the end of the day.
We can get excited about the highway we are
building and delight in the fellowship we share
with all the other road workers.

When it is finished, the dazzling glory of our
God will be revealed so that everyone can see
it. That is well worth a few blisters and bruises.

I Corinthians 4:1-5
As we work, we need to remember that we are
not, so to speak, self-employed. The highway
we build is not a sweeping driveway to our own
private residence, yet it is a temptation
sometimes to behave as if it were. As soon as
we begin to work for ourselves instead of God's
glory the spirit of criticism and judgement creep

in which drastically reduces the efficiency of the
building programme.

Paul urges us to leave all judgement of people
to God, who is more than capable and has a
perfect sense of timing. If we put all our energies
into working as trustworthy servants and
stewards of our Lord and Master, then his
kingdom will be painstakingly established.

John 1:19-28
In this account of John the Baptist's witness we
see the heralding of the long-awaited Messiah,
in images the people — with their sound
knowledge of the prophets — would be likely
to understand. John was fulfilling a role that was
essential in preparing the way for Israel's
Saviour. It would alert many to look for signs
of God visiting his people, and guide them to
see his presence where they may not have been
expecting to find it.

If we join the crowds around John and
wholeheartedly repent of all that is evil, ugly and
damaging in our characters, we too shall be
alerted to recognise Christ and see him more
clearly.

QUESTIONS FOR DISCUSSION

1. Why do you think God planned for John the
   Baptist's ministry to precede the work of
   Jesus? What evidence in the Gospels can you
   find which shows its effectiveness?
2. Read Luke's account of John the Baptist as
   well (Luke 3:10-15). In the light of Jesus'
   teaching, what do you think John would have
   suggested to you, both individually and as a
   parish, as the practical way to 'prepare the
   way of the Lord?'

IDEAS FOR ADULTS

Instead of having the Isaiah prophecy read, have
it duplicated and given out for everyone to follow
while a recording is played of this section from
Messiah. Alternatively, if you have a gifted
instrumentalist among you, have a solo
instrument playing quietly and sensitively as a
background to the reading. In either case the
aim is to alert people to the beauty and hope of
these powerful words.

CHILDREN'S TEACHING

First talk with the children about how their town
or country prepares its streets for important
visitors such as royalty, a winning football team
or a film star. There may be flags hung up,

streamers waving, a red carpet rolled out on the pavement and flowers planted round all the lamp posts for instance. If you have any photographs of such events, or a local carnival, show them around.

Now read them Isaiah 40:3-5 and the first part of today's Gospel, where John the Baptist uses the prophecy to explain his own job. Unroll a length of white material, about a yard wide and four yards long. (A double sheet split down the middle and joined end to end makes the right size: it is important that it looks big.)

The children are going to turn this strip of boring material into a highway for Jesus. At Christmas time it can be laid down in church so that when the Christ child is brought to the manger he is carried along the children's highway.

Have ready plenty of colourful oddments of material, a really efficient fabric glue, scissors, pens and templates. Discuss ways in which we can prepare ourselves for Jesus, and write these at intervals along the highway with coloured pens. On flower shapes they can write thank you messages.

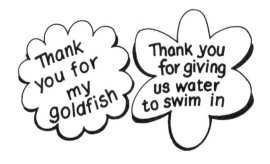

INTERCESSIONS **Years 1 and 2**
Some ideas for prayer

Let us bring to God our loving Father
all the cares that weigh on our hearts,
knowing that he understands us
better than we understand ourselves.

Father, we bring the daily work of those who labour
to spread the good news of Christ
amid apathy, ridicule or prejudice;
may they be encouraged and strengthened.
Pause
Father, hear us: **and prepare us to meet you**

Father, we bring our daily work,
with all the pressures, monotony, enjoyment and mistakes;
help your world to recognise your presence
and trust in your love.
Pause
Father, hear us: **and prepare us to meet you**

Father, we bring all our loved ones
with their hopes and disappointments,
their struggles and their successes;
may they be guided and nurtured
by your love.
Pause
Father, hear us: **and prepare us to meet you.**

Father, we bring all those
whose lives seem to them bleak, painful
or empty of meaning;
please release them, unburden them,
and fill them with your gift of joy.
Pause
Father, hear us: **and prepare us to meet you**

Father, we commend to your unfailing love
all who have died, especially...
Pause
Father, hear us: **and prepare us to meet you**

Filled with thankfulness for all
your many blessings to us,
we offer you our praise.
May we never forget your generosity.
Merciful Father
accept these prayers
for the sake of your Son,
our Saviour Jesus Christ, Amen.

NOTES ON THE READINGS **Year 2**

Malachi 3:1-5
Malachi, speaking to a jaded and disillusioned society, where both moral and religious principles had become badly frayed, looks forward longingly to the Day of the Lord. Although his coming is bound to be caustic and stringent, it will bring about purity and integrity: reconciliation of the people with their God.

John the Baptist is foretold as the messenger who will clear a path in people's hearts so they are receptive and expectant when the Lord comes. For with us, as with them, a path needs to be prepared before we are able to welcome the Christ into our lives. He will remain standing outside our hearts, knocking, until we invite him in.

Philippians 4:4-9

Here, in the full light of the coming of the Son of God into the world, Paul speaks with first-hand experience of the new, purified life rooted in God's love. It is a life radiant with joy, fulfilled and peaceful, constructive and purposeful, encouraging and thankful. And it is not just reserved for a few stained-glass or plaster saints. It is available for us in our world, complete with its violence, work pressures, materialism and corruption — a world in some ways quite similar to the one inhabited by these Philippians.

Certainly we are still journeying forward to the accomplishment of all things at the end of time, but through living in Christ's love the journey itself is part of the accomplishment of God's good plans for us, rather as, on a pilgrimage, the fellowship and expectancy of the travelling is an integral part of the arrival.

Matthew 11:2-15

The Old Testament has been a gradual unfolding of God's character and purpose, and there had been plenty of time for people to form fairly rigid ideas of the Messiah they were expecting.

John the Baptist's preparation of the people had been based on the awesome justice of the Messiah, who would sort out the good from the bad. So, in the harsh and depressing surroundings of Herod's prison, we find John perplexed and surprised at the way Jesus is behaving, wondering, even, if he might have been mistaken in thinking Jesus to be the promised Messiah.

We often find that God works through the most unlikely people and places, and must be on our guard against rejecting his presence because it is not where we expected to find it.

Jesus sets John's mind at rest by pointing to his own 'good fruit' in words described by the prophet in the book of Isaiah that John would have known so well. If the sick are healed, and the blind are given sight, then the evidence is there — God's saving love is at work. We have to make up our own minds as to whether or not we accept the evidence.

QUESTIONS FOR DISCUSSION

1. If all Christians allowed themselves to be 'lived through' by the Spirit of God as described by Paul in this letter to the Philippians, in what practical ways would the world be changed and influenced for good?
2. You can read about the life and work of Elijah in I Kings:17-2 Kings 2. In what ways is John the Baptist similar, both in times of strength and weakness?

IDEAS FOR ADULTS

Ask people to bring with them something of beauty, excellence, purity or graciousness; it may be in the form of a picture or photograph, a cherished book, a child's lovingly made present or a carefully worked piece of carpentry or embroidery. Have a length of cloth draped over a table and on to the floor, with the words of today's epistle clearly displayed. Before the service have the people placing whatever they have brought around the displayed words.

CHILDREN'S TEACHING

Have ready a display of some of the lovely things in our world which enrich our lives and make us thankful. These may include water and food, pictures of the seasons and nature, warmth and light (candles) and photographs of people. Begin with thanks and praise for the God who loves us and gives us so much.

Then, using pictures from an illustrated Bible, tell the children about John the Baptist, sent by God to help people get ready for the Lord's coming. Many listened to what he said and made a big effort to change into more caring, honest and thankful people. As a sign that they were washed clean from evil, John waded into the river Jordan with them and prayed over them while they were dipped in the clean water. This was called Baptism. Remind the children that among those John baptised was Jesus himself. John recognised Jesus as being the Lord.

But then Herod had John arrested and thrown into prison, where he was chained up all on his own. He heard stories about what Jesus was doing and was surprised. He had expected the Lord to unite everyone in a great body that would drive out the Romans so the country would once more be free. Instead, Jesus was talking about loving our enemies, caring for one another — even foreigners — and he seemed to be making friends with bad people as well as good. Could this Jesus really be the Lord?

Poor John must have felt anxious, miserable and muddled. So he sent some of his own followers to Jesus to ask him straight out: 'Are you the one who is to come, or are we to expect some other?'

Jesus understood John's doubts. He thought of the best way to put John's mind at rest. (At this point get out the scroll used last week.) He knew that John had read the prophets' writings again and again and knew them inside out. So he quoted to John's messengers the prophecy about the blind receiving their sight, the lame

walking and the lepers being made clean. The messengers could see that Jesus was making all this come true! John would understand that Jesus' kingdom was to come about by loving rather than fighting, however good the cause.

Help the children make up these figures for a flannelgraph, by colouring, cutting out and mounting on felt. Then, with the children putting the figures on to the flannelgraph, go through the main points of today's teaching.

4th Sunday in Advent

TODAY'S THEME

... is that Mary was chosen by God to be the mother of Jesus, our Saviour. God's great sign of love is that he is carried through a human pregnancy and born into a human family which is descended from David. In this way the prophecies are fulfilled and God's glory revealed to the whole world.

PARISH MUSIC
Hymns
Blessed assurance, Jesus is mine
His name is wonderful
Jesus shall reign where'er the sun
Let all mortal flesh keep silence
Lo, he comes with clouds descending
My God, how wonderful thou art
My song is love unknown

The angel Gabriel
Tell out my soul
Ye who own the faith of Jesus
Wide, wide as the ocean
Take me, Lord
How lovely on the mountains

Recorded music
Messiah (Handel): The Trumpet Shall Sound

For choirs
Jesu, the very thought of thee (T. L. de Victoria)
I sing of a maiden (P. Hadley): SS

NOTES ON THE READINGS **Year 1**

Isaiah 11:1-9
This remarkable prophecy recognises God's capacity for achieving the seemingly impossible. The prophet looks forward to a fundamentally changed world, free from injustice and free from aggression, even in nature. Just as strong, fresh shoots spring from tree stumps, so God's

promised Saviour will appear to transform and renew. And the more we make ourselves right with God, enabling his kingdom to be established in us, the nearer our world will become a God-filled kingdom of peace and love.

I Corinthians 1:26-end
Of course, there is often a huge contrast between Isaiah's vision and the actual world. We, as well as the Corinthians, live in a world which idolises and values the rich and glamorous, and is far more ready to admire someone for intelligence or beauty than compassion or integrity.

But God sees people so differently; to him it is the heart — the inner core — of each person which is important and lovable, and though some may also be rich, famous, handsome or intelligent, these are not the qualities which necessarily draw us closer to our fulfilment in Christ. In fact, he often seems to choose fairly low-attainers on the worldly list and then live so powerfully through them that the world is eventually alerted. Paul himself was no oil painting. Saint Francis was noted for looking so insignificant until he started preaching. In our own time, the world has started to seek out Mother Teresa, while she has never courted the world. And then there is even you and me! If we let him shine in us, he will certainly shine.

Luke 1:26-38a
One in whom the shining grew to be God's Son was Mary. Her ready response teaches us how to react to God's calling in our own lives; it is so important to keep ourselves available, so that when God needs us we are ready. No one person is individually responsible for the success or failure of spreading God's kingdom, but God's great sense of order and timing can be aided or hindered by the individual's response.

For in this gentle and tender moment of the Annunciation, we are witnessing the convergence of many events, many lives and many spiritual journeys. They all merge at this particular point in time to enable the next great stage of God's salvation to be accomplished. And it all depends on Mary's response.

QUESTIONS FOR DISCUSSION

1. Through what stages did God lead his people to prepare them for the coming of his Son? Can you think of any events or relationships in your own life which have made you more receptive to God?
2. Work through the conversation between Mary and Gabriel to see the path leading to Mary's wholehearted acceptance of God's will in her life. What does it teach us, both as individuals and as a parish, about prayer, and response to any challenging call?

IDEAS FOR ADULTS
Today's Gospel reading lends itself particularly well to dramatising. Use Nativity play costumes or albs, with a blue cloak for Mary. Gabriel can carry a lighted candle which is handed to Mary when she responds to the message with total acceptance. Encourage the actors to read the Annunciation in several different translations before rehearsing; otherwise, familiarity can sometimes cloud our perception.

CHILDREN'S TEACHING
Beforehand, prepare a picture of some houses in a street drawn on thin card, and cut round the doors so that they open and close. Also make a simple wooden-spoon or mop puppet.

First talk with the children about any good news they would like to share, and choose someone to knock on the door of each house to tell their news.

At the first house let the puppet say: 'Go away — I'm busy! at the second house: 'Pardon? . . . pardon? . . . I can't hear a word!'; at the third house: 'You don't expect me to believe THAT, do you?'; and at the fourth house: 'Hallo! Nice to see you . . . oh really? How lovely!' Discuss with them the different ways of receiving news, and how we need to welcome Jesus when he speaks to us, instead of being deaf, or too busy, or not believing what he says.

Now show the children a picture of God's messenger bringing some very important news to Mary. Who was the messenger? What was his news? Think back to the ways people sometimes react — did Mary say she was too busy, or couldn't hear, or didn't believe the angel? Read together the way Mary listened carefully and said she would certainly let God's will be done in her.

Unfold the children's 'highway' now (as prepared last week), and complete it by adding Mary's words. Use them as a prayer to make them part of our own preparation for the coming of Jesus into our lives.

INTERCESSIONS **Years 1 and 2**
Some ideas for prayer

Fellow travellers of Christ's Way,
as we walk together through life,
let us pray together in his Spirit.

Father, we bring to your love
all who serve Christ in his church;
that they may not flinch
from responding to their calling,
but rather abandon themselves
to your guidance and protection.
Pause
Heavenly Father: **let your will be done**

Guide all who are in authority
throughout the world;
that they may be strengthened
to stand firm in what is right
even if it is unpopular.
Pause
Heavenly Father: **let your will be done**

Father, in your love we remember
our own mothers,
all parents and foster parents,
all women in labour at this moment
and all who are pregnant;
that they may be
blessed and supported.
Pause
Heavenly Father: **let your will be done**

Father we commend to your love
those who have been rejected or abandoned
by their families or by society;
those who are constantly
ridiculed, criticised or badly treated;
may your love break down prejudice,
disperse hatred and build bridges
of reconciliation.
Pause
Heavenly Father: **let your will be done**

Father, into your hands
we commend all who have died
and those who mourn.
Pause
Heavenly Father: **let your will be done**

Father, our lives are so rich
with all your blessings,
and we thank you for all your love.

**Accept these prayers
for the sake of your Son,
our Saviour Jesus Christ, Amen.**

NOTES ON THE READINGS **Year 2**
Zechariah 2:10-end
Reading prophecy is like looking out over a landscape. The view consists of both foreground and distance. We can focus on either, but in either case the complete view stays in sight. Many prophecies have both immediate and long-term significance, and both are important visions of God's truth. Certainly Zechariah is writing of the immediate and localised return of the Lord to Jerusalem. He also writes of a time which we, through reading the gospels, have all witnessed: the coming of God's Son to live among his people and direct them by his words and example to the loving nature of the Godhead. We are living in a time during which many nations are coming over to the Lord, and are co-workers with Christ in spreading God's kingdom.

Revelation 21:1-7
The ultimate end of all this is the perfect completion of God's good plan for the universe he has created. That is seen here as the new Jerusalem, which represents the entirely new order of God's kingdom, lifting our imaginations beyond the material world as we know it until in the description we can sense something of the incredibly pure and glorious life possible when the whole of humanity is entirely at one with the loving creator.

Advent is a great celebration of hope, which sweeps us joyfully, triumphantly and yet humbly towards the straw-filled manger at Bethlehem.

Matthew 1:18-23
Nothing of this can ever take place without the willing consent of the people created by God. Now, as the world is poised before the Incarnation, we can watch with thankfulness as both Mary and Joseph allow their lives to be used by God. They are prepared to lay aside their own plans and hopes because God asked

them to. Such acceptance and unselfishness can never be dredged from any of us for an important occasion unless we have trained ourselves by making many daily acts of unselfishness. Though none of these may make the headlines, the gradual tuning of ourselves to the Christ-way of living will enable us to be in top condition when we are asked to respond in a Christlike way at times of great importance. If we are available, then God can use us; if not, we actively obstruct his will.

QUESTIONS FOR DISCUSSION

1. From reading today's Gospel and the other references to Joseph and Mary, can you piece together a kind of photofit picture of their characters, and the qualities in them that made it possible for God to use them in his plan to save the world?
2. Tensions often arise between our commitment to our families and our commitment to the Church. Remembering Mary and Joseph, discuss the difficulties you have met, and try to work out ways of resolving them.

IDEAS FOR ADULTS

Go on a carol singing walk around the parish, singing at the homes of any who are ill or housebound. Consider giving a parish Christmas card to those who come to the door, rather than asking for money. Sometimes the Church can give an important message by NOT collecting for charity but simply providing an act of kindness.

CHILDREN'S TEACHING

Talk about all the things they are doing ready for Christmas, and remind them of what we are all getting ready to celebrate — Jesus' birthday. Tell the children about how Mary and Joseph would be getting ready: packing food and clothing for their journey to Bethlehem, loading up their donkey, bringing baby clothes in case the baby arrives while they are away from home etc. Have some bags of nuts and raisins, dry biscuits, brightly coloured rugs, baby clothes and swaddling (length of sheeting). Put these out on the table as you discuss the things Mary and Joseph needed, and let the children pack them into cloth bags.

Now help them to make a small crib to put up in their homes, with a candle to light. Below is a pop-up version to try. The children will need scissors, glue and colouring pencils. Perhaps the finished crib could be offered at the altar before being taken home.

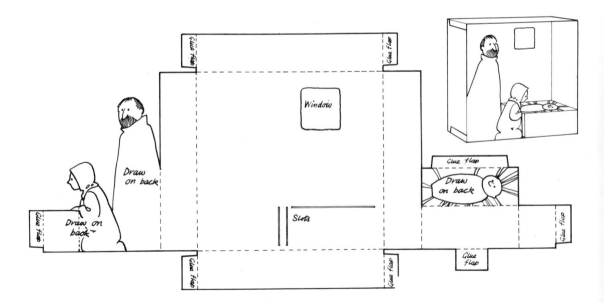

CHRISTMASTIDE

Christmas Day

TODAY'S THEME

... is that Christ, our Saviour, is born. Eternal God breaks into human existence to transform and redeem it. In the darkness of night, God's majestic glory becomes a vulnerable newborn baby. Creator of all is entirely dependent on those he has created. Such is the measure of his infinite love.

PARISH MUSIC

Hymns
Christmas is a time when there may well be visitors who do not go to church regularly; choose plenty of carols that everyone will know.

Recorded music
Music from a Cathedral choir

Anthems
Sing the birth (M. Praetorius)
O ye little flock (J. Amner): SSAATB

NOTES ON THE READINGS **Years 1 and 2**

Isaiah 9:2,6-7
This great prophecy of healing and restoration is fulfilled in the incarnation. Nothing can disperse darkness but light, and now that light has come in the universal sign of hope — a new baby.

With Christ being born, hope springs up, for the darkness can never win or overcome us any more. No wonder it is an occasion for rapturous delight and gladness — nothing can ever be quite the same again.

OR

Isaiah 62:10-12
There is such jubilation and relief in this fanfare of welcome. At last, with the coming of the Lord, all things shall be well. In a rush of enthusiasm and excitement God's people are urged to clear the way for a new era of love and justice. Now, as God, unannounced except by angels, slips into the middle of human life, we can join in the exultant joy of all heaven — for the promised Saviour has just been born.

OR

Micah 5:2-4
Faith seems easier to manage when there is rational, concrete evidence to support what we believe. Yet, in fact, real faith is only begun when that evidence is missing. Like Peter, we

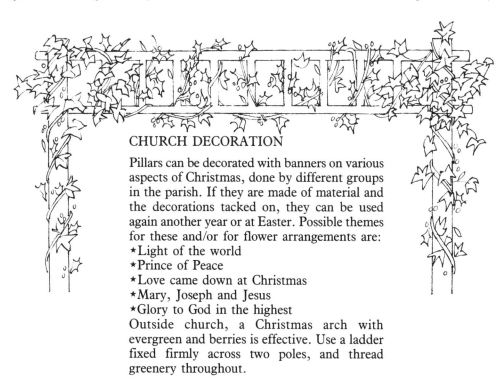

CHURCH DECORATION

Pillars can be decorated with banners on various aspects of Christmas, done by different groups in the parish. If they are made of material and the decorations tacked on, they can be used again another year or at Easter. Possible themes for these and/or for flower arrangements are:
*Light of the world
*Prince of Peace
*Love came down at Christmas
*Mary, Joseph and Jesus
*Glory to God in the highest
Outside church, a Christmas arch with evergreen and berries is effective. Use a ladder fixed firmly across two poles, and thread greenery throughout.

often start sinking at the thought because it makes us feel desperately vulnerable. It was during the blackest times of exile that the prophets remained convinced of God's promise to come and save.

Micah, seeing beyond the fallibility of human rulers, however noble, looks forward to the time when the Prince of Peace will rule over the whole land in a reign of unparalleled integrity and majesty, founded on the majesty of God himself. Like the great king David, he will hail from the insignificant town of Bethlehem, and the fact of his coming is not in doubt, however hopeless the immediate situation appears.

Titus 2:11-14; 3:3-7

No one is let out of this message of salvation; Christ loves every individual in the entire human race, and longs for each one of us to be reconciled to our Father in heaven and to each other, as brothers and sisters in one close-knit family.

Christmas, with all its hope and happiness, is a wonderful opportunity to deepen bonds of love, offer reconciliation where there has been coldness or hostility, and push back the frontiers of our caring a little more, to include a wider circle of 'brothers and sisters'.

OR

Hebrews 1:1-5 (6-12)

Even before the swirling gases of our solar system were formed, God was fully present and active. It is well worth star-gazing, sometimes, to remind ourselves of the vastness of the universe and the immensity of God who had no beginning and will have no end. For that is the power which broke into a particular point in history by being born of a human woman at Bethlehem.

All through the world's development and birth pangs, all through the developing consciousness of humanity, and all through the visions and prophecies of perceptive, prayerful people, God was revealed. But never so clearly as when he lay in Mary's arms as the first-born baby in a human family.

OR

1 John 4:7-14

Simply, yet profoundly, John explains the mystery of the incarnation in terms of God's immeasurable love for us. We do not have to grind ourselves to shreds trying to make ourselves worth saving. Neither can we save

ourselves, however determinedly we may grit our teeth and try. Rather, we need to take a deep breath, relinquish our desire for independence from God and accept the caring love he has for us.

Once we grasp the extent of his love for us, loving care will spill out of us to others and result in some kind of ministry. But because it now grows out of our relationship with Christ, our attitude will be different, less frantic and more lighthearted; less grudging and more generous.

Luke 2:1-14 (15-20)

The first reaction of the shepherds to seeing their familiar hillside filled with glory, is absolute terror. Faced with such awesome and naked power, they recognise their own weakness and vulnerability. Once the angels have reassured them, their amazement at God's power turns into ecstatic joy at the love such a powerful God must have if he is prepared to put aside that glory in order to save the creatures he has made.

Sometimes a glimpse of God's majesty stuns us and may scare us. We may feel tempted to argue it away, so that we can stay in our familiar territory. Many back away from the real God of glory because he is unpredictable and disturbing. They prefer their own, controllable, watered-down version.

But the one, omnipotent God is not only powerful, he is also a God of tenderness and compassion, and if we listen, we will always hear him reassure us whenever he challenges.

OR

Luke 2:8-20

Cataclysmic though the event of the incarnation was, it was worked out in terms of inns and travellers, stables and shepherds — just the ordinary, everyday things among unremarkable people. It was as if God let himself in by a side door, quietly and unobtrusively, just as he often does to many hearts in every generation.

But once we find him there, the pleasure and excited gladness of what his presence means opens our lives to a richness we can hardly believe, and, like the angels and shepherds, there is great rejoicing.

OR

John 1:1-14

Here the full expression of God shines out, as the Word becomes flesh. The incarnation is an impossibility come true; we wonder at the enormity of it, delight in the beauty of it and perhaps balk at the courage of it. Can it really be possible that the creative force behind every galaxy, every bacterium and life itself, is actually here, with the name of Jesus, walking about healing, teaching and listening to us? Yes, says John, incredible though it seems, it is true, because we saw his glory and it was the glory of God himself.

If we, also, are convinced by our experience of Jesus that he really is God, we are bound to accept his teaching and open our hearts to his love. And he will not only make us his disciples, but also his sisters and brothers, all sharing God as our loving Father.

QUESTIONS FOR DISCUSSION

1. Why do you think God chose to enter our world as a baby, rather than showing all his glory?
2. Using a concordance, discover some of the other times that Bethlehem is mentioned in the Bible. Are there any links between these events and Christ's birth?
3. What are some of the biggest risks you have taken? Did they all work out as you hoped? What risks was God taking when he became Incarnate?
4. What difference has Christ's coming made to your life? How can we best tell others about the benefits of living Christ's way?

IDEAS FOR ADULTS

1. At the offertory, the people bring to the altar gifts which they have bought or made for a relief organisation or local centre of need, children's clothes, for instance, blankets and bedsocks or books, games and toys. These offerings will then be seen as the direct result of our love for Jesus, and the giving of presents is fixed firmly in the context of showing Christ's love to others.
2. The Old Testament readings can be read chorally with a small group of voices, and a flute or guitar playing softly in the background. There are opportunities in each of the readings for variety of tone, speed and volume; use individual voices for some phrases. Aim to create an effect that will bring out the meaning and atmosphere clearly.
3. Display the highway that the children have been making (Advent Year 1), fixing it securely to the floor.

CHILDREN'S TEACHING

Many churches find the Christingle symbolism helpful; leaflets providing an outline of Christingle, using the traditional orange (as the world) and candle (as the light of Christ) can be obtained from The Children's Society, Old Town Hall, Kennington Road, London SE11 4QD.

It is important that children feel part of the family worship at the festival. Perhaps they could have practised a special carol which they can sing during the service, or they may present a nativity play or tableau during or just after the Gospel.

Elderly residents in nursing homes love to hear children singing, too. If cards are made and distributed at the same time, the children will be providing a most valuable ministry.

INTERCESSIONS **Years 1 and 2**
Some ideas for prayer

As we gather to worship the Christchild, born today, let us pray trustfully to our heavenly Father.

Father, we pray for all Christians celebrating with us all over the world, in all climates, times and seasons as our planet turns.
Pause
Light of ages: **be born in our hearts**

Father, we pray for all areas of darkness where your light is desperately needed to bring peace, understanding, sensitivity and compassion.
Pause
Light of ages: **be born in our hearts**

Father, we commend to you our homes, families, neighbours and friends; all children and young babies, all being born today.
Pause
Light of ages: **be born in our hearts**

We pray for those who are hungry,
cold or homeless; for all who are
separated from their loved ones;
all who find the festivities of Christmas
emphasising their isolation and misery.
Pause
Light of ages: **be born in our hearts**

We thank you for all who have
worshipped you throughout the ages;
for the lives and examples of all
who shone with your light and now
rest in your peace.
Pause
Light of ages: **be born in our hearts**

Father in thankfulness we praise you;
accept these prayers
for the sake of your Son,
our Saviour Jesus Christ, Amen.

1st Sunday after Christmas

TODAY'S THEME

... is the great love of God which we can see
personally in Jesus, the Christ. All the promises
and hopes are fulfilled by the birth of this baby
in Bethlehem, because he is the one who can set
us free from our slavery to all that is evil. His
salvation, beginning in Israel, extends outwards
to include every created person.

PARISH MUSIC

Hymns
Use plenty of carols again; in particular,
the following carols reflect the readings:

In the bleak mid winter
Angels from the realms of glory
Hark the herald angels sing
O come all ye faithful
Of the Father's love begotten
O little town of Bethlehem
What child is this?

Recorded music
Christmas Oratorio (Handel)

For choirs
Jesus Christ the Apple Tree (Piccolo)
Shepherds loud their praises singing
    (Rowley): SATB

CHURCH DECORATION

Try making some Christmas swags to decorate
pillars or to run along window ledges. They are
very effective and make use of the evergreens
and berries which are plentiful at this time of
year.

I have sometimes seen these made from blocks
of 'oasis' strapped together, but this is quite an
expensive method, and it is possible to make
them more cheaply. First, twist together two
lengths of garden wire and weave into them all
kinds of pieces of greenery until the wire is
hidden. Florist's ribbon can also be woven in
at this stage.

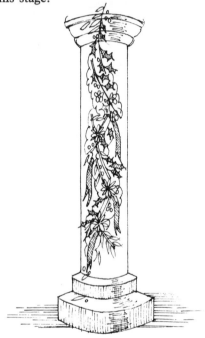

Now cut cubes of oasis (about 5cm × 5cm) and
soak them thoroughly. Wrap each block in
clingfilm and tape these at regular intervals
down each swag. Into these you can arrange
flowers and ribbon, making sure that the oasis
is well hidden. Remember too that if the swags
are going to be hung on pillars then the flowers
will have gravity to contend with!

Alternatively, tissue paper flowers can be
made and threaded among the greenery. This
is also very attractive and has the advantage of
lasting longer.

NOTES ON THE READINGS **Year 1**

Isaiah 7:10-14
In the face of a crisis, Ahaz is shaking like a leaf,
and Isaiah tells him that such terror suggests he
doesn't really trust in God. As an act of faith he
is urged to ask God for a sign, but Ahaz prefers
not to stick his neck out. He excuses his lack of

faith by arguing that you shouldn't put God to the test anyway.

God's response is the affirmation that a new royal child of his own making will be established to put things in order and rectify the wrongs of weak and sinful humanity. With the birth of Jesus, this prophecy is to be stunningly fulfilled at nothing less than the cost of God's own Son.

God is supremely trustworthy; even in times of crisis and panic his power and faithfulness stand like rock. We need not be afraid for he is with us.

Galatians 4:1-7
Often Paul draws our attention to God's remarkably perfect sense of timing. In this letter to the Galatians we are helped to see how God, the Lord of eternity and time, holds and guides his creation in a perfectly ordered and finely balanced movement towards fulfilment and accomplishment. Like an heir waiting to come of age God's people lived expectantly. At the best and right time (both spiritually and historically) God works from within the Law to buy us a greater freedom than the Law could ever give.

John 1:14-18
How do we know that all this was fulfilled in the person of Jesus of Nazereth? What was it about this man which convinced people they were in the presence of something greater than a fine teacher or clever miracle worker?

The two remarkable qualities which most impressed Jesus' disciples were not his power, his intelligence or his looks, but his grace and his truth. It is worth remembering these words to mull over whenever we have the opportunity, because they draw us closer to the character of God. These are the responsive, compassionate, vibrant qualities from which all Jesus' teaching and healing sprang. These are the personal characteristics of a loving and utterly pure God, which could not be revealed through the law alone, but needed to be expressed through a living person.

QUESTIONS FOR DISCUSSION

1. Those who most appreciate freedom are those who have known enslavement or captivity. Do the distractions of our society ever blind us to our enslavement from which Christ could set us free? Consider such areas as our ambitions for financial, intellectual or material success; our fears and anxieties; our full calendars.
2. Look through the Gospels together, picking out examples of Jesus' life and work which

must have led his disciples to recognise in this man God's grace and truth. Share some experiences in your own lives of the living Christ which have led you too, to recognise the presence of God's grace and truth.

CHILDREN'S TEACHING

Discuss with the children what it means to be adopted. Some may have personal experience of being 'chosen' in this way into a family. They may have come across 'Cabbage Patch' dolls which come with an adoption certificate. There are often advertisements in local newspapers about children in care who are hoping to find a family willing to adopt them.

It is important that even young children have the opportunity to talk about such matters in a caring, sensitive atmosphere, and they are often touchingly aware of the importance of belonging to a family unit.

Now give the children lumps of modelling clay and ask them to make some kind of person-creature that they would like as a friend if it were alive. When the creatures are finished, display them and enjoy them.

Wouldn't it be wonderful if we really could bring them to life! Explain how God created beings whom he loved and actually brought to life, and see if they can guess the names of some of them. And not only did he give us life, he adopted us; so that makes us very, very special — we must be children in God's family. He is our parent who loves us enough to want us to eat, sleep, play, work, sing, laugh and cry in his company.

Write this notice to put with the models and bring the whole thing into church.

> God made us, gave us life,
> and chose us as his children

God made us, gave us life, and chose us as his children

INTERCESSIONS **Years 1 and 2**
Some ideas for prayer

Let us pray to God our Father because he loves us so dearly.

We pray that the light of the world
may shine so brightly in our lives
that other people notice it
and are attracted to you
by the way we live and love.
Pause
Father, live among us: **live through our lives**

We pray that our world may stop
its noise, chatter and arguing
long enough to hear the angels
singing of hope and peace.
Pause
Father, live among us: **live through our lives**

Father, we pray for our families
and all our friends and neighbours;
may every relationship we have
be filled with your love.
Pause
Father, live among us: **live through our lives**

We pray for the homeless
and all refugees and exiles;
for children from broken homes,
and all who are destitute,
malnourished or ill.
Pause
Father, live among us: **live through our lives**

We pray for all from whom we are separated
  now
through death;
may they live in your light for ever
and may their loved ones know your comfort.
Pause
Father, live among us: **live through our lives**

Father, we can never thank you enough
for coming to rescue us, and we praise you
now and in our lives;
merciful Father
**accept these prayers
for the sake of your Son,
our Saviour Jesus Christ, Amen.**

NOTES ON THE READINGS **Year 2**

1 Samuel 1:20-end
Hannah had longed desperately for a child, so
now, when she keeps her vow to lend Samuel
to the Lord as soon as he is weaned, we can
appreciate the very great offering she is making.
Sacrifice is always a costly gift; giving from the
surplus of our possessions is not really a sacrifice
at all. But neither is a costly gift given
grudgingly or resentfully. Here, in Hannah's
offering of her son to the Lord, we see a
beautiful example of real sacrifice: the gift is very
precious to her but is given lovingly and
thankfully.

As a result of this Israel was provided with one
of her finest spiritual leaders.

Romans 12:1-8
It is this same attitude to giving that Paul urges
us to have: a generous-hearted giving back to
God our whole selves, complete with our gifts
and talents, our time, our ambitions and our
wills. That kind of giving digs rather deeper than
most of us would wish! What about our right
to self-fulfilment? What about our independent
thinking, our earning potential and our leisure
activities? Surely Paul isn't suggesting any of
these should be disrupted or just abandoned?

These questions, rushing to the surface in the
face of such an all-inclusive challenge, highlight
the differences between God's 'pattern' for
living and the pattern of this present world,
which emphasises the right to happiness and
self-fulfilment and self-possession far more than
the value of giving till it hurts.

Yet the strange truth is that in lovingly
relinquishing our grip on all that in worldly
terms makes for happiness, we find a deep-
seated joy and fulfilment which is otherwise
temporary or just out of reach.

Luke 2:22-40
Both Simeon and Anna had abandoned their
lives to God. They must have been in constant
touch with him and were therefore ready to
recognise, among the daily routines of the
temple, the coming of the promised Saviour,
even though he was only a baby.

Their insight perceived the ancient prophecies
in fulfilment through this small child — the pain
as well as the victory. Joseph and Mary were
given the incredible task of nurturing God's Son.
God chose a home which was not over-
privileged, materially. The family was not
famous, wealthy or well-connected. The best
upbringing for God's Son was a home where he
was loved and cherished, teased and laughed
with, had local children as friends, and trained
in his father's craft.

So we need not worry about how our children
are losing out if we cannot afford the latest toys
or clothes. If we concentrate on the values God
chose for his own Son we shall be giving our
children the best possible start in life.

QUESTIONS FOR DISCUSSION

1. What can the story of Hannah and Samuel
   teach us about giving? You may like to read
   the story from the beginning to place this
   section in context. It starts at 1 Samuel 1.
2. Have you ever found by doing God's will

instead of your own you have ended up more richly blessed? Why is it that greed and selfishness more often bring dissatisfaction than fulfilment?

IDEAS FOR ADULTS

To emphasise the fact that Jesus came to lighten the whole world, have a large globe brought to the front just before the intercessions. (A local school may well be prepared to lend one.) About twelve people bring a nightlight each and place the lights all around the globe. Then have a time of silence before starting the intercessions.

CHILDREN'S TEACHING

Talk with the children about some of the things that have to be done when a baby is born, such as registering the child (show a birth certificate, and suggest they ask to see their own at home) and having a check-up with the doctor (put on a toy stethoscope) and preparing for the baby's baptism (show a christening robe or a picture of a baby being baptised).

Now tell them how, in the Law of Moses, whenever the first son was born, he was brought to the temple to be offered to God, together with a present of two doves or pigeons. (Show two paper ones.)

Using a doll, and four children to be Mary, Joseph, Simeon and Anna, tell today's Gospel reading with the children miming the actions. The other children should mime the parts of the people in the temple so no one is left out. Finally, help the children to make a pair of turtledoves each:

2nd Sunday after Christmas

TODAY'S THEME

... is that God's Son, Jesus, shared with us all the experience of childhood. He grew up in a family which had its share of troubles as well as joys, and his love can fill our family life if we invite him to live among us in our homes.

PARISH MUSIC
Hymns
All that I am, all that I do
All over the world the Spirit is moving
As with gladness men of old
Bethlehem of noblest cities
He's got the whole world in his hands
Jesus good above all other
Once in Royal David's city
O worship the King all glorious above
Peace, perfect peace is the gift
The family of Christ
The heavenly child in stature grows
Forth in thy name, O Lord I go
Lord of all power, I give you my will

Recorded music
Lullaby (Brahms)

For choirs
Sing the birth (Praetorius, ed. Parkinson)
Our Lady's lullaby (Cope)

CHURCH DECORATION

Use bright colours and a theme of childhood in the flower arrangements for today. Try incorporating children's toys, such as coloured

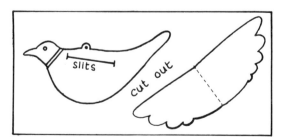

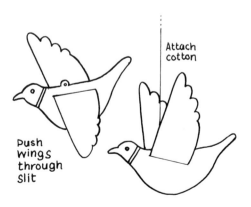

building bricks or balloons, and picking out the colours in the flowers chosen.

One arrangement could interpret the theme of 'The Holy Family'. One idea for this is to begin with fairly long, 'protective' stems at either side (many evergreens are just right or you could use dried grasses or gladioli). In the centre have small-headed flowers such as dianthus or small pompom chrysanthemums in bright colours. Aim to capture a sense of growth in the arrangement — growth which takes place within the area provided by the outer stems.

NOTES ON THE READINGS **Year 1**

Ecclesiasticus 3:2-7
In this passage we find the practical kind of caring love which Jesus taught and showed. It is so much easier to talk about love as a general idea, than to tend patiently to an irritating child, or repeat the same pieces of news time after time to an elderly relative whose memory is failing. Somehow, these mundane, everyday opportunities for loving seem to be especially difficult and demanding.

Yet it is from these threads that the strong fabric of real love is woven. Perhaps if we think of them as opportunities, instead of frustrating time-wasters, we may find them easier to cope with, and even start enjoying the challenge!

OR

Exodus 12:21-27
We all have family traditions and family jokes. Like shared memories they reinforce our sense of belonging. Through looking at the old family photograph albums, too, children learn about the special group they belong to, including those who may have died but are still remembered with affection.

In today's reading we see the family traditions of the Israelites being fixed in the minds of the people so that each new generation will celebrate the Lord passing over their houses and sparing them. The ritual serves both to keep the memory alive and also to prompt the curious young to ask 'Why?' That gives the parents the opportunity to teach their children about God's special love for us. If we go to church each Sunday, sooner or later our children will ask us why we do. We should never evade, suspecting mutiny! God has planned with this in mind; he gives us here an opportunity to tell them about his love.

Romans 8:11-17
Through Christ we have received the Spirit which makes us God's children. 'Abba' is much nearer to the meaning of 'Daddy' than 'Father', so it throws us into the relationship of a young, trusting child with a loving parent. It speaks of dependence, comfort, discipline, belonging and binding love. No longer struggling on our own to uphold moral standards, we are freed from so much pressure and stress. We do not have to go it alone and carry the day's and the world's problems on our shoulders. Those fears are something of the past: in the present we belong to God. His patience, his forgiving nature, and his willingness to show mercy are all there at our disposal to use liberally in all our relationships.

Luke 2:41-end
Jesus' childhood was certainly not without problems. After all, he was born away from home and the family were probably refugees until he was a toddler. When they did get back to Nazareth, no doubt some of the villagers would have gossiped and drawn their own conclusions about them. And Luke's account of Jesus at twelve years old being left behind, his parents searching for him, desperately worried, gives us a glimpse of other special difficulties there may well have been in nurturing a child who was also God.

So it is not an absence of problems which marks out a Christian family from others. It is the way such problems are met; offered in love to God the everlasting Father, accepted and used as an opportunity for growth in patience, unselfishness or compassion.

QUESTIONS FOR DISCUSSION

1. If a child were to ask why you went to church each week, how would you reply? Obviously your answer will depend on the child's age, but it is useful to discuss different ways of explaining our faith, both to crystallise our own beliefs and to prepare us to be better witnesses when we are suddenly called on to answer such a question.
2. Are there sometimes particular difficulties for parents bringing their children up as practising Christians in a secular society? How do prayer, Bible reading and worship help in such times?

IDEAS FOR ADULTS

It is easy to take the blessings of family life for granted. Why not arrange a display board full of family snapshots which capture the fun and laughter, comfort and support which is often much in evidence. Make sure each picture is named on the back, so as to ensure its safe return. The parish family can also be included, but avoid set portraits; catch people in action — caring, rejoicing, praying, working and dancing.

Such an exhibition can develop parish affection and a shared experience of God's blessings.

CHILDREN'S TEACHING

Ask the children to share some of the funny or exciting things their family has done — an outing or holiday, perhaps; moving house or getting a pet — and together thank God for our families. If you have some family photographs, show the children a selection stretching across the generations (so they can see Grandma, perhaps, both as a child herself with her family, and also with her grandchildren in a recent picture). Talk about each person in a family being important and remembered, and link this with us all being part of another family as well: the family of God. He is our Father and we are all his children (even grandparents are children in God's family!) Just as we are special in our human families, so God our Father considers each one of us special.

Ask the children to draw all the members of their own families (extended family members and pets, too, if they wish) and help them to label everyone. Write under the picture 'God our Father, bless my family'. Try singing: *We belong to the family of God* (MWTP, 49).

INTERCESSIONS **Years 1 and 2**
Some ideas for prayer

My brothers and sisters in Christ,
as members of one family
let us talk to God our Father
about our needs, cares and concerns.

We pray for the life, teaching and fellowship
of the Church, our Christian family;
help us to support and care for one another
as true family members,
regardless of physical, cultural
or intellectual differences.
Pause
God our Father: **hear your children's prayer**

We pray for friendship and good will
between all the different nations in our world;
teach us to enjoy the variety as richness,
rather than fearing it as a threat.
Pause
God our Father: **hear your children's prayer**

We ask for your blessing and guidance
in all the homes of this parish;
as each problem and difficulty arises
may your loving wisdom steer us
in the right direction.
Pause
God our Father: **hear your children's prayer**

We pray for all who have been damaged
by a disturbed or violent upbringing;
for children who are growing up
amid hatred and cruelty;
may they be healed by love.
Pause
God our Father: **hear your children's prayer**

We pray for those who have recently died
and commend them into your
everlasting care and protection.
Pause
God our Father: **hear your children's prayer**

We thank you for all the joys and blessings
in our lives; especially we thank you
for the relationships which enrich
our lives so much.
We ask you to make your home
in our hearts and homes,
**and accept these prayers
for the sake of your Son,
our Saviour Jesus Christ, Amen.**

NOTES ON THE READINGS **Year 2**

Isaiah 60:1-6
Israel is to be the focus of the most astounding event of history. Through all her wanderings, escapes, defeat and exile, she has waited. God

has kept by her, encouraged, chided and forgiven her, but still the long-term promise has yet to be fulfilled.

Now the prophet sings with the thrill of conviction and hope, of the time when Israel's greatest hour will come. On her is conferred the privilege of being the centre of God's revelation: like a pulsing light glowing in the surrounding darkness, God's glory will attract all peoples, and the light will eventually flood the whole world.

It is a remarkable privilege, which excites national pride and awe-filled humility. Israel cannot fail to experience a deep-seated hope and expectation.

Revelation 21:22-22:5

Through the incarnation that prophecy came true in the person of Jesus. With him the new age begins; but it is not yet complete. We know this each time we open a newspaper and read of the violence, undeserved cruelty, the greed and the hatred which still run free in our world. We know it in ourselves whenever we sin against God and against each other. No one can pretend that evil was eradicated at the crucifixion.

This prophecy is a vision of the accomplishment of all the good that Jesus made possible by his life and death and resurrection. Painfully slowly we edge towards it, both in our individual pilgrimage and as a species. All the good any one person does, hastens the coming of this kingdom; every loving act and word brings it closer; each time we forgive and promote peace we work with Christ in establishing heaven on earth.

Matthew 2:1-12, 19-23

Even as a tiny child, Jesus begins his work of drawing people to worship God. Here we see him with Mary and Joseph in Bethlehem, being honoured and presented with gifts from these important and mysterious strangers. They have been drawn by signs and promises to pay their respects, for they sense that in Jesus the light of the world has been born.

QUESTIONS FOR DISCUSSION

1. Why is the symbol of light so effective in explaining God? Make a list of the various qualities and use of light, and explore each in terms of spiritual life.
2. The first few years of Jesus' life were fraught with dangers. How did Joseph and Mary work with God in surviving these times? What can this teach us about tackling our own family problems?

IDEAS FOR ADULTS

This dance expresses how a growing awareness of God flows out into our relationships with one another.

Accompany the dance with *The Light of Christ* (ONA, 498). Begin with six dancers placed in a central area absolutely still and staring fixedly straight ahead. Have two sitting, two kneeling on one knee, and two standing; the group should look something like this:

Chorus: During the first chorus they remain completely still, while the whole area is very gradually lit up. A dimmer is ideal for this, but not essential.

Verse 1: Two dancers notice the light and slowly move their heads to gaze in a wide arc to the sides and above; then they raise one arm forward and trace an arc, palm outwards, in the air, as if they can see shape and form around them.

Chorus: Two more dancers notice the light, and the last two start at the second 'light of Christ', each couple repeating the slow smooth actions. The first couple begins to find they can move shoulders, arms and bodies, which they do with a sense of wonder as if the experience is quite new.

Verse 2: The dancers move their hands, studying them as a baby does, fascinated with the fingers, and looking at the hands from different angles. At 'so that all men who believed in him' all faces turn upwards to the light, back to the hands and then up again, bringing the hands upwards as well, in worship.

Chorus: Those who are kneeling stand and turn around as if trying their feet out; at the second 'light of Christ' the seated ones join in; and at the third 'light of Christ' the standing ones join in.

Verse 3: The dancers begin to notice each other and move, hesitantly at first, towards each other into groups of two, then three, exchanging a greeting of peace — embracing, linking hands and kissing. Each should make contact with all the rest.

Chorus: The dancers draw into a circle and all kneel, bowing their heads. Slowly they raise their arms and their heads in a gesture of praise, then stand and walk out among the congregation spreading the sign of peace throughout the whole worshipping community.

CHILDREN'S TEACHING

Prepare a cereal box 'television' and a strip of paper showing the night sky, the wise men on their journey, their visit to Herod, their adoration of Jesus and their departure by another route. Use these drawings as a guideline, or cut out pictures from Christmas cards and

Have six strips of card about 1 metre long and 5 cms wide, lay them down on the floor to make a star shape like this:

Write one of the six guidelines for being a star on each strip of card and let the children decorate them with tinsel and glue. Staple the strips together and carry the star into church, placing it near the altar, if possible.

stick them on.

Tell the children the story of the wise men, rolling the pictures along as you do so; or ask two children to do the spoon twisting.

Talk about how we can all be like the star by shining brightly to lead people to Jesus. With their help, make a list of practical ways we can do this:
- stay close to Jesus
- get to know the Bible
- be kind and loving
- stand up for what is right
- let others know you're a Christian
- enjoy and care for God's world

The Epiphany of our Lord

TODAY'S THEME

... is that wise men from distant countries were led to worship Jesus. The light of the living Christ also leads us, and when our lives reflect his light, many others will be drawn to worship the true God who made us and loves us.

PARISH MUSIC

Hymns

All hail the power of Jesus' name
As with gladness men of old
Bethlehem of noblest cities
Eternal ruler of the ceaseless round
For the healing of the nations
From the rising of the sun
God moves in a mysterious way
Hills of the north rejoice
I am the light
In Christ there is no east or west
Jesus shall reign
Let all the world in every corner sing
O worship the Lord
Praise to the Lord, the almighty
Songs of thankfulness and praise
The King of glory comes
We three kings

Recorded music

Sound track from 2001 Space Odyssey

For choirs

Kings in glory (Shaw): SATB
O God, who by the leading of a star
  (Attwood)

CHURCH DECORATION

Incorporate gold, frankincense and myrrh into one flower arrangement today. Drape a length of gold coloured cloth from a pedestal or over a stone step, and choose flowers to suggest richness and a feeling of mystery. Flowers with an oriental look are also effective. Try using eucalyptus and elaeagnus and ivy for foliage, and chrysanthemums, Christmas roses, lilies or poinsettia.

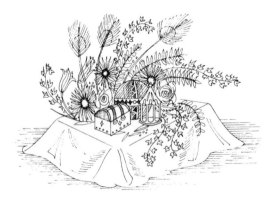

Alternatively, have three main arrangements, each exploring the theme of one of the wise men's gifts. The gold would be predominantly gold and regal, the frankincense blue, grey and silver, and the myrrh purple, magenta and crimson.

NOTES ON THE READINGS **Years 1 and 2**

Isaiah 49:1-6

This reading is one of the so-called 'Servant' poems. It describes a figure who, in the role of God's servant, is commissioned to bring God's people back to him. At times the servant appears to be the people of Israel, who, through their covenant with God, are to be the means of bringing all other nations to worship their creator. At other times the servant seems to be an individual, who, through his example and suffering, will draw many to acknowledge and worship God. It may well be that both meanings are intended, and for us Christians the passage certainly sounds remarkable like the mission of Christ himself.

The important thing is that through his prophet God teaches that his salvation is not just for the people of Israel, but will, through them, flood through the entire world until every scrap of creation is filled with the knowledge of his saving love.

Ephesians 3:1-12

Paul acts an ambassador. Himself a Jew, he is fulfilling Jewish prophecy by reaching out into the world's darkness with the light of God's saving love. The full, rich extent of God's promise had taken quite a time to dawn on Paul, and the dawning had been traumatic. But once enlightened, he worked fervently to spread the news.

Perhaps it has taken us years to realise that Jesus really is the Son of God, and that if we can bring ourselves to 'fall back on him' he does not let us drop. Perhaps a relative or friend has drifted away and seems to be taking anxious years to return.

It is important to remember that it is never too late to bother. However old we are, we can work whole-heartedly, for youth is not a prerequisite for being a full-blooded Christian. Also, some wanderings may be necessary for growth in some people's spiritual development and, if constant prayer is offered for their return to faith, they may well come back stronger and more receptive.

What we must never do is give up on them, even secretly. God never does that and neither must we.

Matthew 2:1-12

This event has always fascinated astronomers, and there are various possible explanations for the great bright light that led these enigmatic strangers to a small child living in Bethlehem. Whoever they were and wherever they travelled from, they knew they had arrived when they saw Christ. Here the searching stopped and the worshipping began. The focus of their lives was readjusted and they responded by giving.

Jesus, when he grew up, promised that everyone who searches will find. Sometimes people fool themselves into thinking that they are searching when really they have their hands over their eyes! Thorough searching involves setting out on a risky journey, asking directions from the scriptures and from those who have studied them, and being prepared for the star being occasionally hidden from view.

Do we provide enough help to those who are struggling through their search? Do we offer accommodation and hospitality on the way? Are we too ignorant of scripture to be able to answer their questions? Perhaps we could do more, as individuals and as a parish, to guide them towards their destination.

QUESTIONS FOR DISCUSSION

1. Talk through the different stages of the wise men's journey, and the events along their way. In what ways is it like a picture of our own spiritual journeys? What can we learn from the wise men's experiences which can help us in our spiritual pilgrimage?
2. How does Paul account for his being a servant of the gospel? To what extent do you think our own efforts and attitudes are important if God is to work through us?

IDEAS FOR ADULTS

Dance

The music for this dance is the beginning of the fourth movement of Dvorak's Symphony: *'From the New World'*.

Into the centre of the church strides an albed figure, holding a lit candle. From four different directions in the church small groups of dancers come towards him when the horns begin, as if being drawn by his light into existence. They stretch their arms out towards the light and move, hesitatingly at first, until they are all grouped round the central figure like this:

Slowly, he turns round in a circle, facing each group in order. As he faces each one he extends his candle outwards, and that group starts busily working. The first group mime building skills, such as chopping wood, hammering, brick laying etc. The second group mime food preparation, such as stirring, kneading dough, tossing pancakes etc. The third group mimes clothes-making, such as sewing, weaving, knitting etc. The fourth group mimes farming — cutting corn, milking, picking fruit etc. The idea is of everyone being involved in their own business, and while they are occupied, the central figure walks away and watches them from the distance.

Then, as the music changes to an oboe solo, he walks back to them. They freeze in their positions watching him, while he extends one arm in greeting. Slowly and deliberately they turn their heads away from him (with the cellos) group by group, and then one member from each group looks at him again, gets up and walks up to him, kneeling before him.

He raises these four to their feet and they bring out candles which have been tucked in their belts. They light these from the main candle and hold them high, facing out from the central figure as the music reaches a crescendo and joyfully move in a 'step, together, wait' sequence round the central figure, four steps one way, then four steps the other way.

Finally, as the groups resume their own, inward-looking 'busy-ness', the central five move down the centre and out into the world, one arm stretched out holding the candle, the other stretched out towards the central figure.

Fade the music as it comes to a natural fall.

CHILDREN'S TEACHING

Tell or read the story of the wise men, with their gifts displayed on the table. If possible, have something of real gold, a thurible with incense burning, and some anointing oil. Talk about these things, and how we use them in our worship (or way of showing the "worth") of our God. How can we give God a present?

Wrap each child in Christmas wrapping paper and give each a label to write and decorate, thread on wool and hang round his neck. At the offering of gifts, let the 'presents' walk up to give themselves. The labels can be collected and blessed before they are returned to the children.

INTERCESSIONS Years 1 and 2
Some ideas for prayer

Fellow travellers of Christ's Way,
let us pray together
for the church and for the world.

Father, may our Christian witness,
in a confused and nervous world,
shine with a piercing integrity and warmth
that awakens people's hearts
to the love of their creator.
Pause
Light of the nations: **shine in our lives**

Bless and protect
all travellers and pilgrims;
teach us to cherish the beauty
of our world and share its riches.
Pause
Light of the nations: **shine in our lives**

Help us to see Christ
in the eyes of all those we meet,
and delight in giving you glory
by serving others without expecting rewards.
Pause
Light of the nations: **shine in our lives**

Direct our vision to see
the best practical ways of providing shelter
for the homeless, safe accommodation
for those who live in fear of violence,
and food for the hungry.
Pause
Light of the nations: **shine in our hearts**

May all who have died in faith
be bathed in the everlasting light
of your loving presence,
and may those who mourn
be comforted.
Pause
Light of the nations: **shine in our hearts**

In thankfulness, Father,
we offer you our lives.
Accept these prayers
for the sake of your Son,
our Saviour Jesus Christ, Amen.

1st Sunday after the Epiphany

TODAY'S THEME

... is Jesus being anointed at his baptism with the Holy Spirit. When we are baptised we are born again into new and lasting life. We are then given the power and all necessary ingredients for witnessing to God's love wherever he sends us. Together we work towards his kingdom which is founded on caring love.

PARISH MUSIC
Hymns
All over the world the Spirit is moving
Hail to the Lord's anointed
Immortal, invisible
I no longer live
Let all the world
Make me a channel of your peace
The family of Christ is growing
The light of Christ
Vaster far than any ocean

Recorded music
The Moldau (Smetana)

For choirs
Psalm 23 (Mawby): U
Hymn to the Holy Spirit (How): 3 or 4
 part choir

CHURCH DECORATION

The font can receive special treatment today. Have a predominantly white theme, surrounding the font's rim and foot with cushion arrangements of flowers. You can extend the idea by adding a mirror on the floor, either near the font or at the front of the church. Sprinkle pebbles and shells around its edges and have small arrangements or clumps of potted plants so they look as if they are growing beside a pool. A few tall, overhanging pieces of willow or irises can be very effective, too.

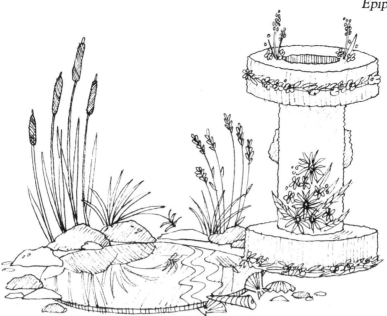

NOTES ON THE READINGS **Year 1**

1 Samuel 16:1-13a

The choice of this king was crucial and, as often happens, God had a particular person in mind for the job. But whether or not his will would be done depended on Samuel's readiness to comply with God's instructions even if that meant waiving his independent judgement. Fortunately Samuel stayed close to God and refused to anoint anyone until he felt God's firm assurance that this was the right man.

If we ever find that setbacks make it impossible to achieve some work we know God desires to have done, we must not make a bodged job with what seems to be available. We must wait and pray for clear guidance — the proper solution may be somewhere else, quite unexpected. The important thing is to stay listening, as God will show his way forward soon enough.

Also, we must bear in mind that outward appearances count for little in God's eyes, so that he often rejects and chooses in ways which take us by surprise. Perhaps we should think twice before judging by appearances!

Acts 10:34-38a

Peter, addressing the centurion, Cornelius and his gathering of family and friends, is a first-hand witness to the remarkable ministry of Jesus which began in full after God had anointed him with the Spirit and with power at his baptism. As Peter now sees, it all began with a chosen few, but it is God's will that through them the news may be spread far and wide; because the promise to forgive sins and set people free is there for every person: past, present and future. It is for the whole of humanity.

Matthew 3:13-end

It comes as a surprise to find how obedient Jesus was to the religious Law and customs. He, after all, had no need to be washed of sin, for he was sinless, so why did he insist on John baptising him?

In sending his Son into the world. God showed his desire to be completely identified in love with the creatures he had made. And now, at the point of baptism, he again shows full identification with the people; he is not above us but alongside us; in our sin and repentance as well as our odd moments of sanctity.

He also needed to be seen to be anointed by God, just as David had been anointed by Samuel. In their culture this expressed God's choosing; his setting apart of someone for a special task.

As Jesus came up from the water, God expressed his confirmation of love and power, both for Jesus himself, and for those whose spiritual eyes were open to understand.

QUESTIONS FOR DISCUSSION

1. Have you ever found that your initial judgement of someone, based on appearance, has been entirely wrong? Our society sets great store by appearances. Is there any way we can learn to look at people with God's eyes instead?

2. When have you been anointed by God with particular (and perhaps surprising) resources which have enabled you to do God's work in difficult circumstances? Do we ask for his resources enough, or are we more inclined to struggle on until our own resources are drained dry before begging for God's help?

IDEAS FOR ADULTS

The reading from 1 Samuel is very striking if acted out, with a narrator working together with players who speak the lines written in the Bible. Use the whole building; perhaps Samuel could set off from the front down a side aisle and then meet the elders from Bethlehem halfway up the centre aisle. (Make sure they really do come hurrying to meet Samuel). The main action can then take place near the altar. Samuel's thoughts can be said as an aside to the congregation, and God's voice could come from the back of the church — perhaps from a gallery if you have one. Obviously details of 'staging' will vary with different buildings, but look at all the possibilities so as to dramatise the reading as effectively as possible.

CHILDREN'S TEACHING

If you have any pictures of the Jordan, show these first, so that the children realise that it is a real place and can identify more easily with events there.

Also have a large baking tray, some earth or sand, metal foil, stones and twigs, and plasticine. Explain that you are all going to make a model of the Jordan and then let the children help assemble it. With the foil make a trough which can be filled with water for the river. Plasticine models of people can also be made, one of whom is John, and one Jesus. The rest are the crowds. Make a dove too.

Then tell the story of Jesus' baptism, moving the models as you do so. Rattle a sheet of thick card as God's voice speaks.

Give the children cards to fill and colour, like this:

INTERCESSIONS **Years 1 and 2**
Some ideas for prayer

My companions in Christ,
let us quieten our hearts
before God our Father,
and pray together for the needs
of the church and the world.

We bring to you, Lord, all who preach
and teach the Christian message of salvation,
and those who hear it;
through your Spirit, may its reality,
truth and hope take root and grow.
Pause
Father of Jesus: **use us for your glory**

We bring to you, Lord, our stewardship
of the world's resources; all discussions
and councils where far-reaching decisions
are made concerning government, conservation,
international relations, methods of harnessing
    power,
and fighting diseases;
may your generous will prevail
over human greed and prejudice.
Pause
Father of Jesus: **use us for your glory**

We bring to you, Lord, all who are apathetic,
mentally exhausted or aimlessly wandering
through life; all who are eaten up with jealousy,
poisoned by hate or weighed down by guilt;
may they feel and know the warmth and depth
of your love, and your yearning for their peace.
Pause
Father of Jesus: **use us for your glory**

We bring to you, Lord, ourselves,
our friends and all we shall meet during this
    week,
however briefly; fill us with your love
so that others may see it
and be drawn towards their Saviour.
Pause
Father of Jesus: **use us for your glory**

We bring to you, Lord, the dying
and those who have already passed
into the next stage of life;
may they live forever
in your peace.
Pause
Father of Jesus: **use us for your glory**

Father, we rejoice in your
uncompromising love for us,
and thank you for all the blessings
we receive from you each day.
**Accept these prayers
for the sake of your Son,
our Saviour Jesus Christ, Amen.**

NOTES ON THE READINGS **Year 2**

Isaiah 42:1-7
The prophet must have been very close to the
mind of God, for the character and actions of
the chosen servant he describes are remarkable
in their breadth, capacity for mercy, compassion
and lack of vengeance, in spite of the general
climate of opinion at the time he was writing.

Jesus, having studied this passage from
childhood, began to see how he must indeed be
the fulfilment of this prophecy.

Holy men and women of all ages and all
regions have always shared this ability to
understand the divine character in some way
which is nothing to do with knowing facts about
him, or observing rules and rituals. Their
understanding grows like a plant that is rooted
in him; by keeping constantly in his company
through prayer and meditation, they 'soak up'
his essence, and it shows.

He has invited us to this close companionship.
If we accept, he will transform us in the same
way, however unpromising the material!

Ephesians 2:1-10
We know only too well our tendency as humans
to be self-centred and self-indulgent. Advertisers
rely on it heavily for their profits. The truth,
confirmed with depressing regularity throughout
human history, is that, left to ourselves, we find
it impossible to escape the hold of evil on our
lives, both in a personal and a social way. One
way to cope with this is to give in to it and jam
the yearning for ideal love and goodness with

a white noise of activity and distraction. Another
way is to erect a fortified wall of cynicism and
bitter resignation, inside which the natural
yearning for reconciliation with a pure and
loving goodness shrivels and dies.

But there is still another way. The God of love
for whom we instinctively long, has come in
person to let us escape from all the evil in and
around us. We cannot buy this freedom; it is
freely given through the abundance of his love
and mercy.

John 1:29-34
John knew that his job was to prepare the people
for the coming of the Messiah, God's Chosen
One, even though he did not know who it was
going to be. No doubt John knew Jesus, his
cousin, and perhaps about him; but he had to
trust God and get on with his own job first, until
God chose to reveal his next task: witnessing that
Jesus was the Chosen One. Accordingly, he was
given the necessary insight and understanding
to enable him to witness with conviction.

We will often find ourselves being led by the
Spirit in a similar way. We may be given some
task to do and wish we knew where it is leading
or how it can be of any use. If we simply trust
God and get on with it, he will lead us step by
step, allowing us to see just enough at a time to
make our work possible. It may not be good for
us to know too much at first; humans are
impatient creatures, and may destroy God's
plans by trying to complete them too hastily. We
need to trust God more: he knows what is best.

QUESTIONS FOR DISCUSSION

1. Read again the kind of methods to be used
   by the servant in the Isaiah reading. Compare
   these with the methods usually used in
   establishing worldly 'empires'. Which work
   best in the short term and in the long term?
   Which methods have you found most
   effective in your own experience of handling
   people?
2. Why did both Jesus and the crowds need to
   see the baptism of Jesus by John?

IDEAS FOR ADULTS

The Isaiah passage is effective when read
chorally. Voices should be grouped into light,
medium and dark.

Medium	Here is my servant, whom I uphold,
Light	my chosen one in whom I delight,
Dark	I have bestowed my spirit upon him,

All	and he will make justice shine on the nations.
1 Light	He will not call out
1 Medium	or lift his voice high,
1 Dark	or make himself heard in the open street.
Dark	He will not break a bruised reed,
Light	or snuff out a smouldering wick;
Medium	he will make justice shine on every race,
1 Light	never faltering,
2 Light	never breaking down,
All	He will plant justice on earth, while coasts and islands wait for his teaching.
1 Dark	Thus speaks the Lord who is God,
1 Medium	he who created the skies
Medium	and stretched them out,
1 Light	who fashioned the earth
Light	and all that grows in it,
Medium	who gave breath to its people,
Medium and Light	the breath of life to all who walk upon it:
All	I, the Lord, have called you with righteous purpose and taken you by the hand;
1 Dark	I have formed you,
Dark	and appointed you
Medium	to be a light to all peoples,
Light	a beacon for the nations,
1 Medium	to open eyes that are blind,
1 Dark	to bring captives out of prisons,
All	out of the dungeons where they lie in darkness.

CHILDREN'S TEACHING

Tell the children the story of John baptising Jesus, and show some pictures or slides of the river Jordan. (Your local Christian resource centre should have these to lend out).

Now help the children make these models, set in shoe boxes. They will need scissors, glue, colouring materials, cotton and sticky tape.

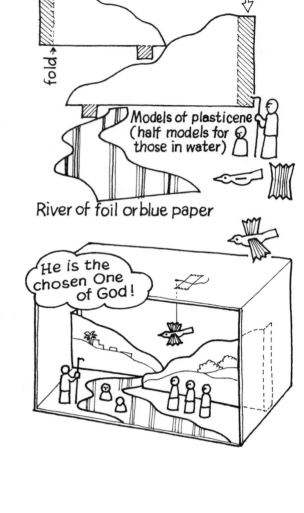

Glue to sides of box

fold→

Models of plasticene (half models for those in water)

River of foil or blue paper

He is the chosen One of God!

2nd Sunday after the Epiphany

TODAY'S THEME

. . . is the calling of the first disciples. Just as the prophets through the ages and the apostles were called by name by God to work with him for the good of the world, so we are chosen and called to work in partnership with God for the growth of his kingdom.

PARISH MUSIC
Hymns
Follow me, follow me
God's spirit is in my heart
He who would valiant be

I no longer live
I will be with you wherever you go
Jesus calls us o'er the tumult
Lord of life you give us all our days
My God, how wonderful thou art
Near the heart of Jesus
O Jesus I have promised
Our hearts were made for you, Lord
Take me, Lord, use my life
Take my life and let it be
Take up your cross, he says
Ye servants of the Lord

Recorded music
Toccata from fifth symphony (Widor)

For choirs
O thou who at thy Eucharist didst pray
   (Wöldike): SATB
I wiil lift up mine eyes (Mawby): U

CHURCH DECORATION

Today's theme of being called by God can be
effectively expressed in flowers, so that as soon
as people come into church their senses begin
to teach and challenge them. Basically, the
structure is a circular burst of white, pale yellow
and peach coloured flowers to represent God's
light. This is mounted on a stool or pedestal.
Lengths of white florist's ribbon are fixed under
the container so that they radiate outwards and
downwards from this 'light'. Each ribbon ends
at a small arrangement whose line stretches
upwards along the line of the ribbon. These
represent those who are called, and since God
seems to delight in calling a very varied bunch,
the arrangements should all have very different

'characters'. What they have in common is their
response to the main arrangement. One way of
ensuring that the small arrangements are varied
is to have each done by a different person,
choosing their own flowers and foliage. Some
may have the main stems in evergreens, others
in driftwood or dried twigs.

NOTES ON THE READINGS **Year 1**

Jeremiah 1:4-10
Jeremiah does not feel up to God's calling: he
is aware of his own inadequacies and the
demanding nature of the job he has been given,
and cannot believe he will have what it takes to
make a good job of it. God reassures him (and
us, too,) that he has set him apart for this even
before his birth, and will himself provide the
means to do well. With the symbolic gesture of
touching Jeremiah's mouth, God consecrates his
speech to be used as a channel of God's words.

Acts 26:9-20
Paul seemed to be another unlikely candidate for
helping the spread of the kingdom. He began
by doing his pretty efficient best to stamp out
the whole community of Jesus-followers before
they could contaminate the world with their
blasphemous teaching.

   Once again, God calls. A witness coming from
someone as hard to persuade as Paul is going to
be a very powerful witness indeed, so God will
actually be using Paul's energetic and misguided
persecution for good. All he needs to bring
resurrection out of death, is Paul's response.
Very probably Stephen's example had prepared
the ground; also Paul was a committed,
prayerful Jew; the blinding realisation that Jesus
really was God's Son flung him into a lifetime
of spreading the Good News far and wide.

Mark 1:14-20
Jesus' call concerns repentance. This is always
the necessary first step; nothing can happen, no
growth can start at all, until we confess that we
are to blame and our sinful way of going on is
our own fault. The buck stops here.

   If you recoil from the unpleasantness of full
repentence you are not alone; neither are you
misguided: taking the blame and renouncing
excuses is a humiliating and painful experience.
It hurts. But, as any dentist will confirm, no
filling will be effective, not even a gold one, if
the cavity is not first drilled clear of all decay.

   After the bad news comes the Good News! A
new life, confident, independent of circumstances, a fresh delight and enthusiasm, an
outlook of hope and challenge. The fishermen
left their old life and followed Jesus' call. Dare
we do the same?

IDEAS FOR ADULTS

At baptism we respond to God's call. Instead of the Creed today, have a space of silence for reflection after the sermon and then use the responses from the service of baptism: 'Do you believe and trust...' A.S.B. page 232.

CHILDREN'S TEACHING

As the children come in, make a point of having various jobs that need doing. In each case say something like: 'Now, we need someone strong to move this table.'; 'We need two people to arrange these lovely flowers Matthew brought.' etc.

When everyone is ready, remind the children of these needs which various people offered to do. God also needs our help to do his work, and he is hoping we will offer our help so that he can use us to make the world a more loving, caring place. Lead the children in prayer —

Heavenly Father,
here I am —
please use me:
I would really like
to help you.

All of us here have been chosen and asked to help, just as the fishermen — Peter, Andrew, James and John — were chosen in Galilee. Tell or read today's Gospel and try singing the 'Follow me' song.

Have a fishing net (or net curtain) and ask each child to make a fish, using templates for the younger children. They write their own names on the fish and decorate them. Then they poke the fish into the net so the names show. Hang the net up in church, putting a notice beside it saying: 'I will make you fishers of men'

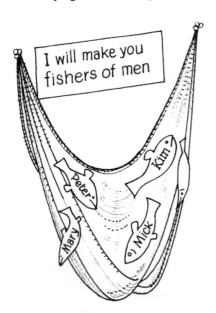

I will make you fishers of men

INTERCESSIONS **Years 1 and 2**
Some ideas for prayer

Bound together in the life of Christ
let us pour out our needs and concerns
before our Lord and Father, who knows
and loves us so well.
Father, we commend to your love
all ministers of your Word and sacrament;
keep them true to their calling
so that their life and work
brings many into contact with you.
Pause
Lord, here I am: **I come to do your will**

Father, we commend to your wisdom
all who wield power;
help them to encourage reconciliation
rather than revenge, friendship
rather than aggression, and flexibility
rather than stubborn intransigence.
Pause
Lord, here I am: **I come to do your will**

Father, we commend to your peace and joy
our homes and all the homes in this parish,
especially any where there is conflict
or distress; dwell with us, so that
our homes speak to every visitor of your love.
Pause
Lord, here I am: **I come to do your will**

Father, we commend to your healing
all who are in pain or danger;
all who are recovering from surgery;
all who depend on others for life and movement;
and who long for a friend who would visit them
and care about them.
Pause
Lord, here I am: **I come to do your will**

Father, we commend to your keeping
those who have left this life through
the gate of death; may they live with you
in the light of heaven for ever.
Pause
Loving Father, we thank you for calling us
and we offer you the rest of our lives.
Accept these prayers
for the sake of your Son,
our Saviour Jesus Christ, Amen.

NOTES ON THE READINGS **Year 2**

1 Samuel 3:1-10

Even before he was born, Samuel had been consecrated to the Lord; and now, while he is still a child, God calls him to prophesy. It would seem that few other people were receptive enough to hear the word of God, for it was 'rare' at that time. The priesthood had degenerated in greed and self-indulgence, with Eli's own two sons the worst offenders, and Eli had already been warned of God's retribution. He had spoken to his spoilt sons but had done nothing to put things right.

Samuel does not recognise God's voice straight away, and Eli, well-meaning but weak, recognises that God is speaking to this child and teaches him how to respond. So begins a lifetime of close communion with God; Samuel treasured the word of his Lord and always acted upon it, however unpleasant or unexpected it proved to be.

Communal worship is essential and of great value, but it is also vital to keep times of silence to commune with God, listen to his presence and respond to his calling.

Galatians 1:11-end
Paul gives us another example of someone who did not at first recognise God's voice. He thought he did. He was thoroughly committed to what he believed was God's will. But, still, he was persecuting the God he worshipped until his dramatic flash of understanding on the road to Damascus.

Having realised the truth of Jesus' claim to be the Son of the living God, Paul's entire life is handed over to the work of spreading the Good News that had taken him so long to grasp.

John 1:35-end
Some time before being called to commit their whole lives to following Jesus, the disciples are directed tò him by John the Baptist, who points him out as being the promised Lamb of God. They trail along behind him, rather than approaching him directly, until eventually he turns and asks them what they want. And isn't that so human? When we have the chance to meet someone we have longed to talk to and learn from, we become quite tongue-tied when we actually see them!

But Jesus is compassionate, welcoming, understanding and straightforward. Whenever he finds us hovering nearby, he will invite us to spend time with him and get to know him better. Then we can go and tell our family and friends news that will transform their lives, too.

IDEAS FOR ADULTS

The reading from Samuel is very effective if dramatised, using a narrator, Eli, Samuel and the Lord. The actions are simple enough to be 'staged' easily and the words will not take long to learn. Make it unhurried and clear.

CHILDREN'S TEACHING

Tell the children the story of God calling to Samuel, involving two of them in the story to mime the events.

Now divide them into two groups to play a game. The children in one line are given a different short message which they have to shout across to their partner on the far side of the room. The trouble is that everyone will shout their message at the same time! See how long it takes before everyone has received the right message. Then gather everyone round in a circle and hold up a pin. Try to hear the pin drop. Once this stillness has been achieved, talk quietly with them about the need to be quiet and still in our prayer if we are to know what God wants us to do.

Finish with a time of prayer based on the sounds we can hear when we close our eyes and really listen. Pray for travellers and drivers when you hear traffic; for those with colds and others who are ill; for babies and those being born; thank God for the wind or the rain, and so on. Encourage the children to add their prayers; there is no better way to learn to pray than by praying.

3rd Sunday after the Epiphany

TODAY'S THEME

... is the way God's glory is shown through signs and miracles. Throughout the Old Testament God proves his love for his people by the care and protection he lavishes on them, and as Jesus heals, feeds and encourages his way through the Gospel, we become aware of his glory — the glory of God himself.

PARISH MUSIC
Hymns
Alleluia, sing to Jesus
A man there lived in Galilee
At the name of Jesus
Christ whose glory fills the skies
God is love: let heaven adore him
God of mercy, God of grace
Hark my soul! It is the Lord
I am the bread of life
I am the light
I cannot tell why he
Immortal, invisible

Listen, let your heart keep seeking
Lord enthroned in heavenly splendour
O for a thousand tongues to sing
Open our eyes, Lord
Oh the blood of Jesus
Take my hands
The King of glory comes
Wander in the sun
Who is this man?

Recorded music
Missa Papae Marcelli (Palestrina): Sanctus
    and Benedictus

For choirs
O worship the Lord (Travers): U
Rejoice in the Lord always (Purcell):
    SATB

CHURCH DECORATION

Year 1
Capture the wedding atmosphere of Cana with
one flower arrangement which includes bridal
ribbon, white and pastel shades of flowers, a
bottle of wine and a couple of glasses.

Year 2
Today's main arrangement develops the theme
of the feeding of the five thousand as a sign of
God's glory. Include in it bread and silver foil
fish, and have the arrangement in a basket, so
as to show God's glory being revealed from
ordinary things. Include some wheat or dried
grasses and try a colour range from brown and
orange, through golds and yellows up to creams
and whites.

NOTES ON THE READINGS **Year 1**

Exodus 33:12-end
One of the things that marked out the God of
Moses as different from the nature gods of
polytheism, was his real presence shown in
actions and events of history (such as the escape
from Egypt, or manna in the desert). In fact,
it was this that made the Chosen People set apart
— not because they were any better than any
other nation (they very obviously weren't!) but
that other nations could see that their God
accompanied them personally.

   This conversation between Moses and his
Lord reveals their closeness and companionship,
which is given special confirmation in the way
God allows Moses a glimpse of his full glory,
while he is shielded from harm by God's own
hand. Our God may be the Lord of all power
and all creative energy, but he is also the God
of tenderness and warm affection.

1 John 1:1-7
John knows this from personal experience; he
has actually witnessed the glory of God as
revealed in the ministry of Jesus. He has seen
something of God's compassion, love and
personal concern for others in the kind of work
Jesus did, the signs and miracles he gave and
the unflinching love he showed. Such goodness
is described as light, and those of us who claim
to follow Jesus are bound to live in such light.
It's no use paying lip-service to the light but
spending most of our time out of it. If we do
that, then we live a lie. But within the light, in
companionship with Jesus, we are given the
resources to live in caring love with one another.

John 2:1-11
In a sense, the miracle at Cana was a speeding
up of the natural creative process. Water, in the
form of rain, does indeed turn to wine through
the slow growing, the sunshine, the fermenting
and the maturing. Here Jesus is showing himself
as Lord of time, who is perfectly in harmony
with all growth and maturing, both in the
natural and in the spiritual.

   He, then, has the power to mature us from
water into wine.

QUESTIONS FOR DISCUSSION

1. What evidence of God's glory is there in our
   world? What signs are there in events and
   relationships which show God to be living
   among his people?
2. Why do you think Jesus involved the servants
   in the miracle at Cana? Does this suggest
   anything about his ability to do remarkable
   things in our own lives?

IDEAS FOR ADULTS

Duplicate these words from Exodus for each person to take home with them:

'I myself will go with you, and I will give you rest.'

Perhaps the text could be put on a weekly handout, or in the church magazine. Encourage people to cut it out and have it with them, stuck on a wall or kept in a purse so it can be used in prayer throughout the week, as a word of comfort, assurance and strength.

CHILDREN'S TEACHING

Display some posters of vineyards — travel agents should be able to supply some pictures — and have a cluster of grapes on the table (seedless are best for young children). Share the grapes out, and talk about how the juice is squeezed out and mellowed carefully in vats before being bottled and drunk, perhaps on a special happy occasion like weddings, or, in some countries, with everyday meals.

Read or tell them about the wedding in Cana when the wine ran out, and Jesus gave them wine from water.

When have they seen wine used in church? Talk about the celebration which we share there — Jesus shares his life with us.

Help the children make a card like this:

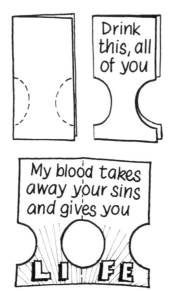

INTERCESSIONS **Years 1 and 2**
Some ideas for prayer

Companions in Christ,
as we remember with gratitude
all that God has done for us,
let us bring to his love the needs and concerns
of the Church and of the world.

We bring to your love, Lord, the daily work
of each member of Christ's body;
that in constant prayer we may learn
your will and your way of doing things,
until we work exclusively for your glory.
Pause
In you we trust: **we look to you for help**

We bring to your love, Lord, the mistakes,
short-sightedness and arrogance of our world;
that in Christ we may learn to respect one another
and the treasures of the planet we inhabit.
Pause
In you we trust: **we look to you for help**

We bring to your love, Lord, the wounded
and the afraid, the despairing and the rejected;
that they may find Christ suffering alongside them
and allow him to restore them to wholeness.
Pause
In you we trust: **we look to you for help**

We bring to your love, Lord,
our busy concern with unimportant things;
that in spending more time in Christ's company
we may learn to act and react in all our relationships
with the character and Spirit of Jesus.
Pause
In you we trust: **we look to you for help**

We bring to your love, Lord,
all our dear ones who are separated from us through death;
that as children of eternity we may always remember
how close they are, linked by your eternal love.
Pause
In you we trust: **we look to you for help**

Almighty Father, hear the prayers we offer,
and use our bodies, minds and spirits
in establishing your kingdom.
Accept these prayers
for the sake of your Son,
our Saviour Jesus Christ, Amen.

NOTES ON THE READINGS **Year 2**

Deuteronomy 8:1-6
As Moses talks to the people of Israel he reminds them of the stages of their journey that have brought them to the present, rather as we might get out the old photograph albums on family occasions and watch the family's growth and change through the years. The relationship of

God to his people is very much a family relationship — he is a kind, firm, wise and loving parent who has been guiding his children's development and cares about their future.

This personal involvement of a loving God is strikingly different from the pagan religions, and marks a new era in the spiritual development of humankind. The God of power and glory, from whom springs all creation, reveals himself in a loving relationship with the beings he has made.

Philippians 4:10-20

If we let ourselves trust and depend on God's parental care, our happiness will become far less dependent on the colour of our bank balance or on material comforts and possessions. Like Paul, we shall be able to enjoy both richness and poverty, and be just as happy whether we have little or plenty. God's glory will make itself known in his practical care of us in all circumstances.

Our society is highly materialistic, which makes it difficult to latch on to Paul's outlook; we are pressurised constantly by the media, advertising and social expectations, to be concerned about achieving better material comforts for ourselves and others, and to see health and wealth as necessary for happiness.

To train ourselves to delight in whatever God provides, it sometimes helps to make ourselves say, 'thank you, Lord' every time we miss a bus, spill our best whisky, cannot afford a new coat or use our holiday savings on repairing the car. Thankfulness is a habit, and when we remember to rejoice in the not-having as much as the having, we shall be much richer and, incidentally, happier.

John 6:1-14

Perhaps Philip needed to learn to rely less on buying answers to problems and more on God's freely given grace. A rapid calculation makes it obvious that in this case, anyway, money is not going to work.

The small boy's quick and willing response, with a prompt offer of his own lunch, shows just the lovely quality of children that Jesus warmed to and longed to find in adults. 'Use mine!' is so often the reaction even from very young children, and as a parent it is touching to find a favourite teddy shoved eagerly in alongside Dad when he has 'flu; or their special comforter shared with Grandma after an operation.

Andrew is obviously touched by the boy's gift, but has natural adult misgivings about the actual use of it! But for Jesus, the willing offering, the spontaneous desire to sacrifice, is what enables

him to feed the vast company of people with God's liberality. As soon as we show we are ready to put ourselves out, God can use us, often with far, far more effect that our meagre offering on its own could have achieved.

QUESTIONS FOR DISCUSSION

1. Trace your way over your own lives — both individually and as a parish — as Moses did with the children of Israel, so as to notice God's parental guidance, provision and help there. Are there any areas which at the time seemed hard, but which now can be seen as times of learning or growth?
2. Jesus could have commanded the stones to become bread, and fed the people that way. Why do you think he asked the disciples about buying bread, and used the boy's lunch?

IDEAS FOR ADULTS

To emphasise the way a small gift was turned into such a wide-reaching service, cover a flower-stand with draped white material and surround the base with a profusion of flowers. But on the stand itself, place only a child's scruffy lunch box.

CHILDREN'S TEACHING

Cut out from card five small rolls and two fish, colour them and put them in a lunch box, and use this as you tell the children today's Gospel. It will help them imagine it all better if you enlist their help in being the crowd walking round the lake, listening to Jesus' words, one boy being Philip and another the one who had a lunch box which he offered and so on.

Then help them make five barley loaves and two fish each, using the card ones and templates. On the back of each item write a word which can be shuffled into a prayer, like this:

4th Sunday after the Epiphany

TODAY'S THEME

... is the way God shows his glory in our lives by renewing us from the inside and transforming us completely. As we increase our availability to the life-giving power of God, we shall become more and more like him, and reflect his glory more and more brightly.

PARISH MUSIC

Hymns
All people that on earth do dwell
And did those feet in ancient time
Build, build your church
Christ is our cornerstone
Father, you are living in us now
Go in peace to be Christ's body
I rejoiced when I heard them say
Jesu the very thought of thee
O worship the Lord
Songs of thankfulness and praise
We have come into this house

Recorded music
The Rite of Spring (Stravinsky): the beginning

Suitable anthems
Jesu, the very thought of thee (T.L. de Victoria)
Christ, whose glory fills the skies (Knight): U

CHURCH DECORATION

In one flower arrangement today have stones or bricks with small pots of ivy, ferns, spider plants

etc. tucked in between, along with a number of tiny flower arrangements. The aim is to create a sense of life spilling out of the building materials.

NOTES ON THE READINGS **Year 1**

1 Kings 8:22-30
The splendid new temple has at last been completed in all its magnificence. The whole population has come to stand before God as it is dedicated. There is an excitement and hope pulsing through Solomon's prayer as he offers the house he has made. Solomon is acutely aware that any building, however beautiful, is insufficient a house for a God who planned and fashioned the vast and intricate universe.

Yet, though he is humbled by this, he is not overcome with despair or futility because he knows God's habit of using what we offer to dramatic effect. What is important, and must never be neglected, is the act of offering. Whatever we build in our lives — marriages, businesses, careers, relationships — all can be in-dwelt by the living God with remarkable effect, providing we dedicate them from the outset to the God who made all our efforts possible in the first place.

1 Corinthians 3:10-17
Foundations are all-important, and in our lives the only foundation possible for an effective and fruitful life is Jesus, the Christ. If we suddenly come to realise with dismay that we have been building with hay and straw, it will be necessary to dismantle down to the foundations before we can begin building again with stronger and better materials, which incidentally, God will always provide.

Sometimes we are so keen to do things our way that we scratch about for bits of straw so busily that we don't notice the fine stone God is offering for our use. Whenever we feel dispirited or overworked, it is worth stopping for a look at Jesus; it may be that we have not been using the best materials.

John 2:13-22
Corruption never happens all at once. Gradually and insidiously the dealing in money-changing had encroached on the holiness of the temple — a sign of greed and selfishness creeping in, taking over the spiritual purity of God's people.

When we read this passage straight after Solomon's dedication prayer of the original temple, so many years before, the sordid difference between high ideals and squabbling, corrupt practice, we can understand Jesus' zeal in driving out all the dealers and money-changers from God's house. It is an anger fired by love for people who are bent on their own spiritual destruction; a sign of how drastic and thorough repentance needs to be, both in an individual and in a nation. As some of the good kings of Israel had atoned for religious corruption by smashing all idols and destroying cult worship, so Jesus publicly cleanses the temple before atoning for all sin by his sacrifice on the cross. Only through systematic crucifying of sin and selfishness can resurrection life in us flourish.

QUESTIONS FOR DISCUSSION

1. What can we learn from Solomon's dedication of the new temple about praying? How does it follow the 'pattern' of the Lord's prayer?
2. When you think of yourselves as temples housing God's spirit, does that direct you to any activities, values or attitudes which really need to be thrown out?

IDEAS FOR ADULTS

To emphasise the different stages of Solomon's prayer, have the passage read by four people standing in different parts of the building. The first reads up to: 'Today you have carried out by your hand,'; the second up to: 'let the words come true which you spoke to your servant David my father.'; the third up to: 'How much less this house that I have built!'; and the fourth up to the end. Practise to ensure that all voices are easily audible and encourage readers to speak quite slowly, so as to give listeners a chance to 'digest' what they hear!

CHILDREN'S TEACHING

Bring along a household repair manual which has clear diagrams in it, a piece of sandpaper for each child and an assortment of wood offcuts or driftwood, and plenty of varnish.

First show the children how important it is to prepare a wall before you paint it — otherwise the paint will not last. Show them how cracks need to be cleaned out before they can be filled and wood sanded down before it is varnished. Explain how repentance is the necessary cleaning out and preparation before any growing can start in our Christian lives. This is made clearer if you have a chart with diagrams similar to the repair

manual like this:

Give the children a chart to use in prayer during the week, which helps them review areas in their lives which need to be sanded down or cleaned up for Christ to make beautiful and useful.

Now let the children select a piece of wood and sand it down smoothly before varnishing it. It may be used as an ornament, or a paper weight.

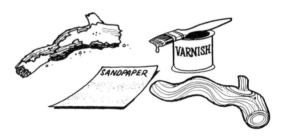

INTERCESSIONS **Years 1 and 2**
Some ideas for prayer

As members of the body of Christ
bound together in his love,
let us pray together now,
confident in God's promise
to be amongst us.

We pray for all who form the church
in its variety and richness throughout the world;
may the weak be encouraged and strengthened,
the wanderers return,
those besieged by doubt be given
the assurance of faith,
and the jaded refreshed by

your living Spirit
Pause
Take us as we are: **and use us, Lord**

We pray for all councils, committees
and governing bodies,
for those serving on juries,
for air, sea and mountain rescue teams;
that in working together in your strength
they may strive for what is good, just and
    honest,
so that your will is accomplished in them.
Pause
Take us as we are: **and use us, Lord**

We pray for our families and our friends,
that we may be transformed and renewed
through the richness of your presence;
give us deeper insight, more awareness
and greater love for one another.
Pause
Take us as we are: **and use us, Lord**

We pray for the poor and for the hungry,
for all frustrated by damaged or crippled bodies;
for those in prison, and those enslaved
by drugs, alcohol, hatred or fear.
Pause
Take us as we are: **and use us, Lord**

We pray for those who have died
and those who are at present
on that last journey;
may they have peace in the
joy of your presence for ever.

Father, we thank you
for all your glory in the world you have made,
for all you have accomplished in our lives
and in the lives of the saints;
we lay the rest of our lives at your feet.
**Accept these prayers
for the sake of your Son,
our Saviour Jesus Christ, Amen.**

NOTES ON THE READINGS **Year 2**

Jeremiah 7:1-11
Jeremiah never minced his words! He was one
of those people who refuse to be lulled into
accepting lax standards just because they have
become the usual practice, and here he derides
the hypocrisy of those who pay lip service to
God's law when at the temple, but whose
corrupt lives are a blatant denial of it.

The hypocrisy of living a lie is a base insult
to the purity and integrity of God, and renders
our worship void and ludicrous. If our worship
seems dead on its feet, no novelties or flashy
gimmicks will revive it; but it will burst into life
spontaneously and become flooded with
meaning and vitality whenever there is a
thorough and rigorous repentance and a genuine
seeking after God.

Hebrews 12:18-end
The writer compares our revelation of God with
God's revelation to Moses and the people of
Israel. The experience of the Old Testament was
awesome and terrifying; for us, in the light of
Christ, the kingdom of heaven itself is open to
us, if only we will take it, and that is something
which should inspire us to utmost reverence and
awe.

It is only when we truly humble ourselves
before God in spirit that true worship can begin,
and our lives can be gradually transformed and
made new through God's power.

John 4:19-26
The new life, with all its vitality, freedom and
peace, is available to everyone of every
nationality, not just the chosen race to whom
and through whom it was first brought. The
Samaritan woman is drawn to question Jesus
about the issues which worry her and make her
angry, until gradually she is led to see that all
these wranglings are submerged in the greater
significance of God's eventual purpose for his
creation. Pure worship begins in the heart, and
its effect on lives is shown personally in the life
of Jesus of Nazareth.

QUESTIONS FOR DISCUSSION

1. What do you think is the breeding ground
   for hypocrisy? Since it leads to spiritual
   blindness, how can we make sure we see it
   in our own lives before it causes our spiritual
   decay?
2. Do we speak out enough to steer the world
   God's way through its crises?

IDEAS FOR ADULTS

Today's Gospel can be acted out. The Samaritan
woman, dressed in biblical costume, holds a
water pot. She stands and Jesus sits; he is resting
after a long walk. Omit the part of narrator and
make the reading a conversation. As Jesus
identifies himself, he stands up.

CHILDREN'S TEACHING

Talk about being honest with God: saying our
prayers and then being unkind, lazy or boastful,

for instance. Explain that this is really lying, and we need to make it up with Jesus by saying we are sorry and having him forgive us — which he ALWAYS will. Have a short prayer time to do this.

Tell the children how God makes our lives beautiful and then builds us into his living church. Give each child an ordinary-looking muddy stone. Have ready several bowls of soapy water and kitchen roll, with protective aprons and scrubbing brushes. The children clean and decorate their stones and then arrange them on an outline of a cross. Nightlights can be placed among the stones. Gather round this cross to sing to Jesus some praise songs.

5th Sunday after the Epiphany

TODAY'S THEME

. . . is the wisdom of God, revealed to us clearly in Jesus. Through all the problems and decision-making of our lives we have God's assurance that he will lead us to make good choices and act wisely and well, provided we remain rooted in the loving wisdom of our Lord.

PARISH MUSIC

Hymns
All creatures of our God and King
All things bright and beautiful
Be thou my vision
Blessed assurance, Jesus is mine
Father, Lord of all creation
Immortal love, for ever full
Jesus is Lord! Creation's voice
May the mind of Christ my Saviour
O God our help in ages past
Teach me my God and King
This world you have made

Recorded music
Symphony no. 5 (Shostakovich)

For choirs
O, praise God in his holiness (Gibbs): 2-part
The earth is the Lord's (Pratt): U

CHURCH DECORATION

Have a very simple, uncluttered line in arrangements this week, to express purity and integrity of God's wisdom. Suggest the natural world with a few large shells or pebbles, chunks of quartz or other minerals around the base of the flowers. Driftwood and bark are also very attractive and could effectively be incorporated. Try using narcissus, pussy willow or young sticky buds of horse chestnut.

NOTES ON THE READINGS **Years 1 and 2**

Proverbs 2:1-9
In these words of advice it is the seeking which is important and will gradually lead to a depth of understanding and knowledge of God. We are reminded of the emphasis Jesus also placed on committed, diligent seeking, along with his promise that if we do seek we shall certainly find.

As Christians, all our life-journey is a seeking after the mind of God, and we are in great danger of complacency if ever we start to think we have arrived. For God encompasses so much that we can never tie him down to a limited space, the shape of our imaginations or hopes. Rather, our search will draw us gradually deeper into fellowship with God, and each new insight will open up new terrain to discover within the loving God who created us.

OR

Ecclesiasticus 42:15-end

This beautiful passage opens our eyes to see God's remarkable creation with the freshness of newly-acquired vision. So often we take it all for granted because we are used to it, and fail to see in the material world all the signs and symbols of God's abundant glory. There are dark, deep and secret places spiritually as well as materially; infinite space reflects the infinite time of eternity; the life-giving brightness of the sun expresses the life-creating power and love of God. We can train our eyes to see only the unsatisfactory, the wrong or the novel; or we can train them to recognise also all the wonder, wisdom and glory of God.

1 Corinthians 3:18-end

Being full of Christ's love, we are like holy temples, filled with the presence of God. When we remember this it can comfort us during danger and strengthen us when we are tempted to abuse our bodies.

For we do not belong to ourselves any more, but to Christ, and when that still point is fixed, all other loyalties and commitments will fall into place. No personality or theory is as important as our relationship with Christ.

Matthew 12:38-42

There is a world of difference between seeking God and looking rather ghoulishly for signs. Signs are exciting, dramatic and 'easy' because they require nothing except a few Ooh's and Ah's. Jesus knew right at the start of his ministry that such showmanship would draw the crowds — hence his temptation to use the technique when Satan suggested he should throw himself off the temple pinnacle and be unharmed.

But Jesus rejected the idea. He prefers to coax and encourage us, step by step, teaching us faith by the very act of our searching, increasing our insight and perception through our desire to see more clearly.

QUESTIONS FOR DISCUSSION

1. Do we, personally and as a church, tend to try and make God small enough to grasp and understand? Do we tend to draw back from our search if it threatens to challenge our lifestyle?
2. How does God's wisdom differ from the worldly view of wisdom?

IDEAS FOR ADULTS

Display a collection of pictures which suggest God's glory in the natural order of creation and in people walking the way of wisdom. There may be landscapes, magnified cells, old and wise faces from a variety of countries, children worshipping with their parents, people reading their Bibles, shadows, camouflage, and people being helped in various ways. Have today's Collect written up among the pictures.

CHILDREN'S TEACHING

Bring along a toy owl, or a picture of an owl, and talk with the children about what we think of as being wise. It's not so much knowing a lot of facts as knowing how to act in the best way whenever you're faced with a problem. Some of them may know the Brownies' story of the wise owl, and there are lots of fairy stories showing wise people solving problems in very practical and effective ways.

Now, using a selection of pictures and objects — whatever you have available — talk with them about the ways in which our God is wise. Explore such areas as animal camouflage, the growth of food, seasons, gravity, electricity and the balance of nature. Jesus showed that he was wise in the way he loved and understood people, and the more loving we are the wiser we shall become, even if some people think we are fools.

Help the children to make a collage of their own and cut-out pictures showing the glory of God in our world. Call the collage:

'the work of the Lord is full of his glory'

INTERCESSIONS **Years 1 and 2**
Some ideas for prayer

Fellow travellers of the Way of Christ,
we know that God our Father loves us;
let us therefore pray to him now
about all that concerns us in his church
and in the world.

We pray for the many groups of Christians
  worshipping
alongside us, but in other communities
and in other countries;
for all who risk persecution for their faith;
that we may support and encourage one another
and serve the world as Christ's body,
whatever the personal cost.
Pause
Take us, Father: **and live through our lives**

We pray for the leaders of the nations,
all members of governments and their
financial and social advisers;
that they may be led in the Spirit of Wisdom
to work in harmony with God's will
so his values are reflected in all policy making.
Pause
Take us, Father: **and live through our lives**

We pray for a lessening of selfishness
and a broadening of our characters,
until we are prepared to welcome, love and care
for whoever is in need,
working hand in hand with God
wherever we are sent.
Pause
Take us, Father: **and live through our lives**

We pray for all in intensive care at the moment;
all undergoing emergency surgery;
all women in labour and their babies;
all who are approaching death;
that God's great healing love
may wash through their bodies and minds
in a surge of peace.
Pause
Take us, Father: **and live through our lives**

Father, we thank you for your constant,
loving provision for us throughout our lives,
and commend to your safe keeping for ever
all who have died, especially. . . .

Merciful Father,
accept these prayers
for the sake of your Son,
our Saviour Jesus Christ, Amen.

6th Sunday after the Epiphany

TODAY'S THEME

. . . is the way God's character is revealed through parables to all who seek to know him more clearly. Jesus often used the form of parables — stories with hidden meanings — as an aid to teaching people about God and the Kingdom of Heaven.

PARISH MUSIC
Hymns
Blest are the pure in heart
Breathe on me, breath of God
Christ whose glory fills the skies
Farmer, farmer
God be in my head
He is Lord
I cannot tell
I danced in the morning
Jesu, Gentlest Saviour
Listen, let your heart keep seeking
Now my tongue, the mystery telling
Tell out my soul
What a friend we have in Jesus
Whom do you seek?

Recorded music
The Four Seasons (Vivaldi)

For choirs
God be in my head (Davies)
O taste and see (Vaughan Williams)

CHURCH DECORATION

Have one arrangement which includes wheat, interspersed with teasles and thorny twigs. Use anemones, dianthus, dimorphotheca and cornflowers among the wheat, so that the effect is of a rich meadow where all grows together until harvest.

NOTES ON THE READINGS **Years 1 and 2**

2 Samuel 12:1-10
Whenever we embark on a course that is wrong, we are very likely to justify our actions to ourselves so as to quieten the nagging voice of conscience. It is quite possible to do this so effectively that we silence our conscience, with disasterous hardening of heart as a result.

Thankfully, before David has accomplished

this, Nathan approaches him through the power of a parable, which forces him to see the truth of his sin objectively. We all tend to be extra indignant about sins which are actually part of our own behaviour, and David is outraged by the behaviour of the rich man in Nathan's story.

Now, when Nathan confronts him with the full horror of his own behaviour, David is challenged. He can either turn away from the truth and run from God into the dark prison of self, or he can repent, and run weeping towards the God of purity and love.

Romans 1:18-25

God's world shows order and discipline from the spiralling galaxies down to the structures of DNA; Paul argues that there is plenty of evidence to point us in God's direction, even if we do not recognise him by name. Our consciences can direct us to respecting one another, caring unselfishly for one another and using the world's riches wisely.

If we persist in self-indulgence, and close our eyes to the truth, we can expect a spread of violence and evil, a sense of futility pervading society; darkness and degradation in a restless world.

Matthew 13:24-30

While in this life we may well find that weeds and thorns seem to be flourishing better than the wheat. Incredible sums of money change hands for things which are of little lasting value; dubious entertainers and money jugglers are highly paid and esteemed by many, while many less glamorous yet infinitely valuable and caring work is poorly paid and unacclaimed.

If we are tempted to be hurt by the injustice of how, often, evil appears to receive all the rewards, we can re-read this parable which acknowledges that good and evil must grow alongside each other until the end of time, when only what is good will survive.

QUESTIONS FOR DISCUSSION

1. Read on in 2 Samuel 12 to see how David reacts to Nathan's parable. Why was it more effective to tell the truth in story form?
2. How does the parable of the weeds and wheat help us to cope with all the evil of our world? Does it affect our attitude to those who have hurt or wronged us?

IDEAS FOR ADULTS

Read today's Gospel with a narrator, house-holder and a group of servants.

CHILDREN'S TEACHING

The Palm Tree Bible Stories series has a very readable version of this story, which could be told to the children first. It is called *Evil Beezel's Wicked Trick*.

Talk about what things they think are like the weeds, and which the wheat, and how sensible God is not to risk damaging the crop by pulling up the weeds before the wheat is strong enough. Then divide them so that some draw and cut out wheat and some thorny weeds. Stick them all on to a poster, on which is written: 'Let them both grow till the harvest'.

INTERCESSIONS **Years 1 and 2**
Some ideas for prayer

Rooted in Christ, let us call to mind now
all those in need, and pray for them
to our heavenly Father.

Lord, we pray that all who teach the Christian faith
may be given appropriate language
to get through to those who hear them,
so that the Word of God takes root in many hearts.
Pause
Lord of life: **teach us your ways**

May all diplomats and negotiators promote
peace and friendship between the nations,
fostering mutual respect and understanding.
Pause
Lord of life: **teach us your ways**

May we and our families, neighbours and friends
become daily more Christlike
and less self-centred;
more responsive to the needs of those around us
and less bothered by what we get out of life.
Pause
Lord of life: **teach us your ways**

May those whose lives have been threatened
or shattered by crippling illness or injury
find new doors opening, new hope appearing
and new meaning transforming their outlook.
Pause
Lord of life: **teach us your ways**

May those who have passed from this life
into eternity rejoice for ever
in the fullness of your glory.

Lord, we thank you for dealing with us
so patiently and with such compassion;
if we should close our hearts to your will
please keep knocking until we open the door!
Merciful Father
**accept these prayers
for the sake of your Son,
our Saviour Jesus Christ, Amen.**

BEFORE EASTER

9th Sunday before Easter

TODAY'S THEME

. . . is Christ as the teacher. Not only with his
words, but in his life Jesus shows us how to live
fulfilled and fruitful lives, realising our potential
and playing our part in bringing the world to
wholeness.

PARISH MUSIC

Hymns
Abba, Father, let me be yours
Be thou my guardian and my guide
Blest are the pure in heart
Children of the heavenly king
Follow me, follow me
Guide me, O thou great redeemer
If you are thirsting
Jesus, good above all other
Lead us, heavenly Father, lead us
Lord, when I turn my back on you
O for a closer walk with God
Seek ye first the kingdom of God
Through all the changing scenes of life

Recorded music
Concerto for flute and harp (Mozart)

For choirs
Ave Verum (Mozart): SATB
Flocks in pastures green abiding (Bach):
   SATB

CHURCH DECORATION

As a central arrangement gather together a
selection of spring flowers in pots, baskets of
seed and grain and bulbs, branches of forsythia
and any other trees and shrubs which are
bursting into new life.

NOTES ON THE READINGS **Year 1**

Isaiah 30:18-21
Isaiah had been given a vision of a world in
which God's kingdom was established and so he
is able to speak to the people with hope and
encouragement. His words were going to be
fulfilled more practically, perhaps, than even
Isaiah himself imagined.

For when Jesus taught his followers in Galilee
so many generations later, he took Isaiah's words
and applied them to himself; he was the voice
which says to us 'I am the Way, follow me'.
Such an offer means that for every individual
there is a personal itinerary through life — we
are offered an individually structured route
together with personal guide and companion. It
is an offer which will lead us to peace and joy.

1 Corinthians 4:8-13
The Corinthian Christians had become
complacent. Their comfortable lifestyle had not
increased their spiritual perception, and their

values had therefore become somewhat distorted. We can imagine them looking down on the vagrant, unglamorous lives of the missionaries like Paul who have often been prepared to look like fools for the sake of spreading the teaching of Christ.

Paul reminds them that Christ's idea of wealth is rather different from the world view. Christians are not promised any kind of worldly security; it is expected that they will often be abused, passed over and insulted. But part of their teaching will be the way they put up with hardship cheerfully, accept criticism patiently, and repay insults with courtesy.

Matthew 5:1-12
When we grasp the meaning of the first beatitude, we find that the others follow on from it in sequence. It we put God first and regard ourselves not as possessors but stewards of worldly goods, we shall be poor (or unpossessive) in spirit. That will make us less aggressive, defensive and ambitious materially, so we shall become more gentle in our dealings with others, having no need to fight to protect ourselves any more.

Those who are gentle are more sympathetic, and that makes us vulnerable, easily affected by the pain we see around us, so we shall find ourselves mourning, due to more loving involvement.

Seeing the causes of suffering will make us long to put right the areas of injustice and cruelty which harm and damage, so that we shall hunger and thirst after righteousness.

Yet, loving oppressors as well as the oppressed, we shall want to act with God's mercy, rather than fighting for good with the weapons of evil. Such involvement will make us increasingly aware of the contrast between God's purity and the chaotic corruption of misdirected humanity, which is bound, in turn, to inspire us to work towards peace, reconciliation and love.

Once we are set on that route, as history bloodily endorses, we are bound for the cross; and it is highly likely that, having stuck our necks out, we shall become targets for persecution.

Yet the journey has been one towards greater and greater closeness to the Spirit of God; towards the peace of knowing we are doing his will; towards finding our true selves and serving him. And that is certain happiness.

QUESTIONS FOR DISCUSSION

1. How do Christians today react to worldly influences? Does our witness slacken in the face of criticism or ridicule?
2. Have you ever felt that the pain and suffering of following the way of the cross is too high a price to pay for Christ's new life? Have you ever found unexpected peace of mind in the very midst of suffering?

IDEAS FOR ADULTS

During the week a group may like to collect slogans and captions from advertisements which encourage greed, self-indulgence and covetousness. (There are plenty to choose from!) These are then displayed against a coloured background as if they are blocks of wood or stone crashing down on some little pin men figures.

Over this have a rainbow superimposed, with the words: How happy are the poor in spirit; theirs is the kingdom of heaven. Here is an idea of what it may look like:

They can bring it up to the altar at the offering of the gifts.

CHILDREN'S TEACHING

Bring along an assortment of advertisements mounted on a board so the children can see them as they come in. You could have some on tape as well from television and radio.

Why do firms advertise? So as to get us to buy their product. Every day we are encouraged to WANT and to GET. The more we GET, the more we WANT. Stick a thin strip of paper over the advertisements which says: GET, GET, GET. WANT, WANT, WANT. GET, GET, GET all across it.

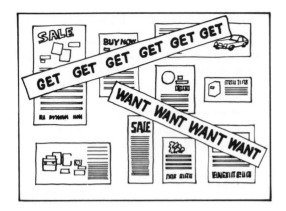

But if *things* are most important in our life, they make life harder, not happier. Have some heavy chains, stone-filled bags with straps etc. with labels on such as:

— I wish I could have...
— If only I could...
— I want...
— Leave that alone — it's MINE.

One by one, hang them around yourself or a child who volunteers, until he is really loaded down.

Jesus says to us: 'Trust in me, instead of in THINGS. You'll find you're much happier.' Then unload your volunteer and pin on him an 'I'm for Jesus' badge. Now he is less cluttered, able to move and run about (let him demonstrate).

When we trust in Jesus we can enjoy what we are given, but also enjoy giving away. We can enjoy owning, but also enjoy sharing. We can be happy when we have lots of toys, but also be happy when we haven't got many.

Let the children make an 'I'm for Jesus' badge to wear, and ask them to try giving instead of getting at least once each day this week.

INTERCESSIONS **Years 1 and 2**
Some ideas for prayer

Chosen by God to be members of his body,
let us gather our cares and concerns and
bring them before our heavenly Father
who loves us and knows us personally.

We pray for the many individuals
comprising the body of Christ,
with all their varied ministries;
for those unsure of God's plan for them;
may your will be made clear to them
and may they be given courage
to accept your call.
Pause
Lord, nourish us: **that we may bear fruit**

We pray for the world and its areas of conflict,
political unrest, decadence and deceit;
that Christ, the Lord of all truth and life,
may lead humanity to desire justice,
peace and integrity.
Pause
Lord, nourish us: **that we may bear fruit**

We pray for a deeper trust in God
among all of us here, and the families
we represent; that we may spend our lives
in getting to know you better,
so we reflect your light more brightly
and can be of greater use to you
in serving your world.
Pause
Lord, nourish us: **that we may bear fruit**

We pray for the bereaved and all who mourn;
for those who have miscarried or given birth
to a stillborn baby; for those who feel uncared
for and unloved;
for those who must watch their children
die from lack of food.
Pause
Lord, nourish us: **that we may bear fruit**

We pray for all the faithful
who have died; may they rest for ever
in the peace and joy of heaven.

We offer you our thanks and praise
for the way you have guided us
and brought us to worship you now;
may we continue to praise you
in the way we live the rest of our lives.

Merciful Father
accept these prayers
for the sake of your Son,
our Saviour Jesus Christ, Amen.

NOTES ON THE READINGS **Year 2**

Proverbs 3:1-8
This is the kind of sound advice we may feel like giving our children as they leave home for the first time! It is like being given a map for a journey, and its instruction would serve well as a basic rule of life because it is both clear and uncomplicated. With God at the centre of life we shall be able to pick our way through all the traumas and disasters, temptations and failures — not avoiding them, necessarily, but growing through them in compassion and wisdom rather than being beaten down by them.

1 Corinthians 2:1-10
The Greeks were used to philosophical arguments. They prided themselves on their civilised discussions and persuasion by logic and, up to a point, the existence of God can be argued in this way.

But when the uncompromising love of God floods into our life in the person of Jesus, culminating in the crucifixion and resurrection, there comes a point at which even philosophy is swept away in the wash.

Accordingly Paul shows the Corinthians how he is quite contented with being a nervous and unremarkable preacher because it has highlighted the evidence of God himself — the outpouring of his Spirit of love. Thus there is less chance of his hearers giving Paul glory; they are are more likely to direct their praise and glory to God, the source of all power and love.

Luke 8:4b-15
Even when God actually walked the earth as a man, the Word was not soaked up by everyone. Their eyes and ears were fully functional, yet they did not notice the obvious, because their inner eyes and ears were shut fast by expectation, complacency and lack of desire to change in any way.

None of this alters the quality of the seed itself, which, if it falls on good, rich soil, can produce an excellent crop. But the parable of the sower does emphasise the other factors involved in fruit production — our own responses, perseverance, capacity to learn to trust and our willingness to be committed wholeheartedly.

It is a good idea to use this parable sometimes during self-examination, as, of course, there is always the possibility of even good soil becoming stony or choked with weeds!

QUESTIONS FOR DISCUSSION

1. Why does Jesus so often speak indirectly, and in parables — would it be better for everyone if he spoke out directly and left no room for doubt?
2. In what ways is Christ's teaching different from an instruction manual or set of rules? Do we sometimes forget to use the resource of his help and guidance?

IDEAS FOR ADULTS

This week is a good time to have a drive to include more people in studying the Word of God in the Bible week by week. Prayerful study of the Bible always leads to a deepening of commitment and richer spiritual life, and if the majority of the parish are praying and reading God's Word during the week, then the worship on Sunday will pulse with vitality.

CHILDREN'S TEACHING

Have some grain (pearl barley will do, if no wheat is available) and a baking tray arranged with the varied surfaces on it like this:

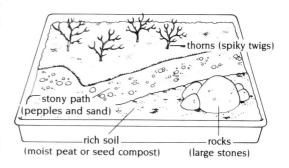

As you tell the story, sprinkle the seed so that some falls on each section. Talk about which will not grow and which will do the best. You could have some fresh plants to press into the good soil to emphasise the point.

Now explain how Jesus used this story to tell us about how people react to God's good news. See if they can work out what some of the images mean. Then help the children to write captions for each section, stick them on lolly sticks and push them into the model. Others can decorate the background and title. The whole model will then look something like this:

A sower once went out to sow...

Bring the model into church and display it where the rest of the congregation can see it as they come to receive Communion.

8th Sunday before Easter

TODAY'S THEME

... is Jesus as the healer. The prophets had foretold the time when God's healing love would renew and restore, and whenever holy men and women became channels of God's power, acts of healing had occurred which directed the people's praise towards the God of creation and renewal. Now, in Jesus, God walks among his people, restoring them to wholeness.

PARISH MUSIC
Hymns
All ye who seek a comfort sure
Bread of the world in mercy broken
Breathe on me, breath of God
For the healing of the nations
God is love; let heav'n adore him
God of mercy, God of grace
Here comes Jesus
How sweet the name of Jesus sounds
Immortal love for ever full

Kum-ba-yah
Lord, for the years
On days when much we do goes wrong
Oh the blood of Jesus
Peace, perfect peace
There's a wideness in God's mercy
Walk with me, O my Lord

Recorded music
Quintet (Beethoven): or any piece of chamber music, where the different threads of melodies weave round each other to create harmony

For choirs
O love of whom is truth and light (Viderö): SATB
Help me, O Lord (Arne)

CHURCH DECORATION

'Healing' is the theme of today's flower arrangement. It is a lovely theme to express in flowers and you will probably have lots of ideas of your own! To start you off, here are a few suggestions: a dual arrangement combining the stark, violent colours of pain, contrasted with the green, cream and pastel shades of the peace of healing; flowers of bright and sunny colours arranged in containers such as kidney bowls, with a bandage, small scissors etc; a wheel chair or zimmer walking frame filled with flowers.

NOTES ON THE READINGS **Year 1**

Zephaniah 3:14-end
This reading proclaims, with exultant hope and joy, that when the Lord our God is right here in the midst of us, all things are well and there is no evil we need fear. We may think of Paul and Silas, beaten with rods and imprisoned with their feet in the stocks; they spent the night praying and singing, and obviously entertaining the other prisoners! When we ask God to give us the assurance of his presence among us he often responds by filling us with a quite unexpected joy, not at all in keeping with the pain we are suffering. For his healing reaches the parts other healing cannot reach: God's healing is wholeness.

James 5:13-16a
James always gives practical help and advice, and when people are feeling weak and vulnerable through their illness, this is just what they need. The Christian community has a responsibility to undertake the visiting of the sick, both at home and in hospital, and not just during the time of a health crisis. In many illnesses there is a long stage of convalescence during which the bustle and activity of emergency has gone, and this can be a lonely and demoralising time.

As Christians, working with God not just for healing but for wholeness, we need to meet the need for companionship and encouragement right through to full recovery.

Mark 2:1-12
Jesus always heals in the way that will bring most lasting good. As in a symphony, many parts are often brought together in superb harmony. So often God's way of answering prayer touches far more lives with blessing than the solution we had envisaged.

Here the remarkable faith of the paralytic's friends provides the opportunity for Jesus to touch the raw nerves of suspicion in the scribes, and gives them the opportunity to believe in him as God's chosen one for whom they have been waiting.

The friends do not murmur when Jesus forgives the man instead of enabling him to walk straight away, because they trust him, and their trust makes them patient and accepting. For the scribes, this met their suspicions head on. They knew that only God has power to forgive sins. What a wonderful opportunity Christ gave them, here, in immediately following his absolution with healing. What joy there might have been if this direct, startling proof had been sufficient for them! We need to pray that our eyes will be able to discern the power of God

in action. Closed minds face the bleak prospect of failing to recognise the only one who can save them.

QUESTIONS FOR DISCUSSION

1. What part does faith play in the healing works of Jesus? Was faith shown by others as well as the patient? What does this teach us about how we can help in the ministry of healing?
2. What do you think — is it easier to heal physically, or to forgive sins?

IDEAS FOR ADULTS

Dance of the healing Christ
This dance expresses the suffering of a person in physical, emotional or spiritual torment. She looks in vain for God and rages at his hard-heartedness, only to find that he is there beside her. He has been suffering with her all the time. The knowledge of his presence sustains her, and he leads her to joy and new life.

The music is the second movement of Sibelius' Symphony No. 5 in E flat. You will need a group of eight dancers to express the torment, and two others: the Sufferer and the Presence of Christ. Play the music through several times, following the dance instructions so that you get the 'shape' of it, as I have left plenty of room for improvisation.

As the music begins the Sufferer enters, running fitfully while the tormenters chase and threaten, blocking her way wherever she tries to go. The group works sometimes in twos and threes, sometimes as a unit. Everywhere the Sufferer goes, the Presence of Christ goes with her and is similarly persecuted, but the Sufferer acts as if she is entirely alone.

As the horns begin their theme the chase should reach the main performance area, and the Sufferer pleads, wringing her hands, trying to push the tormentors away (hands palm to palm). Sometimes they are pushed back a few steps but then they advance and send her off balance, then insolently watch as she staggers to her feet before they claw and jostle again.

They form a large circle and push her from one to the other around it, and then use her and the Presence (back to back) like a rope in a tug of war.

One ties blindfolds on them and they spin them round, teasing, frightening and causing them to stumble. As the music goes quiet, they run to escape, and the tormenters hide; they seem to have gone, but as the Sufferer walks timidly about, they pop out and grab her, or stealthily follow. The horn's theme comes again, and again she pleads for God to hear her. She is bewildered and dazed and seems to have lost her way. The tormenters now slide and slither towards her from different directions until she is cut off. They begin to reach up, as if dragging her down, however hard she resists. At the crescendo she shakes her fist towards the sky, holds her head in agony and collapses from weakness.

With the horn's theme she slowly realises that she is not alone; the Presence of Christ is lying, weak and wounded, beside her. He stands and painfully the Sufferer rises to her feet. As if she cannot quite believe he is real, the Sufferer traces the face and arms of the Presence who puts his arm round her for support and helps her limp towards the altar. In a frenzy the tormenters try to stop them. The Presence of Christ lifts the Sufferer on his shoulder where they cannot reach her. When they reach the altar the Sufferer is lifted down, and finds that she can stand upright. In joy she embraces her rescuer and bends and stretches to the music, delighting in being free.

The music ends with six chords. During the first four of these, the Presence of Christ, holding hands with the Sufferer he has saved, points with authority, all fingers outstretched at the tormenters who are writhing grouped in twos. Each time, the couple pointed at cower and freeze, until by the fourth chord, all the tormenters are still. On chord five, the Sufferer and the Presence of Christ stand facing the altar with arms raised like this:

On the final chord they kneel on one knee, like this:

CHILDREN'S TEACHING

Tell today's story of the paralytic who was let down through the roof, using a simple model which the children make first. One group makes a house from a white shoe box. At this stage do not mention the way the man's friend got him to Jesus; just talk about the typical design of such a house with outside steps to a flat roof in which there was often an opening.

Other children make a stretcher-bed with a paralysed man on it, and others make a large crowd of people. Arrange the model on sand-coloured paper and put a few model donkeys and chickens around, and a palm tree or two.

Place Jesus and his friends in the house first, and add other visitors as you explain how word got around that Jesus could heal the sick. When the men arrive with their paralysed friend the children will see that they can't get to Jesus. Ask what they might do now. Give up? Seeing the problem will help them appreciate the men's faith and their determination and persistence. They may even suggest using the hole in the roof.

All through the story help them to identify with the different characters so that they can, in some sense, become 'eye witnesses' to the events.

INTERCESSIONS **Years 1 and 2**
Some ideas for prayer

My brothers and sisters in Christ,
knowing the deep love that surrounds us
and reaches out to us in every distress,
let us unload our burdens of care
to the healing power of our heavenly Father.

We bring before you the Church's work
among the homeless, the disillusioned
and the apathetic,
in parish communities all over the world.
Pause
Life-giving Lord: **hear us and help us, we pray**

We bring before you all areas of the world
where lack of communication
breeds suspicion and fear;
where lack of understanding
breeds insecurity and a spirit of revenge.
Pause
Life-giving Lord: **hear us and help us, we pray**

We bring before you each member
of this community, each individual anxiety
and sorrow, each hope and dream,
each weakness and special need.
Pause
Life-giving Lord: **hear us and help us, we pray**

We bring before you all whose lives
are crippled by unrepented sin
or the refusal to forgive;
all whose lives are constantly restless
and devoid of peace.
Pause
Life-giving Lord: **hear us and help us, we pray**

We bring before you those who have died
and those who miss them.
Pause
Life-giving Lord: **hear us and help us, we pray**

We bring before you the joy and happiness
of our daily life, the blessings that lift
our hearts to praise you.

Merciful Father
**accept these prayers
for the sake of your Son,
our Saviour Jesus Christ, Amen.**

NOTES ON THE READINGS **Year 2**

2 Kings 5:1-14
If it hadn't been for the little servant girl from Israel, Naaman would never have set off hopefully to find Elisha. When God heals, he uses many people and many circumstances along the way, and we never know when we are going to be in a position to help. If we get into the habit of praying wherever we happen to be, God will be able to use us for his healing work in ways we may never even be aware of. Not just physical healing, either; a letter of appreciation or encouragement may arrive just at a low point in someone's life. Or someone suffering may be quite suddenly eased and comforted because we are praying about them.

Elisha's prayerfulness kept him in close touch both with God's will, and Naaman's need.

2 Corinthians 12:1-10
Often after a deep spiritual experience, which sets us off full of enthusiasm to spread our faith more, we may find ourselves meeting obstacles!

When you think about it, that is not really surprising, as the last thing Satan wants is for us to bring more people to Christ's saving love. Paul's list of insults and sufferings gives us some idea of what to expect, and is not exactly inviting.

However, because it is the God of goodness, power and love that we are volunteering to serve, the strangest paradox becomes evident as soon as we set ourselves to do his will. The more difficult life is, the easier it seems to be to witness to others in an effective way that really draws them to our Lord. Hanging on to his hand for dear life, we experience such overwhelming support and such miracles of perfect timing, answered prayers and peace of mind, that we can witness to actual knowledge of a God who is alive and well, interested in us enough to want to help and remake us. There is only one conclusion we can draw: he must really love us! After that, the difficulties matter less; if they keep us relying on the Lord we love and who loves us, then we are happy to have things that way.

Mark 7:24-end
Spittle was commonly used in the medicine of Jesus' time, so it is interesting that his healing incorporated this. When we pray for healing, our prayer may well be answered via a visit to the doctor or the hospital, for God delights in using us and our gifts in the work of healing. Every time researchers discover new ways to combat pain and disease, that is a victory for the God of Wholeness who enlightens and heals.

If we really want to see Jesus in action, we have only to visit a patient who has been 'prayed through' a major operation; there is an incredible radiance about such people that joyfully proclaims the peace which can only come from God. It shows plainly that wholeness is more than clinical health; that Jesus personally transforms the spiritual, emotional and physical structure of the people he is asked to heal.

QUESTIONS FOR DISCUSSION

1. Look at the different methods Jesus used with different people in order to heal them, and the conversations he has first (which are always a preparation for the healing). Why were these methods appropriate for each particular problem?
2. In our age of great strides in medical research, do you think that physical healing is sometimes overstressed to the detriment of spiritual wholeness?

IDEAS FOR ADULTS

Use the teaching of this week as the basis of a thorough look at the parish's programme for visiting the sick and the ministry of healing. Any fresh ideas growing out of such prayerful study should be treated seriously, even if they break new ground.

CHILDREN'S TEACHING

Palm Tree have a version of Naaman's story of healing, called *Naaman's Spots*. Read this, or another version with pictures, and then go through the story again with the children acting it out. A narrator holds everything together, and children not involved as main characters are servants and interested onlookers.

Children are often very good at praying for others, and are helped by pictures. Explain to them how important their prayers are in making people better, and help them make a praying scrap book. On the first page they stick a picture of Jesus healing someone, and on the others they will be drawing, or sticking in pictures and photographs of any prayer needs for healing. These may be from newspapers and magazines, snapshots etc. Encourage the children to use their books regularly, and from time to time give them the name or picture of others who need their prayers. This becomes beneficial in both directions — the elderly, sick or lonely in the parish gain great support from knowing the child is praying for them, and the child is learning unselfish prayer and a deeper friendship with Jesus.

7th Sunday before Easter

TODAY'S THEME

. . . is Jesus Christ as the friend of sinners. The bad news about being human is that we seem to find it so easy to hurt one another and indulge in our selfishness; with even the best of intentions, we fail and sin. The good news is that in Jesus, God meets us where we are, loves us, warts and all, and brings about reconciliation, forgiveness and peace.

PARISH MUSIC

Hymns
Alleluia, by your Spirit we will sing
All the riches of his grace
Amazing grace
Dear Lord and Father of mankind
Father of heaven, whose love profound
God forgave my sin in Jesus' name
Jesus, lover of my soul
Just as I am without one plea
Loving shepherd of thy sheep
My faith looks up to thee
My God loves me
O Lord my God, when I in awesome wonder
Oh the love of my Lord is the essence
There's a wideness in God's mercy
Vaster than any ocean
Wide, wide as the ocean

Recorded music
Midsummer Night's Dream (Mendelssohn)

For choirs
Be merciful unto me (Blow, ed. Statham): SATB
Nolo mortem peccatoris (Morley): SATB

CHURCH DECORATION

Using deadwood or driftwood, construct a central shape reminiscent of a cross. This will be the basic structure of the flower arrangement, with trailing plants such as ivy, and warm-coloured flowers growing up and around it. You could try using the dark pink dicentra, deep gold narcissus, matthiola or the purple-red malus (crab apple).

NOTES ON THE READINGS **Year 1**

Hosea 14:1-7
The northern kingdom was fast approaching the

threat of collapse after generations of unfaithfulness, self-indulgence and decadence. As the prophet Amos had pointed out, they deserved all they were going to get, for they had rejected God utterly, and God would be quite justified in abandoning them to their fate. But Hosea, personally wounded by his own beloved but unfaithful wife, was able to balance the justice of God's character with his tender mercy and forgiving love. He is the loving and faithful husband of his people, and though deeply hurt and grieved by them, he is always willing to start afresh with them and welcome them back.

Philemon 1-16
Jesus' spirit of forgiveness is seen working here in a way we may recognise from our own experience. Just as paintwork on the house requires a lot of careful preparation before the final coating of gloss can gleam, so forgiveness of deep hurts will take patience, hard work and encouragement before full reconciliation is achieved. We need not be ashamed to admit that it is taking us time to forgive; if we are genuinely working on it in Jesus' strength the time will come when we will know there is complete healing, and this honest approach is far better than pretending our wound is healed when really it festers as bitterness deep inside us.

Like Paul, we can often help ease the way between hurt and reconciliation by looking at the good in people so regularly that it becomes a habit; by refusing to join in critical gossip; and by being positive and encouraging instead of destructive.

Mark 2:13-17
It is such a relief to find that with Jesus, at least, we are totally accepted for what we are, and although he is totally good and sinless, he will happily make himself at home with us, even though he knows our worst as well as our best points.

There is a touch of sarcasm in Jesus' reply to the offended Pharisees and teachers of the law. For by thinking themselves so superior, they were cutting themselves off from the possibility of healing. Even if you are seriously ill, you will never get treatment if you insist you are perfectly well and don't need the doctor.

The truth, of course, is that we all need the healing reconciliation with God that Jesus has the power to give.

QUESTIONS FOR DISCUSSION

1. Why is reconciliation and forgiveness so important? What happens if deep hurts and grievances are not 'treated' and healed?
2. We are bound to hurt others sometimes in our life. As Christians, following Jesus' example, how should we go about putting things right?

IDEAS FOR ADULTS

While the Hosea passage is being read, have a group of six dancers to express the meaning in mime. Boys and men wear plain teeshirts and jeans, women and girls teeshirts and long skirts. I have numbered the lines as they appear in the ASB.

1. Dancers begin in a circle facing outwards, heads bowed, arms at sides. They lift heads and beckon once with wide arm movement.
2. One step forward, wring hands, looking up. Drop down on one knee, arms open.
3. Pluck words from the surrounding air.
4. Get up, turn to face inwards, arms raised to centre of circle.
5. (On 'Take...') Fling arms back, leaning back.
6. Join hands with a partner, swing round once.
7. Kneel with partner like this:

8. Four steps as a group, bowed and arms protecting heads, towards right.
9. Join hands in line and gallop along to left.
10. Two end dancers run to centre front to form statue shape, back to back. Others kneel low and abase themselves.

11. All get up, run forward to this position:

They turn sharply and kneel together, arms raised towards God.

12. Form a circle, facing inwards like this:

13. Rock from right foot to left foot twice.
14. Break from circle and scatter to these positions:

15. Gradually lower hands, fluttering fingers.
16. Step and leap (grand jeté) and form cluster, facing outwards.
17 and 18. Keeping all feet in centre, kneel, lie face down, open arms wide along floor.
19. Two form an arch, others line up ready to come through.
20. Others come through the arch to form this finish.

CHILDREN'S TEACHING

Tell the children the story of today's Gospel as a narrator of a play. Arrange the chairs as an audience and set up one end of the room to be the 'stage'. If there is a screen, or space for a background picture of hills, so much the better. Give the children their parts in advance, but they can sit as audience until needed.

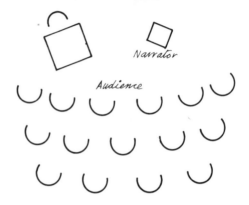

As the characters are mentioned, another helper discreetly tells them to move to the stage, and they act out what the narrator is saying. You may find they join in and speak their own words. If not, they can either use the narrator's words or mime. Speak slowly and clearly, and give enough time for the children to act their parts at each stage of the story. Here is a possible 'script':

On stage: Matthew, sitting at money table, a beggar, two women buying cloth from a man, one man paying his taxes, and Jesus.

One day Jesus was walking slowly through a town, chatting to the people. He saw a man called Matthew sitting collecting money from the Romans. Jonah was poor and told Matthew he couldn't afford to pay today.

Jonah: I can't afford to pay you today.

Matthew shook his fist at Jonah angrily. He told him he had to pay or he would put him in prison.

Matthew: You'll *have* to pay. If you don't, I'll put you in prison.

The man went away sadly. Just then Jesus came up to Matthew and shook hands with him. The other people were surprised to see a good man like Jesus talking to a bad man like Matthew. They told their friends about it.

One of the women to audience: You know that good man, Jesus? Well, he's being friendly with that tax-collector, Matthew! It doesn't seem right to me.

Then Jesus told Matthew he wanted him as one of his followers, one of his special friends.

Jesus: Come and follow me, Matthew.

Matthew was very happy that Jesus had chosen

him. He was quite surprised, too. He jumped up straight away and told Jesus he would love to follow him.

Matthew: Yes, Jesus, I'll come. I'd love to follow you!

He even invited Jesus to dinner that day.

Matthew: Will you come to dinner with me today?

Jesus thanked him and said that he would love to come.

Jesus: Thank you, Matthew. I'd love to come.

So together they went off to Matthew's house. On their way home, Matthew kept inviting his friends to join in the dinner party.

General conversation: Would you like to come to dinner? — Yes please; thank you etc.

Till by the time they reached Matthew's house there was quite a crowd. Matthew showed them all where to sit down, and gave Jesus the seat at the head of the table. Then they all had a lovely feast with lots to eat and drink. There were quite a lot of bad people among the guests, but Jesus was quite happy to be with them. A church leader came and looked at Jesus eating with all the sinners. He asked Jesus why he was with people like that. Didn't he know what kind of people they were?

Pharisee: Why are you mixing with these sinners, Jesus? Don't you know what they're like?

Jesus came over to him. He explained that God loves people whatever they're like, so we must be forgiving as well.

Jesus: God loves people whatever they are like, you see. So if God is ready to forgive, we must forgive too.

He said it was like a doctor — he does not visit the healthy ones, he visits those who are ill.

Jesus: I'll try and explain. A doctor doesn't come to see the healthy people, does he? He comes to help those who are ill. And God comes to put us right, when we go wrong.

And Jesus went back to eat dinner with all the sinners who needed his love to heal them.

INTERCESSIONS **Years 1 and 2**
Some ideas for prayer

Fellow members of Christ,
let us approach our heavenly Father,
acknowledging the wonder of his involvement
with us, and asking him to help us.

We pray for all who labour to spread the Good
    News
especially those who face threatening behaviour,
imprisonment or persecution; for those
who are tempted to remain silent
in order to avoid danger to themselves or their
    families;
that they may be given your courage
and your peace.
Pause
Lord, in our weakness: **we ask for your help**

We pray for all the injustice, cruelty
and oppression of our world;
for its confusion of priorities,
its lost opportunities and misdirected zeal;
that we may be guided unceasingly by
the level-headed, compassionate
leadership of God's Spirit.
Pause
Lord, in our weakness: **we ask for your help**

We pray for our families, friends and
    neighbours;
for the very young and the very old in our care;
for the wisdom to see opportunities
of showing Christ's love,
and for enough energy and time
to do what God needs us to.
Pause
Lord, in our weakness: **we ask for your help**

We pray for all who are wounded and injured —
those in hospital and all in pain;
that they may find Christ among them
in their suffering; we pray for those
who inflict pain on others;
for terrorists, murderers and all who are
fired with hatred; that their lives
may be transformed by encountering Christ.
Pause
Lord, in our weakness: **we ask for your help**

We pray for those on the verge of death
and those who have passed into eternity;
may they rest in your peace for ever.

We give you thanks for all your care
and healing love.
Merciful Father
accept these prayers
for the sake of your Son,
our Saviour Jesus Christ, Amen.

NOTES ON THE READINGS **Year 2**

Numbers 15:32-36

Life in the wilderness was dangerous and hard, and in order to survive at all, self-discipline was essential. The ten commandments gave the people a moral structure which reflected their trust in and dependence on God, and it was vital that God's law was taken seriously and kept faithfully.

So it is in these circumstances that the man is punished so severely for breaking God's law of keeping the Sabbath day set apart, or holy, to God. In context, then, it is a just punishment. Jesus, however, was to show that God's justice is always mingled with compassion.

Colossians 1:18-23

In Christ we are brought into a new understanding of God's cosmic significance. For Christ's actions reveal God's plan to unify, reconcile and overcome all powers of evil and destruction, so that we may no longer be held in their grip.

In Christ we are liberated from any power of the occult, from temporal tyranny and cruelty and even from what grips us most tightly: our own sin.

So we can afford to be filled with joy, laughter, and relaxed peacefulness, because we have just been let out of prison where we were in the condemned cell awaiting death! And the one to thank for it is Jesus Christ, who accomplished it by dying in our place, even though he was innocent. That shows quite a staggering capacity for love.

John 8:2-11

We are now shown an illustration of God's forgiveness in the episode of the woman taken in adultery. She was dragged by the indignant crowd before this new teacher, and she stood in front of him as a convicted person, condemned already to death by stoning according to the law. Jesus does not excuse her, nor does he pretend she has done nothing wrong. He quietly and shrewdly points out to the crowd that all stand condemned by the law, for all have sinned. (Notice how it is the oldest member who is the first to realise this!)

When everyone has gone, Jesus 'redeems' the woman from her conviction and wipes out the sin of her past. Now she is free and told not to sin again in the future: before her is a completely new life.

To have her death sentence removed must have been wonderful enough; but to have her guilt and sin removed at the same time must have been utterly overwhelming.

QUESTIONS FOR DISCUSSION

1. Compare and contrast Moses' reaction to the stick-gatherer and Jesus' reaction to the adultress.
2. What light do these readings throw on the way we should deal with those who wrong us and those who break the country's laws?

IDEAS FOR ADULTS

Have more time for the shared Peace today, so that people can move around and greet others who are not near their 'usual' seats.

CHILDREN'S TEACHING

Have a blackboard, coloured chalk, and an effective board rubber. Have an old dirty sack or bag labelled SINS in nasty looking letters. Inside have separate cards — jagged and irregular, on which are written:
- telling lies;
- stealing;
- pushing someone over;
- spoiling someone's toys;
  etc.

Ask one child to scatter them all around, and each picks one up. Each is written on the blackboard.

Explain how Jesus can wipe them right out, if we are really sorry. (Now rub them out.) How do we show we are sorry?

Let the children copy this cartoon and colour it in.

LENT

Ash Wednesday

TODAY'S THEME

. . . is reconciliation with God. This will involve first admitting our need of God's mercy and forgiveness and then examining our lives in his light to see what needs to be done. God does not simply patch up the bits of us that look bad — he completely renews and restores, giving us the joy and peace of forgiveness.

PARISH MUSIC

Hymns
All that I am, all that I do
All to Jesus I surrender
And now, O Father, mindful of the love
Can it be true?
Come down O Love Divine
If we only seek peace
It's me O Lord
Lord Jesus think on me
My people, what have I done to you?
O love, that will not let me go
O Sinner man
Our hearts were made for you
Spirit of the living God
Take my life and let it be
Thou didst leave thy throne

Recorded music
Jesus, remember me (Music from Taizé):
Vol. I

For choirs
Let my complaint come before thee
(Batten)
Lord, for thy tender mercy's sake
(Farrant/Hilton)

NOTES ON THE READINGS **Years 1 and 2**

Isaiah 58:1-8 or Joel 2:12-17 or Amos 5:6-15
In all these readings, sincerity of the heart is crucial. Outward hysterical drama of tearing clothes or showy breast-beating is not necessary. Other people may be impressed by it, but God is never fooled. He sees clearly the hidden, secret thoughts in our hearts; and it is the complete altering of our values, so that God becomes central, that makes his forgiveness effective.

It is so easy, while life flows smoothly along, to become complacent, almost without realising it.

Although we may deplore the jolts and tragedies that make open sores in our well-ordered lives, they may sometimes do us a great service.

Whenever our timetable is disrupted, it challenges us about whose order really underpins our life; every time material possessions are lost or stolen we are challenged as to where our real treasure is on which our hearts are fixed.

These challenges are very good for us, and provide marvellous opportunities for relinquishing another layer of independence from God and committing ourselves to him more deeply.

From time to time this needs to be a great communal act of repentance and re-commitment. There may be potential within the whole parish which is not being realised; needs which are not being met; opportunities which are not being taken.

The way forward in all Christian communities is through thorough, heart-searching repentance. This alone can open the way to God's forgiveness, leading to stronger, more vigorous growth, and lots more fruit.

I Corinthians 9:24-end or James 4:1-10
These readings deal with the practical business of putting things right. For repentance is not the end of the matter but the beginning. Just as we have to put considerable effort into becoming physically fit, so we need to be rigorous and organised about our spiritual fitness, which has, after all, got to last us not just for a lifetime but for ever!

And just as muscles protest when we start training them, so we shall find it painful at times being re-made as God's children. Don't despair, at such times, but rejoice, because the pain is proof of progress and is making you spiritually strong and healthy.

Matthew 6:16-21 or Luke 18:9-14
Jesus saw around him, among the religious community, some who did the right things for the wrong reasons. To him, looking with the discernment of God, it was quite obvious which ones were acting and what they were really after in their almsgiving, praying and fasting. They were being just subtle enough to take in those whose admiration they craved, and as a result, were highly respected.

Sometimes we use even more subtle ways of pocketing the glory which belongs to God. Perhaps we casually let slip our good deeds in conversation, or recount our news with a heavy editorial slant in favour of Number One. It is quite a useful exercise to attempt to do three good deeds in a day without anyone ever finding out!

Of course, it all stems from the heart; if we are primarily concerned with serving God and pleasing him, we need not become neurotic about what others see or do not see. Their reactions will cease to be so important, and if they do notice us shining, we can gladly and willingly direct the praise to God in whose strength we live.

QUESTIONS FOR DISCUSSION

1. What kind of 'fasting' or self-discipline is still valuable today? How can we guard against hypocrisy in exercising it?
2. Are we ever afraid of Christ transforming us?

IDEAS FOR ADULTS

Consider keeping the church open all day for a day of prayer. People sign up to be responsible for different times throughout the day, which can be · advertised in the local community. There may be those, either formerly committed or hesitantly seeking, who would feel able to come into a quiet, prayerful church without the formality of a service.

Leave around some helpful prayer cards, Bibles and books, and have the day underpinned with the promised prayers of all the worshipping community, whether they are present in church or not.

CHILDREN'S TEACHING

If your church uses the symbol of ashes, try to arrange for the children to be present when the palm crosses are burnt. If they witness the breaking down of matter into dust, they will better understand the symbolism of leaving our past in ashes and of remembering that God formed us from dust : life in him does not end with physical death.

INTERCESSIONS **Years 1 and 2**
Some ideas for prayer

Let us come before God,
our creator and sustainer,
with the needs of the church and of the world.

We bring to your love, O Lord,
all who have committed their lives to your service;
that they may all be one,
bound together by your Holy Spirit.
Pause
Father of mercy: **hear us with compassion**

We bring to your love
all the areas of the world
in which there is hostility and unrest;
that new routes to negotiation
and reconciliation may emerge.
Pause
Father of mercy: **hear us with compassion**

We bring to your love
the members of our human families,
especially any we find difficult
to get on with or understand;
that our love for one another
may enter a new dimension
of warm and positive caring,
seasoned with laughter.
Pause
Father of mercy: **hear us with compassion**

We bring to your love
all who have become hard and aggressive
through years of festering hate or jealousy;
that their unresolved conflicts
may be brought to your light and healed.
Pause
Lord of mercy: **hear us with compassion**

We bring to your love
all those, dear to us,
who are separated from us by death;
may we come, one day, with them
to share the eternal peace
and joy of heaven.
Pause
Lord of mercy: **hear us with compassion**

We thank you for all your blessings
and patient loving,
and especially for coming to save us
from our sin.

Merciful Father
accept these prayers
for the sake of your Son,
our Saviour Jesus Christ, Amen.

1st Sunday in Lent

TODAY'S THEME

... is temptation. Man and woman spoilt God's perfect creation by falling into temptation and disobeying their creator. We are all guilty of sin, but through Christ we are given the strength and grace to resist temptation just as he did.

PARISH MUSIC
Hymns
Alleluia, sing to Jesus
All the riches of his grace
Be thou my guardian and my guide
Father, hear the prayer we offer
Forty days and forty nights
Hear my cry, O Lord my God

How firm a foundation
If you are thirsting
Immortal love for ever full
Lead us heavenly Father lead us
Lord, when I turn my back on you
Loving shepherd of thy sheep
O love how deep, how broad, how high
Praise to the holiest in the height

Recorded music
Raga Bilashkhani Todi — or any
   sitar/sarod music with a similarly
   dignified grandeur, tinged with sorrow

For choirs
O most merciful (Wood)
Forget me not (Bach): SATB

NOTES ON THE READINGS **Year 1**

Genesis 2:7-9; 3:1-7
Nakedness always suggests vulnerability; in our clothes we can, to some extent, choose the image we present to the world, but naked we are just ourselves, as at birth and death. This is why we usually need a relationship of trust before we are at ease being naked in company; yet where this happens, as in family groups, for instance, there is no doubt that the nakedness points to a special, trusting relationship there.

When Adam and Eve were suddenly embarrassed by their nakedness it showed that their special, trusting relationship with their creator had been damaged and spoilt. They knew they had been disobedient and they were ashamed; much as we find it hard to meet people's eyes directly if we know we have wronged them in some way.

Hebrews 2:14-end
In one sense, Jesus came so that we could once more stand naked before God, without trying to hide any part of our bodies or characters; so confident in his love that, as children, we could have a secure relationship with him based on love and acceptance.

The only way this could be done was for the profound disobedience to be reversed. Someone had to go through all the temptations but still resist the urge to disobey God's will, whatever happened.

Someone did it. What happened to that person was the agony of betrayal, torture and crucifixion, resulting in death. But it was, in another way, life; for Jesus went right through to the farthest edge of human temptation and suffering and yet still remained absolutely obedient. He hung naked before his heavenly father at that moment of human death, and in so doing won back for us the long lost relationship with God that Adam and Eve had been created to enjoy.

Matthew 4:1-11
In today's Gospel we see some of the main temptations Jesus had to resist. They were, naturally, aimed at the weakest areas, and they all had just enough relationship with good sense to make them dangerous. After all, if someone approached us proposing a brutal act of murder we should not find that very hard to resist; but if we are persuaded that a dishonest act is going to harm no one and will benefit those we love, then the moral issues blur and it is much harder to see and resist temptation.

As with Adam and Eve, hunger is used, and the great advantage of immediate, dramatic results. 'You will be like gods,' Adam and Eve were persuaded. Jesus, knowing he had power, was urged to behave like a man-god, pandering to our craving for excitement and grandeur, but ignoring our real needs.

In resisting these temptations Jesus was abandoning any possibility of a peaceful end to his life; instead he kept the door wide open for our salvation.

QUESTIONS FOR DISCUSSION

1. Study each of the temptations and Jesus' replies. What do they teach us about how to resist temptation in our own lives?
2. Obedience is not a very fashionable concept in our age, where self-fulfilment is highly prized. Do you think the two ideas can be reconciled in the Christian life?

IDEAS FOR ADULTS

Have a large frame of wood knocked up (about 6' × 8') and stick lining paper all over it. Paint

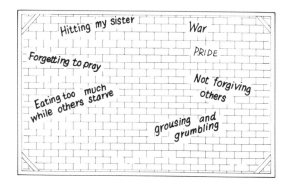

brick markings on it and through the week have all parish groups to write on it the sins that separate us off from God.

Just before the Prayers of Penitence, put the wall of sin between the people and the altar. Directly after communal confession, have a group of people representing *all* ages, to burst through the wall and tear off all the lining paper. Now we are not 'cut off' any more — a symbol of how God's forgiveness demolishes our sin and reconciles us to him.

CHILDREN'S TEACHING

Tell the children the story of Adam and Eve explaining that it was their disobedience which cut them off from the happy life they had before with God. Then help them make a large collage picture of the garden with the tree of knowledge in the middle. Make sure all the other trees have lovely fruit as well as this one; there was, after all, no actual need for them to eat its fruit. Use lots of bright materials, or colours cut from magazine pages, and write on the picture 'Adam and Eve did not do as God told them. That spoilt things.'

Then give them two large twigs each and make them into a simple cross. This is another tree of life. Help them to see how Jesus did obey, even though it meant he was killed. Because he obeyed, he put everything right again. So now, if we do wrong, we can be completely forgiven, all because of Jesus.

Use a prayer of penitence and thanks for forgiveness.
> Heavenly Father,
> we are very sorry
> that we have hurt you
> and each other
> and spoilt your world.
> Thank you for sending Jesus
> to put things right.
> Please forgive us
> because of his goodness.   Amen

INTERCESSIONS **Years 1 and 2**
Some ideas for prayer

Trusting not in our weakness but in God's mercy
let us pray to him now.

We pray for Christians whose faith
is being tested by hardship,
spiritual dryness or any outside pressures;
that they may hold fast to you, Lord Christ,
and emerge stronger in the knowledge
of your loyal, sustaining love.
Pause
Lord, you are the rock: **on whom our security rests**

We pray for those involved in advertising;
broadcasting and journalism,
and for all in the entertainment business;
that they may not encourage
selfishness or violence,
but discretion and insight.
Pause
Lord, you are the rock: **on whom our security rests**

We pray for the people on either side of us now;
for the families represented here,
and all who live in the same street as we do;
that we may live out the pattern
of Christlike loving in a practical way.
Pause
Lord, you are the rock: **on whom our security rests**

We pray for those blinded by prejudice
or self-centred thinking;
for those being dragged down
by a drug or alcohol habit
they feel powerless to stop;
that they may be led tenderly to freedom.
Pause
Lord, you are the rock: **on whom our security rests**

We pray for those who,
having worshipped you on earth,
have now past into eternity;
may they spend eternity
in unending love and praise.
Pause
Lord, you are the rock: **on whom our security rests**

Father, we thank you
for showing us the way to abundant life.

Merciful Father,
accept these prayers
for the sake of your Son,
our Saviour Jesus Christ, Amen.

NOTES ON THE READINGS **Year 2**

Genesis 4:1-10

Resentment can be a killer. Sometimes it results in murder, as in Cain's case. Always it rubs and festers deep inside us, damaging our capacity for love and destroying our peace. Any seething hatred we harbour for anyone, however much they may have hurt us, will probably damage us more than it does them, so it needs to be lanced and healed as quickly and thoroughly as possible.

There are times when we all feel scared by the capacity for evil we suddenly glimpse in ourselves; it can seem far bigger than we are and threaten to crush us. Thankfully, good already has the victory through Jesus, and we can cling on to that strength of his until Satan slinks away.

Hebrews 4:12-end

Jesus can provide such strength because he has been through the very worst possible experience of overpowering evil and remained sinless. It is with the confidence of this knowledge that we are able to approach God and make use of his deep reserves of grace and unlimited mercy.

Luke 4:1-13

It is important to remember that during the fast in the wilderness, Jesus was not only divine but also fully human, so the temptations were excruciatingly real and just as hard to resist as the temptations which face us all. As so often happens, they were couched in such a way that falling into the trap could be rationalised and even appear justifiable.

First, Jesus was experiencing the vulnerability and weakness of the physical body, which craved food. He knew he was entrusted with great power, and at the same time, he was in great need. Surely it would be sensible to use just a little of that power to alleviate physical suffering?

And then there was the desire to draw all men to God. Perhaps, after all, being a kind of Superman might be one way of attracting all those people who wouldn't be interested in things like humility, patience or repentance.

Then there was the urgency of his work; having only a lifetime, if that, to save God's people, perhaps a ministry of worldly power and influence might be quicker.

How, then, did he manage, as man, to resist such temptations? He was able to resist them because he was never, at any point, separated from the power of God.

The temptations were aimed at his humanity; strength and victory came from the Father. We are made co-heirs with Christ, which puts us in the same position. The weakness of our humanity will often be threatened and tempted. But our access to God's almighty power means that in Christ we shall have the necessary strength to cope with whatever happens to us. We have to fix ourselves in his life, and trust him.

QUESTIONS FOR DISCUSSION

1. Using a Concordance, look up the references for the words of scripture Jesus used to answer Satan. What words from the gospels can you find that would help you to stay strong in Christ against temptation? It would be worth learning them by heart — you never know when you may need them!
2. What do you think is the best way to cope with feelings of jealousy and resentment — both in yourself and in helping our children to cope with it?

IDEAS FOR ADULTS

Set up a library of books for people to borrow during Lent, and duplicate a reading list with an introduction to a variety of books on it. Include some for children and young people as well as for adults. Your local Christian bookshop may be able to give some suggestions of appropriate books for your parish.

CHILDREN'S TEACHING

Try to show that the easy ways are not always the best or most effective ways of doing something.

a. Have two pictures of bread. One teacher tears one picture out ('I need to stick it on a poster and tearing is quicker'). The other cuts it carefully ('It took longer but it was much better').
b. Nana's birthday. Two brothers — one makes a card himself, the other asks Mum to buy him one. It may be very smart, and the homemade one may be a bit gluey, but which shows most love? Jesus was tempted three times:

'Use your power
to make bread' —
             be selfish;

'I'll give you the world so long
as you worship ME' —
             take the easy way out;

'Jump off the temple to
show them your power' —
             show off.

Instead, Jesus said 'No, I'll do it God's way
— the hard, good way of love.'

2nd Sunday in Lent

TODAY'S THEME

... is the conflict between right and wrong. We
need discernment to recognise God's will on our
journey through an often confusing and
disturbing world. Following Jesus demands
both trust and calm, level-headed assessment of
anyone setting him or herself up as a prophet
or spiritual leader. If we learn to look with the
eyes of Christ, we shall not be led astray

PARISH MUSIC

Hymns
Abide with me
All my hope on God is founded
And did those feet in ancient time
A safe stronghold our God is still
Be thou my guardian and my guide
Christ be beside me
Cleanse us, O lord
Dear Lord and Father of mankind
Eternal Father strong to save
Father, hear the prayer we offer
Father welcomes all his children
Give me peace O Lord
Guide me O thou great redeemer
I danced in the morning
In heavenly love abiding
My song is love unknown
Peace, perfect peace
Rise and shine and give God the glory
What a friend we have in Jesus

Recorded music
Noyes Fludde (Britten)

For choirs
Day by day (How): 3-part
O for a closer walk (Ives)

NOTES ON THE READINGS **Year 1**

Genesis 6:11-end
Noah put faith in God's promises and survived
with his family in spite of the devastating flood.
No doubt he had had to put up with lots of jokes
at his expense as the people continued to live
corrupt and careless lives while he and his sons
got busy with the wood and pitch. Such concern
with obeying God's wishes would seem to many
a waste of time and energy, while life went on
as usual.

Through his prayer (which, incidentally,
involved quite as much listening as talking)
Noah was able to keep in touch with God's will
even while living among the many distractions
of a worldly society. His example can encourage
us when our faith seems to make us outsiders.

I John 4:1-6
Trustfulness is often emphasised as a Christian
virtue, and indeed we do need the young child's
straightforward trust which is so endearing. But
it is important to remember that this trust is not
a naivety which accepts unquestioningly and is
blown this way and that by different advice, and
is easy prey for the cunning or unscrupulous.

As responsible, rational beings, we are urged
to use our God-given intelligence and common
sense to examine any claims and teaching of
religious leaders to distinguish between those
speaking God's truth and those who are not. We
are not to follow blindly, under pressure or on
an emotional 'high'. God is not shallow; if the
claims are true they will stand up to close
scrutiny. Both the preacher's words and the fruit
of his or her life should bear witness to the fact
that Jesus the Christ, made flesh, came from
God.

Luke 19:41-end
Jesus is heartbroken by the sight of Jerusalem,
set to be the city of light which would draw all
nations to the knowledge of God's love; instead
the people have failed to recognise their king and
redeemer, and their blindness is launching them
headfirst towards destruction.

Surely he weeps still over all the chances and
opportunities we carelessly discard; all the
evidence of his glory we are too busy to notice;
and all the meaningless trivialities that make the
highest claims on our time, talents and money.

QUESTIONS FOR DISCUSSION

1. Notice the practical provision God makes for Noah, his loyal friend. Can you remember times through your life when God has shown his love for you in such practical care?
2. Very few issues are ever sharply defined, with the good and evil neatly labelled for us. Why do you think this is? How does God expect us to cope with arguments, conflicts and dilemmas?

IDEAS FOR ADULTS

Instead of reading the passage from Genesis, play a recording of this section of Britten's *Noyes Fludde.*

CHILDREN'S TEACHING

Show the children some pictures from traditional stories where it is very obvious who is the good character and who is the bad one. You could have a thumbs up sign whenever you point to a 'goodie' and a hiss whenever the 'baddie' appears. Then talk with them about how much harder it often is in real life to decide what is good and what is evil. Think, for instance, of when you make yourself late for school (hiss for bad) because you stopped to help at a bicycle accident (thumbs up for good), or when you offer to carry the shopping (thumbs up) so Dad won't notice a bar of chocolate you have stolen (hiss).

So how can we know for certain what is right and wrong? If you have the recording of Pinnochio, play and sing along with Jimminy Cricket, the voice of conscience. Through our conscience, God shows us which way is right, but we have to listen hard, or we may not hear. When we pray about a problem, Jesus will guide us through it safely. That's what Noah did, and he and his family were brought safely through the flood.

Help the children make this ark to remind them.

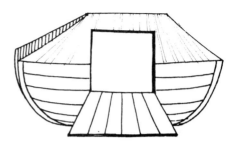

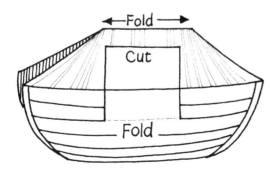

INTERCESSIONS **Years 1 and 2**
Some ideas for prayer

Followers of the Way of Christ, let us bring to the Lord the needs of our times.

Father, we pray for your blessing
on all who confess belief in you;
that they may witness powerfully
to your unselfish love and humility
by the way they act and the lives they lead.
Pause
Father, lead us: **free us from all that is evil**

Father, we pray for your blessing
on all who administer justice;
those working in Law Courts
and serving on juries, and those
who make laws; that they may be given
insight and integrity.
Pause
Father, lead us: **free us from all that is evil**

Father, we pray for your blessing
on us during this Lent
as we examine our lives
and draw closer to you;
that through our self-discipline and prayer

we may enter your stillness
and know your will for us.
Pause
Father, lead us: **free us from all that is evil**

Father, we pray for your blessing
on all in prison or on probation;
on those living in acute poverty
or in refugee camps;
on all who work among them
to heal, redirect, support and encourage.
Pause
Father, lead us: **free us from all that is evil**

Father, we pray for your blessing
on those who have passed through death
especially....
may we one day share with them
eternal life in your presence.
Pause
Father, lead us: **free us from all that is evil**

In silence, Father, we bring to you
our individual concerns and joys.
Pause

Merciful Father
**accept these prayers
for the sake of your Son,
our Saviour Jesus Christ, Amen.**

NOTES ON THE READINGS Year 2

Genesis 7:17-end
Purposely the passage chosen for today finishes
before the flood recedes, with all the hope and
promise of the rainbow glowing in the sky. It
is good to know that all will be well, but at the
moment we are looking at the time such as we
all feel at crisis points in our lives. Noah and his
family have watched the terrible anguish of
many terrified people drowning. Their
compassion and sorrow are mixed with relief and
joy at being alive through God's help. The
familiar world is utterly devastated and the
future completely unknown. So here they drift,
buoyed up but without direction, and all they
are to do is wait for the water to subside. Such
patient waiting can be used as a prayer in itself;
God's love will buoy us up even when we are
adrift because of pain, grief or some shattering
of our lives.

1 John 3:1-10
A person's actions display what he or she is
really like; they really do speak louder than
words. This is why you find out who your real
friends are when times are hard: they will be the
ones who stick around and help instead of fading
conveniently into the distance.

As children of God, loving, caring behaviour
is expected of us because that is the way Jesus
behaved. The more time we spend with him, the
more like him we will become. (You've seen it
happen with dogs and their owners!) It is very
exciting to think that the ordinary, familiar
person you see in the mirror each morning is
gradually being transformed into the likeness of
the most loving, generous, responsive person
ever.

Matthew 12:22-32
As if time is squeezed, we can watch this
transforming process from physical illness to
health, at the hands of Jesus. Amazement and
wonder lead many to dare to speculate as to
whether this healer can possibly be Messiah. His
ability to bring good out of evil is acting as a
signpost. It would be impossible for an evil force
to overthrow itself, so the effective act is proof
of the presence of goodness and love.

QUESTIONS FOR DISCUSSION

1. How do you think Noah and his family must
   have felt at this time? What conflict of
   emotions may there have been?

2. What do you think made the Pharisees accuse
   Jesus of casting out devils through
   Beelzebub?

IDEAS FOR ADULTS

If your church does not have a prayer 'chain'
of people willing to pray in confidence for
anyone going through dark, painful experiences,
whether physical or emotional, this week's
teaching of the word would provide an excellent
basis for setting one up. To work effectively the
chain needs to be quite organised, with a leader
to whom the message is first sent. She/he has
a list of eight names with addresses and
telephone numbers of each 'link'. Only the
minimum information is given, and only first
names are used, so as to protect confidentiality.
Each telephone call should be used only for the
message; phone again later for any other reason.
This will ensure that the message doesn't
become forgotten or misheard. The links jot the
prayer concern down during the phone call and
then immediately phone the next link. The last
link phones the leader to check that the correct
message has got through.

Such prayer support from a group like this has
wonderful effect. It is like providing an ark when
suffering threatens to engulf.

CHILDREN'S TEACHING

Start with a game of Simon Says. Then spread out a number of cards on which are written bits of advice or an order. Some are encouraging selfishness and greed — such as 'You bought those sweets; why give any away?' or 'Don't bother to clear up'. Others reflect the life and teaching of Jesus — such as 'Surprise Nana and Grandad with a letter' or 'Give Dad a hand with the washing up'. Together, sort out which things are what Jesus says, and try to put the Jesus Says game into practice in our lives.

Now tell them about Noah, who did this very well. Read or tell them the story — Palm Tree's version is called *Noah's Big Boat*. Work together on a large picture of the sea raging, and Noah's ark safely floating about on it.

3rd Sunday in Lent

TODAY'S THEME

... is the good news about suffering. In Christ, suffering can become a positive experience; a route to full life and deeper understanding. In fact, Jesus goes so far as to say it is a necessary part of our life in him. He will be there with us all through the very blackest, bleakest times.

PARISH MUSIC

Hymns
Alleluia, Sing to Jesus
And now, O Father, mindful of the love
Farmer, farmer
Follow me, follow me
I heard the voice of Jesus say
In the cross of Christ I glory
Lord Christ who on thy heart
Of the glorious body telling
On a hill far away
Take up thy cross, the Saviour said
Take up your cross, he says
The head that once was crowned with thorns

There is a green hill far away
When I survey the wondrous cross

Recorded music
I know that my Redeemer liveth (Handel)

For choirs
By the waters of Babylon (Pratt): U
Hear my crying (Weldon, ed. Ley): SSATBB

NOTES ON THE READINGS **Year 1**

Genesis 22:1-13
It must have seemed utterly incomprehensible to Abraham that God should ask him to sacrifice the very son through whom the promise of a chosen nation was to be fulfilled. If Isaac were killed, how could God's word possibly come true?

Perhaps Abraham was on the edge of trusting more in the means of achieving results than in the source of the power. Such a drastic threat to the 'means' threw Abraham's faith squarely onto the author of the promise. Since he was prepared to sacrifice even his beloved son, Abraham proved that even his most cherished hopes were second to his desire to serve God faithfully.

It was not any blood-sacrifice that God required; he needed the sacrifice of faith in other things, however closely those things may be tied up with his will. And it is all too easy to start trusting in the means instead of the source. If anything seems to be steering our attention away from God, we may find we are asked to abandon it, even though it is intrinsically good. Perhaps, once we have refocused our priorities, it will be given back abundantly; but by that time we will have sacrificed our faith in it, so our trust in God will have grown.

Colossians 1:24-end
Paul proclaims the fact that Christ is actually among us now; he is our guest and we are privileged to see his glory in a more personal, open way than any of the Old Testament prophets could.

His presence brings great joy and strength, but it also challenges us to join Christ in his redeeming work. This will certainly create problems, hardships and suffering in our lives, but since Christ, in person, has commissioned us, we can take up the work gladly, knowing he will support and uphold us always.

Luke 9:18-27
Not surprisingly, when the people were faced

with the promised Christ in person, they were full of suggestions about his identity which would not demand too shattering a change to their lives and beliefs. When Peter acknowledged Christ as God's chosen one, he was taking a tremendous risk. After all, at this stage there had been no resurrection, and Jesus looked and functioned in a perfectly normal way. To acknowledge Jesus as 'the Christ of God' meant unavoidable and radical change in Peter. The years of waiting had a certain safety about them, but if the Messiah was actually there standing next to him, the waiting was over and humanity had entered a new phase in the relationship with God.

Straight away, Jesus speaks of the inevitable action of suffering and death. There is no possible way to save the world other than the Creator himself submitting to his creation in an entire self-offering of love.

QUESTIONS FOR DISCUSSION

1. What can we learn from the way Abraham responds to God's call? Have you ever found that a course you dreaded and suffered through has actually brought great blessing?
2. Why do you think suffering can be spiritually positive? What changes in outlook does it force us to make?

IDEAS FOR ADULTS

Have a large wooden cross leaning against the wall of the church close to the main entrance. Round it hang the words: 'If anyone wants to be a follower of mine, let him renounce himself and take up his cross and follow me.'

CHILDREN'S TEACHING

Today is a good opportunity to learn about Abraham. To avoid confusion begin by explaining that Abraham lived many, many years before Jesus was born.

Start with a prayer about trusting and being ready, and a song (e.g. *Forward in faith*).

Then use a model and plasticine or card figures to tell the story of his calling. A green towel or cloth spread over various upturned bowls on a table makes a good landscape.

The children can help prepare it, and put on large stones, pebbles, boxes for buildings and the characters needed:

Abraham
Sarah
his son, Isaac
sheep and cattle
a ram
etc. (farmyard models)

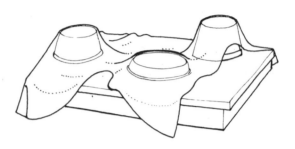

Spend the first half of the session making this model, and when it is all ready, let the children sit round the model while you tell the story of Abraham, moving the figures as you tell it.

At each stage emphasise how Abraham and Sarah trusted God, even when it came to sacrificing their son; and how God rewarded their trust.

Start at Haran, where God makes his promise;   *(Genesis 12)*
go on to the oaks of Mamre, where the three visitors tell him his elderly wife will have a son;   *(Genesis 18)*
and the birth of Isaac;
then to Moriah (in the mountains) where God tests Abraham in asking him to sacrifice his son, but provides a ram.
                                          (Genesis 22)

INTERCESSIONS **Years 1 and 2**
Some ideas for prayer

As children and heirs through adoption,
and knowing that Jesus shares
in all our suffering and joy,
let us confide in our heavenly Father
who knows us so well.

Father, into your enlightenment and perception
we bring all whose faith is limited
by fear or prejudice;
all whose living faith has been replaced
by the empty shell of habit.
Pause
Father, give us courage: **you are our only strength**

Father, into the depths of your wisdom and understanding
we bring those with responsibilities,
and all who have difficult decisions to make;
all those in charge of hospitals, schools,

industry and all community services.
Pause
Father, give us courage: **you are our only
strength**

Into your tireless faithfulness we bring
any who rely on us for help,
support or guidance;
any whom we are being asked to serve
or introduce to your love.
Pause
Father, give us courage: **you are our only
strength**

Into the gentleness of your healing love
we bring all who are in pain;
all those recovering from surgery;
those involved in crippling accidents
or suffering from wasting diseases.
Pause
Father, give us courage: **you are our only
strength**

Into your light and peace
we commend those who have died,
especially any dear to us
who we name in the silence of our hearts.
Pause
Father, give us courage: **you are our only,
strength**

Father, we thank you for supporting us
and encouraging us when life is hard,
and for all the exuberant vitality
of the world you have created
for us to live in.

Merciful Father
**accept these prayers
for the sake of your Son,
our Saviour Jesus Christ, Amen.**

NOTES ON THE READINGS **Year 2**

Genesis 12:1-9
Abram's obedience is so simply told that it
sounds quite easy. In fact, it must have been a
great upheaval and a move which was no doubt
ridiculed as senseless by many; why did he want
to uproot everything and wander off, leaving all
his security behind, for goodness' sake?

Obviously Abram was not like a reed in the
wind, easily persuaded by anybody. So he must
have recognised that this calling, though unusual
and unexpected, was nonetheless full of
authority. He sensed the greatness of God, and
bowed before it, committing his future security
and welfare to God's protection.

If we say that we acknowledge God's
greatness, then we must show it to be true in
the way we willingly submit to changes, new
directions, dangerous or unpleasant
undertakings, without grumbling about what we
have had to give up.

Whenever we are called forward we shall have
to leave something behind. But God will be
going with us, so we shall end up not poorer,
but richer.

1 Peter 2:19-end
People often talk loosely of the cross they have
to bear, when they mean one of the many
hardships which are simply part of being
human. But that cannot be what Jesus meant
by taking up our crosses and following him. For
him and us it signified a willingness to face and
undergo persecution and death if necessary even
when we are not guilty of what our accusers
claim. And that, as Peter says, is where the merit
lies, as far as God is concerned.

We are able to take as our example and
prototype Christ, the suffering servant, who did
not condemn or retaliate or even defend himself;
instead he trusted in an eternal defence against
which death is a powerless weapon. Drawing
together the two aspects of purification
symbolised by the scapegoat and sacrificed goat
of the Jewish people, Jesus is both sent off into
the wilderness, laden with our sin, and also
offered as a pure victim as he dies a sinless death.
He is therefore the complete atonement for
reconciling us to God, for he is both human and
divine.

Matthew 16:13-end
It is quite encouraging, in a way, to find that
Peter, who was so obviously close to God and
had such faith, also had times of blindness, when
his thinking was not aligned with God's mind.
Saints are not born perfect, but are very ordinary
people like us.

Why was Jesus so quick to stamp on what
Peter said? He was, after all, showing love and
concern for Jesus, and it seems a natural reaction
if a loved friend talks of walking openly into
certain death. So why was Peter wrong? He was
thinking with the mind of man; the concern for
his loved friend and master was not wrong in
itself but it did not go nearly far enough. It
became trapped at the immediate instead of
going further to see sacrifice as necessary for the
much wider context of all humanity. And it
therefore pulled the human Christ towards
immediate, smaller gains and away from the very
costly, divine plan for mankind's salvation.

There is, in other words, an element of grit

and rigour in thinking God's way which may lead to a harder, longer and more expensive course of action than seems necessary to those around us. But if we find God asking such costly action of us, it is only because the long-term effects, perhaps on us or perhaps on society, will be immeasurably greater.

QUESTIONS FOR DISCUSSION

1. What sacrifice was God really asking Abraham to make? Is it possible to offer any sacrifice that does not 'hurt' in some way? Is all hurt a sacrifice?
2. What do you think is meant by taking up our cross and following Jesus? In what ways is the weight of a cross different from the usual ills and sufferings of life?

IDEAS FOR ADULTS

A dramatised reading.
The narrator reads the story while others act it out, speaking their own words. You will need:
  God's voice
  Abraham
  Two servants
  Isaac
  Angel's voice
  Length of rope and a knife
  A drum and cymbals
  Triangle

Small handbell
Row of mugs on hooks to play with a fork
  And, if possible, a spot light with punched card shade, to give the impression of stars.
Have God and his angel out of view and as far from the actors as possible. They should both have strong voices which carry well.

Abraham is sitting in the chancel. The drum starts a slow beating and the narrator begins. As God speaks, Abraham stands up and the spotlight shines on his face. All the preparations for the journey are mimed, and the journey itself is from the chancel, round the church and back to a central area, where Abraham leaves the servants.

Abraham and Isaac walk on up to the chancel where a low table is Abraham's altar. As he starts to bind Isaac, the drum beats slowly again, and as Abraham raises the knife high the cymbals clash and Abraham freezes.

He helps his son off the table tenderly and the two begin to walk down to where the servants are waiting. But they are stopped by the cymbals and the angel's voice.

During the promise, triangles play, then mugs join in, then bells, and the spotlight covers everywhere with stars.

CHILDREN'S TEACHING

This is a particularly difficult theme for children to tackle, but if presented in a sensitive way it

provides rich ground for teaching.

Beforehand prepare a duplicated sheet of A4 paper so that when folded it shows Abraham's offering on one side and God's on the other. Give them out and help the children fold them into zigzag books. Then read them through, looking at the pictures and adding details as you go. Help them to see why Abraham had already made his offering without actually doing anything to hurt Isaac. Are they ever asked to give anything up? Sharing toys willingly is offering God a sacrifice. So is giving up viewing time to help at home; offering someone your favourite sweet; sticking up for someone even if you get laughed at; being friendly when you feel like being thoroughly grumpy.

4th Sunday in Lent

TODAY'S THEME

... is God's glory, shown in Jesus at the transfiguration. The disciples were given glimpses of Jesus' divinity which strengthened their faith and upheld them. Through their account, we also become witnesses: Jesus is indeed the Son of God.

PARISH MUSIC
Hymns
At the name of Jesus
Christ whose glory fills the skies
Father, you are living in us now
From glory to glory
Give me joy in my heart
God of mercy, God of grace
Holy, holy, holy is the Lord
Immortal, invisible, God only wise
Let all mortal flesh keep silence
Lord, Jesus Christ
Majesty, worship his majesty
Mine eyes have seen the glory
My God, how wonderful thou art
O Lord my God, when I in awesome wonder
O what a gift! What a wonderful gift
The God of Abraham praise
T'is good, Lord, to be here

Recorded music
Symphony No. 1, final movement (Brahms)

For choirs
How lovely is your dwelling place (Psalm 84): (Oxley)
O love of whom is truth and light (Viderö): SATB

NOTES ON THE READINGS **Year 1**

Exodus 34:29-end
The transfiguration of Christ is prefigured in the way Moses' face glows brightly after talking with the Lord. Their relationship is so close and deep that Moses 'catches' God's glory, and it shows.

Although Moses had remarkable gifts, he also had faults, and there is no attempt to make out that he was perfect. So it was not any freak, inimitable goodness that enabled Moses to draw so close to his God. It was only his longing to serve and love God with his whole being — heart, soul and body — that gradually drew him closer to the mind and heart of God.

2 Corinthians 3:4-end
Handwriting gives away aspects of our character; so do the clothes we feel comfortable in. But, more than anything, our character is shown in the way we behave — the way we act and react in the different circumstances of our daily lives. Perhaps we have sometimes seen a good Christian person we would like to emulate, and tried to graft their way of behaving, like a package deal, on to ourselves. It never works, of course! There is no short cut to being a shining, effective Christian.

But the more we allow his Spirit to write on our hearts, the more effective witnesses we shall be. It will be a testimonial which is unique, since God loves us personally, and the in-dwelling of his Spirit simply makes us more fully ourselves. A lively Christian community, then, will be a very colourful collection of people, with a whole range of variety.

Luke 9:28-36
This great transfiguring power of God was seen by the disciples as Jesus prayed on the mountain. It was beyond their understanding; but it must have remained, simmering in their minds, all through the humiliating crucifixion, till it burst out at the resurrection in an excited realisation that God had fulfilled his side of the promise, and any one who was prepared to accept that promise could now be assured of an eventual transfiguration such as they had once witnessed. God, in Jesus, had proved it would happen.

QUESTIONS FOR DISCUSSION

1. Do you think it is easier to do things for Christ than to allow him to work on us? What is involved, in practical terms, in allowing God's grace to transfigure us?

2. Why did Jesus invite Peter, John and James to see his glory and hear God's voice at this particular time in his ministry?

IDEAS FOR ADULTS

Dance of the Transfiguration
Use two songs as the music for this: *Near the heart of Jesus* (ONA, 340), and *Abba I belong to you* (SONL, 69). Clothing of the crowd can be anything brightly coloured, but Jesus, and the dancers on the mountain expressing his glory, should all wear white. Start at the back of the church.

WORDS	*ACTION*
Near the heart of Jesus here we start with Jesus loving as friends of Jesus tirelessly.	*Jesus walks slowly forward and stops. Two or three come across from other areas to join him. He extends his arms to them and they to each other.*
Near the mind of Jesus here we find what Jesus wills for the friends of Jesus constantly.	*Jesus walks slowly forward. Others come, one brings a stool on which Jesus sits and teaches them as they group, settle and listen to him.*
Near the feet of Jesus here we meet with Jesus guiding the friends of Jesus patiently.	*Jesus stands, beckons, and moves forward, talking and guiding them through imaginary obstacles, checking the last person.*
Near the arms of Jesus here the calm of Jesus comforts the friends of Jesus ceaselessly.	*A crying child runs down from front to meet the group. Jesus lifts him and cuddles him, and puts his arm around another in the group.*
Music only (one verse).	*The group wave to Jesus as they return to the back, except for Peter, James and John, who go with Jesus. He settles them down to watch near the front.*
Abba I belong you. Abba I belong to you. Abba I belong you. Our Father who art in heaven.	*As this begins he moves forward to the centre front and kneels in prayer, facing the congregation head bowed.*
Hallowed be thy name. Thy Kingdom come, thy will be done.	*Slowly raises head to look upwards slowly stands up*
on earth as it is in heaven	*raises his hands. A group of dancers in white join him, three on either side, moving to the chant of 'Abba I belong to you' in a set sequence: Step, together, step and turn. Transfer of weight, swaying.*
give us this day our daily bread	*Jesus lowers arms to 'asking' with palms up,*
and forgive us our trespasses	*kneels on one knee and bows head*
as we forgive those who trespass against us and lead us not into temptation	*stands as if lifting something from the ground as he does so, palms up walks three steps slowly forward and stops.*

but deliver us from evil for thine is the kingdom the power and the glory

for ever and ever.
Amen. Amen. Amen.

steps back with one foot and brings arms up as if to shield his face, then flings open his arms in praise as he is spotlighted in brightness.

The dancers work their way back to the sides, the light fades and Jesus slowly returns to his friends who kneel at his feet. He raises them and they all walk, arm in arm, to the back of the church.

CHILDREN'S TEACHING

Tell the story of *the transfiguration.* (Palm Tree's version is *The Secret on the Mountain.*) This works well on tape with music in the background as Jesus is transfigured. Alternatively, have a guitar playing, or taped music while the story is told.

Have the children sitting in a circle round a table with a white candle on it. Have the candle lit as Jesus is transfigured, and blown out when the cloud passes over and only Jesus is left.

Give each child a candle (unlit). Show how one light can light all of these. In the same way, we can all be lit by Jesus.

Give out squares of paper with candle drawn on and slits above.

Ask children to colour the candle and the flame and wick. Stick into books with a strip of sellotape top and bottom. Above it write: 'The bright love of Jesus can light my life.'

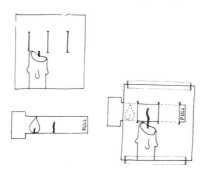

INTERCESSIONS **Years 1 and 2**
Some ideas for prayer

In faith, knowing that where two or three are gathered in your name
you have promised to be among them,
let our minds and hearts be filled
with stillness as we pray.

We pray for the Church;
that all your ministers may be given
perception and understanding,
to lead people into the light of your truth.
Pause
Lord of glory: **make us more like you**

We pray for all councils, committees
and conferences;
that a spirit of intergrity may underlie
all discussion
and a desire for goodness inspire
all decisions.
Pause
Lord of glory: **make us more like you**

We pray for all families,
especially those who have troubles;
that they may not be damaged
through their suffering,
but rather grow in compassion
and understanding.
Pause
Lord of glory: **make us more like you**

We pray for those in pain and distress;
for the mentally, physically and emotionally
    disabled;
that they may be comforted and
    strengthened
by your presence,
trusting in your love which never fails.
Pause
Lord of glory: **make us more like you**

We pray for the dying
and those who have already moved on
from this world into eternity;
may they rest for ever in your peace.
Pause
Lord of glory: **make us more like you**

In thankfulness and praise we remember
all your many blessings, given to us
each day, and ask to help us become
more generous-hearted and appreciative.
Pause
Lord of glory: **make us more like you**

Merciful Father
accept these prayers
for the sake of your Son,
our Saviour Jesus Christ, Amen.

NOTES ON THE READINGS Year 2

Exodus 3:1-6

Fire is frequently used as a sign, or symbol of God's presence, and here Moses is given a powerful sense of God's presence which attracts him and yet fills him with fear. God identifies himself as being personal. He has been involved and concerned with every stage of his people's history. Spiritual experiences of his presence, not only for Moses but also for us, lead on to action which will draw the world closer to its creator.

2 Peter 1:16-19

We have Peter's eye-witness account of the transfiguration. The event has obviously had a tremendous impact on him, and given him assurance of faith which he passes on to his readers. At the time, Peter had wanted to 'fix' the experience, providing holy shrines for Jesus, Moses and Elijah. Of course, he couldn't hang on to it in that way, but this letter makes it clear that the transfiguration had in fact been indelibly fixed for ever by transfiguring Peter himself from the inside!

Matthew 17:1-13

Jesus was quite probably transfigured like this whenever he became rapt in prayer, but normally he sought out lonely places and prayed privately. On this occasion he allowed three of his closest followers to witness his godliness, and the sight stunned and strengthened them with its intense purity, and unblemished loveliness.

Sometimes, when we are deeply touched by a glorious sunset, or our children singing their best, for instance, we glimpse a reflection of God's glory. If we can train our senses to see it in all kinds of small, everyday occurrences we shall be richer, more thankful and happier people.

For our God is so great, so full of purity and perfection that we need not hold ourselves back in lavishing all our worship on him. We have within us an instinctive need and longing to lavish worth and adoration on something or someone.

Here, in Christ, we find the true object for all the love we long to give. We were made for it, that is why worshipping God brings such peace and joy.

IDEAS FOR ADULTS

During the Gospel reading, fade in some flute, guitar or lute music at the transfiguration section.

CHILDREN'S TEACHING

Have lots of candles, flowers and glass in a beautiful arrangement, with quiet music playing as the children come in.

Point out the way the light and beauty is reflected in the glass. Talk about the lovely things in our world which reflect God's glory in this way — sunny days, rain drops, snow-flakes, spring flowers, animals, cobwebs etc. — and thank him for them in a prayer or song.

Then tell them how one day, Jesus showed his glory, the glory of God, not as a reflection but directly. Tell the story of the transfiguration as music plays in the background, explaining that God is full of glory like that all the time, even if we only see it sometimes.

Give each child a card folded like this:

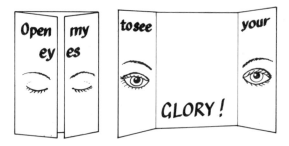

Have the eyes and words already on it. Let them fill the centre with all kinds of lovely things, either drawn, or cut out and stuck on.

5th Sunday in Lent

TODAY'S THEME

... is the victory of the cross. Nothing could look more like failure than the crucifixion, as the promising healer and teacher hung suffering at the mercy of mankind. Yet it was through this anguish and pain, offered in love without sin, that our salvation was secured for ever.

PARISH MUSIC

Hymns

All my hope on God is founded
All the riches of his grace
And now, O Father, mindful of the love
Brother let me be your servant
Can it be true

Farmer, farmer
Firmly I believe and truly
Glory be to Jesus
Hallelujah, my Father
Happy are they, they that love God
It is a thing most wonderful
Jesus, good above all other
Once, only once and once for all
Love is his word, love is his way
Praise to the holiest in the height
We sing the praise of him who died
When Israel was in Egypt's land

Recorded music
Symphony No. 1 (Mahler): final
  movement

For choirs
Ave Verum (Mozart): SATB
Of the glorious body telling (de Victoria):
  SATB

NOTES ON THE READINGS **Year 1**

Exodus 6:2-13
The Israelites had become worn down and demoralised through cruelty and oppression. To them God seemed distant and irrelevant to their troubles. We, too, may well have experienced this, when circumstances are so difficult that we feel we need all our energies just to survive, and any message of hope seems a useless diversion.

But God had not forgotten his people, any more than he ever forgets us. He has watched their suffering and shared in it, waiting only for the right time and receptive hearts in order to act. Now, through Moses and Aaron, the exodus from slavery can begin.

Colossians 2:8-15
Seeing man's sinfulness and his inability to rise above it, God intervenes at his own expense to cancel the great debt of sin. To do this, he does not admit defeat, and lower his standards to accept man's dismal record of habitual sinning. After all, he knows man's potential and longs for him to know happiness and peace. So the only way he can cancel the debt is by paying it himself, in full. In the agony of the passion, we see this sacrifice in action, but this is only the historical focus of it: in terms of eternity, that debt is constantly being paid off; we see the suffering Christ in every starving, maltreated, exiled face.

Having paid the debt, Christ was raised and lives for ever; the first Easter Day was the historical focus, but in terms of eternity that resurrection victory continues too, in every barrier of hatred, broken by love; every act of loving service replacing resentment; every God-inspired rejection of evil and commitment to goodness.

John 12:20-32
When the Greek Jews showed an interest in meeting Jesus, it was the need for complete and willing obedience which he stressed. Philosophical discussion and interest are all very well and can serve as introductions to Jesus, but eventually we are challenged with the requirement to obey, with all the courage and trust that this involves. No longer can we follow Jesus when the mood takes us, or when we approve of the liturgy/music/homily. No longer can we excuse our need for regular times set aside each day for prayer and reading the Bible.

If we really want to follow Christ we have no choice but to become obedient, and lay our ambitions, plans and loyalties down at his feet. We may find that we are enabled to do this in one fell swoop, as Paul did, or we may find it is a question of peeling off skin after skin until we really understand just how much giving is required. But however it happens, it will be done in a supportive and encouraging atmosphere, because God our Father is not a domineering slave-driver but a tender and caring parent who enjoys our company and wills for our salvation.

QUESTIONS FOR DISCUSSION

1. Moses and Paul both describe themselves as rather halting speakers, yet God chose both to be his messengers. Why? What can this teach us about any calling to God's service we may receive?
2. Most of us fight every inch of the way to survive as a grain, rather than risk being 'sown'. What practical changes take place in attitudes and relationships when we abandon ourselves to God, the 'farmer'?

IDEAS FOR ADULTS

During the intercessions have a large globe placed in front of the altar. Have a child and an elderly person, one of each sex, to bring candles and set them down either side of the globe: Jesus' victory is for everyone.

CHILDREN'S TEACHING

Show the children a packet of seeds with a picture of the delicious food they will grow into. Sprinkle them into a tray so they can feel them without spilling them. If we put them back into the packet (do so) will they grow? What if we waited for a month or two — would we get a crop then? No, they would just stay as seeds. What needs to happen to them before they will grow?

Bring out a seed tray and a bag of seed compost, a trowel and a watering can, and let the children prepare the seed bed and plant the seeds. Help them to realise that the original seed has to die in order for all the life to come which brings about the harvest. (Keep this tray of seeds watered and cared for week by week, transplanting when necessary, so the children can watch the growing and eventually share the crop.)

Now read or tell the Gospel for today, relating the seeds both to Jesus and to ourselves. Sing *Love is something if you give it away* and give them all some seeds to plant at home. Put the seeds in an envelope on which is written:

PLANTING INSTRUCTIONS
1. Plant your life in Jesus
2. Water it with opportunities to show love kindness and generosity
3. Watch it grow and bear fruit

INTERCESSIONS **Years 1 and 2**
Some ideas for prayer

In the presence of God,
the giver of all life,
let us lift our hearts and pray.

We pray for all who are training
for ministry in your church;
may they grow in wisdom and humility,
and be increasingly filled
with the life you have won for us.
Pause
Lord, breathe into us: **that we may live**

We pray for all areas of bureaucracy
which frustrate and delay the course
of useful action; for areas where anarchy
undermines stability; for areas of
political corruption; that whatever is good
may flourish and grow, so evil is rendered
powerless and overthrown.
Pause
Lord, breathe into us: **that we may live**

We pray for all who are engaged or newly
  married;
for those coping with family problems,
difficult circumstances or bereavement;

may they lean on your loving presence
which dispels all fear, and
brings life and peace.
Pause
Lord, breathe into us: **that we may live**

We pray that your calming reassurance
will bring peace of mind and spirit
to those worried about the future,
those dreading some difficult event,
and those who are frightened of dying.
Pause
Lord, breathe into us: **that we may live**

We thank you for the life and example
of all who have lived, worked and died
in the joy of your service; may we one day
share with them eternal life in your presence.
Pause
Lord, breathe into us: **that we may live**

Father, with thankful hearts
we offer these concerns for the church
and for the world.
Accept these prayers
for the sake of your Son,
our Saviour Jesus Christ, Amen.

NOTES ON THE READINGS **Year 2**
Jeremiah 31:31-34
Our Bibles are divided into the Old and New Testaments, and there is a very good reason for this. When, at the Last Supper, Jesus offered the wine as the blood of the new covenant, or testament, he was saying that the prophesied new covenant between God and his people was now being made, through himself.

From now on the law would be written on people's hearts, rooted in love and cauterized with the ultimate sacifice of giving up one's whole life freely and gladly. When we share in Christ's dying we give our lives away; we hand over the use of our time, our money and our gifts and energies and allow God to take over and be in charge of our lives. All the richness of communal worship and all the structuring of Christian care emanate from this kind of total, personal commitment to God.

Hebrews 9:11-14
For Christ's sacrifice is so much more effective than any sacrifice of animals, which had to be offered time and again under the old Law in order to cleanse people of their sin. In contrast, Jesus offers himself, sinless as he is, to die as the punishment for our sins. That is why his death frees us from the effects of sin and liberates us from the prison of selfishness. We are now free to get on with living, in the rich, fulfilling, valuable way that God has planned for us to enjoy.

Mark 10:32-45

The wonderful thing about the Christian message is that we do not have to walk around with our faces set in a tight, determined smile. We are not to feel guilty about heartbroken sobs, the ache of missing our loved ones who have died, or the sense of abject misery that may wash over us in a seemingly endless illness. For the central event of Christ's life, the event that saves us, is the slow and lingering death by crucifixion. And we need to remember that Jesus was not anaesthetised. He felt it all. His loving Father allowed it to happen. That is how we know that the result of his suffering was astoundingly good.

It would be wrong to teach people that turning suffering into joy means taking away the pain. Sometimes this may happen, but at other times God allows the suffering to continue, just as he allowed the crucifixion to continue unchecked. But, just as that was the only way to resurrection and wholeness, so God will act through our suffering, if we let him, to enrich us, and bring about a transformation for great good.

QUESTIONS FOR DISCUSSION

1. Which passages in the Old Testament might Jesus have referred to when he taught his disciples that the Son of Man would have to suffer and be put to death in order to save us?
2. Time and again we hear of the importance of sacrifice. What does it mean in practical terms, both for us as individuals and as a parish?

IDEAS FOR ADULTS

As in Year 1, during the intercessions, have a large globe placed in front of the altar. Have a child and an elderly person, one of each sex to bring candles and set them down at either side of the globe: Jesus' victory is for everyone.

CHILDREN'S TEACHING

Show a few pictures of athletes training, mountaineers climbing, an orchestra practising, or any other activities where hard work or discomfort is necessary for the reward of winning, giving a good performance, or some other worthwhile end.

Discuss times in the children's own lives when they have had to put up with pain or discomfort which was worth doing; getting bruised in the process of learning to ride a bike or skate, for instance. Father Damien, the priest who worked among the lepers in Hawaii, was willing to put

up with suffering from leprosy so that the people would be cared for.

When Jesus suffered and died on the cross, it really hurt a lot. But it was worth doing because it led to us being set free from all that is evil and bad.

Help them make this card to take home.

HOLY WEEK

Palm Sunday

TODAY'S THEME

. . . is that Jesus enters Jerusalem as the Prince of Peace, riding on a donkey. At the heart of our rejoicing is the pain he is bound to suffer in redeeming us through unflinching love. Yet we still certainly rejoice, for we know he has won the victory. Jesus is indeed our King.

PARISH MUSIC

Hymns
All glory, laud and honour
At the name of Jesus
How sweet the name of Jesus sounds
Jesus, name above all names
My people, what have I done to you?
O sacred head sore wounded
Ride on! Ride on in majesty
Sing hallelujah to the Lord
The Lord is King
Majesty, worship his majesty
There's no greater name than Jesus
Thou didst leave thy throne
We cry 'Hosanna, Lord!
Were you there
The royal banners forward go

Recorded music
St. Matthew's Passion (Bach)

For choirs
A Palm Sunday Antiphon (Morgan)
Benedictus qui venit (Palestrina)

NOTES ON THE READINGS **Years 1 and 2**

Isaiah 50:4-9a

Philippians 2:5-11

Mark 14:32-15:41

Through his own personal suffering and humiliation, the obedient servant in the Isaiah prophecy is able to teach others about the uncompromising love of God. In Jesus this song takes on a new and astounding reality, for here is the Son of God, with whom God is 'well pleased', undergoing insults, slander, torture, death, and, perhaps most hurtful of all, desertion by every one of his followers and even a sense of isolation from his Father.

However can such a bleak and distressing drama be cherished generation after generation? Why did God not answer Jesus' desperate prayer that the horror might be averted?

When Jesus returned to find the disciples sleeping, perhaps his words applied also to himself: 'The spirit is willing but the flesh is weak'. For here is the essence of what it meant to save us from the prison of sin; God had to empty himself of all rights, privilege and status and become utterly weak and vulnerable; he had to submit to the very worst that evil could throw at him and still continue to love, forgive and trust. Had his flesh not been weak he would not have been able to make this complete sacrifice; had his spirit not been willing, he would not have been able to achieve this ultimate in loving obedience.

Yet even at his most helpless, most cruelly treated and most terribly alone, Christ still loved the world which rejected him, and it is the incredible wonder of such love that draws us stumbling to his feet.

QUESTIONS FOR DISCUSSION

1. Make a list of the people Jesus encountered during his trial and crucifixion. What influence do you think he had on each one?
2. What kind of Kingdom did Jesus proclaim by entering the holy city on a donkey? What kind of Kingdom do our lives proclaim?

IDEAS FOR ADULTS

The procession of palms is a chance to witness to the local community; it is a chance to 'dance with all our might before the Lord' as David did when the ark of the covenant was carried into Jerusalem. Ask everyone to wear bright clothes and bring along percussion instruments (home-made if possible) and branches from tree-pruning that are large enough to wave like flags. Have a practice session during the week to teach the music and dancing and plan a slightly longer

route as the procession will be moving faster than usual! No books will be needed as the words are easily learnt. Such a procession may be different, but it is in no way irreverent; just as the woman lavished expensive ointment on Jesus to show her 'worthship' of him, so we should have times when we move our whole bodies in worship of the king who rides into Jerusalem on his way to achieve our salvation.

The basic step for everyone is:

Step, together, step, hop;

encourage people to improvise on this, introducing turns, swaying and clapping and, of course, waving their branches. The words are a constant reminder of whom we are dancing for. The music is given on page 110.

CHILDREN'S TEACHING

Encourage the children to bring large leaves or branches to wave in the procession, or colourful streamers. They may also join in the crowd sections of the Gospel if they are in the church at this point.

If not, read *Jesus on a Donkey* (Palm Tree Bible Stories) which tells the story of Jesus entering Jerusalem and then help the children make a model of that ride. Use a large tray as the base, with hills of crumpled paper under a green towel. The track is a strip of brown or beige material. Houses can be made from white paper like this:

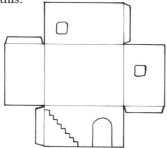

and palm trees from green paper like this:

Have a farmyard model of a donkey and make plasticene figures, waving real leaves. Pieces of material cut out can be laid on the path in front of Jesus.

Display the finished model where the rest of the congregation can see it.

INTERCESSIONS **Years 1 and 2**
Some ideas for prayer

Fellow pilgrims, as we welcome Jesus
and hail him as our King, let us offer
to God our Father in prayer
the deep concerns and needs
of the Church and of the world.

We bring to your love all who are baptised,
and especially those who have lost their faith
or have stopped praying;
may they be brought back through your love,
and put into contact with those
who can guide and reassure them.
Pause
Lord, uphold us: **give us your strength**

We bring to your love every meeting,
demonstration, convention and all large crowds;
may they be peaceful and ordered,
inspiring those present for good,
rather than inciting them to violence.
Pause
Lord, uphold us: **give us your strength**

We bring to your love our own loved ones,
the members of our families, our friends
and especially those from whom we are
    separated,
either by distance or death;

and all who are missing from their homes;
may your powerful love
protect us from all that is evil.
Pause
Lord, uphold us: **give us your strength**

We bring to your love those suffering
from incurable or life-threatening diseases;
those who need medical care, but are either
too poor, or live too far way to receive it;
make us more ready to help
with our time, money and influence,
so that unnecessary suffering and death
are avoided.
Pause
Lord, uphold us: **give us your strength**

We bring to your love those who have died;
may they rest in the light and joy
of your presence for ever.

Father, may we praise you
not only with our voices
but also in the lives we lead.
Merciful Father
accept these prayers
for the sake of your Son,
our Saviour Jesus Christ, Amen.

Maundy Thursday

TODAY'S THEME

... is the new Covenant between God and his
people. The Passover feast was an annual
celebration of God freeing his people from
slavery. The blood of the lamb protected them,
and was both a sacrifice and food before their
journey. Now Christ offers himself in the bread
and wine and in the washing of feet. His sacrifice
frees us from sin's slavery.

PARISH MUSIC

Hymns
A new commandment I give unto you
Bind us together, Lord
Bread of heaven on thee we feed
Broken for me, broken for you
Brother, let me be your servant
Love is his word, love is his way
Make me a channel of your peace
Now, my tongue the mystery telling
Of the glorious body telling
O thou who at thy Eucharist

This is my command to you
Welcome all ye noble saints
We pray thee heavenly Father
When Israel was in Egypt's land

Recorded music
St. John's Passion (Bach)

For choirs
Hail true Body (Byrd)
Love divine (Mozart): U

NOTES ON THE READINGS **Years 1 and 2**

Exodus 12:1-14
The profound significance of this occasion is
marked by the ritual and the reordering of the
calendar. (Every time we write the date we have
a similar reminder of God's great act of
incarnation.)
   The instructions are highly practical for a meal
before a journey, and often the fulfilment of
God's will depends on people obeying his
instructions, however odd or irrelevant they may
seem. For the chosen people, this sets them
apart and protects them from the destroying
plague in Egypt.

1 Corinthians 11:23-29
It is no accident that the Last Supper was a
celebration of Passover. The symbolism would
now be given new meaning, and the new
covenant marks the next stage in God's
relationship with his people.
   And just as the people of Israel were instructed
to celebrate Passover as a festival every year, so
we are instructed to celebrate the Eucharist
regularly until the second coming.

John 13:1-15
There is only a thin dividing line between self-
respect and arrogance. 'No self-respecting
person would allow himself to be treated like
that', we often hear, and we may instinctively
shy away from being helped if we feel it is an
insult to our independence or ability. Peter was
offended by Jesus' behaviour: perhaps he felt
that Jesus was degrading himself by doing a
servant's job, and he wanted no part in it. It
didn't seem right for a Lord and Master to be
washing feet. How would we feel if a bishop
came to the parish and started cleaning
everyone's shoes!
   Jesus again uses a physical act to explain the
love he was telling them about. In the act of feet
washing, in which they were involved, they
could see that his love was not an emotional
feeling or vague affection. It meant renouncing
all right to rank and privileges, and serving

reverently wherever there may be needs.

Those in need are not always the most attractive or pleasant people to deal with; they may smell, insult us, inject themselves with heroin or sleep around irresponsibly. They may encompass all the values we reject. But none of this matters, for we are not asked to like, or fall in love with one another — only to love one another. That involves the will, practical care, generosity and commitment. And we may well find that this leads to deeper, warmer friendships than we had believed possible.

IDEAS FOR ADULTS

The washing of the feet is a very powerful sign. Invite a broad cross-section of ages to take part. They do not need to come out to the front — just make sure they sit on the aisle end of a pew. Have a short preparation session to study the passages of scripture for today, using the notes on the readings, and to pray.

CHILDREN'S TEACHING

Suggest that families have a special shared meal during the day, before which a clear translation of the Exodus and Gospel passages are read, and family blessing is said. Children should be encouraged to help in the preparation of some part of the meal, and to help with the readings. Groups of families may like to get together for this, and invite someone who lives on his/her own.

INTERCESSIONS **Years 1 and 2**
Some ideas for prayer

We belong to the body of Christ.
In his name let us pray to the Father
for the Church and for the world.

We commend to your care and protection
all who are abused, imprisoned or insulted
because of their faith.
Pause
Lord, by your example: **teach us all to love**

We commend to your light and truth
all governments and committees,
every head of state, and all leaders.
Pause
Lord, by your example: **teach us all to love**

We commend to your longsuffering patience
and compassion, ourselves,
with our frequent misuse of his blessings
and failure to serve.
Pause
Lord, by your example: **teach us all to love**

We commend to your healing and wholeness
all who are ill or injured;
those undergoing surgery
and those nearing death.
Pause
Lord, by your example: **teach us all to love**

We commend to your light and lasting peace
all those who have died, especially...
We thank you, Lord, for all your
guidance and loving care; fulfil our needs
in the way which is best for us
in the context of eternity.

Merciful Father
accept these prayers
for the sake of your Son,
our Saviour Jesus Christ, Amen.

Good Friday

TODAY'S THEME

... is that Jesus lays down his life for us. He yearns so much for us to be saved that he undergoes death, allowing the burden of the whole world's evil to rest on his shoulders. Not once does he stop loving and forgiving. His death is no failure, then, but an accomplishment of cosmic proportions, through which we are saved.

PARISH MUSIC
Hymns
Can it be true
I cannot tell why he
I danced in the morning
In the cross of Christ I glory
It is a thing most wonderful
Just as I am
Lord Jesus think on me
My God I love thee
O Love that wilt not let me go
O my Saviour lifted from the earth
On a hill far away
O sacred head sore wounded
Oh the blood of Jesus
Take up your cross he says
There is a green hill far away
The royal banners forward go
Were you there
When I survey the wondrous cross

Recorded music
Requiem: Agnus Dei (Faure)

For choirs
Here lies he now (Bach): SATB
We adore thee, O Lord Christ (Viadana): SATB

NOTES ON THE READINGS Years 1 and 2

Isaiah 52:13-53end
It is certainly amazing, and proof of God speaking through the prophets, that this passage strikes to the very core of how the world was to be saved. The idea of God's obedient servant being prepared to suffer and die in order to bring others to peace and understanding, is taken up and richly fulfilled by Jesus on the cross. The unthinkable insult — of the creator being destroyed by his created — has actually happened: God is being put to death while 'praying all the time for sinners'.

Hebrews 10:1-25 or Hebrews 10:12-22 or Hebrews 4:14-16; 5:7-9
This act, more than any other, points to the end of our hopeless yearnings and desolate loneliness. God is not a distant and unapproachable ideal but a person — warm-blooded and tactile, with pulse and breath. His loving is not a condescending 'playing' but a close relationship with deep affection and empathy. So much so, that he identifies completely with us in all our best moments and our most appalling ones. At the times we come, exhausted, to the end of our strength, and have nothing left to draw on, we find Jesus — not in the distance with his back to us, but right next to us, lifting us up to carry us to safer ground. His willingness to die the crucifixion death is our guarantee that he will never, ever desert us, and no suffering we face is beyond his reach; always he suffers alongside us and leads us through it to new life.

John 18:1-19:37 or John 19:1-37
Dare we pledge ourselves to Christ's way? When we read the account of his crucifixion the example it shows is so daunting. It is relatively easy to say 'use me, Lord' in the safety and fellowship of worship, and certainly this is the right beginning.

But we are bound, as indeed Jesus was, to recoil from the horrors of physical torture, emotional taunting and ridicule, or the call to submit obediently without gaining anyone's approval or praise. When we feel very much alone, and the God-given task weighs heavily and seems to be doing no one any immediate good; when we are tired and mocked for taking it seriously — these are the times we are truly offering ourselves for God's use. Such times must be expected and not resented, for they are the moments when we have the privilege of identifying with the suffering Christ. They are the times when others can be drawn to the strange freedom which owes nothing to comfort or a substantial bank balance, and everything to repentance, forgiveness and love.

IDEAS FOR ADULTS

Instead of having a reader for the Isaiah passage, make sure that everyone has the words and read it aloud, slowly and carefully, together.

CHILDREN'S TEACHING

It is important that children are able to walk their own 'Way of the Cross' today. One way of making this possible is to organise a one or two hour session of teaching, singing and craft activities, with a break for hot cross buns and a drink. A possible programme might be:

10.00 a.m.   Introduction with brief talk *(What happened on Good Friday)*, prayer and a song. Palm Tree's version is called *The Road to the Cross*.
10.25 a.m.   Begin activities
10.45 a.m.   Break; drink and hot cross bun
11.00 a.m.   Resume and complete activities
11.20 a.m.   Gather for short litany, and a song and blessing
11.30 a.m.   End

Possible activities:
a. Make a Holy Week frieze with the crowd, the crosses and the tomb;
b. Make a smaller banner for taking home. Have background material already stitched and figure shapes out of felt. The children assemble it with glue, and thread two sticks through top and bottom, with a piece of wool to hang it up. These could perhaps be blessed at the end.
c. A standing cross could be made from wood. Have ready the base blocks and cross pieces. The children sand the wood down, glue and nail together and varnish. N.B. Very careful supervision necessary!

The atmosphere should be calm and quiet, with the activities being looked on as part of their worship.

EASTER

Easter Day

TODAY'S THEME

... is that Jesus is risen from the dead! Having passed through death to life, Christ has won the victory over everything evil and destructive. Full of glory and power, he enables us to bring the hope and joy of resurrection into the world's problems and tragedies. With God, nothing is impossible.

PARISH MUSIC

Hymns
Alleluia, give thanks to the risen Lord
Alleluia, hearts to heaven
At the Lamb's high feast we sing
Christ the Lord is risen again
Come and see the shining hope
Come let us join the cheerful songs
Come, ye faithful, raise the strain
Earth in the dark
God sent his Son
Hail thee, Festival Day
How lovely on the mountains
I know that my Redeemer lives!
I will sing unto the Lord
Jesus Christ is risen today
Jesus lives! thy terrors now
Lord enthroned in heavenly splendour
Love's redeeming work is done
Rejoice in the Lord always
The day of resurrection
The head that once was crowned with
  thorns
The Lord is risen indeed
The strife is o'er

Thine be the glory
This is the day
This joyful Eastertide
Ye choirs of new Jerusalem

Recorded music
Symphony No. 6: Thanksgiving after the
  storm (Beethoven)

For choirs
Ye choirs of new Jerusalem (Stanford)
Love is come again (Oxley)

CHURCH DECORATION

Why not try constructing a festal archway outside the church using two step ladders with a third ladder lashed across the top? Weave plenty of greenery in and out until the main structure is hidden and then decorate with flowers and ribbons.

Another possibility is to have a festival of flowers in the church this week. Get together a team of about a dozen people to decide on themes and who is going to be responsible for each, ask someone to write labels, and pool ideas and resources. The main theme should be the resurrection; within this, you could either trace God's promises through from creation, the fall, Noah, Abraham, Moses and the prophets; or you could select the main events of Jesus' life. Either way the festival will provide good teaching material both for those involved and for all the visitors.

NOTES ON THE READINGS **Years 1 and 2**

Isaiah 12 or Exodus 14:15-22 or Isaiah 43:16-21
From the very beginning of matter God has been in charge. He chose to fashion the universe, and through his will and command it was created with all its potential for life and variety. Even as it was being formed, God's plans for its direction and purpose were fully developed. Gradually, through history we can see that plan unfolding, as a tentative, halting progress, often spoiled but repaired; often wounded but healed; often wandering but led back to the source of creation, by the creator himself who loves what he has made.

In these readings we see God's faithfulness and abiding love shown to his people. He has provided for them, saved them, comforted them and never forsaken them, in spite of all their waywardness and sin. Neither will he ever forsake us, for not only is he just, but he is also full of love, as we see for ourselves in Jesus Christ.

Revelation 1:10-18 or 1 Corinthians 15:20 or Colossians 3:1-11
Not only has Christ conquered death and sin by breaking through them to unending life. He has also brought us back to life lived in the way God planned when he created us. But there is no way we can half die with Christ if we are to be brought back to true life with him. It simply cannot be done, though often we pretend it can. We submit bits of ourselves but hang on to other bits with a grip of steel. Perhaps we are frightened we may lose our identity along with our companionable sins. Danger and insecurity yawn before us if we contemplate really radical changes in our giving and our life style.

And we are right to count the cost first, for there is no doubt that there will certainly be risks and hardships. Living in Christ is rarely comfortable and never settled; it is full of the unexpected, of constant rethinking, challenge and change. It never allows us to get fixed in a rut or creep into holes when danger threatens.

But then, Christ never promised us a rose garden on the world's terms. We are to look instead for the heavenly things which belong with life in Christ. These treasures — such qualities as truth, joy, compassion and serenity — pour out in profusion, last through all affliction and satisfy as nothing material can. It is infinitely worth taking the risk, and giving ourselves away.

Matthew 28:1-10 or John 20:1-10 (or 1-18) or Mark 16:1-8
As Creator, God has rested on the seventh day after accomplishing his work. Now, as Saviour, God keeps the Sabbath after the accomplishment of his redeeming work. With the beginning of a new week comes the most amazing new life which is forever free of the threat of death. Now Jesus emerges triumphant over humanity's fall from grace. The blockade is down, just as the stone has been rolled away, so that the way is now clear for us to be children of our heavenly Father, loving and beloved in a close relationship which death cannot destroy.

These very human, realistic accounts of Easter morning show us the lovable, varied characters and their predictable reactions to an unimaginably amazing event. We see Mary of Magdala, distressed at finding the physical body of Jesus missing; the petrified guards; the younger John racing ahead, but losing his nerve; the elderly Peter, puffing up behind and impetuously running straight into the tomb. We, too, all react differently and will have different experiences of the resurrection in our own lives.

The important thing is that they all suddenly realised what Jesus had meant about rising from the dead. It was not to be an other-worldly rising from which they were excluded: suddenly they understood that he meant real life — fulfilled, accomplished, physical and spiritual — a total existence. Not only had Jesus become man: he had also brought humanity into the very essence of the Godhead.

QUESTIONS FOR DISCUSSION

1. Has the resurrection really affected our attitude to death — both our own and that of our loved ones? Does that in turn affect our attitude to living?
2. Why is it essential for Christians to believe that Christ rose from the dead?

IDEAS FOR ADULTS

Unleavened bread for today can be baked by one of the congregation, and home-made wine (provided it is suitable) can be used. The makers bring their gifts to the altar.

This recipe makes a soft bread which is not too crumbly:

Ingredients	
1lb of wholemeal flour	¼pt milk
pinch of salt	2oz butter

1. Mix flour and salt together, and make a well in the centre.
2. Warm the milk and butter to blood heat, and gradually add to the flour.
3. Knead well for 2 minutes.
4. Divide the dough into 24 pieces and flatten each piece to a circle, about ¼ inch thick.

5. Cook each one in a frying pan over a gentle heat until speckled brown.
6. Wrap in a clean cloth until needed.

CHILDREN'S TEACHING

Read the first part of *'Jesus is Risen'* (Palm Tree Bible Stories) or tell the story in your own words, acting it out with plasticine models on a tray with a stone 'cave' built on it in a garden.

Sing one of the Easter songs together and give each child a margarine tub with oasis in it, a selection of Spring flowers and a tall white candle.

Help them make an arrangement of joy at Jesus being alive forever. When they have finished, light all the candles, and let the children carry them in procession into the church near the altar.

INTERCESSIONS **Years 1 and 2**
Some ideas for prayer

In the joy of this Easter morning
let us pray to the God
who loves us completely.

We pray that the joy and conviction of Christians
may be so radiant
that all who are lost, weary and searching
may be directed towards your lasting,
inner peace.
Pause
Risen Lord: **live in us all**

We pray that from every world crisis
and tragedy some good may come;
every problem become an opportunity
for development and spiritual growth.
Pause
Risen Lord: **live in us all**

We pray for the newly born,
and for all families,
that the children may be nurtured,
and the elderly cherished
through your wide, accepting love.
Pause
Risen Lord: **live in us all**

We pray that those in mental,
physical or spiritual distress
may recognise in their suffering
a privilege of sharing Christ's passion,
until they also share
the joy of new life in you.
Pause
Risen Lord: **live in us all**

We pray that all those
who have died
may share your risen life for ever.
Pause
Risen Lord: **live in us all**

In silence we praise you, Father,
for your abundant blessings.

Merciful Father
accept these prayers
for the sake of your Son,
our Saviour Jesus Christ, Amen.

1st Sunday after Easter

TODAY'S THEME

... is the life-giving presence of the risen Lord. The disciples began to realise that Jesus was present with them whether they could see him or not. We, too, experience his spiritual presence among us and welcome him with joy.

PARISH MUSIC
Hymns
Bread of heaven on thee we feed
Come to the waters
I am the bread of life
I see your hands and your side
I will sing unto the Lord
Oh come to the water
Shalom, my friend
Whom do you seek?
Walk with me, O my Lord
Without seeing you, we love you
Sing to the mountains

. . . and all the Easter hymns suggested on Easter Day!

Recorded music
Peer Gynt Suite: Morning (Grieg)

For choirs
Alleluia! Hearts to Heaven (Stanton): U
with descant
When the Lord turned again (Batten)

CHURCH DECORATION

The whole church continues to look festive this week, with lots of spring flowers; both cut flowers arranged and bulbs in pots. The Easter garden can be kept fresh by sinking small pots and vases into peat below the moss, and replenishing these throughout the Easter season whenever necessary.

NOTES ON THE READINGS **Year 1**

Exodus 15:1-11
Moses and the people of Israel are jubilant because they have just been rescued from death. Such times make us acutely aware of the splendour of life! They burst into song to praise God who has shown himself in control as their loving parent, involving himself with their misery and intervening personally to save them.

1 Peter 1:3-9
Peter's letter is very encouraging, particularly for any who are finding life difficult. He assures us that any patience or perseverance we practise during rough patches of our lives will be kept in heaven, and form part of the glory that will be revealed at the end of time.

It may look as if we are failures in the world's eyes; we may be hounded by false values, or feel as if we are bashing our heads against a brick wall as we try to bring up our children as Christians in a materialistic and pagan world, hold an unstable marriage together, or cope positively with unemployment or illness.

It is how we respond to these challenges and trials which will make the lasting treasure. Instead of trying to act independently of God we can trust him and use his grace of forgiveness, his patience, his perseverance and his strength. Then we will be building something beautiful with and for God, whether the world sees it or not. The thrill of being privileged to work with God like this takes much of the sting out of the suffering, and an incongruous joy wells up even among the tears.

John 20:19-29
Thomas was not with the other disciples when they were joined by Jesus. Perhaps he needed to sort things out in his mind alone after the death of his leader and friend. It cannot have come as a surprise to Thomas that Jesus would be killed; he had expected it earlier when they returned to Bethany to visit Lazarus' grave. Thomas had been prepared to die with him.

So if Thomas thought of Jesus as a great prophet, and a remarkable man, then an era of his life was now over, and he would have to sort out the rest of his life, trying his best to follow the example of his dead teacher. The prospect would be daunting in its difficulty and loneliness.

He must have had niggling questions about those strange sayings of Jesus concerning new life, and rising again. But Thomas was too dedicated to his human teacher to insult him by believing fairy stories — Jesus being alive again was simply too 'good' to be true: he preferred Jesus to be human, noble and dead.

When he did meet the risen Christ, his amazed acclamation of faith shows what had happened. Thomas had swapped a human teacher for the human son of the all-powerful God; Christ was not only to be loved and listened to, but actually worshipped. It is not idolatry for us to worship Christ, although he has a human face. For his resurrection proves him also to be divine.

QUESTIONS FOR DISCUSSION

1. In what ways is Jesus 'different' after the resurrection? How do these differences alter the disciples' perception of him?

2. Doubt is usually evidence of a longing to believe. Trace the stages of Thomas' growth to faith; what can his story teach us about periods of doubt in our lives?

IDEAS FOR ADULTS
Dance of the Resurrection

Have a group of dancers walking slowly in a highly organised procession, all in step, with their formation strictly kept. Heads are bowed and they are all wearing black cloaks. It should have the atmosphere of a funeral procession.

When they reach the centre front, a line of twelve children, who have been standing in front of the altar, turn to face the procession and, all together, lift up large card brightly coloured letters, which read:

Suddenly the music becomes joyful, the dancers throw off their black cloaks and dance together or separately to the music. If some can put up brightly coloured sunshades or umbrellas, so much the better. The clothes should be colourful as well. The children sway their letters in time to the music. The dance finishes with a great shout of 'Alleluia!' New Orleans jazz music is best for this.

CHILDREN'S TEACHING

Begin by passing round a 'feeling' bag with a couple of objects inside it, such as a sieve and a marble, for instance. Each child has a turn to feel the bag and guess what the objects are, but the guesses aren't shared until everyone has had a go.

Then each one says: 'I believe there's a ... in the bag'. Take the objects out to see who's right, and talk about how they didn't know for sure what was there until they saw it, but they could believe it by using clues, such as what it felt like.

Display a large sign: 'I believe Jesus is God's Son.'

How do we know?

Have we actually seen him?

What clues do we use, then?

Talk about the record of his friends in the Bible, the way Jesus helps us to be kind when we feel like being nasty, (so long as we ask him); the way he helps us through sad or painful times; and the happy feeling we have when we enjoy the lovely world with him.

Then read the Thomas section of *'Jesus is risen'* and give the children a picture of this to colour, with Thomas's prayer on it. Encourage them to use this prayer themselves in church or at home.

INTERCESSIONS **Years 1 and 2**
Some ideas for prayer

Dear friends in Christ,
as we gather here in the presence
of the living God,
let us ask for his help and guidance
in the Church and in the world.

We join in prayer with all other
worshipping Christians;
give us an increasing love and affection
between individuals and groups
in every parish and denomination;
increasing open-heartedness,
outreach and generosity of spirit.
Pause
Unchanging Lord: **we pledge ourselves to your service**

We pray for the breaking down of suspicion,
double standards and hypocrisy in our world;
that the nations may work together
to conquer the problems
of food and water distribution,
so that our planet's resources
are shared and not wasted.
Pause
Unchanging Lord: **we pledge ourselves to your service**

We pray for the homes and families
represented here, with all their particular
joys and sorrows, needs and resources;
that our lives may be
practical witnesses to our faith.
Pause
Unchanging Lord: **we pledge ourselves to your service**

We pray for those involved in medical research,
and all who suffer from diseases
which are as yet incurable;
for any who are too weak
or exhausted to pray;
for any who are desperate or suicidal.
Pause
Unchanging Lord: **we pledge ourselves to your service**

We pray that all who have died in faith may rise
to new life in glory.

Father, we thank you
for your immense compassion,
understanding and encouragement
throughout our lives.

Merciful Father
accept these prayers
for the sake of your Son,
our Saviour Jesus Christ, Amen.

NOTES ON THE READINGS **Year 2**

Exodus 16:2-15

The enthusiasm and excitement of the great escape from Egypt has started to wear off; and the people begin to feel their vulnerability and precarious survival out here in the wilderness, far from their familiar routine. Their panic leads them to grumble at Moses who stirred them up to go in the first place. So what God provides is not just food, which is the immediate problem, but also reassurance, which feeds a much more fundamental need of his children who are frightened and feel threatened.

If we find ourselves doing more than our fair share of nagging and grumbling, it may be worth laying aside all those stupid and terrible things people are doing to irritate and make life difficult for us, and instead ask God to give us reassurance of his love. When he does so, we shall probably find that the urge to nag has disappeared!

And if in our parish there seems to be a lot of carping and petty mindedness, it is often because the critics feel vulnerable and threatened in some way. Ministering to their fundamental need for reassurance of being loved, cherished and valued will promote deeper healing than head-on collisions over spiteful criticisms.

1 Corinthians 15:53-end

Underlying all our efforts and desire to become better, more loving people, is the inspiring fact that God has intervened to save us from our own destructive and mortal nature by becoming man himself and gathering all that experience, including death, into the realm of eternity. Knowing this, we need not be down-hearted, however badly things appear to be going, or however little we are appreciated. As Mother Julian of Norwich said: 'All shall be well, and all manner of things shall be well'.

John 6:32-40

Christianity must never, in any circumstances, become an élitist or exclusive religion; and if we catch even a hint of it, red lights of warning should start flashing in our heads. For when we read the words of Jesus it is quite clear that the good news of hope is freely available to *all* who believe, and no race or class is excluded.

Our spiritual feeding is provided to sustain us on our spiritual journey and we need it just as much as we need food for our bodies. It is also a source of great joy, because through it we experience the individual, personal love our heavenly Father has for each of us.

QUESTIONS FOR DISCUSSION

1. When, and in what way have you experienced Jesus as Living Bread in your own life?
2. What are the similarities and differences between the food provided in the wilderness for the people of Israel and the food offered by Jesus when he calls himself the 'Bread'?

IDEAS FOR ADULTS

Make two banners which can be hung on walls or pillars today, proclaiming Jesus' words not only during the services but also to anyone visiting the church.

The first includes the words: 'I am the bread of life' and the second: 'He who comes to me will never be hungry'. Use appliqué, collage, felt tip pens or curled paper techniques. Here are some ideas for design:

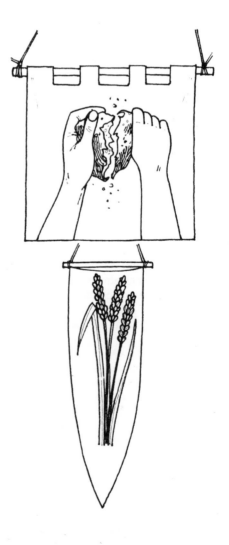

CHILDREN'S TEACHING

Remind the children of how the people were fed by Jesus, and say together the prayer written on the loaves and fishes which were made in the Children's Teaching for the 3rd Sunday after the Epiphany (page 70). Tell them how the people all got into boats and followed Jesus to Capernaum (a map is useful). What do they think the people were hoping Jesus might do? Feed them with a meal again? They may have an uncle or family friend who often gives them a treat, so they hope for one whenever they meet.

Jesus tells them he has come to give them food that will not leave them hungry a few hours later (we may eat breakfast, but we still need more food by lunchtime), and he calls this the 'bread of life'. Now read the last section of the Gospel, from '"Sir," they said'.'

Finish with a bread-making session, using a quick-action bread mix. Each child can then take some bread home to share with the family.

2nd Sunday after Easter

TODAY'S THEME

... is that Jesus leads and teaches us his ways like a good shepherd. We recognise his voice and he knows each of us by name. Just as he led the disciples, on the road to Emmaus, to the point where they recognised him in the breaking of bread, so he leads us, his sheep, to know him and trust him.

PARISH MUSIC
Hymns

Year 1
Bread of the world in mercy broken
Can it be true
Come and be filled
Come, thou long-expected Jesus
I am the bread of life (Toolan)
I am the bread of life (Konstant)
I danced in the morning
The Son of God proclaim
Who is this man?

Year 2
Faithful shepherd, feed me
Loving shepherd of thy sheep
Stand up, stand up for Jesus
The Lord is my shepherd

Recorded music
Cello Concerto (Elgar)

For choirs
Of the glorious Body telling (de Victoria): SATB
Be known to us in breaking of bread (Pulkingham)

CHURCH DECORATION

For Year 1, base one arrangement on the theme of Jesus explaining the scriptures to the disciples on the road to Emmaus so that they understood. Have an open Bible and a candle to represent enlightenment, with the vase of 'oasis' tucked down behind the propped-up book. Choose flowers which continue the idea of light — yellow, white, orange, salmon pink and apricot.

For Year 2 the theme is the Good Shepherd, so incorporate a crook, and a woolly sheep into the main arrangement. Use a pedestal, and have some thorny, prickly branches among the spring flowers and grasses. Cornflowers, almond blossom or rudbeckia, green wheat and cow parsley would all work well to create a pastoral atmosphere.

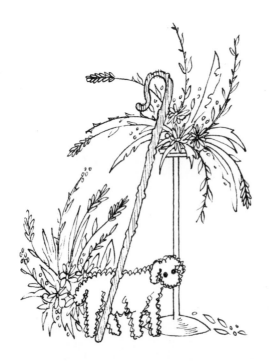

NOTES ON THE READINGS **Year 1**

Isaiah 25:6-9
The cross stands at the centre of the Bible: all the Old Testament looks towards it and all the growth of the Church is based on its foundation. The prophets had foretold that God would rescue his people, and, through them, the world. All through the years and generations the people looked forward to the coming of the Messiah, their understanding of what this meant gradually developing into the Saviour King whose reign would be established and grow for ever.

Revelation 19:6-9
As Christ enters new life at the resurrection, heaven is seen here rejoicing that all the prophecies are fulfilled in a way which goes far beyond the reign of any earthly King, however fine and noble. This Kingdom breaks open the barriers between the physical and the spiritual, between time and eternity, between heaven and earth. It means that while still walking through life in the world, we can also live, think, see and move as citizens of heaven. Christ is our King, and his heaven can now be our 'territory'.

Luke 24:13-35
The two disciples had been full of expectation. As Jesus' ministry progressed they had begun to see that he was not only a great prophet but possibly the Messiah himself. Now, at last, the Roman occupation would become a thing of the past, and Israel would once more be free and powerful.

The nails hammered into Jesus' body on Good Friday had hammered into their fervent hopes and dreams. No angel came to save him from death and when he died, so did their illusions.

Now Jesus approaches them, not abandoning them for having got it wrong, but working to redirect, explain and enlighten. Never mind if they didn't recognise him during the learning — they listened and began to think more openly, to broaden their expectations until, at the breaking of bread, things fell into place and they were filled with tremendous joy.

QUESTIONS FOR DISCUSSION

1. What do you think Jesus might have said to the two disciples on the way to Emmaus? Look up some of the these references to help you:
   Genesis 12:2-3; Psalm 108/109:4; 2 Samuel 7:16; Job 19:25; Psalm 21/22:7,8,16,18; Psalm 70/71:11; Psalm 117/118:22; Isaiah 7:13,14: 9:6,7; 11:1,2; 35:5,6; 40:11; 53; Daniel 2:44a; Micah 5:2-5; Zephaniah 9:9; 11:12,13; Malachi 3:1.

2. Are there any instances in the natural world, too, where suffering is necessary before the good can come about? Or death, before life can come about? How can we make sure that any suffering we may have is fruitful in some way?

IDEAS FOR ADULTS

Make a display for today composed of a selection of quotations from the Law of Moses, the Prophets and the Psalms which are fulfilled in Christ. Write out each quotation clearly on paper of different colours, and using matching cord or ribbon, direct attention from each to a central cross.

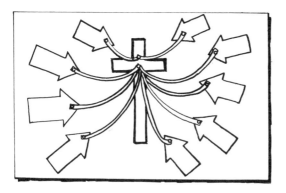

CHILDREN'S TEACHING

Read the Emmaus section of *'Jesus is Risen'* which captures the atmosphere very well. Talk about the story with the children:

- why do they think the disciples couldn't believe Jesus had risen?
- do they sometimes wonder if it is all true, and then later feel certain of Jesus being with them?
- talk about having expectations (for Christmas presents, for instance) which make us feel let down when they are not what we had in mind.
- when have they been surprised by God acting in their lives?

Teachers can give great encouragement in faith by being prepared to talk about some of their own surprises and disappointments; the children are then brought into contact with the real,

living faith, rather than history. Help the children make this pop-up scene of Jesus breaking bread.

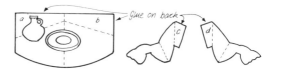

INTERCESSIONS **Years 1 and 2**
Some ideas for prayer

Rejoicing in the amazing love
of God our Father, let us pour out to him
our needs, cares and concerns.

Good Shepherd, as we see, with sorrow,
the divisions between Christian groups,
we ask you to enable us
to become one flock.
Pause
Father, hear us: **and help us to hear you**

As we see the glaring injustices of wealth
and food distribution in our world,
we ask you to give us courage
to work in your strength towards building
a safer and more caring society.
Pause
Father, hear us: **and help us to hear you**

As we watch our children growing up
and our parents growing older
and feel anxious for their future,
we ask you for the assurance
of your steadfast love,
and we entrust their lives to your perfect care.
Pause
Father, hear us: **and help us to hear you**

As we see and read in the news
of all those afflicted by natural disasters,
by terrible accidents and by war,
we ask you, O Lord of life,
to bring good out of every evil
and growth out of every suffering.
Pause
Father, hear us: **and help us to hear you**

As we remember our loved ones
who have passed through death
into eternity, we ask you
to welcome them into your light and joy
for ever.
Pause
Father, hear us: **and help us to hear you**

Loving Lord, we thank you
for the many joys and blessings
you give us each day, and for this
opportunity to worship you.
Merciful Father
accept these prayers
for the sake of your Son,
our Saviour Jesus Christ, Amen.

NOTES ON THE READINGS Year 2

Ezekiel 34:7-16
Yahweh's character of active care and selfless
compassion is being blocked by the very
'shepherds' who are supposed to be acting in his
name. Their self-interest and carelessness has
caused many to wander into danger and get lost.

The good shepherd will be personified in the
person of Jesus, whose care, patient guidance
and loving involvement has won the hearts of
millions for nearly 2,000 years.

1 Peter 5:1-11
Corruption can start anywhere. Nothing is
immune, and certainly not the church, which
is naturally enough a prime target for
temptation. History can supply us with plenty

of evidence that power corrupts, and as soon as
any religious leadership forgets that the power
and the glory belong to our heavenly Father,
there are bound to be destructive and divisive
'shepherds' whose 'sheep' suffer and get led
astray.

So we need to be constantly vigilant and
rigorous with ourselves, re-committing ourselves
regularly, examining our consciences and
checking our priorities. We shall then be
working in partnership with Christ and our lives,
lived in his strength, will draw others to the joy
of his love.

John 10:7-16
Anyone who has walked along behind sheep will
realise what Jesus meant when he talked so often
of humans as sheep. They scuttle out of
immediate danger and immediately start eating,
as if nothing had happened. Seconds later they
see danger catching up with them again so there
is another short-lived scuttle, as they follow each
other however foolishly they are led.

Hence the need for a really trustworthy
shepherd, for sheep are woefully in need of a
responsible leader. (Of course, the shepherds in
Israel always lead, rather than drive the sheep,
as in Britain.)

Some of those posing as the good shepherd can
be very convincing, so that we sheep are
sometimes coaxed into trusting them.

QUESTIONS FOR DISCUSSION

1. Can you find any parallels between the acts
   of a good shepherd described in Ezekiel, and
   events in the Gospels?
2. Humility is not a particularly prized virtue
   in our society — it is often linked in people's
   minds with weakness. What do you think
   Peter means by it here? Why is it considered
   such an important asset in leadership?

IDEAS FOR ADULTS

If there are any photographers (or snapshot-
takers) in the parish, they could start compiling
a collection of photographs for use in exhibitions
and displays.

Today, for instance, a lovely display of sheep,
shepherds and crowds of people could be shown,
with short quotations and prayers. During the
week this kind of display can become a useful
starting point for prayer and a help to visitors.

CHILDREN'S TEACHING

Have a green sheet of paper on the table with
some farmyard models of sheep and lambs, a
sheepdog and a shepherd. (Britain Toys make

a good one.) Talk with the children about what a shepherd's job involves. Some of them may have watched sheep being moved from one pasture to another. What would happen to the sheep if there was no shepherd? Talk about the way they stray into danger, and other ways they are vulnerable.

Now build a model of a sheep fold, or pen, which is used in the country Jesus lived in. Make it from small stones or from plasticine which has been given a stone pattern. The shepherd lay in the doorway to sleep, so he was the door! That kept the sheep all safe inside.

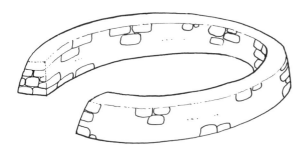

Next read the first part of today's Gospel, and help them understand that Jesus is the Good Shepherd and we are the sheep and lambs.

Then help the children to make sheep headgear on which is written: 'The Lord is my Shepherd'. Perhaps they could process, bleating into church and kneel for a moment of silence in front of the altar before joining their families.

Tie at back of head

White socks

3rd Sunday after Easter

TODAY'S THEME

. . . is that Jesus is the resurrection and the life. Not only does he live for ever — he is actually life. When we put our trust in him, we become part of that full, complete life, which death will not destroy.

PARISH MUSIC

Hymns
Christ triumphant ever reigning
Colours of day
Come into his presence
Fight the good fight
Firmly I believe and truly
God's Spirit is in my heart
I am the bread of life
Jerusalem the golden
Jesus, the joy of loving hearts
Lord, when I turn my back on you
Now the green blade riseth
O for a thousand tongues
Praise my soul the King of Heaven
Seek ye first the Kingdom of God
Thank you, Lord, for giving me life
The Spirit of the Lord is with us
This is the day of light

Recorded music
Symphony No. 8 (Mahler)

For choirs
This joyful Eastertide (Oxley): SSA
Most glorious Lord of life (Harris): STB

CHURCH DECORATION

The resurrection theme continues this week. Keep the Easter garden flourishing with pot plants and cut flowers replenished where necessary. In the main flower arrangement, hide the base in deadwood and rocks to emphasis new life springing from the dead. Try using a riot of colours of spring flowers — red, yellow, blue, orange, purple and pink — in tulips, daffodils, dianthus, and lilies (such as enchantment).

NOTES ON THE READINGS Year 1

Isaiah 61:1-7

The prophets's message is about hope in hopeless situations; restoration replacing decay; vigorous growth and vitality springing out of ruin and desolation. Good news, indeed!

Does it seem too good? Can anything really have such astonishing results? Is it perhaps all just wishful thinking?

The transformation may seem impossible, but time and again God proves it to be real — both in individual lives and in world events, whenever people abandon themselves to God. It may not take place in a flash of magic, but its growth is strong and gradual, just like renewal in nature. Think, for instance, of the abolition of slavery, or the improvement of appalling working conditions in the mines, or the present task of enabling everyone to have access to fresh water.

In all dramatic social improvements, action does not begin until people's hearts are open to see evil and burn to overcome it with good. And it works. Working in tune with the God of Life, we can bring life to every situation, however depressing.

1 Corinthians 15:1-11

Paul's calling was radical and spectacular and he never loses his amazement that God should choose one who had actually persecuted his followers. But having accepted the call, he gets on with the important business of spreading God's saving truth, devoting his entire life and energy to it, and finding that God's rich grace is always sufficient for all his needs.

John 21:1-14

Even his close friends did not at first recognise Jesus. Perhaps their minds were still half-closed to the possibility of resurrection: they had even returned to the boats Jesus had called them from. But once they realise, there is no more doubt, even though the strangeness of it all frightens them.

As so often happens, a deeper knowledge of Jesus gives rise to a deeper responsibility. Peter, gently and deliberately forgiven for his denial, is commissioned as a shepherd, to look after the wayward and feed them. Jesus will never lead us forward so we can bask in the sun and enjoy our private insights. He will always lead us in order to use us, so we should not be surprised, but honoured, if we find ourselves in situations which may be difficult. We are probably there for a reason: God has work for us to do.

QUESTIONS FOR DISCUSSION

1. One of the hardest things to understand is the way we sometimes pray so faithfully for healing, and yet the person dies. How do today's readings help us to understand this? What does complete 'healing' involve?
2. How does our faith in the risen Christ enable us to minister more helpfully to the dying and the bereaved? How does it help in our own bereavements and griefs?

IDEAS FOR ADULTS

Act out today's Gospel, with Mary and Jesus learning their parts by heart and the narrator reading the rest. Jesus can be the minister, dressed in an alb, and Mary wears simple, 'biblical' clothes. She starts walking from the back of the church and meets Jesus, who starts from the front, in a place which is visible to the congregation.

CHILDREN'S TEACHING

Tell the children the story in today's Gospel using an overhead projector or cereal packet 'television'. Explain that God not only brings life, he actually is life. You could sing *Lord of the Dance* which expresses this idea.

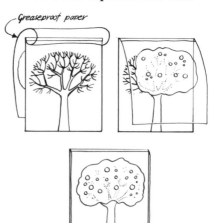

Then let the children cut out, colour and staple together these two pictures to show the effect of God's love.

INTERCESSIONS **Years 1 and 2**
Some ideas for prayer

Filled with the hope and joy
of the resurrection,
let us pray confidently
to our loving Father.

We pray for the newly baptised and their
    families;
for those who are sensing God's call
and need reassurance in it;
for all God's people
in every part of the world.
Pause
Life-giving Lord: **reign in our hearts**

We pray for the areas in which there is fighting,
unrest and unresolved conflict;
for the unprincipled, the corrupt
and those who thirst for revenge.
Pause
Life-giving Lord: **reign in our hearts**

We pray for our neighbours here; in our street;
and at school and at work; for those
with whom we live; for any who may be wishing
they knew someone willing to be friendly
and share their burden.
Pause
Life-giving Lord: **reign in our hearts**

We pray for those finding life very trying
and difficult at the moment;
for those who are coping with personal tragedy,
heartache or mourning;
for all who are ill or frail.
Pause
Life-giving Lord: **reign in our hearts**

We pray for all who have died;
that they may rise to eternal life
in the light of heaven.
Pause
Life-giving Lord: **reign in our hearts**

Father, in so many ways
we have been richly blessed;
give us thankful hearts
and make us more appreciative
of all that is good in life.

Merciful Father
accept these prayers
for the sake of your Son,
our Saviour Jesus Christ, Amen.

NOTES ON THE READINGS **Year 2**

1 Kings 17:17-end
Having been fed and sustained by the widow,
Elijah wrestles with what seems such cruel
injustice. Surely God will not allow her son to
die after she has shown such trust and kindness
to the man of God.

Elijah pleads with God for the child's life, and
his prayer is answered: the child lives, and the
widow's faith is strengthened. Had Elijah not
intervened, the child would surely have died.

Sometimes it takes a state of desperation and
heartbreaking anguish to get us praying — really
praying — with our whole being. God never
rejects such prayer. But, seeing life as he does,
in terms of eternity, restoration to life and
vitality may sometimes involve vitalising
spiritual deadness, rather than physical, and
therefore temporary health.

When we throw ourselves on his mercy in
times of terrible need and despair, we can trust
him absolutely to do what is best for us and the
one we pray for.

Colossians 3:1-11
For in Christ we can at last stop pretending; stop
inventing distractions to keep us from
uncomfortable questions about real values; stop
lurching from one craze to the next for fear of
drowning in the conviction that, though
materialism is all, it is entirely unsatisfying.

Christ is not just a set of ideas, but the living
God with a human face who can show us what
life is really about, and confirm our suspicions
that the material world is not the reason for our
existence.

He can help us break our dependency on the
created world, until we have reshuffled our
priorities. Then we begin to know the relief of
centering our lives on something of real, cosmic,
and ultimate value. This puts our whole
existence in a new perspective and brings with
it an inner peace and order we could never have
believed possible.

John 11:17-27
Jesus deliberately chose to wait until his close
friend had actually died before coming to heal
him. The pathos and overwhelming sadness and
loss of a loved one comes through this account
very powerfully. Jesus feels it to the quick, even
though he knows that Lazarus will rise again.
It is right and important that we feel able to
mourn; squashing our human grief firmly out
of sight in an effort to be brave can actually
damage us emotionally and create long-term
problems of adjustment. Yet at the same time,
beneath the pain of grief, is the quiet reassurance
that Jesus is here, Jesus loves, and Jesus cancels
death.

When he raised Lazarus to life, all those who
witnessed the event could see that God's care
and love did not finish with the pulse, and was

stronger than physical death. Even then not everyone believed. We are each of us shown evidence of God's love in action: whether we believe it or not is a personal decision which no one else can make for us.

QUESTIONS FOR DISCUSSION

1. In what ways have you noticed God is changing you for the better? (It is NOT pride to talk about such things, but an opportunity to praise God; after all, he is doing the transforming, not you!)
2. What parallels are there between this passage and Luke 5:1-11? Drawing on your own experience of the way God works in people, why do you think the disciples were given this particular assurance of Jesus' resurrection presence?

IDEAS FOR ADULTS

The Isaiah passage is full of poetry, and is most effective when read chorally by a group of readers. Use High, Medium and Low voices, with some solo lines. Try to reflect the mood as well as the meaning in the presentation, and introduce differences in pace and volume accordingly.

CHILDREN'S TEACHING

Use the Gospel and tell the story of the disciples fishing and seeing Jesus on the beach.

Divide the group into two. One group prepares the acting out (give lots of help and encourage the shy ones to participate).

The other group cuts out lots of fish, all different colours, shapes and sizes. Have a net (old curtain) and an upturned table as a boat. Then the actors perform to the fish makers.

If this were prepared beforehand, the children could present their performance during the Gospel. Otherwise, let them take a fish home with them to remind them of what happened. Suggest they tell their families, or draw a picture of it to bring back next week.

4th Sunday after Easter

TODAY'S THEME

... is that Jesus is the Way, the Truth and the Life. As we follow in his footsteps we experience the fellowship of his company, which gives us both courage to do his work and also peace of mind, even when life is difficult.

PARISH MUSIC
Hymns
Alleluia, hearts to heaven
All ye who seek a comfort sure
Be still and know that I am God
Be thou my guardian and my guide

Be thou my vision
Come and go with me
Come down O love divine
Father who in Jesus found us
Go in peace to be Christ's body
Good shepherd you have shown your care
Hark! hark my soul
If you are thirsting
I heard the voice of Jesus say
I trust in thee O Lord
Jerusalem the golden
Lord Jesus Christ
O Jesus I have promised
O Lord all the world belongs to you
Thou art the way: by thee alone

Recorded music
Fantasia on Greensleeves (Vaughan
    Williams)

For choirs
Christ is the world's true light (Stanton):
    U with descant
A prayer of St. Richard of Chichester
    (White): U with descant

CHURCH DECORATION

Some churches have a disused door — perhaps
a former side entrance — which is never opened.
Well, today is a lucky day for unused doors! The
famous Holman Hunt picture of Jesus, the light
of the world, knocking at the door of our hearts,

is based on one of today's readings; it would be
very helpful to express the theme in flowers.

Round the sides of the door arrange trailing
ivy and wild flowers and grasses, the containers
hidden with stones and pebbles. The main
arrangement represents the Light of the World.
Drape a stand with a length of pale yellow
material. Tape a tall piece of 'oasis' firmly in
a shallow bowl, so that you can create a circle
of flowers, radiating out from a crimson centre.
Towards the outer part of the circle, blend the
colours through red, orange and gold to yellow.
(That may sound offensive, but in fact the effect
is a brilliant throb of light — try it and see!)

NOTES ON THE READINGS **Year 1**

Isaiah 62:1-5
God's forgiveness is supremely generous; his
loyalty is unswerving. He has promised to save
his people and he will keep his word, so that they
are uplifted and redeemed.

Why will he do this? Simply because he loves
his people.

Revelation 3:14-end
We all do incredibly stupid and unkind things
from time to time, not necessarily through
malice but because we simply don't see at the
time what damage our thoughtless words or
actions are causing. In this passage the church
in Laodicea is given a severe ticking off for such
behaviour, which if we are honest with
ourselves, we can see is a result of the kind of
self-assured complacency which blinds us to the
needs of others. When Mother Teresa visited
London the press tried to draw her into
describing the horrors of poverty in India. She
shocked many people by talking instead about
the spiritual poverty of many in the richer
countries. It came as a surprise to many to find
themselves described as being poor.

We don't have to be, of course. We can open
the door when Jesus knocks, and enjoy the
richness of his company for every day of our
lives. It's just that so often we prefer the squalid,
narrow darkness to the risk of opening up to the
Lord of Light.

John 21:15-22
God's forgiving nature and his yearning for us
to be reconciled with him is illustrated clearly
in this conversation between Jesus and Peter.
We can all understand why Peter had denied
Jesus — it's just the kind of thing that many of
us would do in the circumstances — but that
doesn't make it right, or even excusable. God

never pretends we haven't sinned when we have; what he does is to encourage us to repentance and then offer his complete forgiveness. Then we can get on with our journey together, for the good of the world.

QUESTIONS FOR DISCUSSION

1. Do we sometimes avoid the difficult task of forgiving people by excusing them instead? How is forgiveness different from excusing?
2. How does this commission given to Peter differ from being 'fishers of men'? What can we learn from Jesus' willingness to trust Peter with such an important task even after his denial?

IDEAS FOR ADULTS

If possible, display a copy of the *Light of the World* picture near the altar.

CHILDREN'S TEACHING

Remind the children of how Peter had denied Jesus three times when he was frightened of what might happen to him if he told the truth. Discuss times when we feel scared of doing the right thing (like owning up, for instance) and how we don't feel really comfortable with someone we have hurt until we've said sorry and they have forgiven us.

Now tell or read how Jesus puts things right again for Peter, and even trusts him again. Jesus does the same with us — he will always give us another chance.

Help each child make a zig-zag picture to show how turning away from God makes him and us miserable. Turning back to him makes him and us happy. Each picture is coloured, cut in strips and pasted on to thin card in the order: 1A 2B 3C 4D etc. Fold the finished card like a fan, and the two pictures will emerge when viewed from one side or the other.

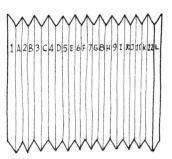

INTERCESSIONS **Years 1 and 2**
Some ideas for prayer

My companions in Christ,
as we gather in the great hope
of our risen Lord who leads us,
let us pray to God who has
shown us such patient love.

We pray for unity among all
who follow the Way of Christ;
that in keeping our eyes fixed on him
we may be enabled to dissolve barriers,
to forgive and be reconciled,
through the healing power
of accepting love.
Pause
Lord, guide us: **to do things your way**

We pray for all in positions of
responsibility and leadership, both
internationally and in our own community;
that they may themselves be led
by your Spirit to make wise decisions
and help create a humane and caring world.
Pause
Lord, guide us: **to do things your way**

We pray for our homes and families,
with their hopes and sorrows,
difficulties and celebrations;
that all our relationships may be

bathed in your love and compassion.
Pause
Lord, guide us: **to do things your way**

We pray for those who incite others
to antisocial or criminal behaviour;
for all involved in drugs traffic;
that they may open their hearts
and allow you to transform and heal;
for the weak, lonely, young and depressed
who are so vulnerable to their temptations;
give them help and strength to resist
the pressures on and around them.
Pause
Lord, guide us: **to do things your way**

We pray that those who have died in faith
may be welcomed into the eternal joy
of heaven, to live with you for ever.

We thank you for all the richness
of this beautiful world, for the gift of life
and time to spend; for the example
and companionship of Jesus.

Merciful Father
accept these prayers
for the sake of your Son,
our Saviour Jesus Christ, Amen.

NOTES ON THE READINGS **Year 2**

Proverbs 4:10-19
The image of a clear, well-lit path is a good one
for describing the right way to 'walk' through
life. It even sounds fairly straightforward, for
we have all the signposts to tell us which way
to go. But whether you are out rambling or
driving through a one-way system in a strange
town, the theory never seems to work out in
practice. Signposts are rarely enough to stop you
making several unintentional detours! Sound
though the advice in this passage is, it highlights
the rather disheartening human weakness of
finding it virtually impossible to obey rules for
long, however fine they may be.

2 Corinthians 4:13-5:5
In Jesus, however, freely given obedience is
clearly visible. Even while on the receiving end
of man's rejection, he submitted willingly to
God's law of outreaching and forgiving love. In
him the rejected God, and the man choosing to
love, are fused together, producing such a highly
potent force that evil can no longer win.

This would only be useful to us if we could
in some way join forces with Jesus, this
man/God; if only there were some way of
soaking up his life-force, we could actually share
the triumph over evil in our own lives!

Happily for us, that is exactly what God makes
possible. The only credential needed is to believe
in Jesus, and then we are given a free pass for
the very qualities which seem so unattainable.
We are promised new, rich, full lives, not just
in this world but in the world to come; in the
light of which, the alluring glitter and neon,
tempting us to sin, are shown up clearly for the
sham and deceitful trash they are.

John 14:1-11
So we can take heart and be encouraged, because
Jesus does not just give us a list of instructions
and directions — he actually comes with us every
spiritual mile of the way. As we travel there will
be conversation, which is prayer. As we watch
how our companion deals with hostility, danger
and weariness we shall learn through experience
the good way to tackle problems, and we shall
gradually become more and more like him.
Then we will realise the joy of what it means to
be truly a child of God — for our companion is
both God's Son and our brother.

QUESTIONS FOR DISCUSSION

1. Do we sometimes try to live a good life by
   following Christian rules rather than setting
   out each day with Jesus as our companion?
   How, in practice, can we walk the Way with
   Jesus?
2. Why do you think Philip wanted Jesus to
   show them the Father? How does this suggest
   he had been thinking of Jesus?

IDEAS FOR ADULTS

Have a series of footprints taped down on the
floor, starting at the door and going up to the
altar.

CHILDREN'S TEACHING

Working on the theme of Jesus being 'The
Way', begin by setting up two model villages,
built by the children in lego or building blocks,
in different parts of the room.

When they are finished, sit down with the
children between the villages and talk about how
the people could get from one to the other,
through the wild countryside. They could have
little arrows at intervals — but in fog you might
get lost between the signs. They could have
instructions, like: 'turn left at the second tree'
— but suppose the wind blew a tree down, or
another one grew up? You could lose your way.

What we really need is a clear road or track
to walk along, which goes directly to the distant
town. (Draw a road in chalk.) Now tell the
children how Jesus said he was the Way, or road,

to God in heaven, so if we want to get there we just have to follow him.

Help them make a spiritual map, with Baptism town at one corner, and The Heavenly City at another. The way winds round all kinds of dangerous mountains, rushing rivers, thick forests etc., but never disappears until it reaches the City. Along the road they write in: Jesus said, 'I am the Way'. Colour in the maps and display them in church if possible.

Try singing: *One more step along the road I go* or *Forward in faith*   (MWTP, 54).

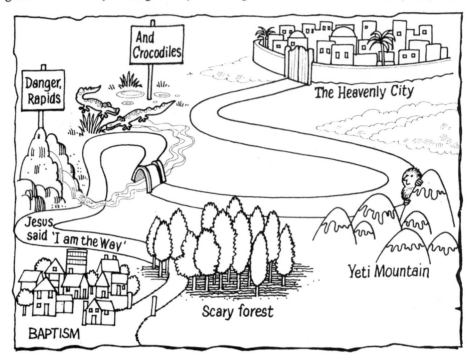

5th Sunday after Easter

TODAY'S THEME

... is that nothing can ever separate us from God's love. Our new life in the risen Christ is a journey home to the Father, and since God is on our side we need not be anxious and afraid, no matter what may happen to us on the way.

PARISH MUSIC

Hymns
A safe stronghold our God is still
At the name of Jesus
Christ be beside me
Comfort, comfort my people
Do not be afraid
Fight the good fight
From glory to glory advancing
Glorify the Lord
God is working his purpose out
Great indeed are your works
How lovely on the mountains
I danced in the morning
Lord, thy Word abideth
O strength and stay
Praise to the holiest in the height
Stand up, stand up for Jesus
The steadfast love of the Lord
Through all the changing scenes of life
Walk with me, oh my Lord

Recorded music
Pavane (Fauré)

For choirs
Now the God of peace (G.H. Knight)
Benedictus qui venit (Palestrina): SAT

CHURCH DECORATION

Today's arrangements need to express the confidence of walking joyfully 'home' to the Father. Use strong, bold lines and clear, bright colour with flowers such as lilies, dahlia, tithonia and gaillardia.

NOTES ON THE READINGS **Year 1**

Hosea 6:1-6
On his side, God is utterly dependable. If he promises us something he will never go back on his word and he never reaches a point beyond which he loses interest in us or feels we are no longer worth bothering with.

In contrast, our love for him is often spasmodic and wavering, as ephemeral as clouds or morning dew. Since we are made in the likeness of God, we are actually capable of much deeper, stronger love, and do often give it to parents, marriage partners or close friends.

This is the kind of love God wants us to have for him, and for those he has made, rather than a casual habit of going through the motions of sacrifice (or, in our terms, church-going and prayer reciting).

1 Corinthians 15:21-28
It is impossible to explain eternal matters in terms of time, or to explain the relationship between Christ and the Father in human terms, since these things are more vast and extra-ordinary than we can ever understand. But Paul does his best, and through his earth-bound words we can glimpse something of the cosmic glory of God's plan surging into a splendid accomplishment, ordered and perfect, bearing along with it, as a huge glacier collects varied rocks and minerals, all sorts of different lives.

Death is the great barrier between time and timelessness and Christ has already broken through it. When all who belong to him in every age have been raised to life, death will itself have died, and the great work of an almighty, loving God will be complete in a perpetual state of joy, peace and love.

John 16:25-end
Jesus is the first fruit and his was the loneliest journey ever made. We sense his human apprehension here, when he knows what is before him and knows, too, that even his most loyal friends will be unable to support him. Almost immediately comes the inner assurance from God, his Father, to encourage and strengthen him — Jesus will not be entirely alone because God will never desert him, even though he may be hidden from sight and insight. The tone of Jesus' words changes from sorrow to confident and inspiring joy as he remembers his Father's unswerving loyalty and love. It can sustain and encourage us as well, because the promise extends to everyone who puts trust in God.

QUESTIONS FOR DISCUSSION

1. What evidence can you see, in the world, of the human capacity for deep, unswerving loyalty or love, lavished on both good and evil causes?
2. Do you sometimes get discouraged in faith because of all the evil in our world? How do the readings today give us confidence again?

IDEAS FOR ADULTS

The first passage can be read chorally, using groups of men, women and children.

All	Come, let us return to the Lord;
Men	for he has torn us
All	and will heal us,
Women	he has struck us
All	and he will bind up our wounds;
Children	after two days he will revive us,
Women	on the third day he will restore us
All	that in his presence we may live.
Men	Let us humble ourselves,
Women	let us strive to know the Lord,
All	whose justice dawns like morning light,
Children	and its dawning is as sure as the sunrise.
Women	It will come to us like a shower,
All	like spring rains that water the earth.
Men and Women	O Ephraim, how shall I deal with you? How shall I deal with you, Judah?
Women	Your loyalty to me is like the morning mist,
Children	like dew that vanishes early.
Men	Therefore have I lashed you through the prophets
All	and torn you to shreds with my words;
Men	loyalty is my desire,
Children	not sacrifice,
Women	not whole-offerings
All	but the knowledge of God.

CHILDREN'S TEACHING

Have ready an assortment of pictures and newspaper cuttings about good and bad things in our world. Talk with the children about some of the very good things in the world. Is it all good? What sort of bad things happen? (Wars, not enough food for some, quarrels, selfishness, crimes etc.) Read them the words of Jesus: 'In the world you will have trouble. But courage! The victory is mine; I have conquered the world.' So although there are bad things, and some of them will happen to us during life, God's goodness has already won over evil, so evil can NEVER win. Sing *I have a friend who is deeper than the ocean* (MWTP, 96) and give each child a duplicated paper, personalised with his or her own name.

>Don't be afraid,...................,
>because I will look after you
>and keep you safe.
>You stick up for me
>and I will stick up for you.
>Together we'll make the world
>a happier place.

They can decorate it and keep it to read whenever they need courage to do the right thing.

INTERCESSIONS **Years 1 and 2**
Some ideas for prayer

My Christian sisters and brothers,
as we rejoice at being called
and chosen by our heavenly Father,
let us speak with him
of our needs and concerns.

Father, we commend to your love
all leaders and teachers in the Church;
that in all they do and say
they may stay close to you,
alert to your will and constantly prepared
to move forward where you guide.
Pause
Father, hear us: **keep us in your love**

We commend to your love
all talks and negotiations in industry
and in matters of international concern;
that they may be marked by generosity of spirit,
and a desire for reconciliation
that comes only from you.
Pause
Father, hear us: **keep us in your love**

We commend to your love
all who are especially precious to us,
and all with whom we find it difficult to relate;
that we may always treat one another
with Christlike love.
Pause
Father, hear us: **keep us in your love**

We commend to your love
all outsiders and outcasts, all who have been rejected by their family or their country;
that rifts may be healed,
relationships repaired

and new bonds of love forged in Christ.
Pause
Father, hear us: **keep us in your love**

We commend to your love
those who have reached the end
of their journey on earth;
welcome them into your heavenly kingdom
and bring us, too, at death,
safely home.

Heavenly Father,
with you beside us
our journey is so richly blessed
with joy and peace; how can we ever thank you
for the generosity of your love
and ceaseless care!

Merciful Father
**accept these prayers
for the sake of your Son,
our Saviour Jesus Christ, Amen.**

NOTES ON THE READINGS **Year 2**

Deuteronomy 34
Moses' great spiritual journey home was matched with his leadership of the great desert journey of the people of Israel to their promised homeland. He is respected and honoured throughout Judaism, Christianity and Islam, and the overpowering mark of his greatness is his closeness to God all along the way.

Romans 8:28-end
When we are down on our luck, feeling at our worst and least pleasant or attractive, or needing the kind of help which involves using people's time and energy — these are the times we find out who our real friends are. Mysteriously, some 'friends' are nowhere around, while others (often those who surprise us) turn out to have accepted us, warts and all, and are prepared to put themselves out to help us.

God's love is of that steadfast, persevering and loyal kind, which means that we do not need to put on any mask in his company. He knows our bad tempers, irritating habits, personal indulgences and particular nastinesses, which we prefer not to be seen too often. He knows us at our very worst, and yet still loves us and tenderly cares for us, boots us sharply if we need it, gives us opportunity for rest when we are getting frayed at the edges, plunges us into hard work when we can cope and buoys us up on a calm sea of peace when everything around us is in turmoil.

That is the kind of love which binds us to Christ, and the bond is surer and firmer than any glue. Nothing can worm its way between us and not even the most terrible catastrophes affect it: not even death itself. He holds out his hand to us; if we take it, we shall never be lost or alone again.

John 16:12-24

Jesus' teaching to his puzzled and rather bewildered disciples speaks of a constantly growing and developing relationship; our faith is not a pickled, preserved entity but a dynamic, living organism, constant and yet flowing. We curb its flow and block its power whenever we forget this.

For Jesus is not only a historical figure living in Palestine during the Roman occupation there. He is also alive now and in every generation, speaking the language of each age and culture, understanding the particular problems and temptations of every time and nation.

So our faith is never outdated or irrelevant; provided we are receptive to God, he will always express himself in ways that humanity understands, and always lead us in truth.

QUESTIONS FOR DISCUSSION

1. Look over the events of Moses' life and notice the way he reacts to difficulties. What can his prayer life teach us?
2. How do you think we can balance the value of changelessness in vital doctrine with the vitality of a living faith whose face is always contemporary?

IDEAS FOR ADULTS

A dance, showing a Christian pilgrim encountering many difficulties on his way, is an effective means of conveying today's theme. The Christian should be carrying a heavy bag or suitcase as he travels round the church towards the altar, and a cross. On the way have groups of dancers providing the difficulties: e.g.

- having a party and coaxing him to stay and join in; — (he stays a while, dancing, then goes on);
- jumping out at him with masks to frighten him and turn him back; (he is scared, then holds his cross firmly and passes them);
- making a dense forest that he has to work hard to get through.

Have some saints to cheer him on (the congregation) and a shout of triumph when he arrives and kneels, arms raised, at the altar. (The case is abandoned just before the finish, so he is free to dance up to the altar.)

CHILDREN'S TEACHING

Talk with the children about how we can keep in touch with people when they are in different places; for example: radio, telephone, radar, letters. Talk about when these aids are used for space travel, docking a ship, in aeroplanes, or at other times when it would be dangerous to act without the guidance of someone who can see better than we can, and who knows all the relevant information.

In life, God is at the base control, and can see the whole picture of what is happening — not just our little bit of it. He is able and willing to guide us through and stay in close contact all the time. Now show them a telephone. What do we have to do to get in touch with someone at the other end of the line? Explain that although God is always in touch with us, we won't be able to talk to him and listen to him unless we keep in touch from our end, too. And that's what praying is.

Help the children make yoghurt pot telephones. Write on them at one end: 'Don't forget to keep in touch with God' and at the other end: 'God always listens'.

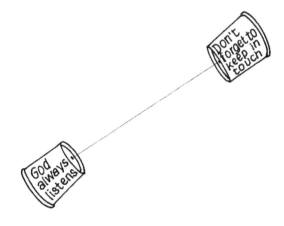

Ascension Day and Sunday after Ascension

TODAY'S THEME

. . . is that Jesus has ascended into heaven. With his ministry complete, and death conquered, Jesus takes his place at the right hand of God. No longer tied by time and place he reigns in glory.

PARISH MUSIC

Hymns

Alleluia, sing to Jesus

A man there lived in Galilee

Angel voices ever singing

At the name of Jesus
Hail thee, Festival Day
Let all the world in every corner sing
Jesus shall reign where'er the sun
The head that once was crowned with
    thorns
There's no greater name than Jesus
Child of the manger, infant of Mary
Christ triumphant, ever reigning
Come into his presence
Come let us join our cheerful songs
Crown him with many crowns
Hail the day that sees him rise
How lovely on the mountains
I cannot tell why he
Immortal, invisible
Lord enthroned in heavenly splendour
Majesty, worship his majesty
O King enthroned on high
Praise my soul the King of heaven
Rejoice! The Lord is King
See the conqueror mounts in triumph

Recorded music
Symphony No. 5 (Shostakovich)

For choirs
Above all praise and all majesty
    (Mendelssohn): SATB
Lift up your heads O ye gates (Amner):
    SATB
God is gone up with a shout
    (Pulkingham)

CHURCH DECORATION

Try decorating the walls and pillars today with bands of flower garlands made like the swags shown in the drawing on page 50. Traditionally the horse chestnut is called the Ascension tree, since its huge clusters of candle-like blossoms are in bloom at this time. If you have a tree near by, why not use its blossom in arrangements. It would be wise to use wire mesh instead of or as well as oasis, as the branches will be heavy.

NOTES ON THE READINGS **Year 1**

Daniel 7:9-14
This amazing vision looks through the darkness of time to the joy of heaven, as Jesus is led into God's presence, having accomplished the saving of humankind. Of course, no pictures can really grasp the meaning, but Daniel's language gives us a wonderful sensation of worth, dignity, grace, truth and rejoicing. Like a magnet, Christ draws many people from all nations into his kingdom which shall never end.

We have the privilege of living in this last age, when all the peoples of the earth are being brought to know and acknowledge him as Lord of All.

Ephesians 1:15-end
When we look at the incredible details of Jesus' life — his teaching and signs, his death and resurrection — we cannot fail to be impressed by the power illustrated there. Thankfully it is a loving power; some of the 'star wars' sagas hint at the terror and devastation that would result from a similarly powerful force of evil. Though fiction, all such stories, both ancient and modern, depict an instinctive human terror of evil taken to the ultimate.

As Christians we are privileged to see glimpses of goodness taken to the ultimate. It is revealed in the person of Jesus, who, through complete unselfishness, has brought mankind into a new relationship with the seat of power — God himself.

His great, universal, cosmic presence draws all things towards the splendid all-glorious harmony of completion. We have been chosen to work in harness with him to achieve it.

Luke 24:45-end
Jesus emphasises the fact that his death and suffering were all a necessary part of his work of salvation. Without his physical presence

which they had always relied on, the disciples needed to understand the mystery of how death is a source of life, suffering a source of joy, and giving a means of receiving. They cannot understand these things without Jesus, so he promises them his ever present life — his Spirit; and the disciples, trusting him, return to Jerusalem full of joy.

QUESTIONS FOR DISCUSSION

1. Does our worship sometimes concentrate too much on the fellowship of the body of Christ and too little on the awesome glory of God? How can we achieve one without losing the other?

2. Jesus had left them and yet the disciples were full of joy. How and why had their outlook changed since the resurrection?

IDEAS FOR ADULTS

Dance of the Ascension
This dance conveys the spread of Christ's power of love as it reaches more and more people, bringing them new life and hope. For the music, use Psalm 97 as set to music on page 139.

Begin with the dancers arranged like this, each one

```
              2
          1       3
      4,5             8,9
              6,7
        10           12
              11
```

crouched down close to the ground and completely still. Together they all say: "Jesus said to them, 'Go out to the whole world, proclaim the Good News to all creation.' " They kneel, sitting back on their heels during a silent count of three, then repeat the words. They kneel up, with arms raised during a silent count of three, then repeat the words loudly and clearly for the third time. The choir and/or congregation now sing the psalm, beginning with the verse, not the response.

WORDS	ACTION
Let us sing a new song to the Lord	*All dancers sit back on heels again, except 1, 2 and 3. They stand facing inwards holding hands, heads bowed.*
for the wonderful things he has done;	*They step forward, swinging joined hands up to the centre; step back, swinging arms back; step forward, swinging arms up; release hands and each turn.*
with his holy and powerful arm	*They join right hands in centre, weight on bent right leg, as left arm is brought up, over shoulder and extended to cover right hand.*
his salvation is brought to us all	*They hop on right foot, step back transferring weight to left foot as left arm is extended like this:* 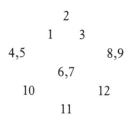

then pivot on left foot as right arm is brought up to 'match', before both arms are brought forward in a gesture of offering.

All the ends of the earth have now seen

They bend knees and lower arms, turn palms upwards and gradually 'unfold' until they are poised on tip-toe (only for a split second!) with both arms raised, palms still flat up and eyes up.

the salvation brought to us by God.

They each run to the nearest group and kneel facing them, arms extended from the elbow.

During the next verse the new groups go through the same action. At the end of the next response they run and regroup like this:

```
            1                    3
         10  4              8  12
                   2
                6  11

                5  7
                 9
```

The actions are now repeated with even more people participating. At the end of the response this time each group of three hold hands.

O sing psalms to the Lord with the harp

They skip 4 steps to the right.

and with music sing praise to the Lord;

They skip 4 steps to the left.

with the trumpet and blasts of the horn

Holding hands in a line, each group skips across to the centre, where they form one circle.

we acknowledge the Lord who is King.

They stand with feet apart, transferring weight from foot to foot 4 times, arms extended up like this:

All the ends of the earth have now seen

They bend knees as before and gradually unfold, facing outwards.

the salvation brought to us by God.

They take 2 steps and on 'salVAtion they all make a great leap of joy with one arm up, as in victory; then slowly kneel down on one knee, raising head and right arm on 'God'.

PSALM 97

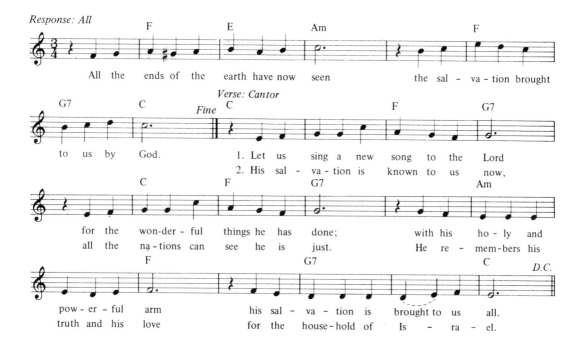

Response: All

All the ends of the earth have now seen the sal - va - tion brought to us by God.

Verse: Cantor

1. Let us sing a new song to the Lord for the won-der-ful things he has done; with his ho-ly and pow-er-ful arm his sal - va - tion is brought to us all.

2. His sal - va - tion is known to us now, all the na-tions can see he is just. He re - mem-bers his truth and his love for the house-hold of Is - ra - el.

3. All the ends of the earth have now seen
   the salvation brought to us by God.
   Shout aloud to the Lord, all the earth,
   as you ring out your joy in his praise.

4. O sing psalms to the Lord with the harp,
   and with music sing praise to the Lord;
   with the trumpet, and blasts of the horn,
   we acknowledge the Lord who is King.

CHILDREN'S TEACHING

It is not widely known that children are still entitled to take time off from school on Ascension Day in order to go to church. If you decide to have a special children's service, make out a form for the children to take into school and use the occasion to witness through courtesy and goodwill.

Keep the service simple and involve the children in the planning, reading, singing and decorating.

For the Sunday after Ascension, start by showing the children a bright cut-out sun, then cover it from sight with a cut-out cloud. Is the sun still there? Show that it is. We do not always see it because it is sometimes hidden from view, but we know it is always there. How?

Talk about life and growth and light and warmth. If we shut ourselves in where the sun cannot reach us we couldn't survive. Can we see Jesus? No. Then what do we mean when we say he is alive? Where is he?

Read them an account of the Ascension as told in Acts. His friends had seen him a lot after he had come back to life on the first Easter Day, and now, like the sun behind a cloud, he is hidden from sight for a time. (Show a bright card with JESUS written on it, and put the cloud in front.) But he is just as much alive as before. As our King he reigns over everything — people, animals, the sun, the stars, the universe!

Ask some children to draw and colour flowers and trees, some animals and people, some stars and planets, mountains, seas and weather. Then mount all their work on a big collage banner, with OUR GOD REIGNS written over the top. This can be carried into the church in procession.

INTERCESSIONS **Years 1 and 2**
Some ideas for prayer

Trusting in Christ's victory over all evil, let us pray to the Father for the world and the Church.

We pray for all who witness to Christ in spite of danger and persecution; all who work to bring others to know and love you; that in your strength they may be blessed, encouraged and bear much fruit.
Pause
King of glory: **reign in our hearts**

We pray for those who have never received the Good News of your saving love; for those areas where violence and terrorism make normal life impossible; that the spirit of Jesus, the Prince of Peace, may filter through to increase love and understanding, respect and goodwill.
Pause
King of glory: **reign in our hearts**

We pray for our families and those with whom we live and work; for particular needs known to us personally; that in everything we do, and every minute we live, your name may be glorified and your will be done.
Pause
King of glory: **reign in our hearts**

We pray for the sick and the dying; that their trust in you may deepen until their fears are calmed and they can look forward with real hope to meeting their Saviour face to face.
Pause
King of glory: **reign in our hearts**

We pray for those who have died; may they wake to the joy of eternal life with you.

We offer you thanks and praise for your constant love and kindness, and especially for the joy of your salvation.

Merciful Father
**accept these prayers
for the sake of your Son,
our Saviour Jesus Christ, Amen.**

NOTES ON THE READINGS **Year 2**

2 Kings 2:1-15
To be allowed to see Elijah taken up into heaven meant that Elisha would indeed be granted his request — to inherit a double share of Elijah's

spirit. We can see the parallels between this account and the account of the disciples who witnessed Jesus' ascension and also received his spirit.

Such insight and perception was only possible because both Elisha and the disciples made themselves available, and were used to seeing God working in the master they followed. Elijah, following in the great tradition of Moses, had been drawn to an intimate relationship with God; it was these two who spoke with Christ at the Transfiguration, which three of the disciples also witnessed. Their lives express the powerful and dramatic use God makes of lives which are freely offered for his service.

Ephesians 4:1-13

After the Ascension, Jesus will no longer be *with* his disciples; he will be *in* them instead, and they prepare themselves to receive his power.

The power they await is unmatched by any other power in any generation. Its potency brought stars and planets into being, generates life, and charges the universe with purpose; in Christ it broke through death and destruction to unsurpassed glory. All time and space is poised in the harmony of that power; and as limbs and organs of Christ's Body, the Church, we have it pulsing through us, vital and glowing. Through us Jesus reaches everyone we talk to, everyone whose lives our lives touch. Through us he restores confidence, soothes and comforts, strengthens and supports, heals and reconciles. Whenever we decide not to co-operate, the whole Body's effectiveness is weakened.

Luke 24:45-end

As witnesses to Christ's ascension, his disciples are commissioned to tell the Good News in Christ's name to all the nations, starting where they are already — Jerusalem. It was a commission which could only come from one who was divine, with full authority over everything, seen and invisible. In his body, Jesus ministered to those living in and around Galilee; in his spiritual body (which includes us) he would be ministering to every person in every country. That is what mission is all about.

We may not need to travel very far before we meet people who do not yet know Jesus. They may be lost, or searching among the dustbins for spiritual food, when there is a meal served up specially for them. It is both our duty and our joy to bring these people to Christ. to introduce them to Christ by our caring behaviour, our forgiveness, open-heartedness and joy.

QUESTIONS FOR DISCUSSION

1. What do we learn of the characteristics of Elijah and Elisha from this passage?
2. The gifts described in Ephesians are not necessarily the inherited gifts we are born with (or without!) but are seen as resulting from the power of the Spirit of God. Can you think of any incidences in the Gospels where this commissioning with gifts to do particular tasks is evident in individuals?

IDEAS FOR ADULTS

Posters on the theme of Christ, reigning in glory, can be made for today, to direct people's attention to God's glory all around us. They can be painted, or worked in collage, and show God's glory in the seas and oceans, stars and planets, hills and mountains, animals and birds.

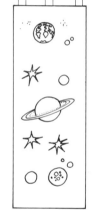

CHILDREN'S TEACHING

In an effort to steer clear of false impressions, we sometimes avoid teaching children about heaven. Today is a good opportunity to put that right. Start with a game. In a box have slips of paper which describe things in terms of other things:

    — a bit like an orange but not so sweet, and coloured yellow;

    — a kind of chair which has no back;

    — a tall sort of cup;

    — a wax stick that you can burn slowly; etc.

Point out that if you had not known before what a lemon was, you would have a better idea now, but not an exact idea until you actually saw a lemon yourself. Show them one. And similarly with the other items described.

It is the same with heaven. Pictures and words in the Bible give us clues but no more.

Show a large round poster with these words written all round the edge;

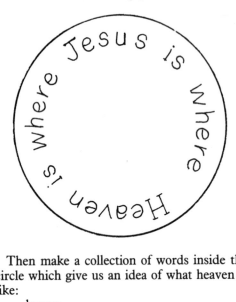

Then make a collection of words inside the circle which give us an idea of what heaven is like:

– happy
– beauty
– peace
– joy
– no worry
– Daddy finds you when you were lost
– like when you give Nana your best drawing and she's very pleased
– like when your friends ask you to join in their game, etc.

Stress that these are only clues, but try to show them some idea of what being with Jesus means in feelings they can understand, rather than looking at the idea of 'place'.

Let the children decorate the words with lovely bright colours and patterns and if possible display the poster in church.

PENTECOST

Pentecost

TODAY'S THEME

... is the Holy Spirit, poured out on the disciples with a rush of wind and with tongues of fire. Ever since, God's Holy Spirit has enriched and empowered all who open their hearts and minds to receive it.

PARISH MUSIC

Hymns
All over the world the Spirit is moving
Blow in me, Spirit of God
Breathe on me, Breath of God
Come down, O love divine
Come, Holy Ghost, our souls inspire
Come thou holy Paraclete
Father, Lord of all creation
Fill thou my life, O Lord my God
Give me joy in my heart
Glory be to the Spirit
Hail thee, Festival Day
I love the name of Jesus
Jesu gentlest Saviour
Listen, let your heart keep seeking
Love divine all loves excelling
O Breath of life
Our blest redeemer, e'er he breathed
Send forth your Spirit O God
Spirit of the living God
Spirit, come and make us new

Recorded music
Symphony No. 6 (Sibelius)

For choirs
Come, thou Holy Spirit (Palestrina, ed. E.C. Gregory)
O Lord, give thy Holy Spirit (Tallis)

CHURCH DECORATION

This is always another lovely festival to express in flowers — the theme of the Holy Spirit coming in the form of wind and fire immediately gets the imagination tingling! Colours will be predominantly red, but not exclusively. Introduce orange, peach, gold and yellow as well and create sweeping lines with lots of movement. Ornamental grasses can work most effectively to give the impression of rushing wind.

NOTES ON THE READINGS **Years 1 and 2**

Genesis 11:1-9

This is not a cautionary tale against progress; it is a story which illustrates humanity's mistake in attempting to 'outdo' God and live independently from him. The ziggurat on which the story is probably based, was an attempt to build a kind of holy mountain artificially in the middle of a flat plain. As we know from Moses and Elijah, mountains were considered special meeting places for God and his chosen; in that context we can appreciate the arrogance and insulting vanity of using the gift of unity for such a project.

OR

Exodus 19:16-25

When Moses leads the people of Israel to meet their God, the whole atmosphere is filled with awe and dread, highlighted by the quaking, fiery mountain, the sound of thunder and the smoke. Moses alone is summoned to the sacred top of the mountain to speak with God.

Acts 2:1-11

The first effect of the Holy Spirit at Pentecost is the breaking down of barriers. All those present are able to understand the ecstatic message of God's saving power and love, unleashed as the Church is born. It is like the first fruits of a great harvest which still goes on today; it challenges the world with a radically new law of love; it is the victorious Christ, alive, strong and in charge. No wonder the disciples were full of such rapturous joy — if God was with them to this extent, then who could possibly be against them?

When we know this experience it is indeed breathtaking, invigorating and tremendously exciting. God has overcome the world. He comes with us in person.

Acts 2:1-21

The apostles have been commissioned to tell all people everywhere about Jesus; the magnificent sign of being understood by everyone without a language barrier serves to encapsulate this task of the apostles and all their successors.

As time passes initial fervour usually fades, but since this fervour is occasioned by the power of a living God, it continues to burst out in every generation of believers. People still find their lives drastically transformed through an encounter with Christ; many still find the Spirit so real and invigorating that sacrifices are undertaken with joyful serenity; unpleasant and dangerous work is gladly undertaken; individuals stand firm to witness in a corrupt society, and countless numbers spread love and peace daily among those around them.

There is still much to be done. But, living in the Spirit, we can work as harvesters and take part in establishing God's kingdom on earth.

John 14:15-26

Wherever people come together to focus their hope on their Lord, and submerge their own selfishness in their longing to be part of him, Jesus stands among them and his presence is powerfully experienced in a wave of joy. Although at such times Christians are aware of their unworthiness, Christ's presence does not give rise to an inward groan of despair as one might expect when he is so loving and we have let him down so often.

Instead there is a sense of contentment and tranquillity; a light-heartedness as all problems are seen in the context of someone who is loving, forgiving, and in full control. Faces relax and eyes soften; many feel great warmth of affection for those around them; many feel very close to loved ones who have died, as if the barrier of death is no longer there.

Such cherished times bind Christians together in the life of our Lord, and it is from such experiences of a real presence that all mission must spring. With the peace of God in us (which is, as Paul knew, quite beyond reasoned understanding) we shall be literally 'inspired' or 'breathed into' by the life of Jesus, so that we shall be able to bring him to each room we visit and each person we meet.

OR

John 20:19-23

The whole purpose of receiving the Spirit, then, is to use it. We are sent out in the Spirit's power to tell others that God loves them in a way they have always longed to be loved: loyally, honestly, uncompromisingly and tenderly. We are to invite others to come and meet Jesus for themselves; to introduce them to him both through our attitudes to people and events, and also by suggesting passages in the Bible to read, praying with them and telling them what Christ means to us and how he has changed our lives.

It is all too easy to assume everyone knows where to come and what to read if they are interested; but we cannot make any such assumptions. There is widespread ignorance today about the good news that means so much to us, and we are commissioned to make sure the news is spread. We never need worry about what words to use; if we live in the Spirit he will give us the best ones.

QUESTIONS FOR DISCUSSION

1. Re-read the conditions under which the Spirit came at Pentecost. Are there any ways in which our preparation, both individually and corporately, could be better?
2. If the Holy Spirit leads us into all truth, how is it we so often disagree? Is it possible to see evidence of God's Spirit even in the middle of disagreement?

IDEAS FOR ADULTS

Fire is a powerful symbol. Consider the possibility of having a preparation time of prayer gathered round a fire near the church, on a beach or in a garden. Invite other Christians to come from other denominations.

Have everyone in the church holding hands in an unbroken chain during the creed or one of the hymns.

CHILDREN'S TEACHING

Tell the children what happened at Pentecost, emphasising that Jesus' friends were keeping in touch with him through prayer, so they were prepared when his life, or Spirit, came to them so powerfully. Explain that we need to keep in touch with him, too, if we want him to live in us.

Talk about qualities the Holy Spirit gives us — love, joy, peace etc. Then help the children to make long streamers out of orange, red and yellow, with these qualities drawn or printed on them. As the children come into church they dance round the aisles waving the streamers and twirling them so they look like fire.

INTERCESSIONS **Years 1 and 2**
Some ideas for prayer

In wonder let us come before the almighty and everlasting God,
to pray in the Spirit of Christ.

We pray for every Christian;
that each may be more receptive
to the Holy Spirit, until every
worshipping community is charged
with the vitality and love
of the living Christ.
Pause
Loving Father: **let your Spirit live in us now**

We pray for the world and its leaders;
for its mistakes and tragedies,
misunderstandings and confusion;
may your active Spirit bring
order, serenity and hope.
Pause
Loving Father: **let your Spirit live in us now**

We pray for a deepening of our own faith,
more understanding of your will,
a clearer awareness of others' needs
and a greater desire to give our lives away.
Pause
Loving Father: **let your Spirit live in us now**

We pray for those whose lives
are darkened by guilt, resentment
or despair; for those who live violent and
cruel lives, and for all who are ill,
injured or abused.
Pause
Loving Father: **let your Spirit live in us now**

We pray for those who have died
in the faith of Christ,
especially . . .
may they enjoy life with you for ever.

Father, in grateful thanks for all
your blessings in our lives,
we relinquish our wills to yours.

Merciful Father
accept these prayers
for the sake of your Son,
our Saviour Jesus Christ, Amen.

Trinity Sunday

TODAY'S THEME

. . . is that the God we worship is Father, Son and Holy Spirit. The qualities of God are revealed in the three persons of the Trinity, and in us, too, when we found our lives on him. Filled with his life, the Christian community will be enabled to show the love of God, the grace of Jesus and the fellowship of the Holy Spirit.

PARISH MUSIC
Hymns
Father, we adore you
Father, we love you
Father, you are living in us now
Firmly I believe and truly
Glory to God
Holy, holy, holy
Holy, holy, holy, Lord God
I bind unto myself today
Jesus, Jesus, never have I heard
O love, who formedst me to wear
Praise to the Father
Three in One and One in Three

Recorded music
Noyes Fludde (Britten): the handbells as the rainbow appears

For choirs
Holy, holy, holy (Palestrina): SATB
Above Him stood the Seraphim (Dering): SS

CHURCH DECORATION

Try a Japanese-style flower arrangement using three flowers and three twigs or branches. Include some clover or shamrock if it is available. Aim to express the idea of three-ness in one-ness. This kind of arrangement is really a visible meditation, and can be very helpful and stimulating.

NOTES ON THE READINGS **Years 1 and 2**

Isaiah 6:1-8
When the prophet sees a vision of God's glory, it brings home to him the shame of man's mean response to God and his corrupt hypocritical life, so empty and pompous.

God shows that he has power to forgive, so that the situation is not as hopeless as it seems. Having experienced the generosity of this forgiveness, the prophet is ready to offer himself as God's messenger.

Ephesians 1:3-14
When you walk up a hill or a mountain, you often head for 'false' summits on the way. They look like the top, but when you reach them you find the real summit is higher than you thought.

Imagining God's power, influence and control is a bit like that: however much understanding and awareness we grasp, there is always more than we can comprehend. But within it is the firm and dependable promise of Christ: that we have been chosen right from the beginning, and stamped with the seal of the Holy Spirit, to be freed sons and daughters of the God whose majesty is beyond us.

John 14:8-17
The most profound way in which God's nature is shown to us is in Jesus of Nazareth, the carpenter turned itinerant preacher, who slept, ate, got tired, knew fear and understood failure. This fully human being was, in some way that is impossible to explain in human terms, also God. In him mankind could see the nature of God expressed through voice, tears, healing hands, and dusty, travel-worn feet. Never before had God's qualities of tenderness and compassion, patience, kindness and faithfulness been so clearly seen.

Having seen Jesus we can understand more of God, and by believing, or putting our trust in him instead of ourselves or man-made commodities, we can be saved and liberated. We can also turn a blind eye to God's offer, and reject it and all the hope it contains. The choice is ours.

QUESTIONS FOR DISCUSSION

1. Obviously heaven is impossible to describe clearly, but what impression of heaven is expressed in Isaiah's vision? What do you think is meant by the burning coal which takes away his guilt?
2. In the creed we profess our belief in the Trinity. Work through the familiar words. In what way are the Creator, Redeemer and Giver of Life all aspects of God? Why is it important in our faith to believe this?

IDEAS FOR ADULTS

Try using this Trinity meditation for the Lord, have mercy.

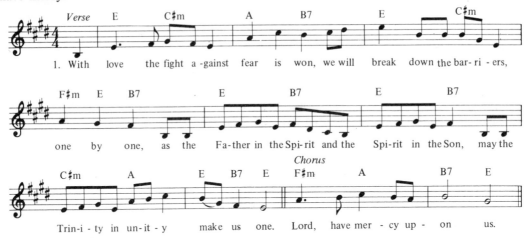

1. With love the fight a-gainst fear is won, we will break down the bar-ri-ers, one by one, as the Fa-ther in the Spi-rit and the Spi-rit in the Son, may the Trin-i-ty in un-it-y make us one. Lord, have mer-cy up-on us.

2. With faith the healing is begun,
   we will break down the barriers, one by one,
   as the Father in the Spirit, and the Spirit in the Son,
   may the Trinity in unity make us one.
   Christ, have mercy upon us.

3. With hope the work for peace is done,
   we will break down the barriers, one by one,
   as the Father in the Spirit, and the Spirit in the Son,
   may the Trinity in unity make us one.
   Lord, have mercy upon us.

CHILDREN'S TEACHING

Begin by exploring relationships in the group, asking the children to stand in the 'daughter' ring, if they are daughters and the 'son' ring if they are sons (use lengths of wool, or hula hoops to make the rings). Now ask the sisters and brothers to go to other rings, such as cousin, grandchild, friend and nephew. Some children will have changed rings several times.

Sit the children in a circle and show them a picture of someone they all know about — it may be the Queen; or a photo of one of the teachers, perhaps. Work out together all the different things the person is, such as mother, daughter, woman, sister, grandmother, queen, horse rider. Write all these down beside the picture.

Now show them a poster with the word GOD in the middle. Uncover the first picture of trees, mountains, animals and flowers.
What is God?
He is our Father, the Creator.
Uncover the second picture of Jesus, healing and teaching.
What else is God? He is Jesus Christ.
Uncover the third picture of wind and fire and the disciples full of joy, which they will remember from last week.
What else is God? He is the Holy Spirit.
Just as they are themselves, although they are also sisters, friends, and cousins, so God is God, although he is also Father, Son and Holy Spirit.

Give each child a triangle of coloured card. They write GOD in the middle and Father, Jesus and Spirit at the three corners to take home with them.

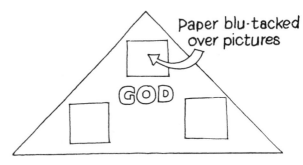

Paper blu-tacked over pictures

GOD

INTERCESSIONS **Years 1 and 2**
Some ideas for prayer

Gathered together in the love
and fellowship of God,
let us speak to our Father
of our cares and needs.

We pray for the work of your Church
in suburbs, cities, slums and villages
all over the world,
especially where there is violent opposition,
complacency or apathy;
that all who work in your name
may be blessed and encouraged,
so many may find peace in your love.

Pause
Abba, Father: **hear your children**

We pray for the world; for all areas
in which there is a breakdown of communication
between individuals, groups or nations;
may your unifying love draw people together,
helping them to find shared interests to build on,
rather than dwelling on hurtful divisions.
Pause
Abba, Father: **hear your children**

We pray for a greater love
and fellowship amongst us here
in this parish and in our families;
live in us, Father, and make us more ready
to respond and forgive, to help
and to listen.
Pause
Abba, Father: **hear your children**

We pray for the homeless
and those living in crowded, inadequate
accommodation; those living alone and
isolated; for the hungry and malnourished;
may your love, working through us, your body,
reach those in desperate need
and give them new hope.
Pause
Abba, Father: **hear your children**

We pray for those who have travelled through
   death
to eternity; may they live in your peace
and joy for ever.

Rejoicing in your strength, love
and fellowship we offer you our
thanks and praise.

Merciful Father
**accept these prayers
for the sake of your Son,
our Saviour Jesus Christ, Amen.**

Alleluia, by your Spirit we will sing
All ye who seek a comfort sure
Amazing grace!
Build, build your Church
Christ is our cornerstone
Colours of day
Come into his presence
For I'm building a people of power
Glorify the Lord
God and man at table are sat down
If we only seek peace
In full and glad surrender
I no longer live
Jesus calls us o'er the tumult
Lord of my life
Make me a channel of your peace
Our hearts were made for you, Lord
My hope is built on nothing less
Take my life and let it be
This is my body (In love for me)

Recorded music
Symphony No. 8 (Dvorak)

For choirs
O thou who at thy Eucharist didst pray
   (Wöldike): SATB
Christ is the world's true light (Stanton):
   U with descant
O taste and see (Vaughan Williams):
   SATB

CHURCH DECORATION

For Year 1 the theme of the true vine is a lovely
one to express. If possible, use some vines in the
arrangement, but if no one grows any, use any
trailing plant for the greenery, and include some
clusters of grapes as well. Pick out the colour
of the grapes with the flowers, and put a pair
of secateurs, gardening gloves and a book on
growing fruit and vegetables, down at the base
of the arrangement.

2nd Sunday after Pentecost (Trinity 1)

TODAY'S THEME

... is that God's people are called to be united
in the fellowship of the Spirit, sharing God's life.
But we are given free will, so we can choose
whether to be part of God's people or not.

PARISH MUSIC
   Hymns
   Abba, Father, let me be yours

Year 2 has as its theme the big dinner party to which many are invited but make excuses for not coming. Have a white lace tablecloth draped over the pedestal and some candle sticks and a 'menu' as part of the main arrangement.

NOTES ON THE READINGS **Year 1**

Exodus 19:1-6

The people of Israel were chosen for a very important mission: their whole nation was to be a light shining in heathen darkness so as to draw the world to acknowledge God as Lord of all. To do this, their unity was crucial; they had to be a people obviously set apart from the cults and religions around them. Hence the binding covenant, demanding strong allegiance on both sides.

1 Peter 2:1-10

Peter explains the role of Christ's followers in terms of the children of Israel who were the chosen race, set apart for God's purpose. Then, the temple containing the ark of the covenant represented the dwelling place of the Almighty. Now that God has revealed himself in the person of Jesus, the temple housing his presence is built of living stones — the followers of Christ. By grace they have become the chosen race, which is no longer bound to any ethnic group but has widened to embrace those from all nations who acknowledge Jesus as Lord.

There are times when it comes as a nasty shock to find that people, whom perhaps we love dearly, are stumbling over the very rock which provides our own foundation. It can be very tempting to try to kick that rock away, for it seems to stand in the way of a precious relationship

Of course, it cannot be discarded, for Jesus is the vital centre of salvation, without whom there is no hope or life or healing. Instead, we are to offer ourselves as a sacrifice so that through our lives being grounded in Christ, even the most cynical, the most unexpected, are drawn to experience the security and joy of living in Jesus.

John 15:1-5

Jesus is quite clear and definite: if we do not live in him as closely as a branch lives on a vine, we shall bear no fruit at all. Not even the occasional grape! If you visit a vineyard, look closely at any succulent cluster of fruit and trace its stem. It may be trained some distance from the main branch, but eventually it joins the true vine with its strong root system (never a weak sucker shoot).

That is how we, too, will bear fruit — fruit in great clusters, like the grapes. But before we can flourish we shall need to be pruned, as any gardener knows. Any side shoots of distractions or weakening habits and sins need to be cut out, so that all our growth and energy are concentrated along the main fruiting branch. We may well dislike this pruning, and not recognise that it proves God's love for us. It can be useful, sometimes, to look again at some disappointment or failure we resent, and see if we can discern in it something that perhaps we needed to learn the hard way; or perhaps it may be the very thing to spur us into action from which great good will come.

QUESTIONS FOR DISCUSSION

1. A grape doesn't actually do much. It grows sweet not through determined effort but simply by being joined on to the vine. Do you think that we Christians can pick up any spiritual hints from this? Is there sometimes too much busy activity in the parish and not enough shared silent 'growing'? What could we change?
2. What is Jesus explaining about both himself and his Father when he describes himself as the true vine and his Father as the vinedresser?

IDEAS FOR ADULTS

Using curled green paper and templates, create a long 'vine' trailing up and around the lectern or pulpit. Grapes are cut out of shiny purple paper.

CHILDREN'S TEACHING

Bring along a gardening book with clear illustrations to explain pruning, a pair of secateurs and gardening gloves, and a bunch of grapes.

First put on the gloves and hold the secateurs, and discuss what kind of job you are ready for. If your church has a garden take the children out into it and show them how the roses have been pruned so they produce better flowers. Also find any flower and trace it back to the main stem and roots, from which it gets all its life. Cut off one twig. Will this be able to produce flowers?

Back inside, show the children how gardeners have to learn to prune all their fruit trees and bushes, so as to produce more fruit. Then read today's Gospel, and help the children understand that we need to be (1) joined on to Jesus and (2) pruned, if we are to produce fruit.

On a large sheet of paper draw a central vine with many branches and some leaves. Let the children stick on lots of clusters of grapes which they have coloured and labelled like this:

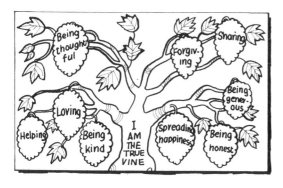

INTERCESSIONS **Years 1 and 2**
Some ideas for prayer

Fellow members of the Body of Christ
full of thankfulness for his abiding love
let us pray to our heavenly Father.

Lord, we ask you to deepen
our personal commitment
so that the life-giving sap
of the true vine
can flow through the Church
and out into the world.
Pause
Live in us, Father: **that we may bear fruit**

Direct and further
all international discussions
so that they lead to peace,
goodwill and mutual understanding.
Pause
Live in us, Father: **that we may bear fruit**

Lord, come and make your home
in us, in our marriages and our families,
our places of work and our local community;
may our characters be forged
by your life within us.
Pause
Live in us, Father: **that we may bear fruit**

Bring healing and wholeness
to those who are ill;
peace to the anxious,
courage to the fearful
and rest to the weary.
Pause
Live in us, Father: **that we may bear fruit**

Give everlasting peace
to those who have died in faith;
may they know the joy
of being invited to your heavenly banquet.

We thank you that we are all invited
to share your life-giving love;
make us worthy of all you have promised.

Merciful Father
**accept these prayers
for the sake of your Son,
our Saviour Jesus Christ, Amen.**

NOTES ON THE READINGS **Year 2**

2 Samuel 7:4-16
The ark of the covenant was a symbol of God's constant presence among his people. He had heard their cries of anguish in Egypt and led them across the Red Sea to freedom; he had supported and guided them throughout their wandering years in the wilderness, and kept faith with them through their grumbles and idolatry. Now, for a while, King David had established peace, and had the leisure to start plans for a permanent building to house the ark.

At first sight it seems to be a very good idea; noble, generous and necessary. But Nathan, being a man of God, mulls it over during the night and begins to see things in God's way. Perhaps a permanent house for the ark would destroy some very powerful symbolism: God is not anchored to one spot, but travels with us in times of danger, failure and victory; God is there among his people where they need him, and he will never abandon them.

In God's eyes the time is not yet right for such

an enterprise, but he reaffirms his promise which spans a far broader plan even than building a magnificent temple: from the family of David will come one who displays God's eternal glory to the whole world.

We, too, need to be wary of planning ambitious works for God. They may not always be what he has in mind, or the timing may be wrong. We would be better advised to ask him first!

Acts 2:37-end

Peter's witness to the resurrection of Jesus is unequivocal and full of conviction, for he has actually seen Christ alive after his crucifixion, and has even eaten and drunk with him. You don't eat and drink with an allegorical character or a vision. There is no doubt about what Peter is saying: Jesus' new life is real and complete. So to believe in Jesus as the living Lord is not something for the gullible and naive, since they are the only ones crazy enough to believe such an impossible tale. The belief is based on the evidence of hard-headed, working men who had themselves taken quite a lot of convincing. Of course it is impossible in purely human terms. That does not mean we need to remould the facts to fit human possibility; it means that we need to acknowledge that God is altogether 'bigger' that the human experience. We are not the god — he is.

Luke 14:15-24

Such teaching is shown in this parable of the invited guests who do not realise the importance of the invitation, and the rabble of poor and crippled who are enjoined to take their place at the dinner instead of those originally invited. At one level, Jesus was addressing the pompous and hypocritical religious leaders of his time, who considered their own petty affairs more important than the kingdom of heaven. At another level he speaks across the centuries of the longing God has to share a meal and fellowship with all his children gathered about him.

QUESTIONS FOR DISCUSSION

1. David was tempted to try and force God's hand, taking it upon himself to build the temple, instead of asking God's advice first. Do we sometimes do this? How does God react?
2. What characteristics of God do we learn from this parable?

IDEAS FOR ADULTS

The Gospel lends itself very well to dramatisation, with actors taking the parts of the excusers and also the poor and crippled.

CHILDREN'S TEACHING

Today's Gospel is good to use for making a 'television' programme. The television is a cereal packet with two wooden spoons for winding the 'film' on, and the story is displayed in a series of pictures on a long strip of paper, marked into numbered frames. Either the words can be written underneath each picture, or they can be read on to tape with a clicker between each frame so that the winder knows when to do his bit.

Tell the children the story first and have each part written on a separate card. These are then given out in order to the children, who work on a particular frame, either drawing or colouring in the appropriate picture. It may be easiest to work on the floor, or to stick separate sheets on to a strip when they are finished.

The finished story can be presented to others, perhaps during visits to the elderly, or those in hospital. It can be kept as useful resource material.

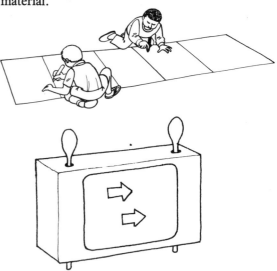

3rd Sunday after Pentecost (Trinity 2)

TODAY'S THEME

... is that through Christ we die to sin and are raised to full life. Jesus, the Christ, the Son of God, is the fulfilment of the prophecies and the only way to salvation.

PARISH MUSIC

Hymns

All to Jesus I surrender
A new commandment I give unto you
Bind us together, Lord
Blessed assurance, Jesus is mine
Bread of the world in mercy broken
Christ is made the sure foundation
Christ is the King! O friends rejoice
Come my brothers, praise the Lord
For our life together we celebrate
Glorious things of thee are spoken
God is love: his the care
Go in peace to be Christ's body
Here comes Jesus
Jesu, my Lord, my God, my all
Joy to the world
Let me have my way among you
Lord, when I turn my back on you
Near the heart of Jesus
Our hearts were made for you, Lord
The Church's one foundation
Who is this man?
Ye know that the Lord is gracious

Recorded music

Symphony No. 9 (Beethoven)

For choirs

Above all praise and all majesty
  (Mendelssohn): SATB
Rejoice in the Lord always (Anon): SATB
Jesu, joy of man's desiring (Bach)

CHURCH DECORATION

Make the link between death to the old life and new life in Christ by paying special attention to the font, and the sacrament of Baptism. If your font has a lid, have it raised today, and flowers and foliage spilling out from the font itself. Put garlands round the font's column and surround the base with small flowers, either cut and arranged, or in pots.

NOTES ON THE READINGS **Year 1**

Deuteronomy 6:17-end

In our age of constant change the pressure is often on to discard the traditions of the past as being irrelevant. Such an attitude is shortsighted and arrogant, for we progress (or regress) as a society as well as in our individual lives.

Here we see the foundation of God's law being passed on from generation to generation so that the whole people can grow and develop as God's people.

Romans 6:3-11

The symbolism of baptism is easier to understand in total immersion, as early Christians would have known it. Wading into water and then being ducked right under it is a powerful reminder of drowning. Anyone who has seen the possibility of immediate death, whether by accident or illness, receding, will know the fresh clarity and thankfulness with which life is suddenly seen. Bird songs seem more lovely than ever, colours brighter, nature full of miracles and the privilege of being alive so great that one feels one will never grumble again.

Dying to sin and being alive to Christ is just

like this; it creates a state of fresh joy and wonder at all that is hopeful, unobtrusively persevering, beautiful or touchingly honest. For it is the relief and heightened awareness that comes from being released from the condemned cell and told that we can go free. That is what resurrection means, and that is why it can be brought with powerful effect into every situation: having found ourselves set free we shall have a different outlook, and that will bring new hope to all areas, no matter how wearying and despairing they may seem.

John 15:5-11

This passage really deals with getting things in proportion, and having our priorities right. When we love God first, our love for others increases by leaps and bounds: we may even find ourselves loving those we couldn't stand before. Our love for God may lead us to see areas of our character which needed to be changed, subdued, curbed or developed in order that we can be more loving; and because we love God we shall be willing to have a go at what he suggests, even if it is a bit humiliating and demands stepping down from a position proudly defended before. It may be only the equivalent of a cup of cold water that we give, but it will serve to increase our love both for God and for the recipient.

On the other hand, if our loving gets trapped in one area — either for a person or a thing — it will not be able to spread and grow in the same way since it is not rooted into the source of all love. It is likely, instead, to become possessive, narrow and exclusive. It must be defended against anyone threatening it, and if it lets us down (as may well happen) our world will seem devastated, for our ground of being will have been devastated.

That is why Jesus urges his followers to give their full allegiance to Love itself: all the rest, and more, will follow us all the days of our life, both here and in eternity.

QUESTIONS FOR DISCUSSION

1. Jesus remained within the old Law in order to fulfill it. What can his example teach us about reform and renewal in the Church? What exactly was he obedient to and which 'laws' did he consider it necessary to break?
2. We all know that, even after baptism, we still commit sin as if we had not died to the old life. What do we need to do about this, in view of Jesus' words in the Gospel for today?

IDEAS FOR ADULTS

After the general confession, or instead of the creed, gather everyone round the decorated font and renew Baptismal vows.

Baptism Dance

To express the cleansing, life-giving properties of water you will need one group of six dancers and one group of three dancers.

1. A group of six dancers starts at the back of the church and moves up the aisle towards the altar. Each dancer holds a length of blue or green cloth or ribbon in each hand. They move in a line, one behind the other, in the following way:
   - one step forwards, raising arms forwards;
   - one step back, sweeping arms back;
   - turn on the spot to the right, arms outstretched;
   - repeat forwards;
   - repeat back;
   - turn on the spot to the left, arms outstretched.
   - When they arrive at the chancel they form a circle, continuing the forward-back-turn sequence until all dancers are in the circle.

2. Standing with feet apart, swing arms and body to the right, then to the left, four times, starting gently and gradually increasing the swing to give the effect of a rising wave.

3. In sequence, with leader beginning, go down on one knee as the arms swing in a circle up over the head and round to the floor. Then stand up. Repeated twice, this should make a continuous waving movement round the circle and it finishes with each dancer swirling on the spot, arms above the head.

4. The dancers form two lines of three, arms stretched in welcome, but constantly rising and falling like a sea.

5. Up the aisle come three dancers wrapped in dark cloaks which hoods (or lengths of dark material). They walk rhythmically and slowly, their heads and shoulders bowed, as if they are heavily burdened.

6. When they reach the water, they kneel down, covering their heads, in a triangle, and the water dancers stand round them in a circle.

7. They move arms backwards and then sweep them up and over forwards (rather like casting a line) so the ribbons should meet in the centre over the kneeling dancers. This is done slowly and deliberately three times.

8. The water dancers then kneel in their circle as the three others slowly stand up, their heads high and arms raised in joy. While they were kneeling, their cloaks were unfastened so that as they stand they are in white.

plain so that the contrast will be greater when they open the card up.

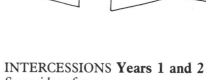

9. Turning together, they walk back down the aisle, upright and confident, leading the water dancers who are in two rows of three, moving in their forward-back-turn sequence.

Any waltz time music will work with this dance. Since its length will vary with the size of building used, a short melody which can be repeated as needed, may be best. If you use recorded music, try Mendelssohn — *Fingal's Cave*.

CHILDREN'S TEACHING

Ask the children to remember some of Jesus' healing works when he was living as a man in Galilee. Explain how he always felt sorry for people who were sad or ill, and wanted to make them well.

Now tell the story of today's Gospel, referring to a picture if possible.

If the children know of anyone who is ill the whole group can pray for them, imagining Jesus comforting them and asking him to make them well.

Then the children can make this pop-up card. They will need a piece of folded paper, and a semi-circle marked with fold lines; coloured pencils, scissors and glue. Decorate the inside as brightly as possible, and keep the outside

INTERCESSIONS **Years 1 and 2**
Some ideas for prayer

Let us pray, my brothers and sisters, in the knowledge of our Father's infinite mercy.

We pray for all Christian people and Church leaders; all whose faith is battered through disaster or suffering; may we know the certainty of your abiding presence which transforms and rebuilds.
Pause
Touch our lives, Lord: **that we may live**

We pray for all world leaders, all administrative bodies and political institutions; may they be always aware of the real needs of those they serve and be effective in providing for them.
Pause
Touch our lives, Lord: **that we may live**

We pray for our local community, for our families and our friends, with all the hopes, fears, problems and needs; make us ready to serve you in our own area and spread your life-giving joy.
Pause
Touch our lives, Lord: **that we may live**

We pray for the dying and those who love and tend them;

for the bereaved and desolate;
may all in trouble and sorrow
draw strength from your life
and your victory over death.
Pause
Touch our lives, Lord: **that we may live**

We pray for those who have died;
that, falling asleep to this life
they may wake to eternal life
in the joy of heaven.

We thank you, heavenly Father,
for saving us from
sin's destruction
and making it possible to live
in such abundant fulness.

Merciful Father,
accept these prayers
for the sake of your Son,
our Saviour Jesus Christ, Amen.

NOTES ON THE READINGS Year 2

Deuteronomy 8:11-end
Even people who do not normally pray will fall
on their knees when there is terrible danger or
suffering. Often it is times of vulnerability that
jerk us back to recognising our dependence on
God. Yet so often, when everything is going
really well, we forget to thank God, or even
acknowledge that he has anything to do with
'our' success. Today's reading reminds us that
we belong to God all the time, and must not
forget him just because we are living in comfort
— such times are opportunities for thanks and
praise. Otherwise, we are really making gods of
the things that surround us in our comfort.

Acts 4:8-12
Peter and John are being embarrassing. They
keep talking about Jesus of Nazareth as if he
were still alive, even though everyone knows he
has been put to death. The priests and elders
just wish they would keep their fanciful,
threatening ideas to themselves and let life go
on in the comfortable, established way it always
has done.

Unfortunately there is this tiresome cripple
standing up in front of the people, large as life
and twice as healthy; in fact, perfectly healed.
Obviously some power *must* have been at work.

Why were they unable to accept the joyful
truth of the resurrection on the evidence of such
'fruit'? Surely because they knew that
acceptance would utterly change their lives (as
it did in Paul's case, of course); and having put
a lot into establishing their life-style, they

reckoned they had too much to lose. Whereas
the cripple, whose life had been held physically
tight and rigid by his handicap, was wildly
delighted at the flexibility and capacity for
movement that God had now given him.

Two things, then, about the resurrection life:
it shows, and it liberates; but not everyone wants
to be liberated. Perhaps some area of our own
life-style is causing us to hobble, spiritually. If
so, the risen Jesus has the power and the desire
to set us leaping!

Luke 8:41-end
If we were to read the creation poem in Genesis,
and then imagine how the God revealed there
might react to a young girl desperately sick and
dying, we would surely come up with the way
Jesus feels deep sorrow, confronts the evil,
overrules it with his authority of intense
goodness, and creates an atmosphere of joy and
wholeness.

Even though he is delayed by another act of
healing (which remade the timid woman who
had suffered for years), Jesus' power to make
whole is not diminished. For Jesus it is never
too late to bother; never too late to transform,
heal and make whole. The wholeness may be
different from what we were expecting, but God
knows and loves us in terms of eternity, and will
make us, and our loved one for whom we pray,
healed in the way which is eternally best for us.
We need to touch him with faith, invite him into
the home or hospital, and listen to his
instructions. He will never refuse to come.

QUESTIONS FOR DISCUSSION

1. How can we make sure that we do not forget
   God except when we are in desperate need?
   How can we use times of need in others to
   introduce them to Christ? (Think about
   follow-up ministry, too.)
2. How can we best pray for the sick and dying?
   Look at the healing ministry in the parish in
   the light of today's readings and pray together
   for God's guidance in your work.

IDEAS FOR ADULTS

Today's Gospel lends itself to a different form
of dramatisation in which the entire
congregation is involved. It gives great
immediacy and reality to the living, healing
Jesus.

The characters of Jairus and his family, the
woman suffering from a haemorrhage, Peter,
James and John, are all trained beforehand, and
need to know their words off by heart. The

narrator stands separate from the action, and the priest takes the part of Jesus.

Warn the congregation in advance that they will be participating; and as Jesus moves out of the sanctuary, ushers invite them all to come out of the pews and crowd round him. Jairus pushes his way through them from the back, and everyone listens to him. As they all begin to follow Jesus and Jairus, the sick woman (no-one should know who it is) touches Jesus' clothes, and the crowd will find themselves reacting naturally: curious and then surprised, happy for her — even hugging her — just as they feel instinctively.

Jairus' house is located at the back of the church, with lots of weeping from the distraught family. This too, will affect the crowd. Let the family ad lib when the girl has been brought back to life. They may bring her outside, and the crowd can cheer and clap before returning to their seats.

CHILDREN'S TEACHING

The children will get a lot from joining in the acting of the Gospel today, along with the adults. If you are not planning to act the Gospel in church, then act it out with the children, after first reading them the story. There are quite a lot of good children's versions of this popular story. Palm Tree's version is called *Becky gets better*.

Have a time, too, to praise and thank God for all his gifts to us, and pray for those who are ill, blind, deaf or handicapped in any way. Discuss practical ways the group can help.

4th Sunday after Pentecost (Trinity 3)

TODAY'S THEME

... is the freedom of the children of God which liberates them to serve others. Whenever we deny God through our words or actions it hurts him, because he longs for us to know the freedom and joy of serving him. When we speak and act as his friends there is great joy both for us and in heaven.

PARISH MUSIC

Hymns
Alleluia, by your spirit we will sing
And can it be that I should gain
Colours of day dawn into the mind
Fear not, rejoice and be glad
Give me joy in my heart
God forgave my sin in Jesus' name
God of mercy, God of grace
Go forth and tell
If we only seek peace
I heard the Lord call my name
I heard the voice of Jesus say
Lord Jesus Christ
Loving shepherd of thy sheep
O Lord all the world belongs to you
Our hearts were made for you
Peace, perfect peace is the gift
Steal away Jesus
Take my life and let it be
The King of love my shepherd is
This is my commandment
We pray thee, heavenly Father
You can't stop rain from falling down

Recorded music
Horn Concerto No. 4 (Mozart)

For choirs
Flocks in pastures green abiding (Bach): SATB
Love one another (Wesley): U

CHURCH DECORATION

Try to express the joy of being with Jesus as his friend. An exuberant arrangement with variety of colour and form will create just the right atmosphere. Use an abundance of garden flowers and sprays from flowering shrubs.

NOTES ON THE READINGS **Year 1**

Deuteronomy 7:6-11
It is very humbling to realise that we are going to church, I am writing this book and others are using it, not because we have chosen to but because God has chosen us. He actually likes our company so much that he has called us all to spend our lives with him!

We are, by adoption and grace, God's children. Not that we are worthy of it; we constantly let him down and allow selfishness to block his power. But if, every time we fall, we are sorry and become reconciled to him, God will bless us and use us in spite of (and even because of) our unworthiness. For he loves us with warmth and affection.

Galatians 3:23-4:7
Paul is stressing here the new-found unity which is a direct result of belonging to Christ. Baptism is like a kind of dying, in that it is a complete break with the world's categorising,

compartmentalised society, divisive by its very nature.

New life in Christ is not the old with a few 'extras' thrown in; it is a complete remaking — more like a caterpillar's transformation into a butterfly.

We are often happiest with things as they are; reluctant to alter what we know and understand, even if there are difficulties. Yet we must risk ourselves with Christ if he is to change us.

John 15:12-17

The transforming power is Love, personified in Jesus, who was prepared to expend his complete life in the service of others. He did not do this sourly, with a self-righteous expression and meaningful glances. He simply lost himself in loving and caring for any who needed his help, wanted to talk to him, or sought his company. He never gave the impression of being too busy for anyone, never missed an opportunity to encourage, sympathise or share a celebration. No genuine enquirer was ever made to feel small or inadequate. No one was made to feel excluded, no matter what kind of life they were leading. And the resultant changed and radiant lives were astounding. They still are.

QUESTIONS FOR DISCUSSION

1. Having read through the Gospel and the notes on it, what do you think of Jesus' way of love? Have you found it to work in your life? When hasn't it worked?
2. What are the differences between a slave and a son? In what way are we slaves? In what way are we sons and daughters?

IDEAS FOR ADULTS

Dance of Reconciliation

To the slow, regular beating of a drum, two men walk up the centre miming an argument which gradually gets more angry and heated until one is thrown to the ground.

Two relatives rush to mourn over the fallen man, one of whom approaches his killer in determined revenge. They face each other, and then the killer falls. Two of his relatives rush to mourn and one of those rises and faces his brother's murderer.

They begin to fight but as they do so, a group of voices starts to chant, with a flute or recorder playing in the background, or you can use the fourth movement of Mahler's *Symphony No. 4*.

The words chanted are from today's Old Testament reading; 'You are a people holy to the Lord your God; the Lord your God chose you out of all nations on earth to be his special possession.'

This is repeated while the two men stand still, look out at the group, back to their dead, then back to each other. Slowly they extend hands to each other and embrace. Together they get the mourning relatives to join hands so they are all in a circle. Finally, they lift their joined hands high and join in with the last two sentences: 'You must love your neighbour as yourself. I am the Lord!'

CHILDREN'S TEACHING

Have on display a selection of things we are given by God which make life possible and enjoyable:
- a glass of water
- lump of coal
- salt
- pictures of a sunrise or sunset
- picture of rain
- plants and flowers

Talk about how much God must love us to give us all these, and many more they can add. Then sing a 'thank you' song.

Now present them with a problem. If they lent a friend one of their toys, and the friend did not use it properly, and broke it, how would they feel? Angry? Upset? What might they do? Take it back? Not lend them anything again? Hit them? (You could write the main points of this discussion up on a board or sheet.)

Then show them some pictures of people spoiling God's world and each other; children quarrelling, being unkind and destructive, people starving while others feast, the aftermath of a bomb explosion etc.

Explain that God sees us all spoiling what he has given us. He feels just as angry and upset, and he could, if he wanted, take the gifts away. As you say this, take away the water, sunlight etc, until the table is bleak and bare.

Why do you think he doesn't do that? Because he loves us so much, even when we are horrid. He hates what we do, sometimes, but he never hates us.

Let the children help put back all the lovely things. If God loves us that much, we must love each other that much.

INTERCESSIONS **Years 1 and 2**
Some ideas for prayer

My companions in Christ,
let us lay at the feet of our heavenly Father
all our cares and concerns
for the Church and for the world.

We pray for those Christians
whom you are calling
to a particular ministry;
may they recognise your voice
and respond to it in trust.
Pause
Lord, hear us: **we offer ourselves to your service**

We pray for all involved with government,
both in our own country and throughout the world;
may the way we govern
reflect the way we are governed by you,
our God of justice, mercy and compassion.
Pause
Lord, hear us: **we offer ourselves to your service**

We pray that we, and all others worshipping
in this city/town, may allow you access
into more of our life and personality;
so you can work through us
to spread healing and wholeness.
Pause
Lord, hear us: **we offer ourselves to your service**

We pray for those who have become locked
in their guilt, resentment, self-pity or hatred;
may they be released
through thorough repentance
to the joy and freedom
of your full forgiveness.
Pause
Lord, hear us: **we offer ourselves to your service**

We pray for all who have been brought home

to eternity, especially....
may they, through your mercy,
live for ever in your peace.

We offer you grateful thanks and praise
for all this life's blessings
which surround us each day;
may we grow in appreciation
and learn to perceive your glory
more clearly.

Merciful Father
**accept these prayers
for the sake of your Son,
our Saviour Jesus Christ, Amen.**

NOTES ON THE READINGS **Year 2**
Isaiah 63:7-14
The people of Israel, being human, did not remain true to their covenant, and there were many times when they hurt, angered and insulted their God by their rebellion and disloyalty. Like a human parent, God is seen here as feeling with them through all their sufferings and hardships, and loving them even in their spitefulness and nastiness. Not that God is blind to their faults: he knows just how mean and nasty they, and we, can be, but he loves us all the same.

Acts 8:26-38
Philip, standing ready and available before the Lord, is therefore able to be used by him just when he is needed. Here was an enquiring, seeking person and through Philip God explained things and brought him to the joy of faith. No doubt the Ethiopian would have then spread the Good News further still.

We, too, need to keep ourselves available for God's use; his life and power is given to us so that we can bring others to share in the freedom of God, so we must never hoard it, or keep it only for those we choose to help. Living in Christ's love means doing things his way, even if his choice of work for us comes as a surprise.

Luke 15:1-10
Those who followed the Law worked hard at keeping God's word. They could see others flagrantly flouting his authority and disobeying the sacred commandments. No wonder it surprised and upset them to see Jesus mingling with those whom the Law condemned. It may not all have been jealousy: some may well have been seriously concerned that it might damage the moral and spiritual values of the most high God.

In none of these parables does Jesus condemn

the scribes and Pharisees or praise the sinners. He simply shows those within the Law that there is a good reason for becoming involved with anyone who has gone the wrong way: caring involvement is the only way to bring them back.

This, of course, presented the religious leaders with a challenge, as it challenges all committed Christians. Do we love God enough to get involved with the hurt, diseased, embezzling, crooked, perverted and cruel? If we don't, then however are they to be made whole?

QUESTIONS FOR DISCUSSION

1. What do you think Philip might have said to the Ethiopian when he explained the Good News of Jesus, starting with the Isaiah 53:7-8 text?
2. How does Jesus' parable of the lost sheep and the lost coin answer the mutterings of discontent among the Pharisees and scribes? Are the 'safe' sheep and coins any less important to their owner?

IDEAS FOR ADULTS

Have a display of missionary work in which your parish is involved. Include pictures, news cuttings of the area, maps and charts to bring it alive, rather than just being a remote 'cause'.

CHILDREN'S TEACHING

There are plenty of good versions of these two parables specially for children. Read them one, showing the pictures as you go. Talk about what it feels like to be lost, and then to be found. Remind them that Jesus doesn't want ANY of his 'sheep' to be lost, and we need to learn to love as much as that. Every person is special to God, and that's why we must treat every person as special and precious — even if we don't particularly like the way they behave.

Together make this model of a lost sheep, with the shepherd out looking for it. They can each make a sheep out of card and cotton wool.

Cut out and stick on cotton wool

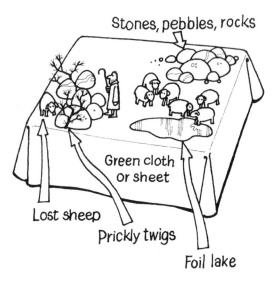

Stones, pebbles, rocks

Green cloth or sheet

Lost sheep

Prickly twigs

Foil lake

5th Sunday after Pentecost (Trinity 4)

TODAY'S THEME

. . . is God's Law, summed up in love. It is this law which undergirds us as we work with Christ to draw all people to the creator, by whom and for whom we were made.

PARISH MUSIC
Hymns
All people that on earth do dwell
And did those feet in ancient times
A new commandment I give unto you
Bind us together
Come down O love divine
Eternal ruler of the ceaseless round
Father welcomes all his children
Forth in thy name, O Lord I go
God gives peace like a river
God's Spirit is in my heart
Help us, O Lord, to learn
I'll turn my steps to the altar of God
In Christ there is no East or West
I will be with you wherever you go
Jesus shall reign where'er the sun
Jesu the very thought of thee
Let me have my way among you

Love is his word, love is his way
O happy band of pilgrims
Rise up O men of God

Recorded music
Use some music from a different culture
— Indian, Chinese, African or
Polynesian, for example

For choirs
O pray for the peace of Jerusalem
(Tomkins): SATB
O how amiable (Vaughan Williams):
SATB

CHURCH DECORATION

Some of our ancient churches have the ten
commandments painted on the wall. If your
church does, accentuate them today, drawing
attention to them with a flower arrangement
beside or under them. Or have a globe which
is enfolded with flowers, to express the love of
God which is for everyone.

NOTES ON THE READINGS **Year 1**

Exodus 20:1-17
If we are to get the full impact of Jesus' teaching,
we need to be familiar with God's Law as
revealed to Moses. Although not the whole
story, the commandments are still worth
learning off by heart, however old-fashioned rote
learning may be! Jesus certainly used them as
the framework of his code of living.

The commandments are a God-given structure
of right attitudes and behaviour, based firstly on
placing God at the centre of life, and secondly
on love and consideration for others. They may
look negative with all those 'You shall not's'
around, but if we look at them in the light of
Jesus' summary of them, we can see that
breaking any of the commandments involves a
lack of caring love towards God and our fellow
humans.

Ephesians 5:1-10
The light Christ brings into our lives is really
'enlightenment' for it means that, in his
presence, right and wrong become clearer, and
we can see how to act for good rather than evil.

One of the most alarming things about evil is
that quite often we have simply no idea how
destructive our well-meant behaviour can be.
Without Christ it is not at all obvious and we
desperately need his guidance, his light, to show
up the areas of our characters which may seem
all right to us, but which are causing others
distress or blocking God's work. If we really
want God to work in us then we must earnestly
pray for his light. When it shines we can be sure
of one thing — we shall not like what it shows
at all, as it will be bound to touch raw nerves.
We must pray bravely, then, in the knowledge
that, even if it hurts to put right, we shall be
stronger, more useful Christians once God has
been let in to heal.

Matthew 19:16-26
The danger of following rules in life is that we
can feel that once we have completed our rules
we have done all that is required. (It is this
attitude, too, which is for ever totting up how
many hours we are working and converting it
into money earned, rather than doing a job
cheerfully, just because it needs doing.)

The young man obviously felt dissatisfied with
rule-following, but was not yet prepared for
what Jesus suggested to him; Jesus' call had
strings attached. Following Jesus will mean
abandoning his wealth, and that is something the
young man finds too hard.

Isn't this often true for us as well? We offer
our day for Christ to use, and then when he
accepts our offer and gives us some unpleasant
job instead of what we had planned, we moan
about what a tiresome day it has been! Our
'wealth' may be our time, energy, plans, and
comforts, our routine, favourite programme,
relaxing company or even the biscuits we were
saving. And God asks us to be prepared to give
them all away joyfully in his service.

QUESTIONS FOR DISCUSSION

1. Work through the ten commandments, looking at them as expressions of loving behaviour towards God and our neighbour. How would life lived according to these commandments create a caring harmonious society?

2. Why do you think the disciples were so surprised at what Jesus said about the rich? How were Jesus' ideas different from the old Law?

IDEAS FOR ADULTS

Today's Gospel can be presented dramatically with the different parts being acted out. The narrator stands where he can be heard clearly, but is apart from the action. The actors mime what is narrated and speak their own parts from memory. The action begins in the sanctuary and Jesus sets out on his journey with his disciples to a central point in the main aisle.

CHILDREN'S TEACHING

Have plenty of Bibles available and help the children to find the verses in which the ten commandments are written. It is important that the children are familiar with these and how Moses received them from God. Older children can be encouraged to learn them, with a small prize given to all who manage to do so.

Talk with the children about good manners, and rules they have at home and at school. These are written up on a board or sheet entitled: 'Remember your manners!' They may include:
Keep to the left in the corridor.
Don't speak with your mouth full.
Please and thank you.
Say 'hallo' and 'goodbye'.
Don't interrupt.
Offer food.
Turn T.V. down or off if visitor comes.
Open classroom door to teacher.
Stand at side for people to pass.
Wait your turn in a queue.

Point out that these are ways of caring for others and respecting them. If you love someone, you do this anyway. The rules remind you to act lovingly however you feel about the other person.

Have a lot of supermarket cartons, with the biggest labelled 'Love God with all your heart and soul and mind and strength'. Label the others: 'Friends', 'Money', 'Career', 'Home', 'Holidays', 'Car' etc. Then place the command-ments box in the centre of the room and ask the children to help build their lives on it, to make a tall tower. What happens if we take away our base of loving God? Have a volunteer to put out that main box and watch all the rest come tumbling down. You could sing *I want to build my life* (SONL, 95)

INTERCESSIONS **Years 1 and 2**
Some ideas for prayer

My sisters and brothers in Christ,
we have been drawn here today
by the power of God's love;
into that love let us now gather
all those for whom we pray.

Father, we commend to your love
all who serve you as ministers
of your word and sacrament
in the church; may all they do
be an extension of your love.
Pause
Father almighty: **let your will be done**

Father, we commend to your love.
all judges and those serving on juries;

those who make laws in our country
and throughout the world;
may our human laws reflect
the unchanging law and love
of your goodness and mercy.
Pause
Father almighty: **let your will be done**

We commend to your love
our own loved ones;
all who will come to our homes this week;
may the welcome they receive
express your welcoming love.
Pause
Father almighty: **let your will be done**

We commend to your love
those whose minds have been poisoned
by exposure to violence;
children who have been abandoned or
    maltreated;
all who crave affection
but are frightened of getting hurt.
Pause
Father almighty: **let your will be done**

We commend to your love
those who have died in faith;
welcome them into your kingdom
and give them everlasting peace.

We thank you for the privilege
of working with you
to spread the Good News
of your saving love;
by your grace may we become
the kind of people you
intend us to be.

Merciful Father
accept these prayers
for the sake of your Son,
our Saviour Jesus Christ, Amen.

NOTES ON THE READINGS Year 2

Ruth 1:8-17,22
This touching story of loyalty is a wonderful
example of the kind of caring love which the God
of love inspires. Ruth is not one of God's chosen
people by birth, for she is a foreigner but
through her, great good was to come for she
became the mother of King David's
grandfather.

Acts 11:4-18
Peter, who had been in Jesus' company from the
start, still found it hard to accept that the Gospel
was also for non-Jews. He was finally convinced
through prayer, as a result of which he was given
fresh insight. He then had to come to terms with

the fact that he had been wrong before. But
Peter does not wallow in embarrassment. As
soon as he realises God's will he sets off to put
things right, plunging straight into a new course
of action. That shows real love for his Saviour;
above his pride and his reasoned arguments for
keeping Christianity Jewish, is set whatever
Jesus wants to be done. If Jesus wants to include
gentiles just as they are, then that is fine by Peter
— he wants it too; even if it means changing his
mind.

Whenever there is disagreement or heated
discussion about any issue, we need to take a
leaf out of Peter's book. First, setting ourselves
to find out God's will by seriously asking him
with prayer and fasting; and then, when we are
receptive, recognising his will and acting on it,
whether we agree with it or not. Obedience to
God's will is what proves the extent of our love
for him.

Luke 10:1-12
This sending out of the seventy-two in pairs to
preach repentance, and to heal, would have been
in some sense a practice run for their commission after Pentecost. It would also have
spread the news of the imminence of God's
kingdom being established on earth. Jesus'
instructions to them, as to us, are clear, practical
and uncomplicated.

The point is not that we should all leave our
families and set off without sandals or any spare
clothes; rather, we need to spend time in the
quietness of Christ's presence to listen to the
instructions he has for us!

QUESTIONS FOR DISCUSSION

1. Are we sometimes less prepared to accept
   people whose age, colour or culture is
   different from our own? What can we learn
   about God's attitude to this, from today's
   readings?
2. Would it be possible to regard Peter's change
   of heart as being weakness? Can his
   experience help us when we find out we have
   been wrong about something?

IDEAS FOR ADULTS

Have the first reading acted out by three women,
dressed in biblical costume. Naomi is elderly,
firm and has quite a sense of humour. Ruth is
obviously fond of her, and is just as firm!

CHILDREN'S TEACHING

Tell the children how Jesus sent out seventy-two
people to go on ahead and prepare others for his
coming. Choose some to be the disciples, and

get them to take off their socks and shoes. Act out the rest of the Gospel, with the other children being the people who are visited; some are ill and are cured, some make them welcome, and some don't. Show some pictures of Israel so the children can see that Jesus' instructions were practical for travelling light in that climate and terrain.

Gather round in prayer to ask Jesus to show us where he wants us to work for him today and through the week, and give them this prayer to colour and hang up in the bathroom at home and use every morning.

Come, thou holy Paraclete
Dear Lord and Father of mankind
From thee all skill and science flow
Glorify the Lord
God forgave my sin in Jesus' name
If I were a butterfly
Jesus, my Lord, my God, my all
Just as I am without one plea
Lord of my life
Magnificat, magnificat
May the grace of Christ our Saviour
My God loves me, his love will never end
My people, what have I done to you?
New every morning is the love
O Love that wilt not let me go
O thou who camedst from above
Thou wilt keep him in perfect peace
We pray thee, heavenly Father

Recorded music
Symphony No. 9: From the New World (Dvorak)

For choirs
Vox ultima crucis (Harris): U
God be in my head (Davies)

CHURCH DECORATION

The restoration and new creation of today's

6th Sunday after Pentecost (Trinity 5)

TODAY'S THEME

... is that in Christ we become a new person. As soon as we turn to approach God, he comes to welcome us; he accepts us just as we are and begins to heal our personalities, increase our capacity to love and to forgive, and enable us to become fully ourselves.

PARISH MUSIC
Hymns
Alleluia, by your Spirit we will sing
All my hope on God is founded
Amazing grace
As we are gathered
Be thou my guardian and my guide
Come down, O love divine

theme is expressed by the story of the prodigal son for Year 1, and by the blind beggar who receives his sight for Year 2. Aim to create an effect of new found hope, incorporating a small arrangement of dried flowers and grasses which leans towards the main display. Choose warm, rich colours and a line which emphasises the welcome.

NOTES ON THE READINGS **Year 1**

Exodus 24:3-11

A shared meal was one way of sealing a covenant between two parties, and here the leaders and elders of Israel share a meal in a literal 'summit' meeting. God is present among them in a very powerful way. They can sense the close bond with him at a time when their wills and hearts are fresh with zeal for keeping his Word. Like a prefiguring of Communion, God and his people eat and drink together in love and fellowship.

Blood, too, symbolic of life, was used in the sealing of a covenant. We can see here the leaning towards Christ's sacrifice, in which, through his spilt blood, we are brought back into fellowship with God.

Colossians 3:12-17

'Wearing' kindness, compassion and humility is quite different from carrying them around. Once on, clothes go everywhere we go, and unless they are definitely unsuitable for our activity we tend to forget about them and concentrate on what we are doing. Having chosen overalls to wear, we can paint the window frames without worrying about accidental spills; having chosen a raincoat and wellies we can take the children to school without moaning about getting wet. In other words, if we choose to wear suitable clothes, our attitudes and outlooks alter.

These qualities of compassionate caring are suitable clothes to wear for living a Christian life. If we mentally put them on when we dress each morning, we shall find them helping us through the day. It will not be an introverted obsession with how our 'clothes' look, but a practical confidence which enables us to fling ourselves whole-heartedly into the business of Christian caring without worrying about any possible damage to us. For these fruits are the loving Spirit of Christ living in us, and they equip us for the task of establishing and forging loving relationships, and making reconciliation a priority.

Luke 15:11-end

It is a great relief to find that Jesus teaches, through this parable, that we can be accepted and saved even when we have made a thorough mess of our lives! There is no sin we may have committed which God will not forgive. Nothing we do will ever make us unlovable to God, our heavenly Father, and he will come running out to meet us even while we are still miles off.

If we feel sorry for the elder brother, we must remember the circumstances in which Jesus told his parable. The Pharisees and Scribes were not wicked men. They had remained faithful through the centuries of history and obeyed the Law minutely. Similarly the elder brother had remained as a good and trustworthy member of his father's house. The trouble is that in our human weakness, we tend to become jealous of our positions, and instead of being delighted when newcomers discover what we have known for years, we are tempted to stand on what we feel are our privileges and rights.

Living in Christ turns this upside down. For if what we delight in is a state in which all men are reconciled to God in one great Kingdom of love, then, when others accept Christ, we will be so thrilled that we'll be feasting and welcoming for all we're worth!

'Thy Kingdom come', we pray. Do we really want the Kingdom of God enough?

QUESTIONS FOR DISCUSSION

1. People often say that unless we love ourselves, we cannot love others. What do you think the Christian version of this would be?
2. We cannot pretend to be filled with the joy of new life and we may not always feel like rejoicing. From today's readings, can you see what we need to do first, in order for the new life to start?

IDEAS FOR ADULTS

Make sure everyone has a copy of the first reading, and have everyone joining in the pieces said by all the people. Have one man to read Moses' words and a narrator to read all the rest.

CHILDREN'S TEACHING

The prodigal son is a lovely story to act out. Have a large assortment of dressing up clothes available (curtains, net, lengths of material, old ties and towels etc.)

Tell the children the story, showing pictures of the son:

(a) asking for money;
(b) waving goodbye;
(c) spending it all;

(d) as a pig keeper;

(e) returning home with Father's welcome. The elder brother can be omitted with young children, as there is plenty for them to grasp without it, and it may make the lesson too complicated.

(f) Angry brother with Father explaining. Having given parts (plenty can be servants, girl friends and pigs) read out the story bit by bit while the children act it out.

The value of this type of drama is in the involvement, rather than the standard of performance, so suggest what the characters might say as you go along.

INTERCESSIONS Years 1 and 2
Some ideas for prayer

Let us approach our heavenly Father
in humility, as we bring to his
restoring love
all our concern for the Church and the world.

Lord, we bring to you
the divided Christian community;
lead us tenderly
to wholeness and unity.
Pause
Jesus! Master!: **You alone can make us whole**

Lord, we bring to you
the divided world,
split between wealth and poverty,
complacency and oppression;
break through all barriers
with your love and reconciliation.
Pause
Jesus! Master!: **You alone can make us whole**

Lord, we bring to you
the wounds and hurts of our own lives;
and of our families;
all unresolved tensions and sorrows,
all reunions, joys and healing;
bless and renew our lives
with your living presence.
Pause
Jesus! Master!: **You alone can make us whole**

Lord, we bring to you
all in pain or distress;
the mentally and physically handicapped
and all whom society prefers to ignore;
may your love nourish and heal,
accept and restore.
Pause
Jesus! Master!: **You alone can make us whole**

Lord, we commend to your everlasting
love and care, all who have died,
especially....

With great joy in our hearts
we offer you thanks and praise
for all the gifts and blessings
you lavish on us; may we
proclaim our thankfulness
by the lives we lead.

Merciful Father
**accept these prayers
for the sake of your Son,
our Saviour Jesus Christ, Amen.**

NOTES ON THE READINGS Year 2

Micah. 6:1-8
In this passage we feel the heartache and sorrow of God which is personified in the anguish of Christ on the cross. So blind, so obstinate and so perverse is humanity that we are forever getting our priorities wrong, and racing at top speed in the wrong direction. Whenever our heads are down, concentrating on immediate satisfaction and self-centred reward, we lose sight of what we are created for. Then even our worship will become hollow and meaningless, and whatever we outwardly 'do' for God will mean nothing if it does not first spring from a thankful and loving heart.

Ephesians 4:17-end
Those who love are bound to get hurt sometimes. Those who love deeply may get badly hurt. And all our loving is only a faint reflection of God's love for us, so every time we turn our backs on what is right, indulge our spitefulness, cause friction or sulk, we reject the one who loves us completely. Anyone who has ever been rejected or slighted will know how much that hurts.

So our sin, our selfishness, causes the Holy Spirit of God to grieve; it fills him with great sorrow and hurts him deeply, in a personal way. And similarly he is personally delighted when we reflect his nature by being responsive, warm and loving people.

Mark 10:46-end
We do not know what made Bartimaeus blind, but when we meet him he strikes us as loud-mouthed, bitter and aggressive. He certainly antagonises some of the crowd, who tell him to be quiet. His cry sounds hard, and full of unresolved resentment at his condition. He demands that everyone should feel sorry for him, for he feels so sorry for himself.

We might expect Jesus to go running over to see him straight away and put things right by making him see. But Jesus understands that the blindness is only part of the problem; healing will only happen to Bartimaeus' personality when he starts to reach out from himself and humble his heart to admit his need and ask for help, instead of nursing his self pity. (In treatment for addiction, healing begins when the addiction is admitted and the need for help acknowledged.)

Jesus sends instructions for the man to make the first move and approach him, and at the invitation Bartimaeus jumps up — he even flings off his cloak in his excitement. When he gets to Jesus there is a significant silence before Jesus prompts him to express his need. It comes out in a new, reverent and respectful manner, straightforward, and simply put. This changed attitude is an important part of the healing; his raw, desperate longing is fulfilled as he receives both sight and self respect.

QUESTIONS FOR DISCUSSION

1. Look at what God says he has done, in the Micah reading. What could he say to his people today — and to us, personally? In other words, what has God done for us?
2. Notice how Jesus first prepares the ground before healing Bartimaeus. What can we learn from this about the kind of healing Jesus offers, and the kind of attitude we need to have before receiving it?

IDEAS FOR ADULTS

The Gospel today is excellent for acting out, and such a dramatisation can open people's eyes to notice things in the miracle which they haven't seen before. Prepare a script with the drama group, putting in lines for 'many people told him to hold his tongue' etc. Don't hurry the action; use pauses, and have some distance for Bartimaeus to walk towards Jesus. He will do this with some difficulty, and determination. Try to express the change of tone in his words at the beginning and when he gets to Jesus.

CHILDREN'S TEACHING

Talk with the children about how difficult it is for blind people to go shopping, cook or even walk along pavements where bikes have been left around. Ask them to shut their eyes for a minute while they try to do an ordinary task like laying a table or putting their shoes and socks on.

Explain how sometimes we can all be 'blind' to other people's needs or to how we are making life difficult for someone. Jesus wants to give us all our sight back.

Now read or tell them the story in today's Gospel, getting a few to mime it as you go. Then help them make these masks to make the point of seeing God's way.

7th Sunday after Pentecost (Trinity 6)

TODAY'S THEME

... is love — the more excellent way of living. God is love, so when we live in love we live in God and he lives in us. In fact, every loving, caring and forgiving act is evidence of God's presence.

PARISH MUSIC
Hymns
A new commandment
Bind us together, Lord
Brother, let me be your servant
Colours of day dawn into the mind
Come down, O love divine
Father, hear the prayer we offer
Father, Lord of all creation
God be in my head
God forgave my sins in Jesus' name
Go in peace to be Christ's body
Help us to help each other, Lord

Hope springs out of every race
If we only seek peace
It is a thing most wonderful
Jesu gentlest Saviour
Let there be peace on earth
Love is his word, love is his way
Make me a channel of your peace
My song is love unknown
O God beyond all praising
Oh Lord, all the world belongs to you
The Spirit lives to set us free
You can't stop rain from falling down

Recorded music
Symphony No. 49 (Haydn): La Passione

For choirs
Day by day (How): 3 part
Beloved, let us love (Joule)

CHURCH DECORATION

Today's theme of loving as the best way to live, needs simple, uncluttered arrangements, in which each flower can be seen and enjoyed. Try, for instance a display of just eight or nine lilies with ivy; or six roses, all of the same colour with twisted willow; or tiny posies attached to the end of each pew in soft mauves and pinks.

NOTES ON THE READINGS **Year 1**

Hosea 11:1-9
In spite of his people's waywardness and lack of fidelity, God loves them with tender, unswerving affection, and whenever they stray he labours to bring them back.

The Northern kingdom was fast approaching the threat of collapse after generations of unfaithfulness, self-indulgence and decadence. As the prophet Amos had pointed out, they deserved all they were going to get, for they had rejected God utterly, and God would be quite justified in abandoning them to their fate. But Hosea, personally wounded by his own beloved but unfaithful wife, was able to balance the justice of God's character with his tender mercy and forgiving love, and though deeply hurt and grieved by them, he is always willing to start afresh with them and welcome them back.

1 Corinthians 12:27-13 end
This most beautiful passage on Christian love is worth reading every day this week. It is so different from the world's values, and reaches to the heart of all Christ's life and teaching.

If we try putting our own name instead of 'love', we shall very quickly see how mean and lacking in love our lives often are.

But there is plenty of hope; by God's grace there are times when we do reveal these qualities, and so often these are the times we feel, surprisingly, not burdened by their weight, but refreshed and full of joy. The way of love is not heavy and oppressive at all — it actually brings the very peace and freedom that selfishness tries desperately to buy. God gives it to us, hands it out for free: can we afford not to accept it?

Matthew 18:21-end

When we hear this story, we probably share the indignation of the fellow servants at such injustice. The issue is clear and easily seen.

Unfortunately, in real life things are rarely so glaringly black and white, and it is quite possible for us to find we have been behaving like the unforgiving servant without even realising it. Often, it happens when we are under pressure: if we have a deadline to meet, we shall probably take out our anxiety on those who hold us up; if money is scarce, we are more likely to flare up at anyone causing expensive damage.

Yet, when you think about it, such pressure is really caused by us keeping a tight grip on our lives instead of giving them away to Christ. If, when we feel the tension, we take a deep breath and remember that, as children of eternity, our lives are now spaces for God to work in, then the irritations and setbacks become opportunities to grow in patience, to spread God's kind of peace which the world lacks, and to put into practice his loving forgiveness.

QUESTIONS FOR DISCUSSION

1. Often the Old Testament is thought of as portraying a God of justice, rather than tenderness and mercy. How does the book of Hosea prove that image wrong?
2. What examples of crime, political unrest and personal misery can you think of which are based on a lack of forgiveness? Why is forgiveness taught by Jesus to be a symptom of love?

IDEAS FOR ADULTS

Today's Gospel is excellent for acting out. You will need:

    a narrator
    the king
    2 or 3 servants
    the man who owes 10,000 talents
    the man who owes 100 denarii
    torturers

You can include a few props, such as a crown, some money, a rope and a whip, for instance.

When the narrator begins, have the king and his servants counting piles of money and looking at long bills. You can alter some of the narrative passages to be direct speech (such as when the king cancels the debt). Try it out first as it stands and wherever direct speech comes naturally, put it in.

At the end, all the actors would walk to the centre and say the last sentence together: 'And that is how your heavenly Father will deal with you unless you each forgive your brother from your heart.' This could either be performed at the Gospel, or just after a straight reading of the Gospel, in place of a homily.

CHILDREN'S TEACHING

Begin by asking them the question Peter asked Jesus — how often do they think they should forgive their brothers and sisters if they keep irritating/breaking toys/teasing etc. It will probably become clear that there is quite a gap between ideals and reality, so help them to be honest!

Then tell them how Peter asked Jesus the same question and how he explained his answer with a story. Tell the story, using different headgear for the various characters, some bills and play money and a pair of handcuffs, or something similar. You can grab hold of a volunteer when the second servant is nearly throttled. If the children have enjoyed an entertaining telling of the story, and been involved in it, they will remember it more.

So having told it and talked about what it says about the way we should behave, let all the children join in an acted version.

INTERCESSIONS **Years 1 and 2**
Some ideas for prayer

My friends in Christ,
mindful of God's steadfast love for us
let us pray to our heavenly Father.

We pray for faithfulness among all Christians,
particularly when conflicts arise
between Christian values and social
    expectations;
for a drawing together towards unity
and an increase of the kind of caring
that should make Christ's followers stand out.
Pause
Father, live in us: **fill us with love**

We pray for all factories, mines, quarries,
all processing and refining plants
and all who work in them or live close by;
may they be safely and responsibly managed
with industrial relations based on
mutual respect, courtesy and goodwill.
Pause
Father, live in us: **fill us with love**

We pray for everyone who has helped us
and forgiven us this week at home, at work
or at school; for anyone in need whom we
could help; make us more prepared
to take the initiative in caring
for others, and taking ourselves
less seriously.
Pause
Father, live in us: **fill us with love**

We pray for the mal-nourished and starving,
the grief-stricken and the bereaved;
for the homeless, and those surviving
in inadequate or dangerous accommodation;
open our eyes to see Christ among all
who suffer, so we are inspired to spend
our lives in helping those in need.
Pause
Father, live in us: **fill us with love**

We pray for those who have died;
that falling asleep to pain and suffering
they may wake to the joy and freedom
of your heaven.

Lord, your glory is everywhere
for us to see, and we thank you for
all the love that brightens our world.

Merciful Father
accept these prayers
for the sake of your Son,
our Saviour Jesus Christ, Amen.

NOTES ON THE READINGS **Year 2**

Deuteronomy 10:12-11:1
Although some of the scribes and Pharisees had
made the Law very narrow and negative by
Jesus' day, we can see here that it is really a
broad, unprejudiced, positive attitude which is
at the heart of the Law. Jesus, interpreting it
as love for God and neighbour, was going right
back to the fundamental values of loving one
another in the same limitless way that God loves
us.

Romans 8:1-11
Once Christ lives in us we shall be alive in four
dimensions, as it were. He will give us the grace
to embrace life with a fullness and generosity
which is unfettered by self-interest or prejudice.
And even death does not mark an end, but an
entrance to the complete fullness of eternal life
lived out for ever in the presence and kingdom
of the risen Christ.

Mark 12:28-34
Regularly through Israel's history the prophets
had declared God's loathing for lip worship
without a committed heart, and hypocritical
sacrifices that were empty of true repentance.
Now, when the scribe approaches Jesus, he is
genuinely concerned to find out where Jesus
stands in relation to the Mosaic Law. Jesus
focuses attention right back at the fundamental
principles, from which all else springs, and the
scribe warmly responds. He recognises that
Christ is not a threat to the Law but is anxious
to centralise what is really important, instead of
looking so closely at the intricate rules and
regulations that the basic rock is disregarded.

The Christian Church is not automatically
immune from a similar near-sightedness. We
need to be constantly rigorous in gazing
steadfastly at our loving God, so as to avoid
getting side-tracked in all the little extras that
can distort our true vision.

QUESTIONS FOR DISCUSSION

1. Does it surprise you to see how 'Christian'
   this Old Testament passage is? (We have had
   Jesus in person to teach us, but they hadn't.)
   How do you account for the spiritual insight
   and maturity shown so early on?
2. How does the Gospel conversation compare
   with most others between Jesus and the
   lawyers and scribes? What makes this lawyer
   different?

IDEAS FOR ADULTS

Have Christ's summary of the Law displayed on large posters in church, worked in appliqué or collage.

Love God with all your heart and with all your soul and with all your mind and with all your strength

Love your neighbour as yourself

CHILDREN'S TEACHING

Beforehand make two simple hand puppets and join them to a piece of stiff card with lengths of string. On the card, stick a sheet of paper with a clearly written script on it. Use different colours for the two characters. Stick the second script on the other side of the card.

Script 1.

Boots   Loopy, you must help me.
I need to do a hard sum.
If you stop talking
I can do it.

Loopy   O.K. Boots. You do your sum.
I will not talk.
Boots   Thank you Loopy.
Now, let me see...
Loopy   (sings) La la la la pom pom pom!
Boots   Loopy, stop it!
You said you would not talk
so I could do my sum.
Loopy   Yes I know I did.
And I have kept my promise.
I was not talking,
I was singing!
Boots   Oh, Loopy!!

Script 2.

Boots   What are you doing, Loopy?
Loopy   I'm sweeping these leaves
for Mr. Tod.
Boots   That is kind of you.
Loopy   I'm just doing it
to make him think I'm kind.
Then he will give me some sweets.
Boots   Wow! That's clever.
I'll sweep too.
He'll never know
we are not really
being kind.

Ask two children to wear the puppets and read the first script so everyone can hear. Was Loopy doing what she was told? Help them to see that in one way she was, yet in another way she wasn't — like when we rush our prayers but have not really talked to God at all.

Ask another two children to read the second script. Mr. Tod told all his friends about how kind Loopy and Boots were. Did they deserve his praise and his sweets? Help them to see that although they had done the sweeping, they had not been honest with Mr. Tod.

Now tell the children about some of the scribes and Pharisees who behaved rather like Loopy and Boots. They did all the right things, down to the very last detail (you could demonstrate all the washing and ritual they went through) but they were not really obeying God's main rule at all.

On a poster, write up God's main Laws, or rules, and see if they can learn them off by heart. Chanting them to a simple melody makes the learning easier, and the Law can be sung to their families in church. *London's burning* works well:

> You shall love the Lord your God with
> all your mind and all your heart and
> all your strength! All your strength!
> And love your neighbour, love your
> neighbour!

8th Sunday after Pentecost (Trinity 7)

TODAY'S THEME

... is the fruit of the Spirit. The kind of tree we are will always be shown by the kind of fruit we bear. If we are rooted in Christ, we shall find that our lives blossom and fruit richly.

PARISH MUSIC

Hymns
All over the world the Spirit is moving
Awake, awake; fling off the night
Breathe on me, breath of God
Come, thou holy Paraclete
Father, hear the prayer we offer
Father, who in Jesus found us
Give me peace, O Lord I pray
Glory to the Spirit of God
Go forth and tell
Go in peace to be Christ's body
Guide me O thou great redeemer
He who would valiant be
I am the light
If we only seek peace
In heavenly love abiding
Lead us, heavenly Father, lead us
Lord Jesus Christ
Make me a channel of your peace
Oft in danger, oft in woe
O Jesus I have promised
Spirit of mercy, truth and love
To mercy, pity, peace and love
Walk with me, O my Lord

Recorded music
Suite in A minor for flute and orchestra
  (Telemann)

For choirs
Lord, make me an instrument of thy
  peace (Rutter)
The Fruit of the Spirit (Oxley): SSA

CHURCH DECORATION

Fruit and vegetables make magnificent displays, and it is a pity to confine them to Harvest Festival. Today's theme of the fruits of the Spirit is a good chance to include some local produce in the arrangements, along with plenty of summer flowers. Try using baskets or trugs as containers, and choose flower colours to enhance the fruit and vegetable colours.

NOTES ON THE READINGS **Year 1**

Ezekiel 36:24-28
Following the fall of Jerusalem, the exiled people of Israel need encouragement and hope. Although they have brought their downfall on themselves by their lax and corrupt behaviour, God speaks through Ezekiel to remind them of his steadfast love, and his promise to save them. It will not be a patched up job, but a thorough remaking — a complete new heart transplant, so to speak — until they are enabled to think and love as God does.

Galatians 5:16-25
We are all prone to self-indulgence, and Paul suggests that the only way to steer clear of it is to be guided by the Spirit. But what exactly does that mean? The Ezekiel passage gives us a clue. In order to save his people from themselves, God knew he would have to give them a new heart; Christ's victory opened the way for this to happen. For the outpouring of the Spirit penetrates our personalities and turns us into a new 'species', with natural capacity for strong growth, good fruit and resistance to disease.

   The good fruit described in this passage, then, is not stuck on to the outside of us, where it would surely decay before long; rather, it grows quite naturally, without exaggerated effort, provided we are first remade by God into fruiting varieties!

John 15:16-end

Jesus never promises us a rose garden. He never pretends that life in his service will be without danger and hardship. Often, in fact, he takes care to warn his friends that they are quite likely to be abused, just as he is. Saint Theresa is said to have been feeling low after such treatment, and heard God explain that this was the way he treated all his friends. No wonder, then, she retorted, that he had so few!

Yet, in spite of hardship, the fruiting goes on, and we still see wonderful examples of fruitful Christian lives whose joy, patience and love spread light among many. And when the going is painful or lonely, and we begin to wonder if God is still there, he is suddenly beside us, with assurance and encouragement, and we realise he has been through everything with us, just as he promised.

QUESTIONS FOR DISCUSSION

1. Why is self-indulgence said to be the opposite of the Spirit? Is it acceptable to 'cut down' on bad habits, rather than cutting them out completely?
2. Why are people in every generation prepared to renounce personal comfort and indulgence and work and live in Christ instead? How is it that such people end up actually happier and more at peace with themselves?

IDEAS FOR ADULTS

Make a set of banners, each depicting a different fruit of the Spirit. They can be done by different groups in the parish, and brought to the altar by a representative from each group before the service. Then they can be leant against the walls or pillars to help people think about the different qualities of love, joy, peace, patience etc.

CHILDREN'S TEACHING

Have ready two money boxes or piggy banks and some pretend money (or real, if you wish.) Read the first part of the Gospel.

Explain how Jesus said that following him might be rather expensive, and we'd better decide first whether or not we're prepared to pay the cost before we join him.

What expenses are there in following Jesus? On another 'Christian Expenses' list, write down what we have to spend or give up to be Christians:

- watching television on Sunday mornings;
- telling lies;
- keeping all our sweets to ourselves;
- joining in the unkind teasing; etc.

What do we pay with? Out of the second money box take money shaped cards with:

- kindness;
- love;
- thoughtfulness;
- helpfulness;
- peace-making;
- self-control;
- patience;
- cheerfulness; etc.

It costs a lot, doesn't it? But we couldn't spend it on anything that would make us happier. And remind them that Jesus has spent everything for us — even his life!

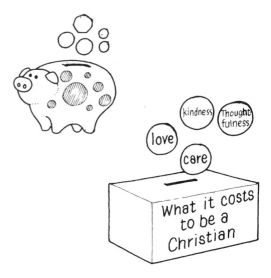

Give each child a box to decorate and cut out 'coins' to put inside.

INTERCESSIONS **Years 1 and 2**
Some ideas for prayer

Led by the Spirit we have come here today.
Trusting in our loving and merciful Father,
let us pray together
for the Church and for the world.

We pray for all Christian ministries,
both ordained and lay;
in mutual love may we learn from
one another, grow closer across denominations,
and keep rooted only in Christ.
Pause
Nourish us, Lord: **so that we fruit in joy**

We pray for all peace initiatives,
all negotiations between nations, and
all attempts at integration;

that, knowing your love for every individual,
we may all respect and honour one another.
Pause
Nourish us, Lord: **so that we fruit in joy**

We pray for our loved ones - our families
and our friends;
for greater understanding of those
from whom we feel distant;
that we may show your love
in the way we order our relationships.
Pause
Nourish us, Lord: **so that we fruit in joy**

We pray for those who are far from home;
for those who are exiled or who fear for their
    lives;
keep them safe, and help them to know
the strength of your presence,
no matter what dangers they face.
Pause
Nourish us, Lord: **so that we fruit in joy**

We pray that those who have died in faith
may rise in glory, and know your presence
for ever.

We thank you for our lovely world
and all the good there is in it;
may we be as generous
as you are.

Merciful Father
accept these prayers
for the sake of your Son,
our Saviour Jesus Christ, Amen.

NOTES ON THE READINGS Year 2

Ezekiel 37:1-14
When hope finishes, it is as if a candle gutters
and dies; as if a heart misses a beat and stops.
Carcasses remain, and many people's lives are
littered with carcasses: their hopes are dead, and
fester to rank bitterness. What chance is there
of bringing such people back to life?

Often their despair is treated with drugs which
may affect the outward symptoms, but if the
cause is deep-seated anger and bitterness,
because hopes have been dashed, the despair and
depression cannot be cured by drugs alone.

This prophecy points to the only lasting and
complete wholeness: the Spirit of God can
awaken new life in the deadest, most hardened,
and seemingly hopeless situations. Nothing is
too dead or beyond his life-giving breath.

We who know Christ must work tirelessly to
open the floodgates for that life to pour in;
wedge a foot of love in the door to keep it open
in those who are in danger of closing it
completely; and constantly clear away all that

clutters and blocks his love in our own lives.

1 Corinthians 12:4-13
His love is outpoured on his followers in a wealth
of diversity, an abundance of gifts and talents,
which are all valuable in building up Christ's
Church.

It is no good wasting our time and God's in
hankering after a different gift. Nor can we
decide in advance our first choices and
recommend God to take our advice!

God is so much greater than we often
arrogantly imagine, and he sees, with complete
knowledge and insight, what the needs are, and
how and by whom they can be met. In some
ways this makes life a good deal lighter and
happier, for we have no need to worry any more
about what we can or cannot do; instead we have
only to love and trust Jesus, the Lord, and he
will bring out in us all kinds of gifts which are
often unexpected and sometimes a complete
surprise and joy. Having been made rich, we can
spend our gifts as liberally and freely as God
wants; then, together, we will be helping to reap
God's harvest.

Luke 6:27-38
Some of Christ's basic teaching has been
gathered here so that we can get a clear view of
what 'loving', in God's vocabulary, really
entails. What we hear is beyond all boundaries
of reason and inclination, and involves becoming
'fools for Christ's sake'.

Since the words are so familiar, it is all too easy
to assume that we know it, in the sense that we
understand and have assimilated such an attitude
in our own relationships.

But what about when we are unjustly accused?
 – unfairly treated?
 – upholding ideals against dangerous
   opposition?

Yet the way that Christ teaches has no list of
exceptions or special cases where the loving can
be waived for expediency; it is an all-inclusive
response to honouring every sordid scrap of
humanity as being God-made and valuable. It
is relinquishing all the independence of self until
our lack of defensiveness leaves us free to serve.

QUESTIONS FOR DISCUSSION

1. What are the parallels between the skeletons
   coming to life in the valley, and God's people
   and their destiny? How does Ezekiel's
   prophecy stretch on, past the Old Testament
   right through to our own time?
2. Is the kind of love Jesus teaches really very
   practical? Is it still possible to practise it and
   work in industry, commerce or politics?

IDEAS FOR ADULTS

At the offering of gifts today arrange for everyone to bring up in the procession a small token of what they do in life. For instance, a builder could bring a brick, a cook a wooden spoon, a gardening enthusiast a trowel. Ask everyone a week beforehand to think about what to bring and explain that we shall be offering our lives for God to use.

As all the people approach the altar with these tokens, it is a moving experience to see the ordinary things of life, and the wide variety of lives presented, being offered. It makes everyone aware of their membership of Christ's body, too.

All tokens are placed near the altar, and taken out into the world again. It is a powerful symbol of our stewardship of God's gifts.

CHILDREN'S TEACHING

Read or tell the children the teachings in the Gospel today, acting some of them out with different children as you go, and involving them in what they think is the right thing to do in each situation. They may well be surprised at Jesus' advice!

Then talk with them about the sort of thing they find starts them off behaving in an unloving way, and together work out some practical way to avoid the temptation. (Perhaps going out to kick a ball when they feel like kicking a sister;

setting a cooking timer to share a toy equally, giving each a set time — until the pinger rings — in which to play; writing a list of daily jobs that need to be done before bed, so things don't get forgotten; asking to sit next to someone in class with whom they are less likely to waste time!)

Give the children paper cups and a pencil. They draw their own face on the side of the cup and punch holes in the bottom. Then, over the grass or a large bowl, pour water from an enormous jug through each child's cup. We are to be channels for God's living Spirit to flow through to the world; we have to work at increasing the flow!

9th Sunday after Pentecost (Trinity 8)

TODAY'S THEME

... is putting on the whole armour of God. On our own we are not powerful enought to fight against evil, but God's power of goodness is sufficient for any evil we may meet, and he promises to give us that power when we put ourselves into his care.

PARISH MUSIC
Hymns
And did those feet in ancient time
A safe stronghold our God is still
Be thou my guardian and my guide
Blessed assurance, Jesus is mine
Christ be beside me
Fight the good fight
Glorify the Lord
Guide me, O thou great redeemer
I bind unto myself this day
Just a closer walk with thee
Lord, when I turn my back on you
My faith it is an oaken staff
Oft in danger, oft in woe
O God of Bethel, by whose hand
O Jesus I have promised
Onward Christian soldiers
O worship the King
Put on the armour of Jesus Christ
Soldiers of Christ arise
Stand up, stand up for Jesus
Take up your cross he says
Through all the changing scenes of life
Walk with me, O my Lord
When a knight won his spurs
With you, O God, my highest good

Recorded music
Romeo and Juliet: The grand ball
 (Prokofiev)

For choirs
O Lord, I will praise thee (Jacob): SATB
When the Lord turned again (Batten):
SATB

CHURCH DECORATION

To suggest the theme of the armour of God, try
using a brass or pewter container today, with
rich bronze coloured chrysanthemums and silver
or bronze foliage, such as copper beech, bugle
or senecio cineraria, eryngium and wormwood.

NOTES ON THE READINGS **Year 1**

Joshua 1:1-9
Joshua, faced with the immense and dangerous
task of leading the people of Israel right into the
occupied promised land, is given great
encouragement: he will be neither on his own,
nor fighting only in his own strength. God
promises to be with him wherever he goes. The
only way he can block himself off from God's
presence and power is by turning away from his
law.

If we sometimes feel cut off from God's
power, it is a good idea to check that we have
not erected blockades of selfishness, greed or
pride which are preventing his power from
getting through to us. It could be that God has
not turned away from us at all; it is only that
we have turned away from him.

Ephesians 6:10-20
There is no doubt that the evil against which we
fight is real, dangerous, and immensely
powerful. (One of the best ways to invite evil
is to pretend it doesn't exist.) Paul was acutely
aware of our need to be constantly vigilant, and
well armed against it. He recognised that it could
otherwise take over. History shows us that he
was right.

So what of the future? Are we ever secretly
afraid that evil is stronger even than God's
influence in our world? Does it sometimes seem
that we are doomed to lose the battle against it?

Whether we tend to dismiss evil or fear it,
God's answer is the same: his power of goodness
and love is infinite, and therefore well able to
win. It is available for us to use, and we do need
to use it — the whole lot, not just bits of it,
which leave bits of us unprotected.

John 17:11b-19
It is great privilege to be given this insight into
Jesus at prayer. We can learn so much from the
way he pours out his heart to his Father, voicing
his fears and talking things through in perfect
trust. His love and affection for the little group
he has trained is protective and deeply caring

but not in any way possessive. Of far more
importance than their personal bodily safety is
that they are kept true to God, consecrated and
set apart to that end. For love is stronger than
death; when we live in God (who is Love) we
live a life that can never be destroyed.

QUESTIONS FOR DISCUSSION

1. Can you see why, in practical terms, we are
more likely to win against evil when we are
in constant touch with God? How does life
in us affect our attitudes and decision-
making?
2. Look carefully at the stages of Jesus' prayer.
What are they? How can they help us pray
when facing some problem, evil or sorrow?

IDEAS FOR ADULTS

In the light of today's readings, discuss the
prayer life in your parish. Groups in some
parishes meet each week to share times of praise,
prayer and meditation; others have times of
shared silence in church, which can be very
fruitful; others have strong prayer chains, which
are used whenever needs arise in the parish.
They may be composed of unemployed, bed-
ridden or elderly Christians who have the gift
of time to spend on this valuable work.

Other parishes have a regular prayer group
which meets specifically to pray for those who
are physically, mentally or emotionally troubled,
and the prayer life extends into hospital and
home visiting, transport for out-patient care or
child care when parents undergo treatment. If
this seems a good idea for the needs in your
parish, be thorough in planning the caring, with
one person organising and centralising.
Otherwise a lack of communication can cause
problems instead of solving them. But the local
church is a wonderful place to act as a centre
for people who care enough about those living
in the neighbourhood to provide prayer support
and practical help in times of crisis and illness.

CHILDREN'S TEACHING

Bring along a selection of protective clothing,
such as a cagoule, umbrella and over-trousers;
crash helmet, leather jacket and strong boots;
white coat and clinical mask; soldier's helmet,
sword and shield. Put them on in turn, getting
the children to help and suggest what each outfit
protects you against. They may be able to think
of some other protective clothing, too.

Now read or tell them what Paul says about
how we can protect ourselves against evil. Go
through the list again, this time putting labels
on each item as you dress one child up in full

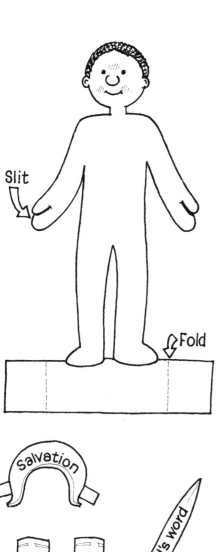

Slit

Fold

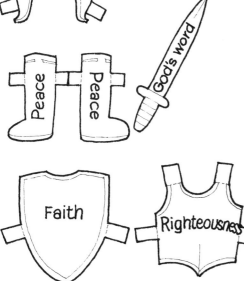

Salvation

God's word

Peace

Peace

Faith

Righteousness

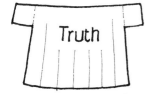

Truth

armour. (If you can't get hold of a dressing up set of Roman armour, make a set from cardboard, using the pattern shown.) Then give each child a picture of a person, and the different items of spiritual armour, each labelled, which they colour and fix on.

INTERCESSIONS **Years 1 and 2**
Some ideas for prayer

Companions in Christ,
knowing that our heavenly Father
has sufficient grace for all our needs,
let us pray to him now.

Lord, we pray for the leaders
and ministers of your Church,
especially those for whom
your work has brought danger
and persecution;
may they never lose sight
of your presence, which
comforts and protects.
Pause
Lord of power: **deliver us from evil**

We pray for clear light and guidance
as our world faces the problems and crises
of another week; for the willingness of leaders
to be wisely advised and courageous
in doing what is right.
Pause
Lord of power: **deliver us from evil**

We pray for a greater willingness in us
to live and work in your strength;
for a deepening trust in your power
to save, heal and overcome temptation.
Pause
Lord of power: **deliver us from evil**

We pray for all addicted to drugs,
alcohol, solvent abuse, violence,
or any other habit that enslaves;
for all victims of war, and abuse;
for the terrified and the suicidal.
Pause
Lord of power: **deliver us from evil**

We pray that all who have passed
from this life
may live in the joy of your presence for ever.

Thank you, Father, for all the evils
that have been conquered, and all the
good that is done through your power

every day throughout our world.
Help us to notice your goodness.

Merciful Father
accept these prayers
for the sake of your Son,
our Saviour Jesus Christ, Amen.

NOTES ON THE READINGS Year 2

1 Samuel 17:37-50
This splendid story speaks of deep, spiritual truth. We see the simple weapons of trust in God and desire to do his will, contrasted with the cumbersome, exaggerated armour of bullying power. We see God-given freedom enabling natural gifts to flourish for good; we see that putting our faith in anything other than God, however technically advanced, may well let us down. We see that goodness can face evil and win; that if God is with us, we need not be afraid.

2 Corinthians 6:3-10
There are extraordinary paradoxes in the Christian life. So many Christians have recorded the odd and remarkable experience of finding wonderful assurance and peace at the lowest, weakest and most terrifying points in their lives; of sensing the great company of the faithful while in solitary confinement, or inexplicable peace before execution. The right words pour out (often to our own astonishment!) when we are called to witness to Christ in a difficult situation; and when we know full well we would normally be exploding, we are buoyed up with patience that can have only one source.

These are the daily miracles that happen to all people of prayer. They strengthen our faith as we see that praying really works, and they witness powerfully to others — especially those who know our weaknesses and limitations all too well. For it all points to Christ's power working in us; and when other people see how our faith allows us to accept disaster calmly (not with a stiff upper lip, necessarily), to remain forgiving in the face of attack, or to stay outgoing during long-term illness, they will be drawn to seek this power for themselves.

Mark 9:14-29
Jesus and three of his disciples had just come down from the mountain where they had seen their master transfigured — an experience which increased their faith in him as the Son of God. Yet back here, Jesus is reminded of what a long way most of his followers have to go before they come anywhere near a committed faith — it must have often been rather depressing for Jesus, working with unbelieving, perverse humanity! Rather like coaxing a bonfire from damp sticks with one match on a windy day.

The prayer that Jesus explains is essential for combatting the evil of this disease, is closely linked with faith. Jesus' prayer, just witnessed at the top of the mountain, had completely transfigured him as he was seen full of God's glory. That radiance now floods out to the boy and heals him.

QUESTIONS FOR DISCUSSION

1. In what way is the combat between David and Goliath like our combats with evil in our lives? What can the attitude and approach of David help us to learn?
2. In what practical ways can praying really help?

IDEAS FOR ADULTS

The Old Testament reading can be acted out today. *Mime* the throwing of the stone! It doesn't matter what kind of armour Goliath is wearing, so long as he is much bigger than David, and is heavily armed. Have them some distance from one another, so they really have to shout across the congregation. Card 'armour' for David can be made from the pattern on page 175.

CHILDREN'S TEACHING

This is a favourite story with children and there are many excellent versions of it with pictures to use. Palm Tree also publish a giant picture of David and Goliath for a whole group of children to work on. Alternatively, give the children modelling clay to make their own David and Goliath. They can set their models in a boxed landscape.

Crumpled newspaper under green paper for the hill

David trusts in God

10th Sunday after Pentecost (Trinity 9)

TODAY'S THEME

... is the mind of Christ. It is, perhaps, his amazing humility which touches us most. For although he understands all things, not only on earth but in the entire universe, and although he is fully in charge, he was prepared to live and die among created beings in order to save them. He, the Lord, serves his people.

PARISH MUSIC

Hymns
Amazing grace!
And now, O Father, mindful of the love
At the name of Jesus
Blest are the pure in heart
Dear Lord and Father of mankind
Help us, O Lord, to learn
If we only seek peace
Immortal love, for ever full
Jerusalem the golden
Jesus, name above all names
Jesu, the very thought of thee
Let us break bread together on our knees
Magnificat, magnificat
May the grace of Christ our Saviour
Near the heart of Jesus
Take me, Lord, use my life
Take my hands
Take my life and let it be
Tell out my soul
There's no greater name than Jesus
Thou didst leave thy throne
We pray thee, heavenly Father
Wide, wide as the ocean

Recorded music
Piano Sonata No 8 in A minor (Mozart):
   second movement

For choirs
Christ whose glory fills the skies
   (Knight): U
Jesu, joy of man's desiring (Bach)

CHURCH DECORATION

One way to express today's theme of the mind of God, is to set an arrangement on a mirror. Aim for soft colours and a sense of peace and calm, pure and reflective. Try using a variety of white flowers, with some mauve and blue.

NOTES ON THE READINGS **Year 1**

Job 42:1-6
Having endured terrible anguish, Job had finally challenged God to account for his suffering, and God had replied by directing Job to look afresh at the wonder and powerful beauty of the created universe. In the face of such overwhelming majesty, Job begins to realise something of the greatness of God, the creator. He understands that fulfilment comes to a person not through

material possessions for the short space of one person's life span, but through the eternal values of dependence on God who is wider even than time, and beyond our complete comprehension.

Philippians 2:1-11

Paul urges us to aim for the sky — to model our behaviour on Christ Jesus. And what shines out in his life is that incredible humility which made him willing to obey and to expend everything at colossal cost in order to help and save those he loved.

So, too, we are encouraged by the strength of Christ's love in us, to be outgoing, caring, generous and willing to put up with hardship and suffering in order to help and save others.

Internal bickering among Christian groups usually results from looking too much at each other and too little at Christ. If friction raises its ugly head, it is usually better if we break off everything we are doing for a while, and all look together at Christ. Then, having been touched again by his humility, open-mindedness, love and obedience, we shall be enabled to put our bickering right and heal our rifts, even if we still do not agree about a particular issue.

John 13:1-15

The washing of the disciples' feet shows how Christ's love turns upside down the worldly structures of rights and privileges. This love means relinquishing everything, even our self-images which we cherish, in the business of serving others solely for love. Impossible? Yes, utterly impossible unless, by dying with Christ, we also live with him. In the eucharist which he has supplied, knowing our weakness, we are able to become one with him and share his life of love.

QUESTIONS FOR DISCUSSION

1. It is well worth reading God's answer to Job (38, 39, 40 and 41). Do you think that in our love for the informal, we sometimes forget the tremendous power of God? Do the findings of science whittle down God's greatness, or rather expose more of it?
2. It is quite startling to look straight from the awesome God of the universe, to Jesus, quietly washing the disciples' feet. What is the signficance of this act, and how does it affect our own life-styles?

IDEAS FOR ADULTS

Have an exhibition of the great wonders of God's creation in pictures, quotations from poetry, facts from an atlas etc. arranged all around a central picture of Jesus, washing feet.

CHILDREN'S TEACHING

Have a display of all kinds of interesting and lovely things in God's world, and give the children some time to examine them, enjoy them and find out about them. (Have magnifying glasses handy, and direct their attention to colours, textures, behaviour etc.)

Talk together about the wonderful world, which shows us something about God, just as the pictures we paint show others something about us. Sing some praise songs, and then tell them how Jesus, in spite of all his greatness, acts like a servant. Explain how the servants of that time washed people's feet because it was a hot, dusty country. Then wash one or two children's feet to show them. What servant jobs can they do cheerfully, to follow Jesus' example? Arrange for them to help with clearing up the coffee cups after church, or doing some other very dull job in a happy, friendly way as an act of praise.

INTERCESSIONS Years 1 and 2
Some ideas for prayer

We are all brothers and sisters in Christ; as children of God, our heavenly Father, let us draw near and tell him of our needs and cares, asking for his help and blessing.

We ask you, Lord, to bless and guide all who serve you; to inspire their teaching, nudge their memories, instruct them through their failures and mature them through their experiences, so that in all activity, your will may be done.
Pause
Merciful Lord: **work on us till we shine with love**

We ask you to direct the people of the world
towards harmony and peace,
mutual respect and appreciation
of one another's cultures and traditions;
make us prepared to learn from one another.
Pause
Merciful Lord: **work on us till we shine with
love**

We ask you into our homes and
places of work, so that all our friendships,
and business transactions, shopping
and leisure times
may be opportunities for rejoicing
in your love and spreading your peace.
Pause
Merciful Lord: **work on us till we shine with
love**

We ask you to ease the burdens
of those bowed down by grief,
depression, pain or guilt;
encourage the timid and frightened,
refresh all who are overworked
or who have not been able to sleep;
break down all barricades
of hatred and revenge.
Pause
Merciful Lord: **work on us till we shine with
love**

We ask you to welcome into your kingdom
all who have died in faith;
may they live for ever in
your perfect peace.

Every day we are given
so many blessings;
we offer you our thanks
and life-long praise.

Merciful Father
**accept these prayers
for the sake of your Son,
our Saviour Jesus Christ, Amen.**

NOTES ON THE READINGS **Year 2**

1 Samuel 24:9-17 (or 1-17)
This is a very graphic description of the noble
young David refusing to take advantage of Saul
in spite of everything he has suffered at Saul's
hands. The fact that Saul was once anointed by
God sets him apart, as far as David is concerned,
and in not taking revenge, David is honouring
God.

If we believe that all people are made in God's
likeness then we, too, must honour God in each
person, whether we like what they do or not.

Galatians 6:1-10
In Christ we have a remarkable example of

humility. As we see in the temptations, he could
have used dramatic power to impress people into
following him as a star; he preferred to choose
the way of love, which never boasts, flaunts itself
or takes advantage of others.

So in this letter to the Galatians, Paul reminds
his readers of Christ's way of behaving. Even
criticism, perhaps the hardest thing to learn to
give lovingly or accept humbly, is under Christ's
law of love and consideration for others. Such
excellent behaviour can only happen through
Christ's Spirit, of course. If only we
remembered to make use of this precious and
essential power, we would find ourselves far
more able to behave in a Christlike way.

Luke 7:36-end
Simon the Pharisee is a respected and
honourable man, dutiful and fully committed to
leading a good life. We may wonder what
prompted him to invite Jesus to a meal at his
house. Perhaps this surprisingly wise teacher
from Nazareth spoke words so profound that he
wanted to know more of him; perhaps he was
merely sounding out a man who people were
beginning to claim as a prophet. His lack of
courtesy suggests that he did not rank Jesus as
anyone very important. Whatever his reasons,
he is certainly taken aback when Jesus seems
quite unembarrassed by the attentions of a
woman of bad reputation. The incident makes
him suspect that Jesus may be an imposter.
Jesus' response, however, proves him to be a
prophet whose vision is wider and more
fundamentally satisfying and practical than any
before him. Simon is led to the point where he
can see the link between love and forgiveness.
The Law went hand in hand with
condemnation; Jesus brings it to life with
reconciliation.

QUESTIONS FOR DISCUSSION

1. What do you think you would have done in
David's position? What do we learn from this
passage about both David and Saul? In what
way is it clear that David understood
something of the mind of God?
2. Notice the careful, gentle way that Jesus
brings Simon round to understanding. Why
do you think he takes this circuitous route?
Do we sometimes pay more attention to the
criticism we want to give than to the kindest
way of giving it?

IDEAS FOR ADULTS

Review the rotas for such jobs as providing
refreshments, gardening, church cleaning and
maintenance, so as to check that it is not always

the same loyal souls who end up doing them. If you find they are, arrange for others to give them a surprise thank you — the work done for them, for a change; flowers or a round of drinks provided; smiles and appreciation. It is a kind of feet washing!

CHILDREN'S TEACHING

Tell the story Jesus told Simon, using the children to help you. First choose a postman, and give him a bag and badge (or hat) with two bills to deliver.

'One morning the postman delivered a letter to Sam Butcher. (Postman gives one bill to him.) Sam opened it (let him open it and show everyone) and inside was a bill for £5.

How do you think Sam felt? A bit fed up/miserable? "At least it's not *too* big a bill," he thought. "I'll have to go without all my sweets this week."

Then the postman delivered a letter to Robert South. (He delivers it.) Robert opened it and looked inside. It was a bill for £5000!

How do you think Robert felt? He was very worried and sad, because he didn't have much money at all. "Oh dear," he thought, "I'll *never* manage to pay this. Not unless I sell my house — and then where could I live?"

He felt worried and sad all day. He hardly slept that night, for thinking about the way he couldn't pay that huge bill. Perhaps he would be sent to prison, even.

Next morning the postman delivered another letter to Sam and another to Robert. They opened them, rather nervously. Inside was an important looking letter. It said (let the children read it our together)

Dear Sir,
I am going to let you off.
You need not pay me
the money after all.
Best wishes,
Tom Smith (Manager)

Well, how do you think they felt? Happy/ delighted/relieved? They felt very relieved and happy. Sam was glad he could buy some sweets as usual.

But who do you think felt most thankful? It was Robert! He had been so worried and sad, and it was as if a great heavy weight was lifted off him. He ran out to Tom Smith's office to thank him straight away. He would never forget Tom's kindness.'

Explain that Jesus is rather like Tom Smith, and we are like Sam and Robert. When we do something wrong or unkind it is like being in debt. When we are forgiven, our debt is paid, and we feel happy and relieved again. Let the children make these cards to remind them.

11th Sunday after Pentecost (Trinity 10)

TODAY'S THEME

... is the serving community. Our belief in Jesus as the Son of God is bound to lead on to serving the world as he did. Through our loving and unflinching service we proclaim to the world the generous, caring nature of God.

PARISH MUSIC

Hymns
A new commandment I give unto you
Bread of the world in mercy broken
Brother let me be your servant
Colours of day dawn into the mind
Come and be filled
Come, Lord Jesus, come
Farmer, farmer
Father, Lord of all creation
Forth in thy name, O Lord, I go
Glory be to Jesus
Go in peace to be Christ's body
Hope springs out of every race
If we only seek peace
I give my hands to do your work
I no longer live

I will be with you wherever you go
Kum-ba-ya
Lord Christ who on thy heart didst bear
Make me a channel of thy peace
O Lord, all the world belongs to you
O Lord, furnace of love
Once, only once
On days when much we do goes wrong
Peace is flowing like a river
Peace, perfect peace, is the gift
This world you have made
When I needed a neighbour

Recorded music
Bridge over troubled water (Simon and
    Garfunkle)
Piano Concerto (Ravel): slow movement

For choirs
Now the God of peace (Knight)
Lord, make me an instrument (Aston)

CHURCH DECORATION

Today's theme of the way God uses us as
channels of his love when we serve others, can
be developed by using earthenware containers
and sprays of gold and yellow flowers and
foliage. Dahlias, yarrow, fennel, roses, and
centaurea are all suitable, as are many more at
this rich time of year. You could also try a rim
of very small gold and yellow flowers along the
edge of the altar, arranged in a series of sections
of 'oasis'.

NOTES ON THE READINGS **Year 1**

Isaiah 42:1-7
God may be powerful, but he is never heavy-
handed or domineering. With great gentleness
he tends the tiny flame of life, never snuffing
it out or dismissing it. With our God there is
always hope, for we are precious to our creator,
and he will never give up on us, however slow
we are to learn his ways, and however often we
make mistakes.

If we, aware of that love, treat others in the
same responsive and encouraging way, then they
will come to understand God's love for them,
too. That is our mission: to be lights that guide
people to the peace and joy of a close relationship
with God.

2 Corinthians 4:1-10
Such a mission is a great privilege but also carries
enormous responsibility. After all, if we directed
someone the wrong way to the Post Office they
would only be lost for a short time, and the
consequences would not be traumatic. But if we
direct people to a false image of God's truth, we
may be preventing them from finding his lasting
joy and peace, which is far more serious.

So it is very important that we treasure God's
light that he has entrusted to us, and never get
illusions that we are anything but earthenware
pots to contain it. That way we shall be able to
help spread the light of Christ into the world's
darkness.

John 13:31-35

The best encouragement of all is that Jesus has been glorified by the Father, and in him we can begin to understand how love transforms and fulfils humanity. But we do not have to gaze longingly from a distance and struggle ineptly on our own: the very love which suffuses Jesus makes him reach out personally to us and help us.

QUESTIONS FOR DISCUSSION

1. What do we learn of God's nature in this Isaiah passage? How did Jesus show such qualities in his behaviour?
2. Paul is constantly reminding us to pass on the glory of any good we are enabled to do in Christ. Why do we find this so difficult as humans? In what practical ways can we make sure that we remember that we are only earthenware pots which contain God's treasure?

IDEAS FOR ADULTS

Ask everyone to bring along an ordinary earthenware pot. It may be a clay flower pot, or a plain mug or small jug. As people come into church they place a small candle in their pot, and at the offering of the gifts the candles are all lit. (Tapers passed down the rows are a practical way of organising this.) They are kept burning for the rest of the service, and afterwards placed in front of the altar as a reminder of how Christ is to shine in our weakness throughout the week.

CHILDREN'S TEACHING

Collect some pictures of missionary work, both at home and abroad, and discuss with the children what the needs are and how they are being met. Point out that the missionaries are telling people about the God of love not only by what they say but also how they behave and what they do.

Discuss with them the kind of things they would like others to know about their special friend, Jesus — who he was, how he helps them and what he is like.

Write down their words on coloured paper which they can illustrate, and then staple the whole lot together to make a book. If possible have it duplicated and used as an aid in mission; children's straightforward and trusting faith is a great witness.

INTERCESSIONS **Years 1 and 2**
Some ideas for prayer

Companions in Christ,
in confidence
let us pray to our heavenly Father.

We pray that all baptised Christians
may pray without ceasing
and work enthusiastically
to serve the world
with love and sensitivity.
Pause
Almighty Father: **may we shine with your light**

We pray that all disputes and misunderstandings
may be brought to a settled peace,
based on mutual respect, honour,
and a concern for each other's grievances.
Pause
Almighty Father: **may we shine with your light**

We pray that every home in this parish
may be enfolded in your love,
brightened by your joy
and calmed by your unbroken peace.
Pause
Almighty Father: **may we shine with your light**

We pray that any who are in great pain

may be granted relief and comfort;
that all who live in constant fear or distress
may be granted a real assurance
of your undergirding and full protection.
Pause
Almighty Father: **may we shine with your light**

We pray that all who have died
may, through your mercy,
rest in your peace.

We thank you for all your blessings
and especially for the example
of Jesus, in whose strength
we offer ourselves for your service.

Merciful Father
accept these prayers
for the sake of your Son,
our Saviour Jesus Christ, Amen.

NOTES ON THE READINGS **Year 2**

1 Chronicles 29:1-9
Years before, David had wanted to build a house
for his Lord, and the time had not been right.
Now, with God's blessing, the work is about to
begin under the care of Solomon, David's son.
Notice how David had never abandoned the
idea, but had patiently waited on the Lord's
time, preparing through those years materials
that would be useful when the building started.
It is David's enthusiasm and dedication to serve
God in this way that inspires all the generous
gifts of gold, silver, bronze and iron which
immediately come pouring in.

Philippians 1:1-11
There is obviously a strong bond of affection
between Paul and the Christians at Philippi. He
draws a great deal of encouragement from the
knowledge that they are working with him for
the spread of the Gospel. Any work is less
daunting and more fun when you know others
are doing their bit as well. Surely that is partly
why Christ founded the Church; working
together for the kingdom, we can encourage one
another along the way, sympathise, inspire and
support. In the process we shall be changing
increasingly into reflectors of Jesus.

Matthew 20:1-16
Humans are often blinkered when it comes to
justice. Generosity in justice rouses suspicions
that we may be losing out, and that would never
do. Being competitive, we usually feel rather
grudging when we meet people who are good
at everything and even look attractive as well;
we also spend time squashing these feelings in
favour of good sportsmanship, but their
existence cannot be denied.

In God's kind of justice there is joy for

everyone who turns to him, especially those who
looked as if they were heading for destruction
but finally received God into their hearts, or
those who have had such a little help and
guidance and yet turn to Christ.

If we are really living in Christ ourselves, we
shall start to share his generous-hearted way of
looking at things, rejoicing in people's gifts and
the good use they are making of them, and
delighting in newcomers to the Church bringing
freshness and different outlooks to enrich and
enliven the worship.

QUESTIONS FOR DISCUSSION

1. Our wealth is often the last thing we are
   prepared to offer to God. Why do you think
   this is? Does it reflect where our real security
   lies? What do you think about the value of
   tithing?
2. Is it possible to be so keen to serve God that
   we object to other people serving in their way,
   too? How does David's attitude to Solomon
   differ from the attitude of the workers in the
   vineyard?

IDEAS FOR ADULTS

Have a display of a bunch of grapes, some
foreign coins, and a carafe of wine, set against
a poster showing grapes growing in a warm
climate — travel posters often have this kind of
picture.

CHILDREN'S TEACHING

First discuss with the children what work there
is in a vineyard, such as grape picking, treading
the grapes, weeding, pruning etc. Everyone can
act out each job.

Without telling the story first, begin acting it
out, with one child taking the part of the
landowner. Narrate it simply, and split the other
children into five groups (or fewer if numbers
are small) to be the workers hanging around the
market place. Make sure that the first group is
quite clear about how much money they will
earn — let them shake hands during the deal.
And make much of those who work hard during
the hot blistering day.

When it comes to the giving out of wages, see
how the children react to the amount the last
workers are given, but don't give away the
surprise. When the first workers receive their
wages it will be interesting to see how they take
it, and it should give rise to some lively
discussion on what is fair and what is generous.

Bring out two points:

1. Jesus never gives up looking for us in the

market place to see if we'd like to work for him.

2. If we do decide to give him our time and energy, then even if we were a long while getting there, Jesus will welcome us and we shall not lose the good reward at the end.

Help the children make a model of a vineyard and workers out of plasticine, and assorted boxes, paper, string, pipecleaners etc.

12th Sunday after Pentecost (Trinity 11)

TODAY'S THEME

... is the Church as a witnessing community. Since we are the members of Christ's body, it is our witness and example that will either repel or draw others to seek God's face. Unless we display Christ's love, many will never see it.

PARISH MUSIC

Hymns
All over the world the Spirit is moving
All people that on earth do dwell
All the nations of the earth
Build, build your church
Christ is the King
For the healing of the nations
God forgave my sins in Jesus' name
God's Spirit is in my heart
Go forth and tell
Gonna lay down my sword and shield
Hills of the North rejoice
I am the light
I danced in the morning
I heard the Lord call my name
In Christ there is no east or west
Let all the world in every corner sing
O thou who at thy Eucharist
Praise we now the Word of grace
Ring out your joy, sing glory to God
Tell out my soul
This little light of mine

Recorded music
Symphony No. 1 (Elgar)

For choirs
Christ is the world's true light (Stanton): U with descant
Let all the world (Gilbert): U, 2 or 3 parts

CHURCH DECORATION

Arrangements today will reflect the theme of witness by being beacons of light and brightness reaching outwards in all directions. Any bright and joyful colours will work well. Try incorporating antirrhinums, delphiniums and gladioli as the expression of light piercing the darkness.

NOTES ON THE READINGS Year 1

Isaiah 49:1-6
God is a personal God — he works through individuals. When a whole nation is chosen to witness to him, it is possible for their light to spread far and wide. Beginning with internal commitment, repentance and reconciliation among the chosen people, God goes on to a far bigger plan, much more far-reaching than the prophet had envisaged; in time every nation will be able to participate in God's work of salvation.

God's power is enormous, and he will use us, if we co-operate, to take on even the deadliest evils of our time and defeat them. When we fail to co-operate, we are limiting his power in our lives and our world; we do so at our peril.

2 Corinthians 5:14-6:2
Whenever we catch glimpses of God's astounding glory, we too are overwhelmed by the sense of our own unworthiness for the patient and loving way he deals with us. For, as Paul points out, if we were to get what we deserve for our sins, we should all be dead! But because the great, creating God was willing to die in our place, it is our sin and selfishness which dies with him, enabling us to live on in a new creation, provided we bind ourselves to Christ.

It is a constant 'dying', whenever sin sidles or charges into our relationships and behaviour; but it is also a constant 'resurrection' as we are tenderly shaped and moulded into new creatures filled with the life of our risen Lord.

John 17:20-end
The kind of unity Jesus prays for in his followers is the same loving relationship he has with and in his Father. They are of the same mind and the same spirit. It is a wonderful vision for us to keep before us as we struggle to mend rifts that have cut deep through history, or stand at the edge of new rifts which threaten to yawn open and divide God's people. God himself is the only power which can bind us in loving unity, even when we disagree about certain issues.

The way we discuss, argue, work towards

change or listen to others' views should witness to the way of thinking which results from living in Christ.

QUESTIONS FOR DISCUSSION

1. Although we agree in principle to witnessing to Christ, do we draw back, in practice, from telling people what we really think and believe? Could some of those reasons actually be excuses?
2. Think back over the strides towards unity there have been in your lifetime. What kind of unity do you think Jesus envisaged here? How can we achieve it? (Take note of any practical suggestions, and act on them.)

IDEAS FOR ADULTS

Use country dancing music to accompany this expression of the gradual witnessing of the people of God until all humanity is united in worship. The sequence is danced through first by one person, then two, then four, then eight. If your congregation is the kind who enjoy dancing as a form of worship, carry on to include them as well. Otherwise, just stop at eight! Begin with one dancer in the centre and 7 round the outside circle.

The sequence is this:

1. Circle to the right, 8 steps, arms high.
2. Circle to the left, 8 steps, arms low.
3. Pas de basque right, then left, twirl round on spot, arms waving.
4. Pas de basque left, then right, twirl round on spot.
5. Four steps forward to someone on outside circle, arms gradually raised to them.
6. Four steps back, arms gradually lowered.
7. Four steps forward to new partner, who also takes four steps forward, both holding out arms.
8. Partners swing.

CHILDREN'S TEACHING

Today offers a good opportunity to learn about some of the famous 'witnesses' to God's love. Make sure they know what it means to witness something — their real experience of something proves it truth, as in car accidents or in court.

Saints are people who have witnessed to God's love; their lives have shown others what God's love is like. The parish church's patron saint will probably be a well-known figure; include a variety of others, such as:

Francis of Assisi Clare
Paul   Margaret of Scotland
Peter   Catherine
Dunstan   Joan of Arc

or any others whose lives are exciting to read about. Have information, books and pictures available, and split the children into small groups to make a display about one particular saint. They can then share their work with the others, and put the whole exhibition up in church entitled: 'You are the light of the world'. 'Let your light shine'.

INTERCESSIONS **Years 1 and 2**
Some ideas for prayer

My friends in Christ,
let us pray to our heavenly Father
trusting in his generous mercy.

We pray for the church as it witnesses
to Christ in the world; may its members be
  always aware
that they are called to be servants,
ready and happy to minister
to the spiritual, emotional
and physical needs of all people.
Pause
Lord of light: **shine through our lives**

We pray for the leaders
of every community and nation;
may governments reflect the values
of responsible caring, compassion
and integrity, so that no individual
or minority group is abused or left in need.
Pause
Lord of light: **shine through our lives**

We pray for a breaking down of any
complacency or blindness in us
until we are able to see the needs around us,
and can work in your strength,
giving our whole lives away
in loving those whom you love.
Pause
Lord of light: **shine through our lives**

We pray for the rejected, neglected,
shunned or despised; for the unwanted
and the disturbed; for the ill
and the injured;
may they be healed, restored and comforted.
Pause
Lord of light: **shine through our lives**

We pray for those who have passed
through the gateway of death
into eternity; may they know the joy
of your presence for ever.

We offer you our thanks
for every opportunity we are given

to witness to your unfailing love;
may our words and our lives
proclaim your glory.

Merciful Father
accept these prayers
for the sake of your Son,
our Saviour Jesus Christ, Amen.

NOTES ON THE READINGS **Year 2**

Micah 4:1-5
Although the ancient prophecies were fulfilled in Jesus, that is not where they end. We always have to remember that we are in the final stage of God's salvation, accomplished through Christ who was the first fruit of the harvest of life. Still to come is the complete accomplishment of God's will. The total establishment of his kingdom which is now growing in the hearts of many in each generation.

Micah's prophecy includes this Day of the Lord which will come at the end of time, brought about by the millions of burning lights of witnesses to the one true light. It is our privilege to be among those light-bearers.

Acts 17:22-end
There were altars to all kinds of deities in Athens. The altar to the unknown god was a sort of spiritual insurance policy, in case someone got angry at being left out. Paul takes advantage of such an opening to tell them all about God. He explains him in terms of their own experience — that he is the creator, from whom springs all the things they have endowed with holiness. He acknowledges their religions but draws on a stage further, to acknowledge the power behind all life. So far, so good.

It is when he starts talking about the raising of the dead — something impossible — that many scoff and go their way. For this is the mind-stretching thing about our religion: the same God who powerfully created the universe also involved himself personally in our world. Once we accept that Jesus is the Son of God, his resurrection is in keeping with what we know of God's power. But the only way to account for God becoming man is to recognise there an unimaginably powerful capacity for love.

Matthew 5:13-16
We, who have been entrusted with the building up of God's kingdom on earth, must, without fail, recognise the source of our power and pass the glory on to God. Otherwise we are not working for him, but for ourselves, and that is both dangerous and destructive.

Salt was not just a seasoning but a food preserver, so that it was actually important for life. Worldly, material values have a powerful grip on many people's minds. The greed and selfishness they engender can cause decay and rot in family life, society, and in individuals. We, the Church, are the salt which can preserve, purify and decontaminate: that is how vital our work as Christ's body is. It is desperately important for our world that we are effective grains of salt.

Similarly with light: we may all be burning brightly with God's love due to our worship and communion with our heavenly Father, but if we share his love only with other Christians we shall be hiding our light under a tub. We Christians are supposed to be the world's light: is its darkness due to our wasted, under-used or dim light? If we do not shine, how will anyone see?

QUESTIONS FOR DISCUSSION

1. Do you think we ought to let people of other faiths alone to worship their way, or should we make contact with a view to bringing them to accept Christ? Try to avoid a 'gut' reaction to this question; use the spirit of Jesus' teaching to work out God's will, rather than ours.
2. Look again at the different uses of salt. What spiritual parallels can you find between the use of salt and the use of Christians? Where do we fail?

IDEAS FOR ADULTS

The gifts today could include salt and light, as a sign that we are intending to be used by God for the good of our world. Salt and light can also be the theme in flower arrangements this week. If you live near the coast, some seashore plants and pebbles may be included.

CHILDREN'S TEACHING

Bring along the following:
- some sea salt;
- something preserved in brine (e.g. frankfurters);
- some small cubes of cheese (enough for one each)
- a candle;
- a large metal saucepan.

First sprinkle some grains of salt on a plate and talk about what it is (they can taste it if they like). Explain how it was used to keep food before anyone had freezers and fridges. Sometimes it is still used like that (give examples) and in hotter countries it is still used to preserve meat and fish. See if they can taste the saltiness in cheese — the salt keeps it fresh.

Now read what Jesus said about us being salt. Discuss with them what this means for us: how can we be salt in the world? It may be helpful to have this question on a board or sheet of paper, and jot down their ideas to keep track of them.

Then light the candle, and talk about useful lights such as torches, street lamps, car lights etc. Cover the light with the saucepan, and help them see how silly this is, if we want to light the room.

Now read the seond part of today's Gospel and jot down ideas under a second question: how can we be the light of the world?

Sing *I'm gonna let my little light shine* and help the children to make these Chinese lanterns from stiff paper. They can carry these into church.

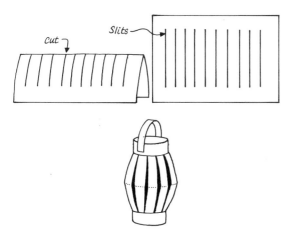

13th Sunday after Pentecost (Trinity 12)

TODAY'S THEME

... is that, just as Christ suffered, so we also will suffer. But the suffering is not negative and demoralising; it is even cause for rejoicing, because through the crucifixion and death of Christ came the resurrection. As we share his suffering we shall also share his glorious life.

PARISH MUSIC

Hymns
Abide with me
Be still my soul
Be thou my guardian and my guide
City of God how broad and far
Do not be afraid

Farmer, farmer
Father, hear the prayer we offer
Follow me, follow me
Hark! hark my soul
He who would valiant be
In heavenly love abiding
Lead us, heavenly Father, lead us
Lord, when I turn my back on you
Nearer, my God to thee
Oft in danger oft in woe
O God our help in ages past
On a hill far away
Peace, perfect peace, in this dark world of sin
Put thou thy trust in God
Take up thy cross, the Saviour says
Take up your cross, he says
The Lord's my shepherd
Through all the changing scenes of life
You shall cross the barren desert

Recorded music
Cello suite (Bach).
Earth Mass: Kyrie, based on the sounds of howling wolves (Paul Winter)

For choirs
Ave Verum (Mozart): SATB
We adore thee, O Lord Christ (Viadana): SATB

CHURCH DECORATION

For today's theme of suffering, try using purples, mauves and crimsons. Sweet peas, roses, sweet scabious, lavatera, delphiniums and stokesia are just some of the flowers around at the moment which would express anguish and sorrow, yet also life and hope. Include some sharp leaved foliage such as holly.

NOTES ON THE READINGS **Year 1**

Isaiah 50:4-9a
The physical and psychological cruelty endured without retaliation here, foresees the mocked and crucified Christ, in heart-rending clarity. We sense the terrible rejection, the jeering and lack of understanding; but there is also the help and strength from God which empowers the suffering servant to submit to his agony in the knowledge that it is necessary for a greater good.

Suffering in our own lives can provide really fertile conditions for growth, much as we may laugh at the stupidity of such an idea in our initial anger, distress and hopelessness. The value of suffering is partly in the way it can nudge us into trusting God instead of our own strength which is in short supply. It helps us learn what it means to be dependent on God and draw help from him. It heightens our awareness of the suffering of others and will in the future enable us to be more sympathetic and useful. It gives us a glimpse of the suffering that Christ was willing to undergo, in order to buy us back from sin; and it can concentrate our attention on what is of lasting value, rather than living from one distraction to the next.

Suffering is bound to be acutely painful; but with Christ it can become a positive pain.

Acts 7:54-8:1
Stephen was so convinced of Jesus' eternal presence that death was a gateway to a life more rich and fulfilling than anything this world could offer. Sometimes we confess this belief with our words, but the way we behave denies it. Are we really convinced that God will keep his promises, even when a loved one is at the point of death, or when witnessing to Christ threatens our popularity or our lifestyle?

Being children of eternity does not preclude grief and heartache: in the person of Jesus we see that love is often compatible with tears. Yet it does mean that at bedrock level when we are confronted with the bleak, barren landscape of despair, Jesus alone, Lord of earth and heaven, time and eternity, reaches across death, across annihilation and keeps his word to be one with us for ever, in this world and the world to come.

John 16:1-11
Knowing this gives us hope and courage, even in the face of Jesus' warnings here. Anyone who loves becomes vulnerable, so if we are set on course to love in God's way, we are bound to get involved with suffering, even apart from such dangers as persecution. But Jesus does not only warn, he also provides. The Helper, or Comforter, will give us whatever we need to cope, survive and rejoice.

QUESTIONS FOR DISCUSSION

1. Why do you think such suffering was necessary for Christ in saving us? Why couldn't there have been an easier, less painful way?
2. Have you ever experienced God-given help and assurance during suffering which has enabled you to bear it? Why is suffering sometimes called 'privilege'?

IDEAS FOR ADULTS

During the intercessions, nightlight candles are placed on the floor before each concern. Have a short space of silence after the prayers and then have the candles placed on or near the altar for the rest of the service.

CHILDREN'S TEACHING

Jesus was not just a good man but actually the Son of God. Draw a large cross as the sign of Jesus, in the centre of a sheet of paper. The prophets in the Old Testament spoke about what Jesus would be like and what he would do. Now draw in (or stick on) some people on the left side of the cross, looking towards it. Write in some speech balloons with quotations referring to the Christ:

Daniel 7:13-14
I saw...there came one like a son of man...and to him was given dominion and glory and kingdom.
Micah 5:2
From you, Bethlehem, shall come a ruler...who shall feed his flock in the strength of the Lord.
Isaiah 60:3
Kings shall come to the brightness of your rising.
Isaiah 53:5
He was wounded for our wrongdoing.
and discuss with the children how these fit in with Jesus' life. They will see that his suffering for us is mentioned; the cross is part of the loving.

Jesus told his friends that if they wanted to follow him they would have to be prepared to suffer as well. Ask the children to colour and cut out pictures of themselves to stick on the right side of the cross, looking towards it.

Speech balloons above them can say things like:

'Don't worry — I'll help you.'
'I'll share my chocolate with you.'
'There's no need to be nasty to her; let's
ask her to join in our game.'
'Please don't say those horrid things
about Jesus — he happens to be a friend
of mine.'

When we follow Jesus we have to learn to give
up our time, money, plans or wishes whenever
we are needed by our friend Jesus to help
someone, or stand up for what is right.

The completed poster can be brought into
church so that everyone can see it.

INTERCESSIONS **Years 1 and 2**
Some ideas for prayer

My sisters and brothers in Christ,
let us bring to the Lord of life
our concern and care for the Church
and for the world.

Lord, we bring before you
all Christians, especially church leaders
and pastors; may they remain faithful
in times of trial, trusting in
your everlasting love;
may all who take risks to witness
be given courage and inspiration.
Pause
Lord, in mercy: **hear our cry**

We bring before you
all the diverse societies of our world;
may your living Spirit be spread
to purify the corrupt, inspire the apathetic
and unlock the hearts of the bigoted.
Pause
Lord, in mercy: **hear our cry**

We bring before you
our own circle of family and friends;
all our desires and attempts to follow you;
live within us to protect, guide,
and bring us to perfection
in Christ.
Pause
Lord, in mercy: **hear our cry**

We bring before you the weak
and the frightened;
all who are suffering in any way;
may they find you there with them,
and draw hope and courage
from your presence.
Pause
Lord, in mercy: **hear our cry**

We bring before you
those who have died in faith;
may they know the joy and peace
of your heaven for ever.

We thank you and praise you
for all you were prepared to
suffer for us; bring the light
of resurrecton to all our suffering,
until we learn to praise you
even through dark times.

Merciful Father
accept these prayers
for the sake of your Son,
our Saviour Jesus Christ, Amen.

NOTES ON THE READINGS **Year 2**

Jeremiah 20:7-11a
Things were not going too well for Jeremiah. He
was ridiculed, belittled and abused; the message
of gloom and doom did not go down well,
however true it was, and he was very tempted
to give up the whole business, keep quiet and
let people get on with their destruction
unchecked.

The trouble was, he knew that God needed
him to speak out, and since he loved God, that
placed him in a tricky and painful dilemma. His
love for God won and he was then prepared to
put up with any insults and ill-treatment for the
sake of following the God he worshipped.

If we find ourselves in the minority, with
values that are despised and scorned by many
around us, and pressures on our children to
conform to different standards of behaviour, we
may well feel like Jeremiah. It will test our
reasons for standing out; if we have been
working towards gaining adulation and respect,
then these difficulties will probably dissuade us
and cause us to falter. If, on the other hand, we
are giving our lives for our love of God, then we
shall find that the difficulties deepen our resolve
and give us clearer understanding of how
important the work is.

Acts 20:17-35
Paul is no stranger to suffering, either. He lives
a very insecure life, by most standards, and
insists on sticking his neck out to say and do
what he believes is God's will, even when it
results in hardship and risk. So why does he
bother?

Paul lives both in time and in eternity since
receiving the ever-living Spirit; so physical safety
and a long life no longer hold the same
importance for him. It is spiritual life that lasts
for ever which is more important, and he is quite
happy to do anything to help others believe it.

For Paul knows that when you do, it gives you freedom and peace and joy that you wouldn't have thought possible.

Matthew 10:16-22

So we do not have to fear any more. If Christ wants us to witness with words we can be sure he will give us the right, suitable words to say. He will give us an uncanny sense of calm as we stand up for what is right or speak out against what is wrong, even if some ridicule us for it.

That is because it is not us speaking at all; it is none other than the holy Spirit of God.

QUESTIONS FOR DISCUSSION

1. Do we ever keep our mouths shut for fear of being unpopular, when we really ought to speak out? How can Jeremiah's attitude encourage us?
2. Have you ever experienced the words being given to you when you are speaking in God's will? — Perhaps dealing more sensitively with someone than you thought you could?

IDEAS FOR ADULTS

Keep a folder of newspaper cuttings about people imprisoned or suffering for their faith. They are in great need of our regular prayer, so have the book available in the church for times of private prayer.

CHILDREN'S TEACHING

Read today's Gospel — God's work sounds rather frightening, but he promises to come with us and tell us what to say. Jesus doesn't pretend it will be easy, but he still asks us to stay with him for the good of our world. What will we do?

Help them make this moving picture.

14th Sunday after Pentecost (Trinity 13)

TODAY'S THEME

... is the family. God loves and cares for us, his children, wth parental love, and we are a spiritual family, with Christ our brother. Our own relationships should reflect this strong bond of love and affection; the kind of love which is not possessive but liberating.

PARISH MUSIC

Hymns

Abba, Father, let me be yours
Children of the heavenly King
Come, my brothers, praise the Lord
Dear Lord and Father of mankind
Faithful shepherd feed me
Father I place into your hands
Father welcomes all his children
He's got the whole world in his hand
In bread we bring you, Lord
Now thank we all our God
Oh the love of my Lord is the essence
Our hearts were made for you, Lord
Reach out and touch the Lord
Seek ye first the Kingdom of God
Thank you Lord for giving us life
The family of Christ
The King of love my shepherd is
Thine for ever! God of love
Through all the changing scenes of life
To mercy, pity, peace and love
We pray thee heavenly Father
What a friend we have in Jesus
When all thy mercies, O my God

Recorded music
Peter and the Wolf: Peter's music
   (Prokofiev)
Swan Lake: the love duet (Tchaikovsky)

For choirs
O Jesu most kind, O Jesu most mild
   (Bach): SATB
Beloved, let us love (Joule)
The Father's Love (Lole): SS

CHURCH DECORATION

The theme of the family is a lovely one to express
florally. Aim to combine mutual love and
support with a sense of fun. You could try this
crescent-shaped arrangement which 'cradles'
small, bright flowers; or incorporate a child's
brick house and pick out the colours of the
bricks with the flowers.

NOTES ON THE READINGS **Year 1**

Proverbs 31:10-end
In spite of the fact that few wives work
assiduously at their distaffs these days, there is
something in this account of the perfect wife
which has a lot to say to all modern members
of God's family.

It is the thoughtful care for others, shown in
work; or, as Kahlil Gibran puts it, 'work is love
made visible'. A carefully prepared meal, a well-
ironed shirt or a newly decorated room —
whoever does these things and whoever they are
done for, tell a great deal about love.

There is little value in love being expressed
in words if no demonstration of practical caring
is ever forthcoming. Christianity is a 'body'
religion; after all, our God wore a body in order
to show his love for us. And, using our bodies
to work, carefully and lovingly, we are making
our lives a prayer of praise.

Ephesians 5:25-6:4
Paul uses marriage as a beautiful illustration of
the kind of relationship Christ has with his
Church. At first sight it may look as if Paul's
concept of marriage is irrelevant in our age of
sexual equality, and is one of those bits of the
Bible we can skip lightly over, looking the other
way.

Look again. Obedience sometimes gets stuck
in the groove of grudging duty, and love in the
groove of emotion and instinctive desire; but
what happens when Love becomes Law, as it
has in Christ? Now, duty and obedience become
full of delight and joy, freely chosen and always
appreciated. This can only occur when both
husband and wife live in obedience to the Law
of Love, with all the patience, acceptance,
kindness and humility that it entails.

And that is the sort of marriage Christ has with
his Church: bound by love, the Church becomes
one with the body of Christ; our obedience to
him springs out of our love for him and his rich
love for us.

Mark 10:2-16
It is clear from Jesus' teaching here that God's
will concerning marriage is that it should be
between one woman and one man and that it
should be a life-long partnership. Just as Jesus
had developed the Mosaic law, about loving your
neighbour, to include loving your enemy, so he
develops the Mosaic rule concerning divorce.
Under the new covenant, based on unlimited,
selfless love, we are called to be so responsive
to God and each other that our marriages work
for life.

Unfortunately, it is very obvious that
'hardness of heart' still tears marriages apart,
resulting in misery and heartbreak for parents
and children alike. The break-up of strong
family units is damaging the whole structure of
our society; and there are many pressures to
accept marriage as only a temporary state, valid
until it becomes tiresome or inconvenient.

As with all Jesus' teaching about real loving,
we are being asked the impossible. It only
becomes possible when our whole life is founded
not on our partner, our emotions, our instincts
or society's expectations, but on the rock of
Christ. He can reinforce crumbling marriages,
heal deep hurts, refresh our love, promote

forgiveness and soften hardened attitudes, so he is an excellent guest to invite to the wedding!

But we also need to remember that our God is loving and compassionate, understanding our weakness and willing to forgive. So if we have a wrecked or failed marriage in our past, we are not unredeemable; when we confess our failure and determine to build our future on Christ, he will not only forgive us but also give back the years that the locusts have eaten.

QUESTIONS FOR DISCUSSION

1. In what ways is a Christian marriage different? Why do you think so many people choose to get married in church? Do we provide enough follow-up support and contact for those who use our church to get married in? How could we use this opportunity better? (Act on any helpful suggestions.)
2. How does Jesus' example in the Gospel help us get our priorities right in our attitudes to one another?

IDEAS FOR ADULTS

Organise today as a family day, with an outing, shared meal, teaching film strip or video about family life; have discussion groups and a party. Include non-churchgoing partners in the invitation and stress that as members of Christ's family, single people and married ones are all part of the family.

CHILDREN'S TEACHING

Bring along a selection of toy farmyard and zoo animals and people and let the children group them into families of mother, father and baby.

Or you could use a Happy Families set of cards to sort into families.

Now read the children the story of creation; *Palm Tree Bible Stories* has a version called *God makes the world*. They will see how God started the family idea right at the beginning of humanity's creation. Show them some wedding pictures and point out that it is God who joins the couple in marriage.

Using card tubes, scraps of net and other material, colour pens and glue, help them make a bride and bridegroom holding hands.

INTERCESSIONS **Years 1 and 2**
Some ideas for prayer

My brothers and sisters in Christ,
let us come before God our Father
with our burdens, cares and joys.

Father, bless our Christian family,
both in this parish and throughout the world;
may we witness to your love
by the kind of lives we lead
and the work we do in your name.
Pause
Father, live among us: **keep us in your love**

Bless and guide the leaders
of each country and each community;
may we not wander as sheep without a shepherd
but rather be led and directed
by you in the path of peace.
Pause
Father, live among us: **keep us in your love**

Father, bless our own homes
and our relationships with our parents,
marriage partners, brothers, sisters
and children; may we learn to see and experience
Christ in one another, and cheerfully love
and serve with generosity of spirit.
Pause
Father, live among us: **keep us in your love**

Bless and protect all families at risk
from evil and danger, either within or without;
for children born with brain damage or
    deformity
and for their families; for marriages which are
strained and difficult;
that wherever much is demanded,
much strength and support may be given.
Pause
Father, live among us: **keep us in your love**

Welcome into your kingdom, Father,
all your children who have died,
especially . . .
may we one day share the joy and peace
of coming home to you for ever.

We thank you for the everyday blessings
and fun of family life;
both in our own and in our spiritual family.

Merciful Father
**accept these prayers
for the sake of your Son,
our Saviour Jesus Christ, Amen.**

NOTES ON THE READINGS **Year 2**

Genesis 45:1-15
This is a very moving account of a family
reunion and reconciliation. Joseph is so
overwhelmed with love for his brothers that he
has completely forgiven them for all their
mistreatment of him so many years before. His
concern now is to care for them in the future,
and he dismisses their former cruelty in a way
which makes it clear that no resentment or
bitterness has been harboured through the
intervening years.

If there are any estrangements in our family,
perhaps this passage can give us the courage to
set about reconciliation. Perhaps, as here, the
first move must come from the wronged, rather
than the offender.

Ephesians 3:14-end
All necessary courage, determination, humility
and strength will be supplied for any act of love
or reconciliation we decide on when Christ lives
in us. For the great Father of us all is like a
loving parent of a huge, sprawling family; the
archetypal parent who embodies selfless love,
creation and nurture. The glory we give him
witnesses to the unlimited power he is able to
set working in our lives.

Luke 11:1-13
The disciples could see that when Jesus prayed
it was an altogether different experience from
the praying they knew. What he taught was not
so much a form of words as a new relationship
with God. Just as we would expect our children
to be given good things from their earthly father,
so we, as God's children, can trustingly ask and
expect to receive good things from our heavenly
Father.

It is sometimes helpful to think of the Lord's
Prayer as headings, and spend much longer on
each phrase than is usual, remembering
throughout each phrase and silence, that God
is our loving Father and we are conversing with
him as his loving children.

QUESTIONS FOR DISCUSSION

1. Joseph had allowed God to use the bad times
   of his life as well as the good. How has this
   attitude helped him forgive his brothers?

Does God sometimes use family rows for
good? Can reconciliations lead to a new depth
in a relationship?

2. Work through the Lord's prayer phrase by
   phrase. What does each part mean? Why do
   you think Jesus uses the pronoun 'us' rather
   than 'me'? How can praying this prayer
   sincerely actually change our outlook,
   attitude and priorities for the better?

IDEAS FOR ADULTS

Have a complete family offering the gifts and
leading the intercessions today. Have a parish
family party with shared food after the service.

CHILDREN'S TEACHING

Talk with the children about asking. Suppose
they would like a friend round to play or some
help with a tricky model they are building, what
would they do? Ask Mummy and Daddy, and
if they can help, they will. It's no good just
thinking to ourselves, 'If only I could have my
friend to play.' We have to ask, and then we've
got a good chance of our hopes coming true. (At
this stage show the first sign: 'Ask and you will
receive.') Point out that it's the same with our
heavenly Father; it's no good just thinking to
ourselves, 'If only I didn't get bad-tempered so
often!' or 'If only I wasn't so scared of owning
up!' But if we ASK our heavenly Father, he will
help us to change!

Have ready hidden an object in the room. Tell the children something is hidden. How can they find it? By looking! (Let them hunt till they find it. Then show the second sign: 'Seek and you will find.') Point out that in the same way we will never find out about Jesus, or ourselves or other people unless we get up and make an effort to find out, by reading the Bible, asking people, thinking and being aware.

Show a picture of a front door. How can you get someone to open it? By knocking or ringing the bell — no one will answer unless you do! (Show third sign: 'Knock and the door will be opened to you.') It is the same with God, our Father. He is there, alive, strong and he likes us — in fact, he loves us! But he will never push into our lives; if we want his help, or if we want to know about his way of living, we must ASK, SEEK and KNOCK at the door.

Let three groups colour and decorate the three signs, to be put in church where everyone can see them. Then join in prayer together, encouraging the children to add their prayers too.

PARISH MUSIC

Hymns

All hail, the power of Jesus' name
All over the world the Spirit is moving
Be thou my vision
Christ is made the sure foundation
Come, praise the Lord, the almighty
Eternal ruler of the ceaseless round
For the healing of the nations
Forth in thy name, O Lord I go
Forward in faith
Glorious things of thee are spoken
God is love: let heav'n adore him
God save our gracious Queen
He's got the whole world in his hand
How lovely on the mountains
In Christ there is no east or west
I vow to thee, my country
Jesus shall reign where'er the sun
Let there be peace on earth
Lord, for the years
Oh the love of my Lord is the essence
Praise, glory, to you, O Lord
The Church of God a Kingdom is
The Lord is King!
This world you have made

Recorded music

Coronation anthem: Zadok the priest
   (Handel)

For choirs

God is gone up with a shout
   (Pulkingham)
Above all praise and all majesty
   (Mendelssohn): SATB

CHURCH DECORATION

Today's theme of authority springing from

15th Sunday after Pentecost (Trinity 14)

TODAY'S THEME

... is about those in authority. All authority stems from God, and when temporal leaders remember this, good government results. Corruption in authority begins when God's supremacy is ignored, rejected or usurped. For us, as citizens of heaven through God's grace, loyalty to God's kingdom must always come first; that may well be shown by our loyalty to others in authority.

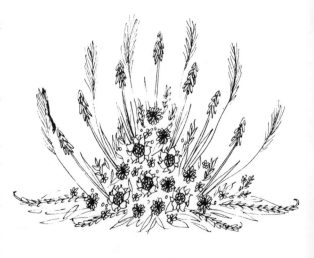

God's authority can be expressed in bold, dramatic arrangements with strong lines and colour. Try using chrysanthemums, gladioli, dianthus and the kniphofia variety of red hot poker. Pampas grass, laurel and ferns are useful for foliage.

NOTES ON THE READINGS **Year 1**

Isaiah 45:1-7
The powerful Cyrus was about to break Babylon's rule; perhaps this would be the way in which the people of Israel could be freed from Babylonian captivity. It seemed to the prophet that Cyrus would actually be used for God's will to be accomplished.

It is certainly true that God works through many and varied means, using a far wider spectrum than those who know him. They may not believe in him, but he believes in them; and if many of us pray fervently for all those who lead and influence in national and international affairs, God's plans will be put into practice in the most unexpected ways and through surprising people.

For God is more powerful than any individual or group, no matter how important or aggressive it may temporarily seem. Even in the worst horrors of war and disease, some shaft of hope and goodness lights up among the terrible shadows; even evils can be used by the one creative and caring God to bring about the birth of hope and understanding. This is because our God reigns — over all time, in all places and throughout all existence, whether excellent or appalling.

Romans 13:1-7
When any state upholds justice and order, respect for people and property and maintenance of personal safety, it will be acting under God, whether using his name or not. And we are to respect and keep within its laws, not just for the sake of steering clear of punishment, but because our consciences guide us to do so.

Obviously Paul is not advocating blind obedience even when a corrupt state demands action which is contrary to Christian teaching. At such times we need to be among those who stand up for what is right. But as far as possible we are advised to show that as followers of Christ we can obey cheerfully, respect others' positions and values, and be responsible citizens.

Matthew 22:15-22
The Pharisees have been faced directly with the need to turn their expectations and thinking upside down if they are to be saved. But they have, like Dives, the wealthy man, too much to lose, and so begin scheming for the downfall of this man who threatens their comfortable lives.

Cleverly, they lay the trap for Jesus to fall into: Roman taxes are a volcanic issue and if he denounces them the authorities will be enraged; but if he does not, his integrity as a Jewish teacher will be in question. The scheming is particularly ironic, since it hinges on the forfeiting of esteem — the very thing the Pharisees themselves could not cope with.

So Jesus not only confounds them, but also uses the situation to teach, if they will only listen. The real question is one of priorities, and whereas what Caesar both represents and requires is money, or materialism, what we owe God is on a different plane altogether — more costly, more demanding, more far-reaching, but also more fulfilling and rewarding.

QUESTIONS FOR DISCUSSION

1. In what way was Jesus' expression of authority different from that of the religious leaders of the time? How did Jesus' authority show?
2. Are there political or social policies in our country which are at variance with Christian values and beliefs? If so, what should the Christian way be of solving the problem? (Make sure you discuss this question as the loving Christians you are called to be!)

IDEAS FOR ADULTS

Have a time of prayer set aside during the week for all governments in countries all over the world. Have posters, news cuttings, and an atlas available for people to use, and the names of the leaders written out clearly, so people can pray for them by name, in the context of their country's needs and problems. We so often say, 'If only THEY did this or that...' Here is a chance to help them positively by placing them into God's care and guidance.

CHILDREN'S TEACHING

Jesus' lifetime can sometimes appear like a fairy tale to children, and today's Gospel provides a good opportunity to fasten it firmly in history, with the Romans.

Have a book on the Romans (the local library will have some available) and show the children how they lived, and which countries they ruled. Point out that the people of those countries (Britain as well as Israel) disliked paying taxes to foreign rulers. Also show the children some pictures of Roman coins, and some of our own coins to see whose head is on those.

Now tell the story of the Pharisees' clever

question, pointing out how difficult it was for
Jesus to answer without getting into deep
trouble, either with his people or the Romans.
Tell them how Jesus answered, and have this
answer written out clearly ready to display: 'Give
back to Caesar what belongs to Caesar — give
back to God what belongs to God.' They can
all say this together, or even learn it for next
week.

What does belong to God, that we can give
him back?
- our time
- our life
- our thanks
- our praise...*ourselves!*

Sing *Father, you have given us a bright new
day* (MWTP, 105) or *The clock tells the story
of time God gives us* (MWTP, 16).

INTERCESSIONS **Years 1 and 2**
Some ideas for prayer

Our heavenly Father assures us that
wherever two or three meet in his name
he will be with them; in confidence, then,
let us bring him our needs and cares.

We pray that your love will spill out
through your Church to the world,
filling all teaching, all advice and council,
all authority and correction.
Pause
We are your people: **hear us, Lord, we pray**

May your spirit of forgiveness and justice
permeate the social and political fabric
of our world, till we are able to rule wisely,
discuss differences calmly and be prepared
to negotiate rationally.
Pause
We are your people: **hear us, Lord, we pray**

May your light shine in our hearts
to show us our faults and enable us
to admit them; to shine through our lives
in the way we treat one another,
especially when we disagree or feel hurt.
Pause
We are your people: **hear us, Lord, we pray**

May your comfort and consolation
soothe those who are afraid or in great pain,

refresh those who are mentally
or physically exhausted
and be a life line to those who are
broken hearted or in despair.
Pause
We are your people: **hear us, Lord, we pray**

May those who have passed into eternity
be welcomed into your heavenly kingdom
to live with you for ever.

We praise you, Lord, for all
the joy and gladness of our lives;
for the beauty of your world
and the affection of our loved ones.

Merciful Father
**accept these prayers
for the sake of your Son,
our Saviour Jesus Christ, Amen.**

NOTES ON THE READINGS **Year 2**

1 Kings 3:4-15
Solomon's legendary choice of gift, and God's
pleasure at it, has been echoed in stories of
similar nobility in many other cultures. It does,
after all, show man at his possible best, rather
than in his more usual human petty-mindedness.
We may hope we would choose a similarly noble
gift, but have a sneaking suspicion that, on the
spur of the moment, we might well have
plumped for a repaired car (to make us more
useful, of course) or a bigger house (so as to be
more hospitable).

Solomon was feeling rather vulnerable. He
was conscious of his raw youth, aware of his
inexperience and probably very nervous about
the daunting prospect of ruling the people of
Israel. In some ways all that put him at a
disadvantage; yet in another, important way, his
misgiving gave him an advantage, because
whenever we are at our most vulnerable, and
most aware of our weakness, we are also at our
most receptive. There is no play-acting about
trusting in prayer, when people are confronted
with the possibility of immediate death in an
accident or disaster. Desperate people are driven
to pray, and there are many stories of fervent
prayer during shipwrecks, or while waiting for
rescue.

In Solomon's vulnerability he asks for what
he needs, instead of what he wants. It is
something we need to cultivate in our prayers,
so that, instead of thinking of short term answers
we would like to suggest God tries, we
acknowledge the actual difficulties of our own
weaknesses, and leave it in his hands. Things
are far more likely to fall into place if we do.

1 Timothy 2:1-7

We are encouraged to pray for all those in authority; not merely as a dutiful lip-service, but with the deeply concerned Christian love which supports and is prepared to act and become involved.

There are two reasons for this prayer. One is that, obviously, good government allows us to live peaceful lives, free from terror and violence.

The second reason is that, whether we agree with our leaders or not, whether they are Christian or not, whether they are interested in us or not, they are in God's eyes loved beings whom he has created. God longs for everyone to be saved — that, after all, is why he bothered with the humiliating business of becoming man!

If we live in Christ, we shall start to see all men through his eyes, and that will urge us to pray.

Matthew 14:1-12

Herod's obsessive guilt is typical of the misery which results from using authority for corrupt and cruel acts. Herod had known that what he did was evil; yet he had been too weak to follow his conscience, and instead had given in to the request of his jealous and bitter wife.

For us, too, there are times when we may have to refuse to follow the law because it would be against God's law. If this happens, we can be sure that, however much hardship, exile or danger it brings us, we shall be eternally safe, buoyed up by the encouraging presence of God.

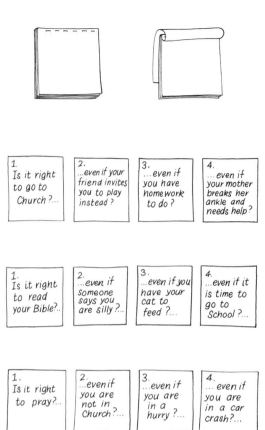

QUESTIONS FOR DISCUSSION

1. How can we make sure that any authority and power we are given in this life is used as an extension of God's power, and does not lead to bossiness, distancing or corruption?
2. What were the factors that persuaded Herod to give in to his daughter's request? Did his action silence his fears or add to them? What can we learn from Herod?

IDEAS FOR ADULTS

Have a world map displayed with tapes going from various countries out to the full names of their leaders. We cannot pray effectively unless we make an effort to understand the people and needs. Encourage everyone to pray as they read their newspapers each day.

CHILDREN'S TEACHING

Prepare three large posters each with four sheets of paper staples at the top, like this:

Look together at the one about going to church. The answer to the first two questions is going to be YES; the third circumstance is more difficult. In the end the answer should still be YES, as long as they plan to rearrange other activities that day to make sure the necessary jobs get done as well. The fourth circumstance helps the children explore the kind of situation when a good rule has to be broken in order to do God's will. Obeying God's law of love must always take precedence.

Next, deal with the question of Bible reading in the same way, and finally the question of prayer. This one will be different, because there is no time at all when keeping in touch with God is wrong; in fact, the more difficult the situation, the closer we cling!

After this discussion, show the children a picture of Jesus healing the man with the withered arm. Was it a good thing he was doing? Tell or read how the Pharisees reacted and how Jesus showed that even the best rules are not as important as living life in God's loving way.

16th Sunday after Pentecost (Trinity 15)

TODAY'S THEME

... is about loving our neighbour. Since God made all of us — even those we may not like or whose behaviour we may disapprove of — we are to love one another and help those in need, regardless of whether they are friends of ours or not.

PARISH MUSIC

Hymns
Bind us together, Lord
Brother, let me be your servant
Christ is the King! O friends rejoice
Christ is our King, let the whole world rejoice
Colours of day dawn into the mind
Come and be filled
Farmer, farmer
Give me joy in my heart
Go in peace to be Christ's body
Good shepherd you have shown your care
Help us to help one another, Lord
I am the light
If we only seek peace
I give my hands to do your work
In bread we bring you, Lord
Joy to the world
Kum-ba-yah
Love is his word, love is his way
Make me a channel of your peace
Oh Lord all the world belongs to you
Peace is flowing like a river
The spirit of the Lord is with us
Thus! says the Lord
We find thee, Lord, in others' need
When I needed a neighbour

Recorded music
Lyric Suite (Grieg)

For choirs
O Lord, give thy holy Spirit (Tallis): SATB
Lord, make me an instrument (Aston)

CHURCH DECORATION

To express today's theme of loving our neighbours, try a twin arrangement where two displays interact with one another. Use soft, pastel colours and feathery leaves that produce an open, airy feeling.

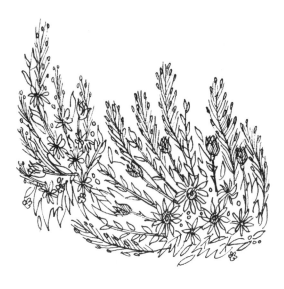

NOTES ON THE READINGS **Year 1**

Leviticus 19:9-18
The message which Moses is given for the children of Israel concerns God's call for them to be holy. Holiness will be expressed by love, and love will be expressed by forgiveness.

Such a message is reassuring, for although the ideal of holiness is distressingly impossible, the path towards it does not presuppose perfect beings who never irritate each other or offend. Since we know we all spend considerable time (and even effort!) in irritating and offending each other, it is good news to find there is hope for us yet.

For the holy loving to which we are called is about how we react to our own sin and that of other people. It is about forgiving, in the sense of really wiping the offence away; if we dredge it up years later in a spiteful argument we have not really forgiven at all. Nor must we tot up the injustices we have suffered and store them ready for some mammoth explosion of rage and 'righteous' indignation. Far better to talk about what has upset us, being ready to hear the other point of view, recognising that, unlikely as it may seem, we may actually be mistaken or be over-reacting. Then, with full forgiveness, our loving will have developed, and we shall have progressed along the road to holiness.

Romans 12:9-end

This passage is one we could usefully fix up on the kitchen, office or factory wall, or even learn off by heart. There is really practical advice here for living under God's authority in a positive and inspiring way. The whole idea is really summed up in those last words: 'Do not be overcome with evil, but overcome evil with good,'

As Christians we need to do positive good, rather than being simply mild, inoffensive people. God's power can give us authority and confidence to inspire others by our behaviour.

Luke 10:25-37

This Gospel shows us how, all too easily, our mouths can utter honourable vows of commitment which our lives belie. We can probably think of many vows we have made which we thought, at the time, we understood, but only later discovered what was really entailed. Perhaps we may regret ever having promised anything, at that point!

But if we have kept the vow even in the hard times, we can look back gratefully to the way the difficulties have enabled us to grow. The lawyer who approaches Jesus thinks that he understands the Law inside out and back to front. He is really hoping to make a fool of this new upstart.

Jesus shows him, in the story of the Good Samaritan, what the Law really entails when it has soaked into a person's whole being. It is no longer a case of doing certain things and not doing certain other things. It involves the much more open-ended and therefore far costlier commitment which sees with eyes of love, recognises needs with insight, and works for another's good without counting the cost.

QUESTIONS FOR DISCUSSION

1. How can we train people, from an early age, to be kind and considerate to one another? What is more important — rules or example?
2. Although we wouldn't dream of walking by on the other side in this case, are there cases where we do just that by refusing to get involved in others' problems in case they become too demanding on our time?

IDEAS FOR ADULTS

If there is no Good Neighbour scheme operating in the area, today is a good time to launch it. Have a chart with the names of roads written on it, and during the week ask people to sign up against the road for which they will take responsibility. Any needs which become apparent can be met more effectively, matching needs with those prepared to offer help in different ways. The list of helpers should be duplicated and made available for each street representative, and help can range from shopping and cleaning to reading, ironing or baby sitting.

This is a fairly simple means of enabling Christians to carry out practical care. The lists can be brought up and the work blessed at the offering of the gifts.

CHILDREN'S TEACHING

The Good Samaritan is an excellent story for the children to act out, but it needs to be clearly explained first.

If the priest and the Levite touched a dead man they would be considered 'unclean' by the Law. The man looked dead, so they passed by, pretending they hadn't noticed.

The Samaritan came from another country so it was extra strange for him to bother with the man. But because he saw the man needed help he felt sorry for him, and helped him as best he could.

There are several book versions of the story which can be used. Give the children lots of help with what to do and say, setting out the room first with a road, an inn, Jerusalem and Jericho. Have strips of material for bandages and some pretend ointment in a small pot, some play money in a bag and some plastic cups for the people at the inn.

INTERCESSIONS **Years 1 and 2**
Some ideas for prayer

My companions in Christ,
humbled by the wonder of God's love
for us all, let us lay before him
our needs and concerns.

We lay before you all Christians,
especially Church leaders, our bishops
and all in ordained ministry;
Christians who have lapsed from worshipping
or whose prayer life is dead;
may all be touched and strengthened
by your caring love.
Pause
Father of all: **increase our love for one another**

We lay before you the heated arguments,
industrial action, blinkered vision
and stubborn behaviour of our world;
may the power of your love soften,
ease and coax us all to be more
understanding, wise and forgiving.
Pause
Father of all: **increase our love for one another**

We lay before you the areas of
our own lives which are in shadow and
darkness; that in the light of your love we may
   see
our faults and weaknesses more clearly,
notice the good in those we live with,
and recognise the needs around us.
Pause
Father of all: **increase our love for one another**

We lay before you widows, widowers
and orphans, all broken families
and all the lonely; the disfigured,
incapacitated and neglected;
those who daily persevere in tending
a physically or mentally sick relative;
may the warmth and joy of your love
comfort and transform.
Pause
Father of all: **increase our love for one another**

We commend to your keeping
all those who have died;
may they rest in your peace.

We thank you for all the blessings
which enrich our lives; for the
opportunities to show our praise
in loving service to one another.

Merciful Father
accept these prayers
for the sake of your Son,
our Saviour Jesus Christ, Amen.

NOTES ON THE READINGS Year 2

Deuteronomy 15:7-11
Even the best rules tend to get frayed at the
edges after a time, and need tightening up again.
This seven year rule, whereby every debt is
cancelled, and slaves can go free, is an efficient
way of checking that no one is left destitute.
Unfortunately, some of the people are keeping
an eye out for the approach of the seventh year,
and are noticeably less willing to lend to their
poorer relatives as the time draws near for all
debts to be cancelled. Rules only work when the
generous spirit of them is adhered to.

1 John 4:15-end
We are so used to seeing the power of hatred
in action. Terrorism, violent crimes, child
abuse, revenge killings — the news is packed
with details of destructive behaviour by
individuals and nations based on hatred and fear.

At first sight it does look powerful. Innocent
people lie dying as the murderer escapes with
both life and money; aggressive threats extract
secrets; brutal selfishness can pile up easy money
quickly.

Yet through the history of the chosen people

of Israel, and in the person of Jesus, God unfolds
a much stronger power, which not only makes
living more joyful and secure, but actually works
better as well. Loving our enemies annihilates
them more effectively than any gun can, because
the door is then opened towards friendship.
Rebels can be won over by kindness and a
genuine concern for their cause, while repression
and strong-arm tactics are more likely to turn
them into underground revolutionaries. Love
has inspired people to great acts of loyalty and
courage and prolonged self-sacrifice; love has
succeeded in uniting families and countries when
war has weakened both and failed to bring
lasting peace.

God's way of living by love, through every
situation without exception, is both profound
wisdom and sound good sense.

Luke 16:19-end
People often express the view that they do not
need to go to church because they are happy as
they are and don't do anyone any harm. Dives,
the rich man, didn't do anyone any harm. His
sin was that he didn't do anyone any good either.
Opportunities for helping and caring simply
went past unnoticed: he did not realise they
existed until it was too late. How can we be sure
that we are not also missing opportunities to do
good? It is very difficult to look at ourselves
objectively but we need to train ourselves to do
it regularly if we want to find out in time.

The more closely we live to Jesus, the more
enlightened we shall become about where the
needs are and how we can help. For we have not
only Moses and the prophets to guide us, but
also Jesus, risen and glorified, so we cannot say
we have not been told. The ball is in our court.

QUESTIONS FOR DISCUSSION

1. One reason for ruling out exploitation as far
   as possible was the people of Israel's
   experience of slavery. Do you think that
   hardship can be beneficial?
2. Love in the abstract is much easier than
   demanding, practical, caring love. Are we
   sometimes liars about loving God, because of
   our attitudes to other people?

IDEAS FOR ADULTS

A display about world poverty, particular areas
of need, and how we can help will focus
attention on possible help. Include in it the good
as well as the bad news, and try to borrow some
examples of clothes, jewellery, food, musical
instruments etc., of the areas concerned.

CHILDREN'S TEACHING

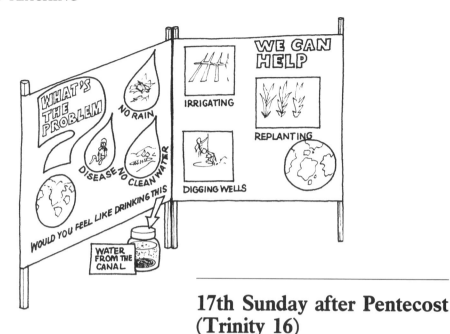

17th Sunday after Pentecost (Trinity 16)

Continuing our practical involvement with those in need, make a display board of something like the Clean Water project, or Famine relief, tree planting and mud stoves or a sponsored village.

Supply bright background paper and pictures from newspapers and magazines. Many of the relief organisations are happy to supply excellent material: a selection of addresses is below.

Begin the session with a song of thanks.

Then tell the story that Jesus told about the rich man and Lazarus, and follow up last week's activities for helping before arranging this week's display.

Make it as clear as possible by headings, questions and maps. Coloured wool pinned between areas of the map and relevant information may be helpful.

Display the board where the rest of the congregation can see it, possibly bringing it in at the offertory.

Useful Addresses

Action Aid, 208 Upper Street, London N1 1RZ
Christian Aid, P.O. Box 1, London SW9 8BH
Oxfam, 274 Banbury Road, Oxford OX2 7DZ
Traidcraft, Kingsway, Gateshead NE11 0NE
U.S.P.G., Partnership House,
  157 Waterloo Road, London SE1 8XA
V.S.O., 9 Belgrave Square, London
  SW1X 8PW

TODAY'S THEME

... is that the kind of life we lead proclaims the kind of faith we have. We may say we believe in God, but that is only true if we live a life compatible with belief in the God of love. It will be our kindness, thoughtfulness, self-control and generosity which best prove our faith real.

PARISH MUSIC
Hymns
Alleluia, by your Spirit we will sing
All my hope on God is founded
All to Jesus I surrender
Bread of the world in mercy broken
Cleanse us O Lord
Come down, O love divine
Dear Lord and Father of mankind
Faith in God can move the mountains
Father, you are living in us now
Firmly I believe and truly
God is love, his the care
Holy, holy, holy, holy
If we only seek peace
I now no longer live
Jesus, my Lord, my God, my all
Just as I am
Lord Jesus Christ
Lord of my life
Lord, when I turn my back on you
My God, how wonderful thou art
O Jesus I have promised
O Lord all the world belongs to you

O thou who camest from above
Revive thy work, O Lord
The Spirit lives to set us free
Thine for ever! God of love
You touch my soul

Recorded music
Enigma variations (Elgar)

For choirs
Christ is the world's true light (Stanton):
  U with descant
Thou shalt show me the path of life (Day)

CHURCH DECORATION

Today's theme of our faith showing in our loving behaviour, would be effectively expressed in this display of three cascading arrangements on different levels. For the main line, choose arching stems, such as tamarisk, willow, forsythia and ivy; sweet peas, asters, cosmos and alstroemeria are among the flowers which look well in this kind of arrangement.

NOTES ON THE READINGS **Year 1**

Jeremiah 7:1-11
Hypocrisy can so easily slip into our religion without our noticing, and we all have to guard against it constantly. As humans we tend to be lazy, and as soon as we get slack about our self-discipline in prayer and worship, we can find ourselves starting to behave the way 'everybody else does', while still singing our praises lustily each Sunday.

The people of Israel were just the same, and had begun to adopt the ways of the heathen cultures around them, probably without noticing. Jeremiah's words remind them and us that God will not tolerate double standards. If we are going to proclaim faith in him we must

ditch all behaviour and attitudes that are contrary to his values of love, respect for one another, and purity of heart.

James 1:16-end
The practical James knows that the Word must always be a spring-board to action, and not a substitute for it. It is quite possible to be swept up on to an emotional 'high' during some inspiring worship, and feel so good about it that we fail to notice glaring needs and opportunities for serving when we get out of the church. Or we can get so used to talking 'God-language' that we deceive ourselves into thinking we are practising the words we spout, when we have actually got stuck in a complacent rut.

Another temptation is to busy about all the *doing*, without any hearing first. (Or during, or afterwards!) God's word is our treasure, our strength and our foundation, and if we really steep ourselves in it, by attentive reading and receptive contemplation, we shall find ourselves urged to take positive action in ways which may surprise us. So long as we do not let Self plug up the channels, God's Word will flow through us for the good of the world.

Luke 17:11-19
The lepers must have had faith in Jesus. They all asked him to take pity on them, and did not hesitate to set off to show themselves to the priest as cleansed men while their bodies were still covered with sores.

It is a mark of Jesus' immense love for us that he never sets our thanks and adoration as a condition of helping us, even though he longs for it. He loves us enough to leave us free to make our own decisions and never forces us to honour him.

Yet how mean and small-minded, how arrogant and discourteous we are if we fail to give God the thanks and credit he deserves, when we have cried to him in distress and he has taken pity on us and healed us.

People pray when they are suddenly aware of their frailty and vulnerability. If we stay with him right through to thankfulness we shall be doubly blessed and the Kingdom of God will be that much closer.

QUESTIONS FOR DISCUSSION

1. In what ways does Jesus proclaim God's love? In what ways does the Church proclaim its faith in God? In what ways does it proclaim its lack of faith?
2. How can we express our faith in practical ways in our own lives and as a parish? Are there any areas which should be altered straight away in the light of today's readings?

IDEAS FOR ADULTS

Today's Gospel can be acted out, or mimed while it is being read.

CHILDREN'S TEACHING

Palm Tree Bible Stories have the story of the ten lepers which can be read aloud to the children today, or the story can be told in your own words. It lends itself well to being acted out, with the help of some sheeting bandages for the lepers which can be flung off as they are healed.

Then talk with the children about when we give presents and enjoy it so much when the person is pleased and thanks us — it draws us closer.

Make a 'thank you' poster by having some pictures of things we want to thank God for, and let each child add to it his own thank you prayer.

Sing: *If I were a butterfly* (ONA, 214).

INTERCESSIONS **Years 1 and 2**
Some ideas for prayer

In the Spirit of Christ
and taught by his example,
let us pray trustingly
to our heavenly Father.

We pray for Christian witnesses
throughout the world, with all their
weaknesses, gifts, victories and
    disappointments;
May all Christians reflect your brilliant light
to direct others to worship you and
experience the joy of your peace.
Pause
Lord, we believe: **help our unbelief**

We pray for all inhabitants of our planet
in the daily routines, the work and leisure;
for the silent majorities and all
elected to govern; may all leaders
truly represent the needs of their people,
and may we live in peace with one another.
Pause
Lord, we believe: **help our unbelief**

We pray for our loved ones;
for friends with whom we have lost touch;
for any we have let down;
and for ourselves; may the Spirit
we have been so privileged to receive
burn more brightly in our lives.
Pause
Lord, we believe: **help our unbelief**

We pray for all who are undergoing
long-term or chronic illness,
slow recovery or mental anguish
with no end or hope in sight;
may they hold on to you,

receiving your strength and love
and knowing that in you they are safe.
Pause
Lord, we believe: **help our unbelief**

We pray that those who have died
may rise to eternal life in you,
and that at our death, we too
may share your peace for ever.

We offer you all our thanks and praise
for your generous love and kindness
to all your people; may we show our praise
in our generosity to others.

Merciful Father
accept these prayers
for the sake of your Son,
our Saviour Jesus Christ, Amen.

NOTES ON THE READINGS **Year 2**

Jeremiah 32:6-15
Jeremiah is in prison; Jerusalem is under seige; all immediate hope for the people of Israel living freely in their own land is quite dead. And yet, at this lowest point, Jeremiah proclaims his faith in the future of God's people by putting his money where is faith his: he buys a plot of land at his village of Anathoth from his cousin. Since there is no chance of using it yet, the deeds are preserved in an earthenware jar, ready for the time Jeremiah is convinced will come, when the land will once again belong to God's people. It is a remarkable act of trust in God.

Galatians 2:15-3:9
Paul had been a very committed and conscientious rabbi, following the Law astutely. He is therefore well qualified to speak on this question bothering the Galatians: the importance of the Law in being saved and liberated from one's sins. If anyone could find salvation by strict adherence to God's Mosaic Law, it would be Paul himself.

Yet he confidently asserts that the Law, though valuable as a guideline, creates its own type of prison; for although it suggests a good, noble and godly way of living, it does not provide the strength and power which weak humanity desperately needs in order to achieve such a life.

With the coming of Jesus Christ, all this changed. God, humbling himself in becoming man, accepts the duties and confines of the Law, but also breaks through them to suffuse them with his own life and power. So, when we accept Christ, we too are enabled to plug into that power which can at last take us just as we are, without pretence, and make us new creatures, able to do all things; for it is no longer us, but Christ alive and working in us and through us.

Luke 7:1-10

Recognising in Jesus a fellow figure of authority, the centurion is able to trust his authority in a way that puts many to shame.

He was obviously a man sensitive to needs, as he commanded wisely and had made friends with the people, even contributing to their synagogue. In many ways he was already touched by the grace of Christ.

Now, out of surprising concern for a servant, he sees Christ in action, even though he never actually meets him personally. It does not seem to occur to the centurion that Christ would need more than a command to make the servant well again.

When we pray, do we really expect our prayer to be answered? Are we afraid to expect in case our God lets us down and proves impotent? Yet time and again Jesus says: 'Your faith has saved you.' He acts when we trust him to act.

QUESTIONS FOR DISCUSSION

1. Do our lives and the activities of our parish proclaim the faith we have in God? In what practical ways could we change for the better, so as to show our faith in action?
2. Why does Jesus so often state that his healing is dependent on the faith of those who ask for his help? What does praying in faith mean, exactly? How can we increase our faith?

IDEAS FOR ADULTS

Try having a time of worship outside one evening this week with other Christian groups to praise God and ask for renewed and increased faith. Have a bonfire to remind everyone of God's burning love, and light candles or torches from the fire and then pass the light from one to the other during the worship. Finish with a shared pledge to proclaim the faith by passing the light of God's love to others in our actions and words.

CHILDREN'S TEACHING

Tell the story of the centurion, using flannel-graph or plasticine models to illustrate it.

Begin with a game of 'Simon Says'. They only obey if Simon gives the order. Talk about who gives orders that are obeyed:
  — policemen in traffic;
  — teachers at school;
  — doctors about medicine;
  — Mums and Dads about looking after the home;
  — soldiers in battle.

It is necessary for safety and peace to have someone *in charge*.

Now tell the story of the Roman centurion (if possible, have a picture of one commanding his men) showing how he was used to being in charge, and recognised Jesus as being in charge as well. Use a flannelgraph or models to illustrate the story.

Using coloured pencils or pens, let the children decorate these words on a card:

'Lord, I am not worthy to receive you.

But only say the word and I shall be healed.'

Do they recognise it from the communion service? And from the centurion story?

Encourage them to read this from their card next time they are in church and remember how the centurion trusted Jesus to be in charge.

18th Sunday after Pentecost (Trinity 17)

TODAY'S THEME

. . . is about offering our lives to God's service. God has given us so much that our thankfulness prompts us to show our love in acts of generosity, both to God in worship, and to one another wherever there is need.

PARISH MUSIC

Hymns
All that I am, all that I do
All to Jesus I surrender
Come and praise him
Come, Lord Jesus, come
Father, we adore you
From thee all skill and science flow
Great indeed are your works O Lord
How great is our God
If I were a butterfly
I give my hands to do your work
In bread we bring you, Lord
Jesu gentlest Saviour
Lord of my life
My God accept my heart this day
Oh! how good is the Lord
Our hearts were made for you, Lord
Praise God from whom all blessings flow
Take my hands
Take my life and let it be
Thank you, Lord, for giving us life
The wise may bring their learning

Recorded music
Piano concerto No. 2: (Rachmaninov):
  last movement

For choirs
A prayer of St. Richard of Chichester
(White): U with descant
O for a closer walk (Stanford)

CHURCH DECORATION

To represent the tithe offering of the first fruits, have as the main arrangement either a basket or cornucopia filled with fruits and flowers, spilling out to express both God's bounty and our gratitude. Any seasonal fruits and flowers can be used — the effect is to be a richness and abundance.

NOTES ON THE READINGS **Year 1**

Deuteronomy 26:1-11
The people are reminded here that, during their hardship and suffering in Egypt, God heard them and acted powerfully to rescue them. It is both a duty and a pleasure then, for them to acknowledge this by an annual thanksgiving and harvest offering. Thankfulness and gratitude find expression in practical ways, and generosity often awakes generosity in the recipient.

2 Corinthians 8:1-9
Here again, suffering that the Church in Macedonia has undergone seems to have made them extra generous to others in need. Suffering can have this power of making us more aware of others' needs and more sympathetic. Their giving, we notice, does not stem from a desire to look good, but from their offering of themselves to God. He translates that offering

into cheerful, loving service to others.

Matthew 5:17-26
Jesus was not punctilious about observing the exact letter of the Law. On a number of occasions he healed on the Sabbath instead of resting from all work, and this raised doubts and righteous anger in others.

So Jesus takes pains to explain the purpose of God's Law. He shows the people not only its limitations but also its demands. Instead of conserving narrow, pedantic behaviour, the Law is now thrown open so that in one sense we are freed from exclusive and rigid rules and in others we are given the grown-up responsibility of observing God's loving will in all its awesome ideals.

Our whole selves are to be brought under his Law in this way — what we think as well as how we act; what is hidden as well as what is seen by others.

Since rules define limits, the temptation is to go no further than they explicitly demand. That gives us a sense of having 'done our duty' and 'arrived'. When Jesus speaks of the Law as complete loving, the limits are swept away, and we can see that there is no point at which we will have completed our duty, for the duty of love in God's terms has no boundary.

QUESTIONS FOR DISCUSSION

1. How can we offer our first-fruits to God? Think in terms of offering the first minutes of the day; the first hour's wages; the first day of the week etc.
2. Do we sometimes get hung up on the idea of giving only *money*? What other riches do we have that we could share in God's service?

IDEAS FOR ADULTS

Are there ways your parish could be ministering to local needs more effectively? Consider having a coordinator who can put people with time, skills or experience in touch with those who have needs in the parish. Often these will not be very onerous things; for lonely people a friend to visit can make all the difference to their lives; taking a child home with yours after school sometimes can give a tired parent a rest — on another day, when you are the tired parent, you can swap over!

CHILDREN'S TEACHING

Tell the children (or remind them) of how God had helped the people escape from Egypt where they had been slaves, and how, when they reached the promised land, they thanked God every year by bringing a basket of their harvest to his altar. At our harvest festival we do the same. If we remember that God is the provider of all we have, our lives will be rich and full; God holds everything together. Spread out the five sections of this jigsaw puzzle and ask two of the children to make the puzzle up.

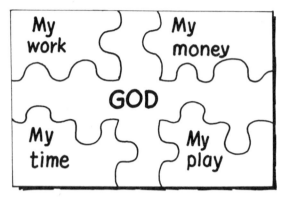

If we have God at the centre, all the different parts of our lives can be part of our thanks and praise. Give out pieces of thin card, paper with the puzzle drawn on, scissors, glue and crayons, and help them make their own jigsaws to take home.

INTERCESSIONS **Years 1 and 2**
Some ideas for prayer

Brothers and sisters in Christ,
in the knowledge of God's love for us
let us pray for the Church and for the world.

We pray for all clergy serving in deprived
or violent areas of the world; all who are
in personal danger for teaching the faith;
may they be reassured and their service blessed
by the power of your love.
Pause
Abba, Father: **we belong to you**

We pray for all who serve in
positions of authority in this country
and throughout the world;
for all debates and international talks;
may the power of reason you have given us
lead us towards your truth and wisdom.
Pause
Abba, Father: **we belong to you**

We pray for those we serve each day,
and those who serve us; for relationships
we find difficult, and for situations which
tend to make us irritable; increase our
generosity of spirit, and our delight
in serving others.
Pause
Abba, Father: **we belong to you**

We pray for the resentful, and all who
suffer injustice or neglect;
for all in need from natural disasters,
war, famine or disease;
may your love reach them through our care.
Pause
Abba, Father: **we belong to you**

We pray that all who have died in faith
may know the joy of heaven for ever.

We rejoice in all the goodness
and generosity your love has inspired
in so many people; for the way
you encourage and guide us.   .

Merciful Father
**accept these prayers
for the sake of your Son,
our Saviour Jesus Christ, Amen.**

NOTES ON THE READINGS **Year 2**

Nehemiah 6:1-16 or Ecclesiasticus 38:24-end
Both these passages praise the perseverance that is shown in working long hours, often in the face of difficulties, in order to complete a valuable piece of work. Their patience and concentration becomes in some way an act of prayer and praise to God whom they serve.

With us, too, our work can be part of our praise and worship; we should not cut that area off as being 'secular'; with God, all the different parts of our life can be used, and all are an extension of our life in him.

1 Peter 4:7-11
Although Peter's advice springs out of the expectation that the end of the world was imminent, it is still good advice which will remind us we are only travellers through this life, and not dwellers in it. We are not owners but stewards, so it is only right that we pass on any gifts we have received in service to others.

Matthew 25:14-30
Some people keep their best china permanently behind glass doors; some have precious jewellery in bank vaults instead of round their necks; some keep a large 'nest-egg' of money and rarely dip into it, even if the carpet is threadbare.

All these precautions are taken because greatly valued things are precious, and we want to preserve them from damage. But the need to preserve can get out of hand, until, since we are not using something, we come to value its value, rather than itself. And then, in a way, its possible use is being wasted.

Gifts and talents are often under-used and hidden away as well. Sometimes this is because of an inverted vanity, rather than real modesty; perhaps other people will not appreciate our gift sufficiently — they may even laugh at our efforts.

Sometimes we hold back because our sophisticated society brings a slick professionalism into every home through the media, and home-grown talent is thought of as second best.

What Jesus wants us to know is that we are all valuable and have all been given talents which can be used to good effect in our world. We really ought to see them, or the world will suffer — yes, even if one, seemingly meagre talent is wasted, the world will be poorer.

If we are willing to have a go, try anything once, or make fools of ourselves in a good cause, we might well unearth talents we did not even know we had!

QUESTIONS FOR DISCUSSION

1. Do we sometimes forget that our working hours are all part of our life in Christ? When we remember, how does it affect our attitudes, actions and responses to colleagues?
2. What gifts and talents do we have which could be used in service for the good of God's world? Has God actually nurtured any gifts in our lives for particular jobs he has wanted to be done?

IDEAS FOR ADULTS

At the offering of the gifts today, use this as another opportunity to arrange for everyone to bring up in the procession a small token of what they do in life. For instance, a builder could bring a brick, a cook a wooden spoon, a gardening enthusiast a trowel. Ask everyone a week beforehand to think about what to bring and explain that we shall be offering our lives for God to use.

As all the people approach the altar with these tokens, it is a moving experience to see the ordinary things of life, and the wide variety of lives presented, being offered. It makes everyone aware of their membership of Christ's body, too.

All tokens are placed near the altar, and taken out into the world again. It is a powerful symbol of our stewardship of God's gifts.

CHILDREN'S TEACHING

Have three boxes with slits in the lids, and some play money. Label the boxes as follows:

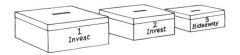

Secretly place five pounds inside box 1, two pounds inside box 2 and nothing in box 3.

Tell the children the story of today's Gospel, using more play money. Post five pounds into the first box, two pounds into the second box and one pound into the third.

When you tell the children about the master's return, open each lid. There will now be ten pounds in the first (give him a round of applause), four pounds in the second (another round of applause), and still only one in the last.

Explain how Jesus needs us to use the gifts he gives us, otherwise they will be wasted. Talk with them about their own gifts and things they are good at or advantages they have been given. These may include, for instance, being friendly, strong, a fast runner, musical, clever, artistic, sympathetic, good with animals, a clear reader, funny, or a good listener. They may also include having enough money to share, outgrown toys which could be given away, or time which might be used in helping.

19th Sunday after Pentecost (Trinity 18)

TODAY'S THEME

. . . is about living by faith. Faith is what gives us hope and certainty about things we can't actually see. It enables us to step out confidently into the future, and it gives us courage in the face of threats and danger.

PARISH MUSIC

Hymns
Alleluia, sing to Jesus
All my hope on God is founded
Blessed assurance, Jesus is mine
Christ is made the sure foundation
Do not be afraid
Faith in God can move the mountains
God moves in a mysterious way
God sent his Son
How firm a foundation
Immortal, invisible, God only wise
Jesus, these eyes have never seen
Lead us, heavenly Father, lead us
Lord, let me know
O God of Bethel, by whose hand
Put thou thy trust in God
Seek ye first the kingdom of God
Thou wilt keep him in perfect peace
What a friend we have in Jesus
With you, O God, my highest good

Recorded music
Dream of Gerontius (Elgar)

For choirs
Psalm 23 (Mawby): U
A song of trust (Stanford): U

CHURCH DECORATION

Year 1 has the story of Jacob's ladder, as Jacob is led to increased faith; a series of small arrangements at different heights develops the theme. Use white, gold and yellow flowers and aim to create a sense of movement and grace.

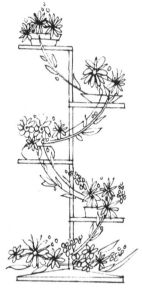

Year 2 includes the story of Daniel in the lions' den, so there is lots of scope here! Try reds, orange and gold with powerful lines and spiked shapes to express the fierce lions, contrasted with a foliage arrangement of different green tones to suggest serenity in the face of danger.

NOTES ON THE READINGS **Year 1**

Genesis 28:10-end
God chooses the strangest people to be his close friends! The character we have been shown in Jacob up to this point in his life hardly suggests a man of goodness, honesty or responsibility. But God could see the man he would make him into, and chooses him to be the next link in the chain of Promise.

Having cheated his brother Esau out of their father's blessing, Jacob is on the run. And here, God makes himself powerfully known, confirming the blessing and making it clear that, faults or not, God has chosen Jacob. The effect on the guilty, scheming Jacob is utter amazement, reverence and the beginning of a new, deep faith; from now on he is going to trust God.

Hebrews 11:1-2, 8-16
Faith, or trust in God, is the firm ground on which we stand as we journey towards a deeper relationship with our Creator. It is unaffected by our moods, feelings, state of health or the weather. It is not altered by hardship, suffering, success or failure.

How can anything so constant exist in us who, being human, are generally inconstant? The reason is that it is nothing man-made or man-invented. It is a present which God will give us if we ask him for it. His close friends, from Abraham onwards, have known it and lived in its hope, and that is why it is so strong — it is based on a hope which is certain and goes deeper and further even than death.

Matthew 6:24-end
In fact, we are easily put off by outside influences. So many trivial things seem important, and we are not helped by the vast amount of advertising, which aims to create a need and then fill it. An offshoot of this is that many cravings and expectancies are roused which give rise to guilt and anxiety when they cannot be fulfilled.

Many of us waste time and energy worrying about what shape we are; which clothes we should wear; whether our children are intelligent, brave, relaxed, fat, thin, noisy or quiet enough; whatever would happen if...and so on.

Life is not only more pleasant, but a good deal healthier if we take this teaching of Jesus to heart. It only demands a change of attitude, not necessarily life-style. If we begin every day by consciously submitting our energy and resources to working with God, and putting our worries into his capable hands, the pressure is immediately eased. Praying people have been found to acquire the therapeutic alpha brain waves, so praying is good for you in many ways!

Worrying is also connected with pride and selfishness. We may feel very self-righteous about worrying for those we love, thinking that it proves our love. But isn't it sometimes an inflated sense of our own importance which makes us worry, assuming that we have the key to other people's happiness and survival? If we acknowledge that the key really belongs to God, then we can start seeing that the world will not crumble if we forget the peas, or our children do not make the grades we hoped for, or we have to get used to new neighbours.

With God at the helm, problems can become exciting opportunities, and we shall be able to face whatever life throws in our way with confidence and enthusiasm.

QUESTIONS FOR DISCUSSION

1. Read through the life-story of Jacob this week (Genesis 25:19 onwards). Can you trace the growth of Jacob's faith through God's patient guidance and all the events, both bad and good?
2. Is it harder for people to have faith when their lives are financially and materially secure, or not? Do you think faith is just a question of temperament, or can everyone have it? How?

IDEAS FOR ADULTS

I have suggested in the discussion questions that Jacob's early life is read this week. One way of doing this is to have a communal reading one evening as part of a social gathering — as these stories would have been passed on through the generations in biblical times, by firelight and candles after a barbecue, for instance. Use a good, modern translation so everyone can enjoy the story without any obstacle to the meaning.

CHILDREN'S TEACHING

Make up a story about Mr Worry-a-lot, illustrating it with flannelgraph pictures. He might worry about what he's going to wear, what he's going to eat, who he's going to invite, where he should go on holiday etc.

Then he meets Mr Trust, who finds him in a bad state of nerves. One by one he sorts out Mr Worry-a-lot's problems with him, showing him that he is worrying unnecessarily because God is sure to look after him. When the next worry arises, they remember to stop and ask God to help them and are then much happier, knowing that God will not let them down. You could make the characters look something like this:

Mr Worry-a-lot   Mr Trust

and give the children cut-outs of each character to colour in and take home.

INTERCESSIONS **Years 1 and 2**
Some ideas for prayer

In the Spirit of Jesus Christ, our brother, let us draw near to our heavenly Father and pray to him together.

We pray for all who labour
in the painstaking work of
building up the kingdom of heaven;
guide them in uncertainty,
encourage them in apparent failure,
and train them in trust through perseverance.
Pause
Father of great mercy: **we trust you to help us**

We pray for the leaders of our country
and of all peoples throughout the world;
for newspaper editors, film directors and all who influence
our nation through the media;
may our world be led to understand
your values, and know your peace.
Pause
Father of great mercy: **we trust you to help us**

We pray for those we rely on and those
who rely on us; for an increase of loyalty
and trust; for guidance in the way we use
our time, money and abilities; for courage
to commit our lives to you more deeply.
Pause
Father of great mercy: **we trust you to help us**

We pray for those who have lost their way
in life, and long to be rescued

and loved back to wholeness;
for those suffering through illness
or handicap or accident.
Pause
Father of great mercy: **we trust you to help us**

We pray for those who have passed
through the gateway of death
into eternity; may they abide
in your peace for ever.

We thank you for the many blessings
of life which you give us each day;
for the wonder of your creation
and the joy and comfort of your presence.

Merciful Father
**accept these prayers
for the sake of your Son,
our Saviour Jesus Christ, Amen.**

NOTES ON THE READINGS **Year 2**

Daniel 6:10-23
The Bible is full of inspiring stories, and this
must be one of the best loved. Daniel's quiet
trust in God pulses through it like the rythmn
of his daily prayers, unswerving even in the face
of danger. He has obviously influenced King
Darius for good already, and Darius is clearly
very fond of his friend, who has such faith in
his God. We feel for him as he works till sunset
to negotiate Daniel's case for freedom from the
rules but in the end he submits to higher
authority and has to treat Daniel like everyone
else. We can imagine him pacing the palace floor
through the night, fasting and no doubt praying
to Daniel's God.

So it is the faith of two fine people which
protects Daniel. It results in relief and delight
as Daniel's familiar voice pipes up from the
lions' den and there is great rejoicing all round.

Romans 5:1-11
Paul reminds us that we are not in a state of
grace through our own efforts but through the
person of Jesus, so we must always guide
people's praise for any good we may do towards
Christ, in whose strength we live and work.
Even suffering provides opportunities to boast
of God's love, for out of suffering can spring
patience, perseverance and hope: the strong
hope which comes from trusting in the all
powerful, loving God.

Luke 19:1-10
Zacchaeus must have presented rather a comic
picture to the citizens of Jericho, standing on
tiptoe to peer over the crowd and then climbing
a sycamore tree in spite of his wealth and status.

Why was he so curious? Perhaps he was a
lonely man, for all his riches. Perhaps he already
felt vaguely uneasy about his life-style, but
hadn't the courage to change without some firm
outside incentive.

Whatever his reasons, Jesus' heart goes out
to him when he sees him. He senses Zacchaeus'
need to be useful and valuable, his longing to
be wanted. So he gives him a practical job to do,
and then there is no stopping Zacchaeus who
cannot wait to get started.

Jesus' outgoing friendship gives him the
impetus to respond to others and put right the
wrongs Zacchaeus has done. We can almost see
the chains of misery dropping off him as he
begins his new life of freedom through love. As
Christ's ambassadors, we can set other
Zacchaeuses free.

QUESTIONS FOR DISCUSSION

1. What can we learn from the behaviour of
   Daniel and Darius to help us in our spiritual
   awareness and growth? Look at areas like
   faith, patient trust, prayer, authority.

2. Is it possible that our conversation, behaviour
   — even our body language — can block or
   encourage others to spiritual growth? What
   can Jesus' friendship with Zacchaeus teach
   us about loving people to faith?

IDEAS FOR ADULTS

The poem 'Daniel Jazz' is very effective in
choral speaking; there is also a musical version
to try, if you are feeling more ambitious. Or have
the story mimed as it is narrated, or acted out
with speaking parts.

CHILDREN'S TEACHING

Both the Daniel and the Zacchaeus stories
provide excellent teaching material. There are
many good, sensitive books to use first. Palm
Tree has both stories: Daniel and the lions and
Zacchaeus and Jesus.

After the reading make a model of the story
on a base, such as an old tray. Use modelling
clay for the figures (and the lions), twigs stuck
in cotton reels with tissue paper leaves for trees,
painted boxes for houses, sandpaper and stones
for the terrain. Bring the finished models in to
display in the church with the heading: Trust
in God can change your life!

20th Sunday after Pentecost (Trinity 19)

TODAY'S THEME

... is steadfast endurance. By his own example and encouragement, Jesus inspires us to continue faithful even through the difficult and rough passages of life; in fact, it is often through such perseverance that we are enabled to mature spiritually, and grow to fulfill our potential.

PARISH MUSIC

Hymns
Be thou my vision
Children of the heavenly King
Christ is made the sure foundation
City of God, how broad and far
Fight the good fight
Follow me, follow me
Forward in faith, forward in Christ
Glorify the Lord
Guide me, O thou great redeemer
He who would valiant be
How firm a foundation
Lord Jesus Christ
Mine eyes have seen the glory
Moses, I know you're the man
My hope is built on nothing less
Oft in danger, oft in woe
O Jesus I have promised
On days when much we do goes wrong
Onward Christian soldiers
Rise up, O men of God
Take up your cross he says
Thine for ever! God of love
Through the night of doubt and sorrow
Walk with me, oh my Lord

Recorded music
A rousing march, played by a brass band or the theme music from Chariots of Fire

For choirs
Exultate Justi (Viadana): SATB
O love of whom is truth and light (Videro): SATB

CHURCH DECORATION

Year 1 uses the burning fiery furnace story to teach about steadfast endurance. Fiery colours for flower arrangements reflect the theme. In the main arrangement, have the 'flames' of flowers and foliage surrounding three yellow lilies. Try incorporating chinese lanterns, burning bush or stags horn.

In Year 2 the athlete's laurel wreath of victory can provide the focus for a flower arrangement today. Aim to express the sense of victory.

NOTES ON THE READINGS **Year 1**

Daniel 3:13-26
Shadrach, Meshach and Abed-nego are faced with death if they refuse to worship Nebuchadnezzar's god or the idol he has set up. Their determination to stay true to God's command is put to the test, and their steadfast faith is remarkable; they refuse to worship the idol even if their God does not rescue them!

Such endurance under pressure provided just the kind of role pattern needed by the people of Israel, who were exiled and living among pagan worshippers. Such examples would have inspired them, in their own endurance tests, to stay loyal and true to God through everything.

Romans 8:18-25

Paul's life was full of hardship, danger and deprivation as he spent it in spreading the Good News of Jesus. The patient hope which he describes is not a grim determined stoicism but a joyful acceptance of being part of a larger plan than immediate problems; a plan which is totally in the hands of the loving God he trusts with his life.

Luke 9:51-end

In this reading we see both Jesus' and man's commitment. Firstly, Jesus, fully aware of the distress and agony he is certain to encounter, nevertheless resolutely takes the road to Jerusalem, obedient to his calling, regardless of the risks and costs.

Secondly, we see several examples of men offering to follow or being called. 'I will follow you wherever you go,' says one. We sense in Jesus' reply that perhaps the man was not fully aware of the hardships and discomforts his decision would entail.

Others make excuses for not immediately obeying their call. Their reasons may seem humane and valid, but this is not really the point. They serve to point out how radical and absolute our approach to Christ must be: we are little use to him unless we are prepared to commit ourselves wholeheartedly.

QUESTIONS FOR DISCUSSION

1. Why do you think the three men were prepared to disobey the king even when they were not certain that God would save them from death?
2. James and John obviously still thought in terms of retribution taking place in this life. How is this attitude different from Paul's as shown in his letter to the Romans?

IDEAS FOR ADULTS

The first reading can be acted out to enjoy its drama to the full. Use the passage like a script to work from, and emphasise the calm of the three men contrasted with the uncontrolled rage of the king. For the fire, have five dancers, whose twisting, flickering movements get wilder as the furnace is made hotter. Their swirling will contrast with the men walking about calmly within the fire. The fourth person can be imagined by the congregation, if you wish. Or one member of the fire dancers can mingle with them, and revert to being part of the fire with Shadrach, Meshach and Abed-nego come out unharmed.

CHILDREN'S TEACHING

Tell the children the story of Shadrach, Meshach and Abed-nego bringing out their determination to do what they know God wants them to do, even when it puts them in danger. Then help them to make this moving model of the three men in the fire out of card, a lolly stick, sticky tape and colouring pens.

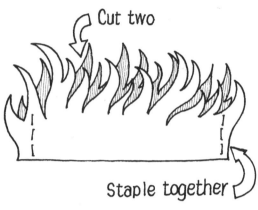
Cut two

Staple together

lolly stick

INTERCESSIONS **Years 1 and 2**
Some ideas for prayer

Fellow members of Christ,
we have been drawn here,
united in his love;
let us pray together,
confident in God's faithfulness.

We pray for every newly baptised Christian;
for all recently confirmed and ordained;
may they be strengthened and encouraged
to witness faithfully and bravely,
strong in your strength.
Pause
Give us courage, Lord: **to do your will**

We pray for our world, so richly blessed
and so full of potential; give us the grace
to persevere in what is right,
to use the world's resources for good.
Pause
Give us courage, Lord: **to do your will**

We pray for all of us here,
for our families and our friends;
inspire us to work at our relationships
and remind us to welcome you
into every situation we meet.
Pause
Give us courage, Lord: **to do your will**

We pray for those whose bodies or minds
are weak and diseased; for those too ill
or exhausted to pray; for all who nurse
and care for the chronically or terminally ill.
Pause
Give us courage, Lord: **to do your will**

We pray for the bereaved
and those who have died;
may they wake to the eternal joy
of your heaven.

We give you our thanks and praise
for your steadfast love which
gives us strength and courage.

Merciful Father
**accept these prayers
for the sake of your Son,
our Saviour Jesus Christ, Amen.**

NOTES ON THE READINGS **Year 2**

Genesis 32:22-30
Having had the reassurance of God's blessing
in the dream of the ladder to heaven some
twenty years before, Jacob now encounters God
very personally, as he wrestles with a spiritual
agony throughout the night until he finds peace
in the knowledge of God's acceptance of him and
the years of penance he has given. He has learnt
so much during the years of working for Laban,
and his perseverance and dedication have
brought him to this point of full 'conversion'
characterised by the new name he is given.

1 Corinthians 9:19-end
People today are highly aware of what they
consider to be their 'rights'. Righteous
indignation inflates every issue where our rights
are threatened or violated, and sometimes we are
so concerned with protecting our rights that we
fail to remember our privileges.

Paul is not in the least concerned with his
rights; he is more than willing to sacrifice them
all if it means gaining more souls for Christ. We
may not live under the Mosaic Law any more,
but we do live under God's law of love; and that
can often cut clean across the worldly view of
rights. Our unselfish caring, our willingness to
forgive completely, our self discipline (all of
which should be hallmarks of our life in Christ)
may often be regarded as weakness and
foolishness by a world which is obsessed by what
it can gain rather than what it can give. And we
are required, as part of our allegiance to Christ,
to work for the spread of his kingdom using his
methods. They are, in the end, the only methods
which work.

Matthew 7:13-27
Since the man who built on sand is called
'foolish', we can assume that he had the choice
of rock for his site, but for some reason decided
against it. Perhaps the sand involved less work,
and would provide quicker results. Both as
individuals and in society and the Church we are
often guilty of similar short-sightedness, and pay
for it later.

Spiritually, we are particularly loath to dig
deep foundations into hard rock, since it is
painful and humiliating. And the house will look
just as impressive from the surface what ever it
is built on. Through history 'Christians' have
been notorious for this: singing hymns while
slaves died below decks; using their faith as an
excuse to wage war and plunder; using their
status as respectable people to lead self-indulgent
or cruel lives. The whole body of the Church
is weakened by the shame and sadness of such
hypocrisy.

Tragically, many fine, sensitive people, and
many longing for faith, have rejected Christ
because of our pathetic building on sand. Jesus
offers us strong rock on which to build lasting
houses; lives built on Christ work — for the good
of the whole world.

QUESTIONS FOR DISCUSSION

1. What does building our house on rock entail? How is it different from building on sand?
2. Do you think that our concern to protect people's rights can sometimes blind us to the outrageous path of love which Jesus teaches? How can we influence others, by our example in daily life, to see the value of living by spiritual, rather than material security?

IDEAS FOR ADULTS

All spiritual endurance grows out of a strong prayer life. Consider having a parish retreat or quiet day in which to pray, reflect under God's guidance, and practise listening as well as talking to God.

CHILDREN'S TEACHING

Bring along two sets of building bricks (not interlocking ones). Divide the children into two groups and let each build a house. One is based on a firm block of wood, the other on a thick layer of sand in a tray.

When both are finished, tell the children Jesus' story of the two houses. At the point of the stormy rain, pour water round the bases of each in turn. The sand will cave in and the 'rock' will not.

Make sure you explain what Jesus told the story for, or they will not understand. Point out how silly it was not to have a good strong foundation, (they may have seen houses being built with foundations deep in the ground) and that we can choose to build our lives on strong rock or slipping sand. Sing 'I'm gonna build my life'.

Build on God — put him first

21st Sunday after Pentecost (Trinity 20)

TODAY'S THEME

... is our Christian hope. As adopted children of God, we know that this world and this life is not the whole story. We are children of eternity, living in the faith that this life does not finish at death, and our true spiritual home is in heaven, towards which we are walking as joyful pilgrims.

PARISH MUSIC

Hymns
Alleluia, sing to Jesus
A man there lived in Galilee
At the name of Jesus
Blest are the pure in heart
City of God, how broad and far
Come and see the shining hope
From glory to glory advancing
God is working his purpose out
Happy are they, they that love God
Hark! the sound of holy voices
I cannot tell why he
I will sing the wondrous story
Jerusalem the golden
Light's abode, celestial Salem
Lord, when I turn my back on you
Mine eyes have seen the glory
O Jesus I have promised
Once in Royal David's City
We pray thee, heavenly Father
When came in flesh the incarnate Word
Ye holy angels bright
You shall go out with joy

Recorded music
Brass band playing: When the saints
Symphony No. 6 (Tchaikovsky): 'Pathetique'

For choirs
Lift up your heads O ye gates (Amner): SATB
The souls of the righteous (Marchant): SATB

CHURCH DECORATION

The theme of today's readings is hope — the joyful Christian hope of risen life in heaven, so the flowers need to be full of exuberance and hope. Make the main arrangement very broad-based, solid and secure, and 'overflowing' as

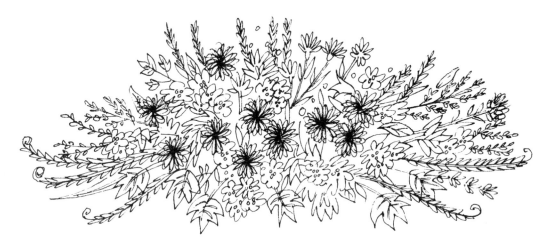

well as uplifting. Choose rich colours which reflect this idea — chrysanthemums are splendid and usually plentiful at this time of year. Choose richly shaped foliage, too, with ferns, rhododendron or richly coloured autumn leaves.

NOTES ON THE READINGS **Year 1**

Habakkuk 2:1-4

Habakkuk sees apparent injustice all around him. Evil often appears to be rewarded rather than punished, and it seems as if God's plans and promises are not being fulfilled. He lays these questions and doubts before God, and receives the assurance that God is indeed in control, even when our limited vision cannot see how things can possibly work out.

We need not worry about staging our own retribution or attempting to do God's planning for him. His timing is best, and we can rest assured that in God's good time all things will be fully accomplished in the way which is best and in accordance with God's nature of merciful love.

Acts 26:1-8

Having been accused by the Jews of preaching against God, Paul couches his defence in terms which the Jews, and Agrippa, will recognise. He speaks of his hope as being the hope of all Jews — the hope foretold by all the prophets — of a time when all God's people would worship with God's chosen one, Messiah, among them. They would be the nucleus of light which would spread out to give light to the world.

The point of difference is that Paul claims Jesus to be the fulfilment of that hope, proved by God raising him to life after death, and thus opening to us all the chance of being raised to eternal life.

Luke 18:1-8

The need for persistent prayer is illustrated here by Jesus in his story of the widow nagging a judge to give her justice. The judge is a thoroughly unsympathetic man, who would never help her but for her persistence, which finally drives him to act on her behalf. Jesus couldn't have chosen anyone less likely to grant a request, and yet in the end, justice is done. The contrast between this miserable judge and the all-loving God highlights the certainty of God being prepared to listen to us and see justice done. However long it takes we need never worry that God will turn down our request — it may well be that we are being taught perseverance and gaining a deeper faith in the process.

QUESTIONS FOR DISCUSSION

1. Do you ever feel, like Habakkuk, that evil seems to be ruling our world, rather than good? How does today's reading help? How can our lives help?
2. Persistence is a mark of hope. Do we tend to give up praying for something if we don't seem to be getting answers? How does God train us to be patient?

IDEAS FOR ADULTS

Using the reading from Acts make the church into a court, in which the congregation are witnesses. Agrippa sits near the altar and Paul is brought in by two guards to stand in a central position so that the congregation are spoken to as well as Agrippa. Spoken, rather than read, these words drive home the secure hope Paul has.

CHILDREN'S TEACHING

Talk with the children about working hard at something until at last it is finished. They may have found it difficult making a model, mixing a cake, tidying their bedroom or learning to swim or skip, for instance.

You could bring to show them something you had to persevere with, such as a knitted jumper, loaf of bread, or piece of music, and tell them you sometimes wanted to stop and give up, but decided not to.

Help them to see that perseverance is not always easy, but it is always worthwhile.

Now tell the story of Moses, using plasticine models or pictures to illustrate it.

Give each child a card to split into days and with a prayer they have made up to say every day. Perhaps their parents might like to say it with them.

Ask them to bring their cards back next week with a tick drawn each day they remembered to do it.

INTERCESSIONS Years 1 and 2
Some ideas for prayer

As sons and daughters of our heavenly Father, let us pray together, trusting in his love.

We pray that the Church and all its members may not be stagnant, but flow forward in the direction you want it to go; may the Christian hope burn brightly in our lives and may your kingdom come.
Pause
Lord, you are our hope: **we believe and trust in you**

We pray that we may all tend and care for the world you have given us to live in; may we share its food and riches, and use them wisely and safely without waste or destruction.
Pause
Lord, you are our hope: **we believe and trust in you**

We pray for the sick, the injured and the distressed; for the dying and for those who mourn; may your healing presence bring wholeness and comfort.
Pause
Lord, you are our hope: **we believe and trust in you**

We pray for our own circle of family and friends; for personal spiritual growth; may we be more watchful, preparing ourselves more thoroughly day by day to meet you face to face.
Pause
Lord, you are our hope: **we believe and trust in you**

We pray for those who have died in faith and live with you in glory; may we one day share with them the joy of being in your presence for ever.

We thank you, Father, for all your goodness and kindness to us; for the hope of heaven and the comfort of your love.

Merciful Father
accept these prayers
for the sake of your Son,
our Saviour Jesus Christ, Amen.

NOTES ON THE READINGS Year 2

Ezekiel 12:21-end
If you have ever watched time-lapse photography in action you will have appreciated the wonder of how seemingly still things move, and plants grow. Much goes on imperceptibly under the earth during winter; we only see the glorious result burst out in the spring flowers.

So it is with spiritual things: much growth happens during times we may be considering dead or unproductive times. Much later we may be able to look back and discern the painstaking development which has taken place, and for which the 'barren' section was necessary. God works all the time; he is working now; we can trust, even when we cannot see.

1 Peter 1:13-21
Until Christ came to live among us in person we could not know God or hope and believe in him in quite the same way, because he had not yet been revealed to the world.

But Jesus changed all that, for in him we see the power and love of God acted out in human terms that we can understand.

Having acknowledged God as our Father, through seeing and listening to Jesus, we must be careful to act out our faith scrupulously as we journey through life to our heavenly home; not following meticulous rules of conduct, but living closely with Christ who will save us from evil.

John 11:17-27
Mary, Martha and Lazarus had come to know God's love in person, through the time they had spent in Jesus' company.

When Lazarus dies, their faith in the living saviour is, as it were, brought to a head. This is the time when all their growth in spiritual understanding comes to flower. Martha recognises the power of Jesus' life-giving presence, and is convinced that if Jesus had been there her brother would still be alive. She is now led on by Jesus to see that he is not only the one who gives abundant life to his friends and followers — he is also life itself, divine as well as human, whose power of love is stronger even than death.

QUESTIONS FOR DISCUSSION

1. How would you describe the Christian hope? What do you base it on? This may be either teaching or example, from the Gospel or from other Christians who have influenced you.
2. How can we best give others we meet the chance to share such hope? Have any methods you have tried failed? Can you now see why this was?

IDEAS FOR ADULTS

Use a section from the *Dream of Gerontius* where the angel brings Gerontius to a glimpse of God, and he sings:
'Take me away, and in the lowest deep
There let me be'
Give the congregation copies of the words to follow (there are about ten lines) and use it as a time for reflection.

CHILDREN'S TEACHING

Tell or read the story of today's Gospel. Palm Tree's version is called *Martha, Mary and Jesus*. Then make a frieze that shows the events and fix it up on the wall in church for everyone to see.

22nd Sunday after Pentecost (Trinity 21)

TODAY'S THEME

. . . is that we cannot serve two masters — if we choose to serve God we shall not be able to continue as slaves of money and materialism. We should be as astute about our spiritual lives as the dishonest steward was about keeping his job.

PARISH MUSIC

Hymns
A safe stronghold our God is still
Be thou my guardian and my guide
Christ be beside me
Dear Lord and Father of mankind
Father, hear the prayer we offer
Father, you are living in us now
Forth in thy name O Lord I go
He who would valiant be
Immortal love, for ever full
Lead us heavenly Father lead us
Lord Jesus Christ
Lord of my life
O for a closer walk with God
O God our help in ages past
Oh Lord all the world belongs to you
Our hearts were made for you, Lord
Take up your cross, he says
Thy way, not mine, O Lord
With you, O God, my highest good

Recorded music
Last section of 'Libera me' (Lloyd Webber): from Requiem

For choirs
Let all the world (Gilbert): U, 2 or 3 part
Thou shalt show me the path of life (Day)

CHURCH DECORATION

The theme of following the narrow path which leads to heaven is expressed in an arrangement with a broad base which tapers upwards into a column. It needs to have an upward sweep in the line, and colours lighten towards the top.

NOTES ON THE READINGS **Years 1 and 2**

Deuteronomy 11:18-28

We must never listen to the whisper of temptation which tells us we have done our choosing and our turning to God, and can sit back and relax. We may suddenly find that we have been worshipping all kinds of idols for quite some time.

We may find that some of our worst problems are actually the result of worshipping (or 'considering of great worth') the wrong things, and if we turn ourselves back to God, the problems may be solved or healed.

It is best to acknowledge our capacity for getting side-tracked, and set regular, thorough times for examining ourselves in the light of God's law of love. Then we can start to be reconciled with God before we have blundered too far in the opposite direction.

Moses well understands the way human memories are short and easily side-tracked. He knew from experience the initial bursts of enthusiasm gradually sinking into slackness. Few of us can keep going with sustained vigour for long; mostly we get distracted, and progress by lurching fitfully from resolution to resolution.

That is why Moses suggests fastening the Law, quite literally, to our bodies, and the Law itself is a memory aid, useful for keeping us pointing in the right direction and turning us

back if we have turned away.

1 John 2:22-end

John, too, urges us to keep the faith we hold alive. We need to run over it in our minds regularly: recite our faith together regularly, and then we will continue to live in Christ and he in us. This will also help to strengthen us against the temptation to rush off and get involved in the latest cult, in order, perhaps, to experience something emotional, rather than spiritual. This is certainly not suggesting stagnation. It is suggesting the anchor of true faith which will stop us drifting on strong currents which may look interesting but take us in the wrong direction.

Luke 16:1-9

At first sight Jesus seems to be praising a steward for his dishonest behaviour. In fact he is comparing the shrewd, thorough way in which a dishonest man prepares for himself a settled future, with the vague uncommitted way we often go about preparing ourselves spiritually for our eternal future.

If we gave even a quarter as much attention to the development of our relationship with God as we give to the planning of a holiday, say, or the decorating scheme of the bathroom, we might start to really feel the effect of God's presence in our lives.

Suppose we prepared as carefully for communion as we do for arranging a dinner party for an important guest? Or spent as much time talking with God as we spend chatting to our friends at the pub or over a cup of tea?

Yet Jesus warns us that if we only use our time and energy pursuing money, material comforts and personal power, we shall not be serving God.

If, on the other hand, we regard all money and possessions as things to be used for good, and for God's glory, then our shrewd, wise handling of material goods may actually help us learn how to be responsible in spiritual matters.

QUESTIONS FOR DISCUSSION

1. What kind of obedience is encouraged by the threat of punishment? What kind of obedience does God require of us?

2. What attribute of the dishonest steward was the master applauding? Do we take more time and care over our financial, social or intellectual interests than over the growth of our spiritual life?

IDEAS FOR ADULTS

If you have a gate in the church yard, place today's Postcommunion sentence on it. Otherwise, write it by the door into the church.

CHILDREN'S TEACHING

First give the children a maze to do, individually with a pencil. Here is one you could use:

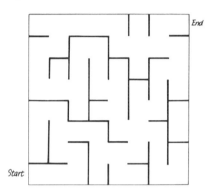

Talk about what happens when they go down a dead end:
— they are out of the main route
— they can't make any progress
— the only way out is to retrace their steps
— if they just stay there they may be imprisoned with no freedom.

Now show them a large picture of the maze either on a blackboard or sheet of card. The beginning of our maze, as Christians, is when we are baptised. (Stick a picture of baptism, or a font at the start of the maze.)

All the time we go on the right route we are putting Jesus first. In his love we can enjoy loving Mum and Dad, playing with brothers and sisters, enjoy football, painting, going on holiday, helping Nana, having friends to tea etc. (Write these, and their ideas, in coloured pencil along the route, with a cross, as Jesus' sign, in between each one.) Because Jesus is Love, he helps us love and appreciate other people.

But suppose one thing starts to be more important than our love for Jesus? (Write one item, such as 'football' or 'having friends to tea' at a dead end.) It will cut us off from the supply of Love, and our lives will be stuck at a dead end. So what can we do if that happens? We have to go back the way we came, meet up with Jesus, and then we can live in his love again.

INTERCESSIONS **Years 1 and 2**
Some ideas for prayer

My companions in Christ,
having promised to commit our lives
to God, let us pray to him now.

We pray that all Christians
may stay true to their calling;
may they witness to the value
of caring, selfless love, and draw others
to acknowledge you as Lord.
Pause
Lord, take us: **help us to live**

We pray for all monarchs, presidents
and those in positions of power;
for those whom they rule, and those
with whom they negotiate;
that peace and justice may prevail
over all our earth.
Pause
Lord take us: **help us to live**

We pray for ourselves, our families,
friends and neighbours; may we acknowledge
our failings as well as our strengths,
and serve you in serving one another.
Pause
Lord take us: **help us to live**

We pray for the poor, the weak and
the oppressed; for the abandoned,
neglected and abused;
may all obstacles to their healing
and wholeness be removed,
through the outpouring
of your love and hope.
Pause
Lord, take us: **help us to live**

We pray for those who have died;
may they know the eternal joy
of living in your presence for ever.

We thank you for the fresh joys
and challenges of each day;
for the love and encouragement
your Spirit gives us.

Merciful Father,
accept these prayers
for the sake of your Son,
our Saviour Jesus Christ, Amen.

Last Sunday after Pentecost

TODAY'S THEME

. . . is that we are citizens of heaven, gradually making our way home. Before anything was created, and after the end of time, our God continues to reign. All who love him have been promised a share in his Kingdom of heaven.

PARISH MUSIC

Hymns

Alleluia, sing to Jesus
Be still, my soul
Bright the vision that delighted
City of God, how broad and far
Come down O Love divine
Father, we adore you
Father, we love you
From glory to glory advancing
Glorious things of thee are spoken
God of mercy, God of grace
Hark! the sound of holy voices
Immortal, invisible, God only wise
Jerusalem the golden
Jesus, the joy of loving hearts
Light's abode, celestial Salem
Lord, enthroned in heavenly splendour
Love divine, all loves excelling
Loving shepherd of thy sheep
My God, how wonderful thou art
O love that will not let me go
Tell out my soul
There is a land of pure delight
Thy loving kindness is better than life
To the name that brings salvation
We pray thee, heavenly Father
Whom do you seek?

Recorded music

The Planets Suite (Holst): Neptune.

For choirs

Holy, holy, holy (Palestrina): SATB
How glorious Sion's courts appear (Tye)
I will lift up mine eyes (Mawby): U

CHURCH DECORATION

In both years the flowers need to express the glory of heaven, with a sense of majesty, light and joy. Go for a large scale, either arranged like a sheaf of abundance, or like a brilliant star. In

year 2 there is the parable of the wise and foolish bridesmaids, so you may like to express this in one arrangement, incorporating into the design a clay oil lamp and a length of bridal material.

NOTES ON THE READINGS **Year 1**

Jeremiah 29:1,4-14

God's word through Jeremiah to the exiled people of Israel is that they should contribute to the life of the community in which they find themselves, living caring lives to include the welfare of the Babylonians. They are to live in the present, in other words, doing good where they are, but at the same time looking forward to the time when they will be able to return to their own country.

In a way, this illustrates our own position: we are to live in this world to the full, but we are not to feel we belong to worldly values, since our home is the spiritual kingdom of heaven.

Philippians 3:7-end

Paul has realised that his own efforts, however determined, will never be able to provide the lasting joy and peace which Christ offers, so nothing else is worth striving for.

Although living for Christ may well mean physical and spiritual hardship — even agony — it is worth every drop of suffering because the reward is so great. And the closer we get to being Christ-like, the more joy we shall find, and the more thankful we shall become.

John 17:1-10

As Jesus nears the end of his saving work on earth, he prays for all his followers — us included — for whom he feels such love and for whom he is willing to undergo all the suffering of the cross.

When Jesus wrestles with burdens and problems he never does it alone. Always we read of his many hours of prayer in a solitary place where he could communicate with his heavenly Father. All his ministry was under-girded with the strength of this prayerfulness.

If we find ourselves having sleepless nights worrying about something, we ought to follow Jesus' example and worry it through with God instead of keeping it to ourselves. The difference is amazing. Instead of going round and round in circles with no glimpse of a solution anywhere, the whole process becomes manageable and productive. We may still spend sleepless hours thinking, but they are no longer chaotic and tense. Solutions may spring to mind which we had not even considered. (God, after all, can see the whole picture, not just the little section our human eyes are aware of.)

QUESTIONS FOR DISCUSSION

1. How can we live fully in the world without being worldly? Jesus' ministry will provide some suggestions.
2. What kind of qualities and resources can the Church offer the world which are in short supply or lacking in the secular, materialistic way of life? Does your parish tend to compete with the secular, rather than offering these things?

IDEAS FOR ADULTS

Have an instrument, such as a flute, guitar or cello, playing softly in the background at the Gospel, beginning at: 'I have glorified you on earth'.

CHILDREN'S TEACHING

If there is an outside area available, this could be used for today's teaching, based on races. If not, have the indoors area clear of chairs and tables for the first part of the session.

Tell the children you are going to have some races, and choose two or three to race first. Have the others cheering at the side lines.

For the next race, give the runners baggy clothes to wear, which will slow them down.

For the third race, have obstacles to get round, over or through. In each case encourage the runners by cheering.

Then gather the children round for prize giving. A nice surprise — everyone who finished gets a prize (small sticker or badge).

Now arrange the chairs in a circle, or several if numbers are large.

Show a large sheet of paper with 'The Race of Life' on it. Talk about what sort of obstacles life has (people nasty to us; moving away from friends; illness etc); how cheering crowds help us (the saints, other people, and we can cheer on others); how the heavy clothes and baskets in our life are our sins (being greedy, unkind, selfish, wishing for what we cannot have, being lazy) so that they relate their races to life. Now each child can make a plasticine model of him or herself running, and put it somewhere along the track.

INTERCESSIONS Years 1 and 2
Some ideas for prayer

As sons and daughters
of our heavenly King
let us ask our Father's blessing
on the Church and on the world.

We pray for the world of Christ's body, the
  Church;
that all may labour zealously
for the establishment of your Kingdom on earth;
till the world is flooded
with your peace, joy and love.
Pause
Lord, our heavenly Father: **may your kingdom
  come**

We pray for the work of all peacemakers,
all who work for justice, reconciliation
and harmony; that you, Lord God of peace and
  love,
will bless, support and encourage them.
Pause
Lord, our heavenly Father: **may your kingdom
  come**

We pray for our own work in this life;
that we may dedicate our energies and resources
more fully to your will,
undertaking every task and activity joyfully,
trusting in your strength.
Pause
Lord, our heavenly Father: **may your kingdom
  come**

We pray for the work of those who heal
and tend the sick, the injured and the dying;
for all in their care;
for all involved in medical research
and those whose lives depend on drugs,
dialysis or radiotherapy.
Pause
Lord, our heavenly Father: **may your kingdom
  come**

We pray for all who have passed
through the gate of death to eternity;
may they live for ever in your heaven.

We rejoice for all the wonder and beauty
of your creation; in the constant miracle
of life and renewal; in your amazing
and undeserved love and affection for us.

Merciful Father
**accept these prayers
for the sake of your Son,
our Saviour Jesus Christ, Amen.**

NOTES ON THE READINGS Year 2

Isaiah 33:17-22
Living in turbulent times, with human weakness
glaringly obvious, the prophet is led to see this
vision of a different kind of rule in a kingdom
of God's making.

Under such a reign there is justice blended
with mercy, purity, and integrity. God is
personally involved with his people and will care
for them in an atmosphere of order, tranquillity
and mutual respect.

The kingdom of heaven, later described so
often by Jesus, is the fulfilment of such a vision,
and directs us to a quality of life which will even
continue beyond death.

Revelation 7:2-4, 9-end
In this vision of heaven, the seer senses the
awesome majesty and glorious beauty of
everlasting life, suffused with purity and light.
There, where there is no trace of sin any more,
the fragments of perfection we have glimpsed
throughout our lives are concentrated in
immeasurable, unlimited joy and worship and
praise.

There we see, with a thrill of excitement, the
countless numbers of faithful people from all
over the world, and from every nation, pouring
into the courts of heaven, to share its joy for
ever.

Matthew 25:1-13
As we have seen, the early Christians expected
Jesus to come in a matter of weeks or months,
He did not, and here we are, nearly 2,000 years
later, still waiting.

So this story of long waiting, yet still being
prepared, is very useful. There is no doubt in
the bridesmaids' minds about whether the
bridegroom would come or not, and they had
all brought their burning lamps with them. The
only difference is that the five sensible ones had
an extra oil supply with them so that their lamps
would not go out after the initial burst of
enthusiastic preparations.

We do need to refuel regularly if we are to stay
'alight', alert and ready to welcome Jesus. But
we must do it ourselves — it is no good resting
on other people's prayer lives, good works or
depth of commitment to worship and care. Just
because we are all members of the Church does
not mean that we can jog casually along, not
getting too involved while others dedicate their
lives to serving Christ. If we do this, we shall
find that our lamps are out when we need them
most, and no borrowing of beautiful lives is
possible.

In other words, how we live every second and
every day determines how bright our lamps will

be. Seconds may not seem very important, but life in Christ is painstakingly built, piece by piece, and a few grand gestures followed by months or years of complacency will not enable us to be made new in Christ. If we treasure each moment as an opportunity to refuel, then, when we meet him face to face, he will welcome us with joy.

QUESTIONS FOR DISCUSSION

1. How do you imagine heaven to be? Try to build a picture of the kingdom of heaven, based on Jesus' teaching and the ideas behind the visions of the seers. Don't feel that this is childish. We need to develop a sense of heaven as a real experience which we will one day know fully.
2. How can we 'refuel' regularly during our life, so that when Jesus calls us we are ready, with our lamps lit?

IDEAS FOR ADULTS

We, creatures of clay, are given the light of Christ. A rather unusual way of exploring this idea is to meet as a group some time this week to make clay oil lamps, which can be filled with oil and a wick, and lit during the service on Sundays. It is not difficult, and the working hands become part of our prayer.

As the group works, either have silence, or taped Christian music. Give instruction beforehand and work, if possible, in a circle. Have bowls of soapy water and old towels available. All ages can take part together.

1. Any sticky mud can be moulded, and as the bowls will not be fired, there is no need to use first class clay. But many areas have a good supply quite near the surface.
2. Knead thoroughly, moistening with water as necessary. It will gradually become more pliable.
3. Make a lump into a ball, push in your thumb, and widen the dent bit by bit by pressing your thumb on the inside and first finger on the outside.
4. Decorate the outside using a small twig or spent match. The finished bowl should be large enough to hold a night light or a floating wick.
5. Leave the bowls to dry out slowly in an airy place. They will be ready to use in church on Sundays in Advent.

CHILDREN'S TEACHING

Tell the children today's Gospel, making it clear that it is a story Jesus told, not a real event. To help in the telling, have two strips of card, each with five bridesmaids on it.

Five have extra oil in a flask, five do not. At the point where the lamps go out, pull the strip along, so that the wicks show instead of the flames.

When they have heard the story and what it tells us about keeping ourselves ready for Jesus, the children can make their own strip of bridesmaids with flames that go out. Write on each: 'Keep my lamp burning Lord' with one word on each bridesmaid.

Dance of the Bridesmaids

Ten bridesmaids, with long dresses and flowers in their hair, carry their lamps during this dance. The lamps are small bowls with nightlights inside.

As the music begins they dance up the centre in two lines of five, doing basically a quick waltz step but free within this to turn and sway or join hands sometimes in pairs. They adjust their hair, smooth each other's dresses, check their lamps in an atmosphere of excited preparation.

Gradually they start to fidget and yawn, resting in different positions — some leaning, some sitting, some lying down. The lamps go out.

From the back comes the trumpet call to announce that the bridegroom will soon be here. The bridesmaids nudge each other awake, flutter about getting neat again, and then the five with extra oil mime their refuelling. The other five kneel and beg them to lend some oil, which the first five refuse to do, pointing out where the oil can be bought.

The five foolish bridesmaids scamper (in contrast to their waltzing) off to buy oil, as the bridegroom, bride and guests come in grand procession up the centre.

The wise bridesmaids dance down to greet him, curtsey and light the way to the centre front. As the bridegroom goes to 'close' the door, the foolish bridesmaids run up with their lamps alight again, but are turned away and walk to the back, dejected, and looking wistfully behind them at the others enjoying themselves.

Handel's *Water Music* has three sections which reflect the three moods of this parable.